METHODS ANALYSIS AND WORK MEASUREMENT

McGraw-Hill Series in Industrial Engineering and Management Science

Consulting Editor

James L. Riggs, *Department of Industrial Engineering, Oregon State University*

Barish and Kaplan: *Economic Analysis: For Engineering and Managerial Decision Making*
Blank: *Statistical Procedures for Engineering, Management, and Science*
Cleland and Kocaoglu: *Engineering Management*
Denton: *Safety Management: Improving Performance*
Dervitsiotis: *Operations Management*
Gillett: *Introduction to Operations Research: A Computer-Oriented Algorithmic Approach*
Hicks: *Introduction to Industrial Engineering and Management Science*
Huchingson: *New Horizons for Human Factors in Design*
Law and Kelton: *Simulation Modeling and Analysis*
Lehrer: *White-Collar Productivity*
Love: *Inventory Control*
Polk: *Methods Analysis and Work Measurement*
Riggs: *Engineering Economics*
Riggs: *Essentials of Engineering Economics*
Wu and Coppins: *Linear Programming and Extensions*

METHODS ANALYSIS AND WORK MEASUREMENT

Edward J. Polk
GMI Engineering and Management Institute

with contributions by
John J. Mariotti
Joe McGinnis
Cecil Peterson
Richard B. Harmon

McGraw-Hill Book Company
New York St. Louis San Francisco Auckland Bogotá Hamburg
Johannesburg London Madrid Mexico Montreal New Delhi
Panama Paris São Paulo Singapore Sydney Tokyo Toronto

This book was set in Press Roman by Jay's Publishers Services, Inc.
The editor was Rodger H. Klas;
the production supervisor was Diane Renda.
Project supervision was done by The Total Book.
The cover was designed by Suzanne Haldane.
R. R. Donnelley & Sons Company was printer and binder.

METHODS ANALYSIS AND WORK MEASUREMENT

234567890 D O C D O C 8987654

ISBN 0-07-050378-8

Library of Congress Cataloging in Publication Data

Polk, Edward J.
    Methods analysis and work measurement.

    (McGraw-Hill series in industrial engineering and
management science)
    Bibliography: p.
    Includes index.
    1. Work measurement. I. Mariotti, John J.
II. Title. III. Series.
T60.P64 1984   658.5'42   83-11283
ISBN 0-07-050378-8

CONTENTS

PREFACE

Much of the material in this book is taken from a manual published by and for General Motors Institute. This manual has served General Motors Corporation and GMI Engineering and Management Institute admirably and in a variety of ways since it was written 20 years ago. It is based on the combined experience, knowledge, and expertise of many practicing supervisors of industrial engineering who, through participation on committees and task groups, devised many of the specific models presented and laid the basic philosophical foundations for their application to the never-ending search for "the one best way." Fortunately, the coauthors and I have been contributing members of these various committees and task groups through the years.

In the intervening time, the manual has been revised and expanded, thus benefiting from the viewpoints and varied perspectives of more recent additions to the faculty of the Industrial and Systems Engineering Department at GMI. This book, constituting a major revision, should continue to function well as a basic text for methods analysis and work measurement courses at the sophomore or junior class level. This purpose has been well served at GMI for both industrial engineering and industrial administration students for whom the course is a requirement. Portions of the text are also used for a two-week continuing engineering education program which has been operating in its present form for over 15 years, and is intended to provide newcomers to this aspect of industrial engineering with some fundamental "tools of the trade," or to provide some polish for those whose skills may have become a bit rusty. In addition, selected sections have been used in seminars and training programs conducted in various plant locations throughout the United States and in Canada, England, France, West Germany, and Brazil. The usual emphasis in these latter uses is on cost reduction and productivity improvement, involving a wide cross section of personnel from production and staff support groups. Many millions of dollars in savings have been documented as a result of these efforts.

This book has been organized to present the material in a sequence corresponding to the typical order in which the various topics are presented in teaching the course. Alternate sequences are certainly feasible and are left to the discretion of the instructor. An instructor's guide offers several alternatives, as well as specific chapters recommended for short courses, seminars, and similar purposes.

The overall thrust of this book is to first establish a solid philosophical base, recognizing the historical precedents for the profession of industrial engineering and reestablishing a too-often forgotten notion that the ultimate long-term success of any enterprise, however measured, depends on the properly directed and adequately rewarded efforts of people. With this foundation we move on to cover a big-picture view of systems analysis, followed by the tools of methods analysis and design, and proceed to work-measurement techniques and other related topics. It is no accident that the latter two topics appear in that sequence. We have long recognized the concept of inseparability of method and time; thus, if time, the dependent variable, is to be conserved and used wisely, one must first deal with the method and all factors affecting performance. This is not an industrial engineering handbook; its scope is limited to only basic tasks of methods analysis and work measurement which are essential elements of the industrial engineering function. It is our desire that this book may offer in some respect a different or new insight into the ways, whys, and worth of competent and professional approaches to these responsibilities, upon which so much of the business depends.

Finally, we would be remiss in not expressing our appreciation to several individuals whose efforts and influence over the years are still evident in some fashion in this text. To Ed Allen, Art Wright, Ned Gene Jones, George Reynolds, Walter Friess, Larry Cooper, and Robert Dettinger, former colleagues on the faculty of GMI, our thanks and appreciation are extended. Also, a debt of gratitude is owed by all who may derive benefit from this book to John Duncan and Ted Gobeske, formerly of GM Manufacturing Development Engineering, who were instrumental in organizing and guiding the early committee work upon which much of the original manual used at GMI was based. Sincere gratitude also goes to all the committee members who made contributions to this book.

Edward J. Polk

ONE

INTRODUCTION

From beginnings rooted primarily in the areas of methods analysis and work measurement, the industrial engineering profession has moved outward from this narrow-base concentration to encompass a widely expanded sphere of concern and influence. This trend is clearly evident on the one hand by the growth in numbers of practitioners found throughout the world of business, industry, government, and academia. It is further indicated by the variety of specialties represented in the field and included within the curriculums of most degree programs. Such areas of concentration as computer systems design, ergonomics, quality control and reliability, manufacturing and assembly systems design, production and material control, project management, and the economic evaluation of engineering alternatives are but a few which might be cited.

This expanding breadth of interest has been accompanied and facilitated by a similar expansion in the body of pertinent knowledge as well as by a phenomenal growth in technology applicable to the measurement and quantification of the characteristics of all types of systems. In particular, modern computer systems have revolutionized data-processing capabilities, permitting the application of mathematical tools of analysis and computation to real-world problems on scales of magnitude and complexity that had previously been unapproachable; in fact, this progress may be only a hint of what may occur in the next few years.

There is, however, a common factor or thread running through all the problems which face the managers of most organizations producing goods or services, whether private or public. This ubiquitous component is the cost of labor, which must still be measured, controlled, and utilized efficiently. Placing an accurate value on the time taken to perform work is still an essential part of the industrial engineer's responsibility. The successful management of any enterprise involves cost control, planning and estimating, development of budgets, and other activities, all of which involve great dependence on the reliability of these values. Decisions about making or buying a component, installing labor-saving machinery, or withdrawing from a particular line of business demand a solid information base, including the real cost of labor. The consequences of such decisions are often far reaching, not only touching upon the people directly involved but often rippling throughout an entire community.

It is particularly appropriate, therefore, to present a reprise of the basic elements of these traditional tasks with special emphasis on an organized approach to problem solving, critical analysis, and careful measurement. Underlying all these tools and techniques is a constant awareness of each worker's needs, capabilities, limitations, dignity, and value as a human being. No amount of effort by any staff or service group can guarantee the success of the enterprise unless the worker and the workplace are given top priority in the scheme of things. That in large measure is where the long-term success of any organization, as measured by profitability, begins and ends.

HISTORICAL PERSPECTIVES OF INDUSTRIAL ENGINEERING

As in most endeavors, a look backward at the beginnings often provides light for the future and appreciation for the efforts of the pioneers who opened some doors to the present and may most importantly provide the insight necessary for avoiding pitfalls and errors which were discovered early and forgotten of late.

One of the earliest references to sound management principles is found in the Bible, Exodus, chapter 18. An overwhelmed Moses is counseled by Jethro to relieve himself of petty details and minor matters by delegating to carefully selected subordinates the authority to render decisions on routine matters. Implementation of this principle of management by exception, hinges on the establishment of operating rules and policies within which the subordinates are empowered to act. Managers are thus able to apply their special skills and talents most effectively to the disposition of non-routine matters (the "exceptions") which do not meet the criteria for action by the subordinates.

Testimony to an even earlier achievement in technical skill and organization of resources is offered by the pyramids of Egypt. These massive structures, built by people and animals with only the most rudimentary machinery, raise a number of technical questions, many of which have not yet been answered. Given the size and precision of these massive structures, one is led to speculate that the architects supervising the design and construction must have used scale models (simulations) to avoid errors and devise methods of construction. The magnitude of this achievement is in no way diminished by the fact that unlimited human effort was used in lieu of machinery. Not only do the architectural and technical riddles remain, but the puzzle is compounded by new problems. The questions raised and still unanswered revolve around managing the concerted efforts of tens of thousands of people, providing direction and control, and solving the logistical problems of providing food and water for such numbers. Considerable executive and administrative talents in supply and distribution were clearly required.

The pictorial writings of that era also suggest an awareness of a need for organizational structure and identification of levels in the organization. Various kinds and classes of workers are distinguishable by their dress. An awareness of some principles of motion economy is also evidenced by the illustrations of the gang bosses responsible for enforcing order and, no doubt, generating dedication to the task at hand. They are repeatedly shown with one large club held high in the right hand and a long dagger held in the left hand. A second long dagger is positioned and located on the body so that it can be grasped with the least amount of motion in the event that it instead of the club was desired in the hand.

That the Roman Empire came to dominance and prevailed for so many years is attributable in part to great administrative skills in government and successful management of the military organization. Perhaps the Romans recognized the truth of an observation about the management of people reported in the Discourses of Socrates: "Those who know how to employ men, conduct either private or public affairs judiciously, while those who do not know will err in the management of both." One is thus led to speculate that when "employment" of men ceases to be a prime concern in any society, the resulting "mismanagement" leads to the eventual downfall of that society. There may be a lesson here for all of us.

It is clear in any case that the attempts to define management and to develop a science of management certainly predates Frederick Taylor and others who followed the scientific management principles which he espoused.

In 1776, Adam Smith wrote *An Inquiry Into the Nature and Cause of the Wealth of Nations,* not only a masterpiece on the economics of enterprise but also a clear statement of the basis for industrial efficiency. In 1832, Charles Babbage in his *Economy of Machinery and Manufacture* presented a masterful description and analysis of conditions in industry of the time and furnished a model method of studying those conditions. These efforts clarify the nature and bases for intelligent operation of business and industry and have been paralleled by many learned people in other parts of the western world at a time when industrialization was just beginning to emerge as a driving force which would have tremendous impact on society throughout the world.

SCIENTIFIC MANAGEMENT

The term "scientific management" was devised to describe principles of management developed and espoused by Frederick Taylor which were intended to bring to the industrial scene new problem-solving methods based on investigation and measurement. The purpose of these new ideas was to promote increased productivity and derive maximum benefit from all resources for the greatest good for the greatest number, with justice, increased opportunity, comfort, and happiness for all.

In preparation for hearings before the Interstate Commerce Commission and Congress relating to a request by the railroad operators for freight-rate increases, a group opposing the increases, including Louis Brandeis, later Justice Brandeis, expressed a need for a short name by which the subject of "science applied to management" could be identified more conveniently. Brandeis and his group were preparing to argue for better management and improved operations rather than increased freight rates. The

Taylor system among others was to be presented as an alternative approach to the fiscal problems of the railroads. The term scientific management was finally selected as being free from personalities and embodying the essential ideas of this new style of management of decision by measurement.

As often happens, however, the best intentions of well-meaning individuals may become entangled in politics, sensational journalism, and misinterpretation by the technical writers of the day. Many argued that there was a lack of scientific basis for Taylor's theories. In truth, if one requires a methodology by which hypotheses are developed and systematically tested against factual evidence acquired in a totally unbiased manner, much of Taylor's work would fall short. The term thus acquired a negative connotation and much adverse publicity. Taylor himself objected to it and would have preferred a term such as "measured functional management," also suggested at the time. This would perhaps have better served the cause of science in management, as well as being closer to what Taylor and his associates were advocating—a thoughtful and systematic approach to solving the problems of management.

The "science of management" implies much more than what the term scientific management came to mean to most early industrialists. It has evolved into a broad-based field of knowledge and applied technology firmly anchored in quantitative measurement and analysis. The discipline of industrial engineering continues to grow as a profession, with continuing emphasis on research to develop new tools and new applications of old ones, always dedicated to the proposition that effective utilization of all factors involved in an organization providing goods or services is essential to the survival of that organization, the well-being of everyone associated with it, and in the broader view, the ultimate well-being of the nation and society.

HISTORICAL FIGURES IN INDUSTRIAL ENGINEERING

Though any list of people who have in any way contributed must inevitably be incomplete, mention of a few seems entirely appropriate to further demonstrate the roots of the body of knowledge and the scope of applications as the profession has evolved over the years.

Adam Smith

Adam Smith, a British economist and author of *Wealth of Nations* (published in 1776), recognized and stated the principle of division of labor, which Babbage later restated, emphasizing its importance. Smith also recorded the divisions of work for manufacturing pins, listing 11 operations and the standard time and cost for each operation.

In his book, Smith discusses three basic economic advantages resulting from the division of labor: development of a skill or a dexterity when a single task is performed repetitively; a saving of time normally lost in changing over from one activity to the next; and invention of machines or tools that seem normally to follow when people specialize their efforts on tasks of restricted scope. The book was a milestone in the development of production economics, both because Smith's observations probably accelerated the division of labor and because this great scholar recognized that there existed a rationale for volume production.

Frederick Winslow Taylor (1856–1915)

Taylor came from a well-to-do Philadelphia family. He attended schools in France and Germany and New England's Phillips Exeter Academy, where he graduated at the top of his class. He had planned to study law at Harvard, passing entrance examinations with honors but at the cost of seriously impaired eyesight. Forced to give up the idea of further study at the age of 18, he obtained a job in a machine shop at the Cramp Shipyard in Philadelphia, where he served the apprenticeships of patternmaker and machinist.

In 1878, when Taylor's apprenticeship ended, he became a laborer at Midvale Steel Company, remaining there for the next 12 years. The friendship between Taylor's family and the W. W. Clark family, which owned a majority of the Midvale stock, probably helped his early advancements in the company. Though he started as a laborer, he became gang boss after 2 years and chief engineer after 4 years, when he was 28 years of age. During his early years at Midvale, Taylor studied at night and received a degree in mechanical engineering from Stevens Institute in 1883.

As a supervisor, Taylor first became aware of such problems as what was the best way to do a job and what constituted a day's work. Taylor thus realized that it was the employees rather than the employers who were running the various shops.

Taylor observed that "the workmen together had carefully planned just how fast each job should be done; they set a pace for each machine throughout the shop— limited to about one-third of a good day's work."

Taylor tried every expedient to get his workers to turn out more work. He fired stubborn employees and even hired untrained men and tried training them himself. Even though he urged his workers to produce more, he fully sympathized with their reluctance. Since the company reduced the piece rate as output increased, earnings were fixed regardless of what they produced.

That management hadn't the slightest idea what constituted a proper day's work shocked Taylor. So he set out to discover for himself just what the ingredients were. Taylor believed it was management's obligation to understand the workers and their jobs. He wanted individual jobs surveyed and a program worked out to ensure an orderly system guaranteeing maximum production at minimum cost.

After 12 years at Midvale, Taylor left to test his management theories with other firms. The most important of these was Bethlehem Steel Company. Here Taylor attempted to systematize management-employee communications, gather information on the qualities of cutting tools, and assess "correct" work methods.

One of Taylor's most noted experiments centered around the simple job of carrying pig iron (castings from a blast furnace) from yard pile to freight car. No one could conceive a more elementary example of mere physical effort. After watching his men load pig iron into freight cars from the storage yard, Taylor decided that they were not doing it the best way. He thought that they used the wrong motions and that they worked too hard and too long, becoming overtired and having to rest too long. He believed that the work would be less tiring if the workers did it differently and took frequent short rest periods.

The men were paid $1.15 a day, loading an average of $12\frac{1}{2}$ tons of pig iron per man per day. One person in the group named Schmidt was offered the opportunity to earn more money if he would follow directions on how to pick up, carry, and put down the pigs of iron, and to take frequent short rests. Taylor believed that in this way Schmidt could load more pig iron.

The results obtained were startling, as the figures in the table indicate. Schmidt

	Before tests	After completion of tests
Output per day per worker	$12\frac{1}{2}$ tons	$47\frac{1}{2}$ tons
Wages per day per worker	$1.15 per day	$1.85 per day
Labor cost per ton	9.2 cents	3.9 cents

followed the directions, loading 47 tons in one day and earning $1.85, and continued to do so thereafter. Some of the workers could not handle that much pig iron, but the company soon had many applicants for the $1.85 job.

With respect to the fatigue element, Taylor found that a worker handling 92-pound pigs should be under load less than 45 percent of the working period for best efficiency. Of course, this percentage would vary with the physical demand and would be higher with lighter loads.

A similar experiment was conducted on shoveling work. Taylor was not the first to study shoveling, but his study made the headlines. Taylor had a flair for the dramatic and received widespread attention for some of the things he did. He found that each person in the gang furnished his own shovel, and that the shovels were of various sizes. Sometimes the yard laborers had to shovel coal, sometimes iron ore, sometimes ashes. Hence the weight per shovelful varied considerably, depending on the material lifted. By experiment, he found that most work was done when a load of about 21 pounds was moved per shovelful. He had the company buy a stock of shovels of various sizes. No matter what the material shoveled, the appropriate size shovel could be furnished to the workers. Large shovels were used for ashes, and small shovels for iron ore. In such a way, the load was always about 21 pounds. As a result, the work done per worker increased and costs were reduced.

Significant conclusions were drawn from these and similar experiments. They demonstrated the importance of regulated rest periods (related to the human energy expended); standard methods of working; standard tasks (output quotas); adequate wage incentives; and proper selection and training of workers for each type of job.

With respect to the wage incentive, Taylor believed that the worker's best effort could be obtained only with wages based on output, and that the wage rate should enable superior workers to exceed their former earnings by 30 to 100 percent. Inadequate incentives would discourage extra cooperation and effort. Many employers who adopted the Taylor method of setting time standards and piece rates but failed to provide sufficient reward could not achieve desired objectives. Dissatisfied workers refused to cooperate.

Taylor's standard tasks were not easy ones; he placed dependence on *superior labor*. He believed that superior workers could be found for each class of work and that adequate wage incentives would reward such individuals for this superiority. He also believed that no one should be kept on a chance-assigned job for which he or she was ill-suited. He assumed that all workers could be placed at jobs within their individual capacities.

Experiments such as those conducted by Taylor pioneered the modern science of operation analysis, which includes motion study and time study. The experiments involved more than the simple process of cut, try, and record results. Methods and conclusions were *scientific* because of exhaustive investigations, extensive accumulation of factual data, analytical studies, and derivation of principles.

Taylor arrived at four fundamental principles which remain important today. Referring to managers and their duties, he summarized as follows:

> First, they develop a science for each element of a man's work which replaces the old rule of thumb method.
> Second, they scientifically select and then train, teach, and develop the workman, whereas in the past he chose his own work and trained himself as best he could.
> Third, they heartily cooperate with the men so as to insure all of the work being done in accordance with the principles of the science which has been developed.
> Fourth, there is an almost equal division of the work and responsibility between the management and the workmen. The management takes over all work for which they are better fitted than the workmen, while in the past almost all of the work and the greater part of the responsibility were thrown upon the men.[1]

Taylor developed a number of systems which he put into practice as manufacturing executive and consultant. These included forms of organization and a wage system. He emphatically pointed out, however, that basic principles were the essence of scientific management and that systems and detail procedures must be fitted to individual conditions and must be revised to accommodate new developments. This important concept was neglected by some efficiency experts who tried to obtain quick results by employing some elements of Taylor's methods while disregarding others. The results in such cases were not satisfactory. Taylor's differential piece rate and functional foremanship are now obsolete.

Taylor is sometimes referred to as the father of scientific management, but to credit him with originating it is claiming too much. He certainly did a great deal to develop the field of management as a science, but his greatest contribution was that of developing and dramatically publicizing the field of management. He was the movement's catalytic agent. His imagination and zeal in carrying through his investigations were perhaps equal to the task of originating the ideas. The fact is, however, that he arrived too late on the scene to be credited with the whole job. He himself said: "Hardly a single piece of original work was done by me in Scientific Management.

[1] F. W. Taylor, *The Principles of Scientific Management,* Harper & Bros., New York, 1929.

Everything that we have has come from a suggestion by someone else." However, Taylor is undoubtedly the outstanding historical figure in the development of the production management field. Others were observers and writers, but Taylor was both a thinker and a doer.

By the turn of the century, interest in improved shop-management technique had become more general. During this time, Taylor, who by then had become a consulting engineer, was prominent in management activities. In 1906, he was president of the American Society of Mechanical Engineers. He wrote numerous articles, most noteworthy of which were "A Piece Rate System" (1895) and "On the Art of Cutting Metal" (1906). His two books, *Shop Management* (1903) and *The Principles of Scientific Management* (1911), are classics in the literature of management.

Henry Laurence Gantt (1861–1919)

Gantt was born May 20, 1861, in Calvert County, Maryland. He graduated from Johns Hopkins University with a bachelor of arts degree at 19. He then taught for 3 years at the McDonough School in Baltimore County. In 1884, he received a degree in mechanical engineering from Stevens Institute of Technology.

Gantt began his industrial work at Midvale and Bethlehem Steel Companies in association with Frederick W. Taylor. This early union lasted for only a short time, because Gantt felt that Taylor's approach was too restrictive, owing to its mechanistic ideology. Gantt believed that there was far more to the industrial complex and went on to develop a concept that visualized industrial problems as national problems, with the human element being of prime importance. He placed strong emphasis upon properly trained management. Trained workers, according to Gantt, would not be sufficient if management lacked proper direction. He believed that business must produce service first, with rewards (profits) the by-product, because "reward according to service rendered is the only foundation on which our industrial and business system can permanently stand."

These principles were radical departures from the philosophy of his day, and it becomes apparent to the student of Gantt's teachings that modern devices do not always correct the situations which he encountered, but merely hide them from the untrained eye.

Gantt is remembered for initiating the concept of a task and bonus system, based on the notion that a reward for a good job would mean more in the long run than a penalty for a poor job. During his work with the Ordnance Department at the time of the first World War, the Gantt chart technique was developed.

In a talk before the ASME on November 30, 1961, Professor David B. Porter of New York University, a former associate of Gantt, described the Gantt chart's principles as follows:

> Mr. Gantt recognized that these charts were more than tools to aid in production planning and control. They are, in reality, effective measures of performance of those at all levels from workman to manager. The record is clear and the responsibilities for either good or poor performances are accurately placed. This is truly a democratizing performance force which causes

control to gravitate from weak to strong hands, or as he (Gantt) put it, "to those who know what to do and how to do it." This reflects the philosophy of Gantt, who was impatient with any system which covered up the shortcomings of management and caused frustration and ill will within the organization.

Gantt was much interested in the new type of management as applied to all aspects of a business. He placed heavy responsibility on management and emphasized the principles of training, helping, and leading people rather than merely directing and driving.

Gantt was a close associate of Taylor, but later branched out as a consultant on his own. Gantt's and Taylor's viewpoints on management were in many respects the same, but Taylor emphasized analysis and organization of the work in solving problems and Gantt gave major attention to the people who were doing it. He insisted that willingness to use correct methods and skills in performing a task are as important as knowing the methods and having the skills in the first place. He thus perceived the weight of the human element in productivity and approached the concept of motivation as we understand it today.

Gantt described a task and bonus system of wage payments, which exemplified this point of view and had a far-reaching effect on compensation methods. As time passed, Gantt became increasingly interested in management's broad obligations to society. In *The Parting of the Ways,* published in 1919, he called for the return to a philosophy from which he felt management had departed—a return which gained momentum in the 1930s and has been strongly influential ever since.

Frank B. Gilbreth (1868-1924)

Gilbreth is the most prominent figure in the history of operation analysis, or motion study. Ably assisted by his wife Lillian, Gilbreth developed methods and principles which are the foundations of modern practice in this field. As Lillian expressed it; Frank was absorbed in "the quest for the one best way"—a search which was to lead far beyond the experiments of Taylor and other contemporaries.

Gilbreth's first classic experiment was in bricklaying, a skilled trade. As originally performed, this was a job exceedingly wasteful of skill and effort. Gilbreth was able to increase output per man-hour from 120 bricks to 360. He accomplished this by elimination of unnecessary movements, by full utilization of both hands, by simple new apparatus, and by the introduction of low-cost helpers. A special scaffold was devised, easily adjustable in height so that the bricklayer could work continuously at a convenient level. The unskilled assistant working below the scaffold sorted the bricks with best faces out and stacked them on standard pallets, which were then elevated to the masons. For various reasons, Gilbreth's and similar efforts to increase productivity did not appeal to labor organizations in the construction field. It seems probable that if labor had adopted his methods, construction costs could have been greatly reduced.

The bricklaying achievement was the first of a long series of experiments. Gilbreth later adopted a research tool not available to Taylor—the motion picture. Motion studies were formerly dependent on the stopwatch and the capacity of an observer to perceive, time, and record the various steps in a work operation. The movie camera detects details of motion too fast for the human eye to catch and produces a permanent record which can be studied in slow motion or frame by frame. As a result of extensive motion studies of many types of work, the Gilbreths developed two new and exceedingly important devices for operation analysis: (1) basic elements common to all human work operations and (2) principles of efficient motion. The basic elements of motions as defined by the Gilbreths were named "therbligs" (Gilbreth spelled backward, with the *th* transposed). Originally, there were 17 therbligs. Examples are search, select, grasp, transport (the hand) empty, transport (the hand) loaded, assemble, plan, and inspect. Although industrial engineers have changed or combined several of the original therbligs, the analysis of therbligs and their combinations is the basis for detailed motion studies of the present day.

The Gilbreth laws of efficient motion embody scientific principles which serve as guides to the analyst in determining the one best way for handling any manual job. As originally developed, there were 16 of these laws. To cite one example: "Motions of arms should be in opposite and symmetrical directions, instead of in the same directions, and made simultaneously." (This principle is based on the fact that by its observance, the body of the operator is kept in balance by the opposing arm movements, which eliminates the fatigue of turning or resisting motion at the shoulders, back, and hips.) Gilbreths' laws of efficient motion have also been revised and supplemented since their days.

The Gilbreths paralleled Gantt in their interest in human beings and human effort, applying to this interest an enormous capacity for organized detail. They explored many other important new areas of management. A common characteristic of their thinking was emphasis on the employee, as an individual, whose productivity depended on attitude, opportunity, and physical environment as much as the use of correct methods and ideal equipment. The Gilbreths' three-position plan of promotion proposed in 1916 anticipated by almost 40 years what is now called systematic management development.

The Gilbreth family of 12 children often participated in the work being done by this remarkable husband-wife team. They often served as subjects for studies ranging from bathing and brushing teeth to the touch system of typing.

Their books *Motion Study, Applied Motion Study,* and *The Psychology of Management* still make interesting and useful reading for the industrial engineer. In a lighter vein, *Cheaper by the Dozen* and *Bells on Their Toes* are amusing accounts of life in the Gilbreth family circle written by two of the younger Gilbreths.

Walter A. Shewhart

Shewhart, a young physicist of the Bell Telephone Laboratories, is credited with the development of the statistical control chart in 1924. Wrestling with a problem made complicated by the presence of random variation, he came to realize that the problem was statistical in nature. Some of the observed variation in performance was natural to the process and unavoidable. But from time to time there would be variations which could not be so explained.

He reached the brilliant conclusion that it would be desirable and possible to set limits upon the natural variation of any process, so that fluctuations within these limits could be readily explained by chance causes; but any variation outside this band would indicate a change in the underlying process. There followed the development of charts for measurement and control on attributes and variables, the concept of the rational subgroup and its use in most effectively letting the process set the limits of natural variability, and a large amount of practical experimentation in trying out the new methods on actual plant problems. In 1931, Shewhart produced his great text, *Economic Control of Quality of Manufactured Product,* in which the whole topic was laid out, including the theory, philosophy, applications, and most importantly, economic aspects. The field of industrial quality control gets its name from this book and control charts are often called Shewhart control charts.

L. H. C. Tippett

Tippett described a statistical method which he had developed in the English textile industry to measure operator and machine delays in 1934. He called his method the snap-reading method, finding it particularly effective for determining the causes of loom stoppages in the textile factories he was studying. Tippett states that around 1927 he was making time studies in the weaving sheds to discover how much of the productive capacity was lost for various causes.

As Tippett was observing his weaving sheds, he was on the lookout for methods of observation to collect data. One day a weaving manager remarked: "I can tell at a glance whether the weaving in the shed is good. If most of the weavers are bent over their looms mending a warp break, weaving is bad; if the weavers are mostly watching running looms, weaving is good." It became clear that a snapshot of the state of the looms in a shed taken at any instant was in some way an indication of the rate of production in a short interval surrounding that instant, and of the losses in output due to various causes.

Tippett saw at once that a snapshot of the looms taken at any instant would enable him to determine the production of the looms at that instant. Further study led him to develop the snap-reading method of analysis which later became known as ratio-delay studies. The current name for this technique is work sampling. Tippett, an outstanding mathematician and statistician, has a long list of articles and publications to his credit in mathematical and statistical journals and texts.

Although presented from a variety of perspectives, each of these people was concerned with some measure of the efforts of people to achieve the goals of an organization. As suggested by these brief accounts, the basic principles of work design, method analysis, and work measurement have long been recognized as essential to continued improvement in productivity; similarly, there was a perceived need for administrative and management practices emphasizing leadership rather than drivership, based on mutual recognition of a shared responsibility for the long-term success of any organization.

The material presented in this book is essentially a reprise of proven techniques aimed at practitioners who continue to search for the one best way, which in truth can exist only momentarily. Changing conditions require continuous effort to reevaluate, update, and review; thus a continuing need for these basic tools of the industrial engineer is assured.

It is obviously beyond the scope and intent of this book to treat the matter of management practices and policies as they have an impact on the work force and the industrial engineering function to measure, control, and predict labor cost. It must of necessity be a given that total management support and commitment is assured, and that all concerned are prepared to work a bit harder to achieve their common goals at no sacrifice of human dignity and worth in the process.

QUESTIONS

1-1 What is the common factor involved in cost control and planning, estimating, and establishing budgets?

1-2 Name four areas of industrial engineering typically found in college curriculums.

1-3 Explain the principle of management by exception.

1-4 What were the three basic economic advantages stemming from the division of labor as reported by Adam Smith?

1-5 Frederick Taylor became aware of a number of problems in management style early in his career. What were some of these problems?

1-6 What were the principal factors involved with Taylor's successful effort to improve the handling of pig iron? With that of the shoveling jobs?

1-7 What are the four principles of good management proposed by Taylor?

1-8 What was the basis for H. L. Gantt's task and bonus system?

1-9 According to Gantt, what was the first concern of business in order to guarantee long-term success?

1-10 The Gilbreths are credited with pioneering what special aspect of industrial engineering?

1-11 In what respect did Gilbreths' work parallel that of H. L. Gantt?

1-12 What were two of the contributions attributed to Walter Shewhart?

1-13 Who is credited with developing work sampling?

PROBLEMS

1-1 Aside from those examples cited in this chapter, what other examples might give evidence of very early recognition of the basic principles of motion economy, efficient organization, or the assembly-line concept?

1-2 What are the arguments in favor of the cost-of-living allowance (COLA) feature of many labor agreements? To what would you ascribe the success or failure of these COLA agreements to meet the objectives for which they were written?

1-3 What are the characteristics of management style and industrial organization in Japan which are different from those in the United States? In what respect do you think their methods could be successful in this country? What would be unlikely to succeed in this country?

TWO

SYSTEMS APPROACH TO METHODS ANALYSIS AND WORK MEASUREMENT

In recent years, various concepts of system analysis have been developed. With continued development, these new concepts become more involved and of greater scope as more is being learned and applied to the many categories of activities. Normally, a problem of communication exists in the development of concepts and their peculiar language. Therefore, an introduction to systems concepts is presented as an introductory part of this chapter, leading to an explanation of the methods analysis and work-measurement philosophies. Each of these important functions are involved in system analysis, so a more thorough understanding of the systems concept is therefore necessary.

CONCEPTS OF SYSTEMS

In the historical development of industrial engineering, the pioneers researched or analyzed activities, leading to the development of problem-solving approaches and techniques of study. For the most part, the results brought forth means of studying individual components of a system for improvement of productivity and thus better utilization of human beings, materials, space, and equipment. However, the interplay and interactions between components of a single system and between related systems further complicated the analysis of any one component by itself. Therefore, today an awareness of the total system—its function, components, and operation—is a necessary part of any study involved.

The use of the terms "system" or "total systems" can be misleading. One edition of the Webster dictionary defines a *system* as

A set or arrangement of things so related or connected as to form a unity or organic whole.
A set of facts, principles, rules, etc., classified or arranged in a regular, orderly form so as to show a logical plan linking the various parts.

Based on such a definition, there is a tendency to view any activity of single and multiple components as a system. Expressions such as information system, data-processing system, production and inventory-control system, accounting system, marketing system, quality-control system, packaging system, manufacturing system are a few examples. Under these circumstances, an individual reasons that the sum total of an activity must be a system of some sorts. However, the system as referred to in this text is defined as

An integrated group of interacting physical and human resources designed to process material or information to the desired state of product or service.

Thus, by definition, the higher the system level, the more complex the study becomes, since more components are involved. One concept would be that the organization and its many interrelated activities is one system, a system encompassing the policy, financial, and top-management decision functions through the design, improvement, installation, operation, and control of a manufacturing facility to the inclusion of packaging, shipping, and eventual sales of the product. Another concept is that each function of the organization has a system of accomplishing its specific objective in view of the total organization's goals. Since a wide variation in interpretation is possible, it is reasonable to first separate the activities of the organization into three broad categories, or types, of systems—administrative, manufacturing, and control system (see Fig. 2-1).

Within each broad category can be found functions or groups of activities, each of which is frequently identified as having its specific subsystem.

The very existence of industrial enterprise is built upon the multitude of systems integrated and coordinated to achieve its purpose and further to accomplish the objectives established for its mode of operation. Each enterprise must have reason to exist and must, in turn, establish objectives in line with external and internal influences. An example of external influences may be competition, business trends, marketing, and consumers wants. On the other hand, the internal influences of the design, operation, coordination, improvement, and maintenance of systems will likewise influence the functioning of the enterprise. It should be noted that the influences and their intensity will vary as business cycles change. Therefore, in order to counteract these influences and keep the enterprise in balance, a need exists for continued

Research
Design or planning

Analysis and improvement
Control
Administrative and/or management communications and decisions

Since the same resources are basically available to all enterprises, the difference between competing enterprises has to do with how well they use their basic resources of human beings, materials, and equipment to manufacture a product in view of the external and internal influences. Methods analysis and work measurement, in turn, influence this resource utilization. They should permeate the system in order to achieve realistic objectives suited to the organizational capabilities. Management, in turn, uses the output of methods and work measurement to make decisions that lead to action on the physical and human resources of the organization to produce the desired output.

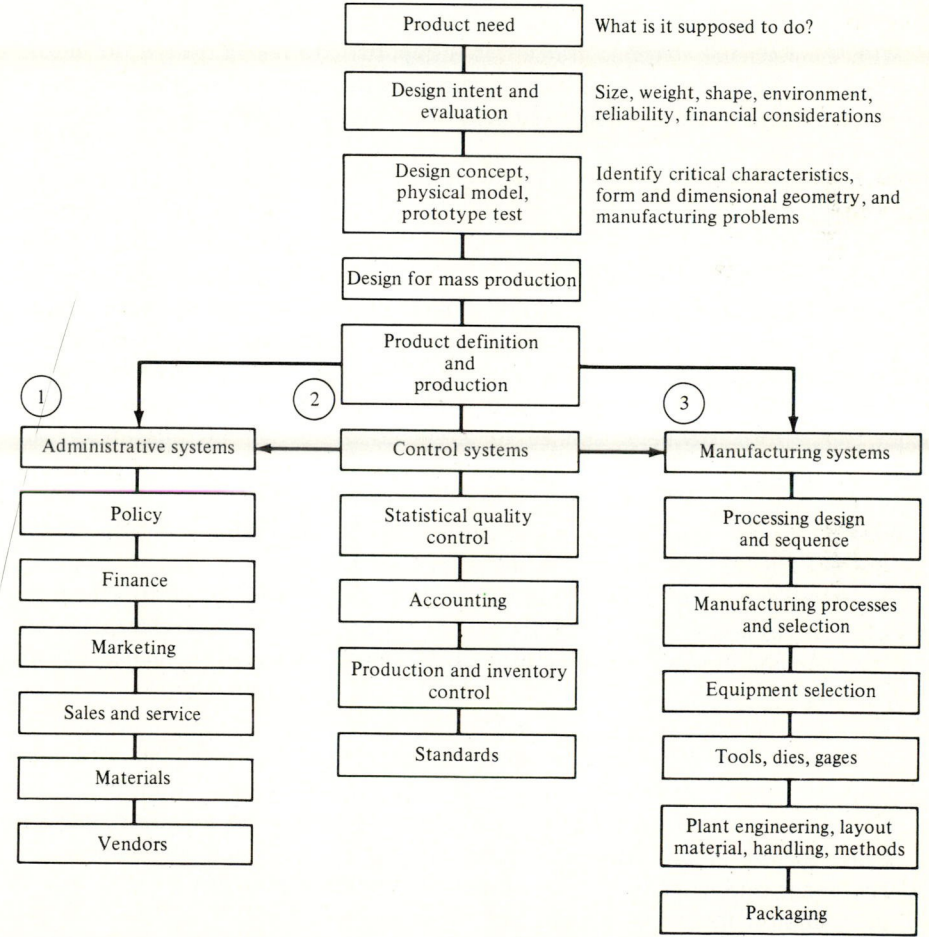

Figure 2-1 Typical example of categories of systems in a manufacturing organization and their functional components.

Systems and their components are to be studied continually. Knowledge of the common characteristics of all systems is therefore important to the analyst. These are

1. The function or purpose of the system
2. The input to the system to achieve the function
3. The output specifications required of the system
4. The facilities and equipment and accompanying controls constituting the system
5. The methods employed by the human resources in working with the physical resources of the system

Since a system involves a multitude of components, it would appear that each function of the enterprise through its specific systems would take a segregated part of the total project or study and accomplish its function within the framework of its specific objectives. In theory this should work; but in practice, coordination of effort becomes the most frustrating task.

With these general concepts in mind, it is important to take a look at the underlying philosophies behind methods analysis and work measurement to gain insight into why they are part and parcel of any system.

METHODS ANALYSIS

Methods analysis, or the method function, has evolved from the initial efforts of people such as Frederick W. Taylor and Frank Gilbreth. Through the years methods analysis has become a more respected and valued addition to management resources for design, planning, improvement, and operation of systems. Initially, methods analysis was focused on the production facilities. Today the problem-solving approaches, techniques, and efforts are being applied to all functions of the enterprise. However, growth has been slow, owing to the inability of people to see the application of methods-analysis principles and fundamentals to other functions as well as the reluctance of people to engage in the total methods-analysis effort. Resistance to change and the blocking of the analysis of one's own method of operation are continual struggles within the enterprise, but times of past and present show the steady growth of methods analysis and its integration throughout the many functions of the enterprise.

The basic philosophies of methods analysis in view of the total system concept are the following.

1. Increasing productivity and developing manpower, facilities, and effectiveness are the objectives for studying systems.
2. Methods analysis is concerned with all phases of system design, development, installation, operation, control, and maintenance.
3. The design and planning of systems should consider alternatives from models of automation to integrated worker-machine systems.
4. All aspects of the system under study regardless of extent or scope should be considered in methods analysis.

5. The design or analysis of systems is enhanced through recognition of people and their abilities and talents as an integral part of the process.

These philosophies form a basis for study. The first establishes the objectives for methods analysis. The second defines the scope of the activity. The third points out the development and range of alternatives to be considered. The fourth brings out that methods analysis today includes in its processes the study of all factors of the system including the manual content. Finally, the fifth establishes the importance of people and their contributions to the design, or analysis, process.

Methods analysis is a function that is not limited in its range of application. It is a part of all designs or operations of systems in all of the administrative, control, and manufacturing activities. The success of the methods-analysis function, although guided by specialists, is primarily owing to the acceptance of its philosophies by all people of the enterprise and their applications of the principles and fundamentals of methods analysis in discharging their responsibilities. This is not to imply that there is no need for the methods analyst. As in other functions, there is a definite need for personnel skilled in methods analysis who plan to provide management with the specialized data necessary for design, development, installation, operation, improvement, and maintenance of a system. Likewise, it should not be construed to mean that methods analysis is an answer to all management problems. Rather, because of the understanding and inclusion of people in its philosophy of conduct, methods analysis encourages the team approach to problem solving with due respect for all functions of the enterprise. It can be said that methods is everyone's business.

To many analysts, the question arises about how the methods function itself can improve and thus better serve management. Improvement evolves from the activities of the total function, as depicted in Fig. 2-2.

More specifically, the activities in Fig. 2-2 include

1. *Research* of (*a*) organizational activities for problem conditions worthy of investigation and study and (*b*) means of solving problems in varied and diversified areas.
2. *Education* of management personnel in methods philosophy, principles, tech-

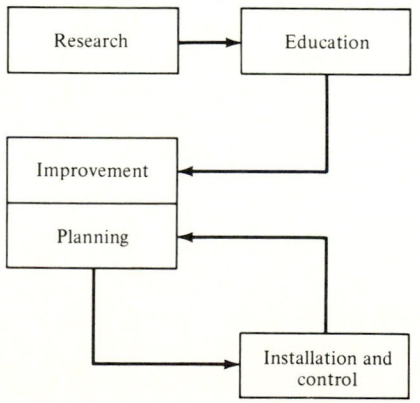

Figure 2-2 Phases of methods analysis.

niques, and service for appreciation and understanding of its purpose as well as encouragement of application of these in their areas of responsibility.

3. *Improvement* of existing systems and their components through logical and organized problem-solving approaches.
4. Participation in *planning* and design of systems as a part of the team effort.
5. Participation in the *installation and control,* or maintenance, of plans in the system operation.

As can be seen, these activities provide a wide range of endeavor. The development of methods consciousness and an improvement attitude must be a continuous effort of the methods function. The participation in all these phases is directly dependent on success in gaining acceptance of the function, its purpose, and finally full participation of all members of management in the total methods effort.

To further emphasize the breadth of these activities, here are some typical objectives concerning situations in which the methods function will be involved.

1. The design of the manual components and establishment of physical specifications for a manufacturing system development
2. The design of methods and procedures for information-handling systems
3. The analyses and improvement of a manufacturing system for varied production rates involving integrated worker-machine components
4. The conduction of studies in search of potential improvement possibilities in better use of physical and human resources
5. The development of alternatives and their specifications for automated versus integrated worker-machine processes
6. The design of packaging system methods for collecting, sorting, wrapping, and storing diversified products
7. The analysis for improvement potential of an assembly system for an anticipated production increase

THE METHODS-ENGINEERING APPROACH

When used effectively, the methods function almost always follows a sound engineering approach to problem solving, frequently labeled the methods-engineering approach. This approach is generally basic to all engineering analysis and design functions and more logically should be labeled an engineering approach. Nevertheless, it can be a guide to analysts in all types of problem solving (see Fig. 2-3).

This outline for problem solving was refined into seven steps by the General Motors Methods Engineering Committee and the Work Standards and Methods Engineering Section of the manufacturing staff. Each of the seven steps of the approach are proven steps in problem solving. To emphasize one step as being more important than another would be misleading, since each must be undertaken and completed for the problem concerned. However, it should be recognized that the first step is most important in getting underway in the problem-solving approach.

Step 1 Determine Problem or Objective

The first impression is that this step consists of two different considerations. However, the analyst may or may not know what problem conditions must be studied in order to accomplish the objective. In a line of operations, one step may be the bottleneck. Improvement of that one step could lead to the achievement of the objective stated for the entire line. In another case it is possible that the first step would be to become familiar with conditions, define the problem(s), and then state the objective for the study. As a result, the definition of the problem may precede or follow the statement of the objective. Of most importance is that the problem conditions be brought to light and carefully analyzed so that the scope of the study can be identified.

The thought of "what comes first—the chicken or the egg" can be applied to this step. Interaction of the problem definition and the objective will frequently occur at this stage of problem solving. The important point is that a study cannot be undertaken without some objective in mind; and the objective cannot be accomplished without a thorough understanding of the problem.

Step 2 Study Conditions

The second step appears to overlap the first in that the study of conditions may precede the problem definition or statement of the objective. The study of conditions in this step implies that once the problem conditions are identified, the analyst can proceed to apply the questioning attitude and the fundamental principles of engineering analysis to determine cause and effect. Questions such as the following should be asked:

What is being done?	Why is it being done at all?
When is it being done?	Why is it being done at that time?
Where is it being done?	Why is it being done at that place?
How is it being done?	Why is it being done by that method?
Who does it?	Why is it being done by that person?

The analyst should gather the pertinent facts relating to the functioning of the components involved and try to determine their interactions. From these facts he or she should be able to find the cause of conditions and/or the effect of one or more components on the total. Completion of this step provides a detailed understanding of the problem, the interactions of the components, and possible causes and effects of conditions relating to the problem.

Step 3 Plan Possible Solutions

From the understanding gained through the first two steps and the mass of information gathered, the analyst is prepared to plan possible solutions. A normal tendency is to consider one method, whereas many alternatives are possible answers to the problem. How any solution can be called the better or best solution without something to compare it with is difficult to understand. Still, in many instances, the analyst is trapped by lack of knowledge, guided or misguided by experience, or thwarted by lack of initiative or creativeness in developing solutions. The objective of the study is the first factor to consider when generating alternatives, since if it is stated clearly and concisely, it may have placed limitations or alternatives. For example, if the stated objective includes "with minimum expense," the consideration of automated methods may be out of order.

Regardless of the range of alternatives, the development of the first alternative is based on what can be done with present components or facilities without or with little expense. Since most activities are normally not operating at peak efficiency, the resulting alternative provides a new base for evaluating other alternatives. In addition, other alternatives may not be justified in view of the improvement obtained by this first solution.

Another approach would be to develop alternatives based first on ideal methods and then gradually back off from the specifications until a range of alternatives are developed. This approach is referred to as the creative method of planning alternatives. Again, development of alternatives will follow the process of analyzing components, developing the first alternative to obtain greatest efficiency out of existing components, and then developing further alternatives to compare with the first.

Step 4   Evaluate Possible Solutions

As noted in Fig. 2-3, four basic factors should be considered in the evaluation of solutions or alternatives. In addition, we can include the economic factors listed previously: product design, material specifications, processing sequence and process selection, equipment and facilities, tooling and devices, plant design and layout, and worker utilization. Also quality and quantity specifications should not be overlooked in the evaluation process. The evaluation should therefore consider all possible aspects of the proposed alternatives. Many times the development of proposals are limited to savings or minimum costs relating to one specific factor, such as labor savings. It is not necessarily wrong to consider such savings, but other savings may be overlooked. In addition, some managements will practice a policy that requires that all improvements pay for themselves within a prescribed period of 6 months or 1 year. This places a serious limitation on many proposals, especially if the investment involved will be of value for a much longer period of time. By all means, the analyst should attempt to evaluate completely the alternatives, noting their advantages and disadvantages, and then compare them before making a recommendation. One or more alternatives may be left to management's decision.

Step 5   Recommend Action

Development of alternatives and their evaluation based on criteria established for the problem brings the analyst to the point in problem solving where conclusions and recommendations are to be drawn. The recommendations presented provide management with the technical data necessary for decisions.

Figure 2-3 shows three suggested factors to include in the recommendation. Bene-

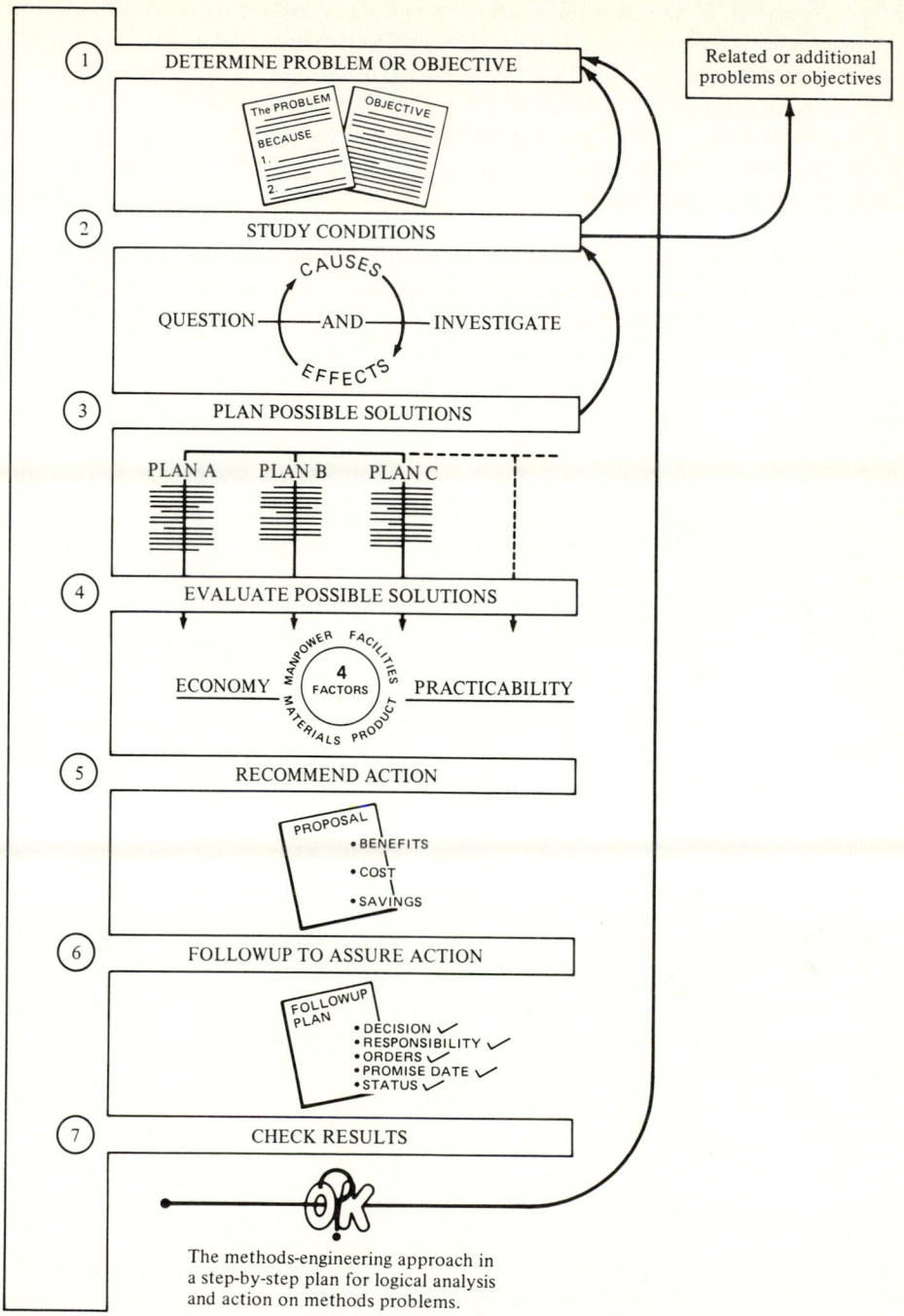

Figure 2-3 The methods-engineering approach. *(Developed by the General Motors Methods Engineering Committee and the Work Standards and Methods Engineering Section Manufacturing staff. © Copyright 1953, General Motors Corporation.)*

fits are indicated, inasmuch as these are factors which show management what will be gained by the installation of the alternative(s). The analyst should keep in mind the statement of benefits as viewed by the reader. For example, if efficiency and downtime are a constant problem or explanations for which management is more receptive, it would be better to point out the possibility of increase of efficiency from 87 to 95 percent and decrease of downtime by 18 percent than to explain the savings of 0.005 minute in a manual method.

Costs involved in acceptance and installation of the alternative(s) are always a necessary part of the recommendations. This is basic to any proposal. However, establishment of benefits aids the receptiveness of management to cost.

Savings are additional data that management will be looking for in improvement-type projects. From total savings and the necessary expenditures for the improved plan or design, management can see the length of time necessary to obtain a return on an investment. Management will frequently withhold acceptance of a proposal because the length of product run remaining during a model year will not provide the necessary savings to pay for the expenditure. In other cases, the installation is held over and the proposal slightly altered to allow for its installation at the beginning of a new model year.

Benefits, costs, and savings are traditionally the concern of any good sales person. Unlike the sales person, the analyst is not necessarily selling a proposal but rather providing pertinent technical data in such a form that management can readily comprehend to thereby help the decision-making process. Still, any proposal has some of the sales gimmick in it.

A word of caution: decisions based on other factors may outweigh decisions based on benefits, cost, and savings; in some cases, quality or other criteria are of more importance, even at a slight increase in expenditures.

Step 6   Follow Up to Ensure Action

Nothing is more discouraging and frustrating than this step of following up to ensure that the design or improvement alternative is detailed and eventually installed. The frustration factor seems to be a part of the coordination of the functions and their system of operation. Since one or more functions are usually involved in detailing the components of an alternative, decisions must first be made to proceed on the design; and then the responsibilities should be assigned for design of components, the necessary orders issued, promise dates determined for design of components or purchased components, and a continuous check made on the status of the design and installation.

Step 7   Check Results

Logically, the engineer should be concerned with the functioning of the design once it has been installed. Many plans or designs do not function exactly as planned. A debugging and test or trial runs must normally be part of the total problem approach. In addition to achieving the proper functioning of the design, it is always wise for the analyst to again check the benefits, costs, and savings predicted in the recommendation. Naturally, since management has decided to proceed on the project, it expects the outcome to be equal to or better than that predicted.

Also at this step, the analyst should recheck the problem definition and objectives to ensure that the proper action was taken and the objectives were achieved. To get off course is easy. For example, an analyst with visions of or experience in designs in material handling may get involved in the design of one factor and lose sight of the total operation analysis.

To have knowledge and a problem-solving approach is no assurance of success in problem solving. Abilities of observing, questioning, recording, analyzing, reasoning, and synthesizing are important in application of the problem-solving approach. These abilities are further explained as follows:

Observing.   Mental questioning of the activity; questioning the what, when, where, how, and who of each integral part of the situation under study.

Questioning.   Intelligent questioning of those who may provide facts regarding the situation under study so as to aid in the collection of facts not obtainable through the observation process.

Recording.   Recording information gathered in a logical, factual, and systematic manner.

Analyzing.   Analyzing data gathered and recorded for problem definition and cause and effect; breaking data down into component parts.

Reasoning.   Determining and solving problem areas.

Synthesizing.   Creating alternatives and their specifications for management decision and evaluation.

WORK MEASUREMENT

The measurement of work goes hand in hand with methods analysis. Whereas methods analysis is directed toward the study of the components of a single or multiple operation of a system, work measurement is a means of measuring the interaction of the components. Measurement, therefore, provides the analyst with a time relation between worker and job components. Previously, the importance of evaluation of alternatives in the application of the engineering approach was pointed out. Time and cost are two criteria most often used for evaluation, although other factors of quality and effectiveness of components are likewise used.

The importance of time has not been suddenly thrust upon the enterprise. History records the use of the sundial, the calendar, and other means to give the measurement of time. In past years, during the initial growth of complex industrial enterprises, time was a factor to consider, but it was not as important as it is today. Many tasks were based on the individual's concept of work and most often measured in terms of a day's work. Even though research of past history would bring forth concepts of work measurement, it wasn't until Taylor's time that interest was shown in the relation of worker and job conditions to time. Taylor's study of shoveling coal, coke, and iron indicated a need for study of all components of worker-job factors and some measurement to determine what constituted a fair day's work.

Years have passed, but the philosophy of work measurement is still misconstrued as it was in Taylor's time. Misunderstanding of the philosophy of work measurement is the root of most labor-management disagreements. Therefore, an understanding of the philosophy involved is important before we enter the discussion of various techniques.

The modern-day philosophies regarding work measurement include the following.

1. Method and time are inseparable.
2. Human work forms the focal point in work measurement because of the difficulty in establishing appropriate expected output levels for human tasks.
3. Time of human performance of assigned tasks plus the interaction of related physical or mechanical components of a system is a basis for determining the effectiveness of the system.
4. The development of a work standard is a science and an art: a science in that depth and breadth of knowledge of a multitude of system components and an inquisitive approach to gathering reliable information and time data are required; and an art, in that skillfully relating worker-job-time components in view of external influences of sociological and environmental factors and internal influences of psychological and physiological aspects of the persons involved is necessary.
5. The enterprise in order to function effectively in view of business trends and competition must continually sense, govern, measure, and predict the performance of the physical and human resources.

Because of a misunderstanding about the needs for methods analysis and work measurement, there are many who look upon these functions as being of little importance, as creating mistrust and labor-management difficulties, and as consisting of practices which are out of date and not reliable. Despite these criticisms, there are many effective methods-analysis and work-measurement functions in industry. Modern management would find it difficult to operate effectively in the many aspects of planning, estimating, and controlling multitudes of human and physical resources without such functions.

As with methods analysis, work measurement and the development and maintenance of ethical and reliable work-measurement practices are based on the acceptance of its philosophies by all people of the enterprise. Furthermore, it is important that these philosophies and practices be continually reviewed, updated, and installed in all phases of operation of the function—phases of research, education, improvement, planning, installation, and control.

Whereas the past emphasis has been on the study of production operations, today's needs point to an ever-expanding acceptance of work measurement by all activities of the enterprise. The gradual equalizing of direct and indirect labor personnel and the trend toward automation have shifted the labor costs from that of being primarily direct labor to that of being indirect labor, which in most cases is paid at a higher rate. Management is definitely concerned with the lack of means of measuring effectiveness of those involved in indirect areas. An organization cannot endure with outdated practices or opinions. Facts are needed for the effective structuring and handling of indirect areas. The resulting work-measurement data are used directly or indirectly in the decisions of many functions. They include the following.

The production and inspection function
    Provides a measure of what constitutes a fair day's work
    Provides a basis for decisions regarding requisition, release, or transfer of personnel
    Provides a basis for determining efficiency of operations
The processing and tooling function
    Furnishes a means for determining machine, tool, and equipment requirements
    Provides a measure of alternatives in the planning of or improvement in operations and operations sequence
The production and material control function
    Furnishes a means for establishing production schedules
    Provides cost data relative to in-process inventory
The accounting and time-keeping function
    Furnishes a means for determining labor costs of a product
    Provides the data necessary for determining labor and system efficiencies
Cost-estimating function
    Provides the data necessary for determining cost estimates of labor content
    Yields a feedback of data for determining actual cost versus estimated costs
The sales and service function
    Provides data for aiding in establishing a selling price for products
    Indirectly aids the function in order to work more closely with production capacities
The purchasing function
    Provides cost estimates of internal production versus purchase possibilities
    Furnishes a means for determining cost incurred in reworking vendor products
The engineering area
    Furnishes a means for comparison of engineering design alternatives
    Furnishes a means for determining costs of engineering changes

The work-measurement function is an important function. It has been condemned, belittled, and looked down upon, but never eliminated. Today there is a real need for more understanding of the function, participation by all functions of the organization directly or indirectly in the development and use of reliable data, and a continuous effort to further refine the techniques and their applications. To say that industry has found the ideal practices or approaches or is adhering to the philosophies of work measurement would be wrong. As with all functions, improvement can be realized.

Within this chapter, the explanation of methods analysis and work measurement has been treated separately. As explained previously, method and time are inseparable. The functions are likewise inseparable, even though some organizations' structures do not show this. Accompanying methods analysis is time and accompanying the development and use of work measurement data is methods analysis. Both are important functions for the continued operation of the industrial enterprise and must work together to provide management with the technical data so necessary for decision processes.

QUESTIONS

2-1 What is the definition of a system as referred to in this chapter?

2-2 What are the common characteristics of all systems?

2-3 What are the five basic philosophies of methods analysis in view of the total systems concept?

2-4 Explain how each philosophy forms a basis for study.

2-5 What is meant by the expression that methods is everyone's business?

2-6 What are the basic activities of the methods function in serving management?

2-7 What are the seven steps in the methods-engineering approach?

2-8 What are some basic questions to be asked during the study of conditions?

2-9 What are the four basic factors to be considered in the evaluation of possible solutions?

2-10 What basic abilities are important to the application of the methods-engineering approach?

2-11 What are some modern-day philosophies regarding work measurement?

2-12 What is the general trend of labor costs in the enterprise?

THREE

MANUFACTURING SYSTEMS ANALYSIS

Even though methods analysis has been traditionally associated with the analysis of operator movements, another equally important aspect of methods, that of flow analysis, has received relatively less attention. Although some of the early developments in methods and standards included tools for flow analysis, the performance of the operator at his or her work station appeared to be more susceptible to analysis and improvement.

FLOW ANALYSIS AND CHARTING TECHNIQUES

More recently the systems concept has emerged. It is essentially a way of looking at the operations and activities in an industrial organization as interrelated parts of a system. The importance of the interaction between activities is thus emphasized. In the broadest sense, the whole organization can be considered as an operating system. Within the organization there are many other systems. For example, consider a materials-handling system or a manufacturing department. As management becomes more technically oriented, more activities will be scrutinized, operating patterns will be recognized, and variables will be controlled. Hence, in the future more activities will be subjected to the systems approach. The systems concept when applied to manufacturing operations results in what might be called manufacturing systems analysis. Thus, a renewed emphasis has been given to flow analysis and other related techniques. More specifically, manufacturing systems analysis includes such techniques as the flowchart, process chart, flow-process chart, fabrication chart, and precedence chart. Many variations of these charts also exist. The techniques are simply ways of organizing information and emphasizing certain aspects such that the system in question can be more readily analyzed.

The Symbols Used

Before discussing techniques of flow or process analysis, we must recognize that recording the characteristics of a system can become quite involved. A suitable short-hand system is therefore needed. This need for a standardized and simplified approach to flow and process analysis was recognized by the Gilbreths around the turn of the century. The symbols they developed in conjunction with suitable forms were the first significant steps toward standardizing the method of recording and analyzing. The Gilbreths were comprehensive in their effort, wanting a system that would be applicable to all forms of flow and process analysis in an industrial organization. But their thoroughness was actually a deterent to the widespread adoption of the system. They had developed 40 different symbols. An attempt was made to convey an appropriate meaning with each symbol. This quantity of symbols made it necessary for people to memorize a great deal and resulted in needless discrimination between basically similar operations. By using 40 symbols, the technique became cumbersome. However, from the 40 Gilbreth symbols, an abbreviated set of symbols were developed.

Abbreviated Gilbreth symbols   The abbreviated Gilbreth symbols are as follows:

◯   A large circle to denote an operation performed.

○   A small circle to denote a movement of workers, materials, or paper work.

▽   An inverted triangle to denote filing, storage, or any form of delay in movement.

▢   A square to denote inspection for quality or quantity.

Whenever a relatively few number of symbols must cover a wide variety of activities and conditions, there is much controversy about their appropriateness. One of the criticisms of the abbreviated Gilbreth system was the likelihood of confusion between operation and move.

ASME symbols   The American Society of Mechanical Engineers (ASME) reviewed the variety of symbols in use. A committee was formed and a set of acceptable symbols were developed. These were proposed as the ASME standard.

◯   Operation

▽   Storage

⇨   Transportation or move

▢   Inspect, (quantity or quality)

D   Delay

⊙   Combined activity

The ASME symbols are widely used today and a respectable analysis can be made with the use of them.

GM symbols Many years ago the General Motors Corporation (GM) also sensed a need for standardization of the symbols to be used for analyzing the movement of a part throughout a system. This resulted in the development of the GM version of the process symbols. These symbols are as follows:

○ Move. All steps in a process where the object under observation moves from one location to another, outside of fabrication

△ Store. All steps in a process where the object remains at rest, either temporarily or permanently, outside of fabrication

◇ Fabrication. All steps in the process where the object undergoes a change in form or condition

□ Inspect. All steps in the process where the objects under observation are checked for completeness, quality, or quantity, outside of fabrication.

△c Change of carrier. All steps in the process where the object is transferred from one type of carrier to another.

    Note: The change of carrier indicates essentially instantaneous transfer. Since it does not account for movement, it is always preceded and followed by a move.

 Area of fabrication. Only the fabrication symbol should appear within the fabrication area. When a large fabrication area is shown, this area is essentially eliminated from detailed study. A similar notation can be used to designate an area of inspection or storage.

From this point on, the GM symbols will be used, because the change of carrier highlights excessive handling of a product, and there is flexibility of more or less detailed analysis possible with the use of the area of fabrication. However, the following charting techniques can be used with either the GM or the ASME symbols.

The Fabrication Chart

The fabrication chart shows only fabrication and inspection steps and does this by means of the appropriate process symbols. The information is developed in symbolic form to conveniently display a series of fabrications and inspections. The fabrication chart shows the sequence of steps and reveals the possibilities of changing the sequence and eliminating or combining operations. It facilitates communicating process information to others, and may serve as a rough guide to actual physical location of machinery and equipment. It is a useful planning tool in the development of the plant layout. See Fig. 3-1 for an example of a fabrication chart.

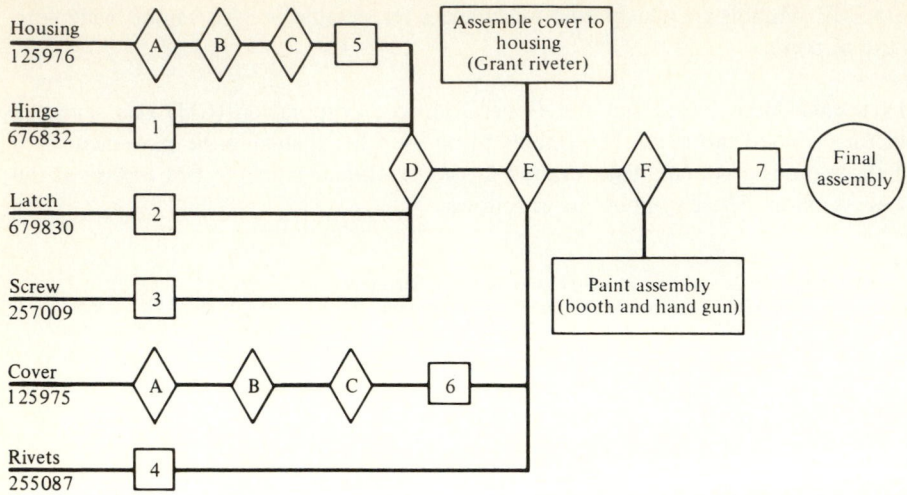

Note: 1. Inspection operations 1, 2, 3, and 4 are inspections of purchased parts.

2. Fabrication operations A, B, and C are blanking, forming, and piercing operations, respectively.

3. Inspection operations 5, 6, and 7 are inspection after processing or assembly.

4. Fabrication operations D and E are assembly operations.

5. Fabrication F is a paint operation.

Figure 3-1 A fabrication chart of a sheet metal box.

Following are some items to consider in construction of a fabrication chart.

1. A fabrication chart is developed directly from the information on parts lists, routings, and/or drawings.
2. The name and part number of the component parts of an assembly to be charted are listed (widely spaced) along the left-hand edge of the page.
3. Successive inspection and fabrication steps are plotted to the right with lines and symbols (see Fig. 3-1).
4. Additional information in the form of notes may be incorporated to suit specific needs, such as operation description, type of equipment, pieces per hour, etc. (see Fig. 3-1).

The fabrication chart is a useful tool for planning and/or analyzing a system of assembly operations or manufacturing operations.

The Process Chart

The process chart is often developed in conjunction with the flow-process chart. These two techniques provide for a thorough analysis of a system for improvement. The process chart is a sequential listing of brief descriptions of each of the steps in a system. In

PROCESS CHART

Process Description: _Timing Gear Cover Plate Assembly_

Object Followed: _Gear Cover Plate_

Name: _John Doe_ Date: _8/7_

Present Method ☒   Proposed Method ☐

Remarks: _Normal operation -- two operators_
utilized

SUMMARY	
Number of "Fabrications".. ◇	5
Number of "Moves"....... ○	13
Number of "Stores"....... △	8
Number of "Inspects"..... ☐	1
TOTAL STEPS	27
DISTANCE TRAVELED	$57\text{-}\frac{1}{2}$

Step	Fabrication / Move / Store / Inspect	Description	Distance Moved	How Moved	Parts/ Move
1	◇ ○ △ ☐	Rough stock in gondola			
2	◇ ○ △ ☐	To reinforce assembly area	13'	hand	8
3	◇ ○ △ ☐	On table			
4	◇ ○ △ ☐	To assembly reinforce	$1\text{-}\frac{1}{2}'$	hand	1
5	◇ ○ △ ☐	Assembly reinforcement and bolts assemblies to cover plate			
6	◇ ○ △ ☐	To press for restrike	$4\text{-}\frac{1}{2}'$	hand	1
7	◇ ○ △ ☐	Restrike assembly			
8	◇ ○ △ ☐	To storage bench	$3\text{-}\frac{1}{2}'$	hand	1
9	◇ ○ △ ☐	On storage bench			
10	◇ ○ △ ☐	To spot weld machine	4'	hand	1
11	◇ ○ △ ☐	Spot weld reinforcement and bolt assembly to cover plate (four spots)			
12	◇ ○ △ ☐	To storage bench	3'	hand	1
13	◇ ○ △ ☐	On storage bench			
14	◇ ○ △ ☐	To inspection area	$9\text{-}\frac{1}{2}'$	hand	$\frac{4}{2}$
15	◇ ○ △ ☐	On inspection bench			
16	◇ ○ △ ☐	To inspection operation	2'	hand	1
17	◇ ○ △ ☐	Gage bolts for width and straighten if necessary			
18	◇ ○ △ ☐	To storage area on bench	3'	hand	1
19	◇ ○ △ ☐	On bench			
20	◇ ○ △ ☐	To oil supply nozzle area	3'	hand	1
21	◇ ○ △ ☐	Assemble oil spray and crimp to cover -- assemble nuts to bolts			
22	◇ ○ △ ☐	To high cycle wrench	$2\text{-}\frac{1}{2}'$	hand	1
23	◇ ○ △ ☐	Tighten nuts to bolts			
24	◇ ○ △ ☐	To bench for storage	1'	hand	1
25	◇ ○ △ ☐	On bench			
26	◇ ○ △ ☐	To finished stock gondola	7'	hand	$\frac{4}{2}$
27	◇ ○ △ ☐	In gondola			
28	◇ ○ △ ☐				
29	◇ ○ △ ☐				
30	◇ ○ △ ☐				

Figure 3-2 A process chart for a cover-plate assembly.

comparison, the flow-process chart is a graphical illustration of a system. However, the process chart provides information in addition to the graphical flow of a flow-process chart.

1. A more detailed description of the steps of the system, hence a better understanding gained

2. A specific indication of the ratio of significant fabricate steps to the noncontributory move, store, and change-of-carrier steps
3. The distance that the part moves recorded

The completion of a process chart on a manufacturing system yields a comprehensive tabulated description of the flow through the system. See Fig. 3-2 for an example of a process chart.

Several rules should be adhered to in the completion of the process chart form:

1. The heading and periphery information of the form should be completed.
2. The symbol corresponding to the step being described should be outlined or highlighted.
3. The chart should start and end with a store. Every other step is a move.
4. Numbers should be entered in the symbols. Each set of symbols should be numbered independently to match the numbering on the flow-process chart.
5. Diagonal lines should be drawn joining the symbols in succeeding steps to indicate flow.
6. The description for steps in the system should contain the following information:

Move	From what location to what location
Store	In what kind of container, at what location
Inspect	For what features, quality, or quantity
Change of carrier	From what carrier to what other carrier
Fabricate	A description of the process

7. Additional columns are provided to enter such information as distance moved, how moved, number moved, time for fabrication, etc.
8. The summary section must be completed at the top of the form.

The Flow-Process Chart

The flow-process chart is easy to create when plant layout prints of the area under observation are available. All that remains to be done is to place the process symbols at the proper locations on the layout and draw connecting lines between the symbols. In Fig. 3-3, note that the symbols are numbered independently; these numbers should correspond to the numbers inside the symbols of the process chart. Note further in Fig. 3-3 that the area of fabrication is shown and that only the fabrication symbol is shown in this area. A layout print is drawn to scale, so distances moved are easily attained from the print.

When analyzing a system for improvement you should develop both the process chart and the flow-process chart together for a thorough analysis. The process chart states in detail what is being done, whereas the flow-process chart shows where the work is done. In addition, the flow-process chart shows the path of the flow of a part throughout a system. Crisscrossing, retracing of steps, or some other haphazard flow are all indicators of potential for improvement, such as changing the layout or combining operations.

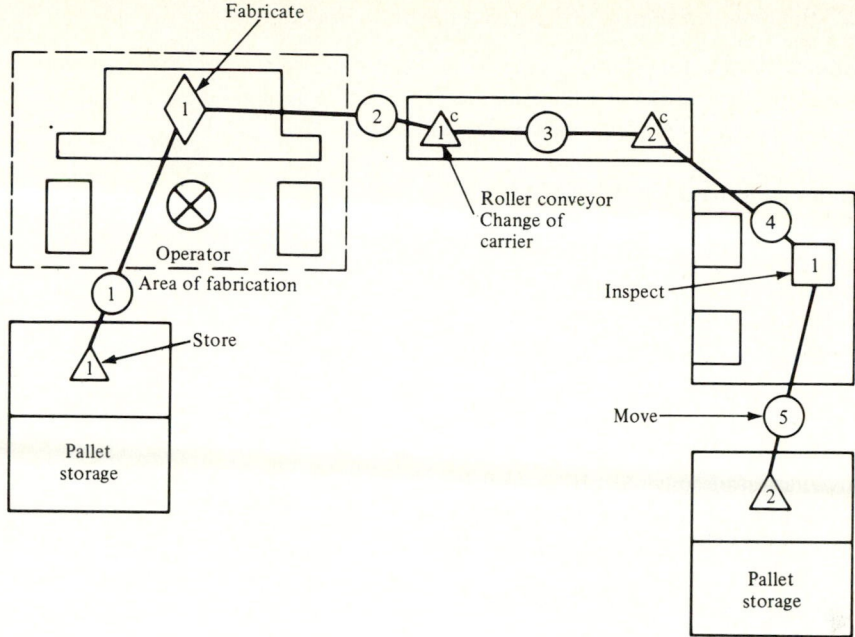

Figure 3-3 A flow-process chart.

Certain rules should be followed in creating a flow-process chart in addition to some of the rules already stated (rules 3 and 4) for a process chart which are common to both. The additional rules for a flow-process chart are:

1. The symbols must be located at the point where the steps occur, so that the flow lines on the layout portray, as nearly as possible, the actual flow path of the object.
2. The flow must be charted as if the movement of a single object is being followed, even though the object is being produced in quantity and stored in batches.
3. All areas of fabrication must be indicated with a dotted line. Areas of fabrication may include entire departments in a plant or be limited to a single work station. When studying the movement of a part between several plants, treat an entire plant as an area of fabrication.

The Flowchart

The flowchart is similar to the flow-process chart except that on it no process symbols are used. The path of travel is shown merely as a line with periodic arrowheads to indicate direction on the layout. If the process symbols were removed from Fig. 3-3, then only the line would remain to indicate the direction of movement. This example would then be a flowchart. For a more thorough analysis, the flow-process chart is recommended because of the use of the symbols.

Flow and Process Analysis for Improvement

Upon completion of a flowchart, process chart, and/or flow-process chart on a manufacturing system, further analysis for improvements can be guided by a set of pertinent questions. Some suggested questions are offered below.

1. Can movement paths be shortened by
   a. Changing sequence of steps
   b. Changing location of particular operations or inspection points
   c. Regrouping related operations
   d. Creating new aisles
2. Can material handling equipment and procedures be modified to advantage by
   a. Design of special racks
   b. Standardization of containers
   c. Centralization or dispersion of storage points
   d. Installation of conveyors for material movement or material storage
   e. Change of quantities handled at each move (batch size)
   f. Introduction of chutes, hoppers, and other equipment to reduce manual handling
   g. Installation of wheels on containers, hoppers, racks, and other storage devices
   h. Use of gravity to advantage
3. Can the process be modified by
   a. Combining certain operations such as fabricate and inspect
   b. Improving tools to make the operation more automatic (example—automatic eject)
   c. Changing the scheduling of parts or the operation times
4. Can the product be modified by
   a. Eliminating nonfunctional details
   b. Substituting one process for another equivalent process
   c. Reducing unnecessary quality requirements

The preceding charting techniques are very helpful when analyzing existing systems for improvement. Creating a process chart and a flow-process chart together would offer the most potential for improvement when the analysis is made. These techniques are also very helpful when planning a new system.

The Precedence Chart

The precedence chart has a different purpose from that of the previous charting techniques that have been discussed. In addition, the process symbols are not used in precedence charting. In the flow- and process-charting techniques, a sequence of operations were analyzed for improvement of such things as the layout and handling of the product. In contrast, the precedence chart displays all possible sequences in a series of elements of work or operations that are performed in manufacturing and/or assembly. It is used to allocate the work by selecting the one sequence which results in the most efficient use of labor and a minimum amount of idle time. This is discussed in detail in the chapter on Line Balancing.

In the construction of a precedence chart, there are no vertical connecting lines and the chart reads from left to right. In Fig. 3-4, elements *A, B, C,* and *D* are in parallel, which illustrates that there is no precedence restrictions between these elements; they can therefore be performed in any sequence. Since these four elements of work are independent elements, there are 24 (*N* factorial) possible sequences; however, *A* through *D* must be done before *E* can be accomplished. The less desirable situation is the series chain of elements *E, F, G,* and *H,* where the sequence of performance must be *E,* then *F,* then *G,* and then *H.* After *H* is performed, then *I* or *J* or *K* can be done next. Last of all, *L* cannot be done until *I, J,* and *K* have been completed. It should be evident from this discussion that having elements in parallel whenever possible is highly desirable. However, some elements must stay in series, because of such restrictions imposed by the following.

1. Product. Parts internal to a product that must be assembled before external parts.
2. Process. Drilling that must be done before tapping, priming before painting, etc.
3. Plant layout. Large machines or facilities too costly to move.
4. Quality. Work performed earlier or later instead of now that might impose quality problems incurring rework or scrap.
5. Method. Doing the element later that may cause extra time because of such things as restricting the work area for fingers or tools.

Sometimes there are imagined restrictions, so that every precedence chart should be checked to see if additional elements can go in parallel without causing problems. To make this check, it is sometimes helpful to list the immediate predecessors and then determine if certain predecessors are necessary. In Fig. 3-4, *A, B, C,* and *D* are the immediate predecessors for element *E.* Also, *E* is the immediate predecessor for *F; F* for *G; G* for *H; H* for *I, J,* and *K;* and *I, J,* and *K* for *L.* Incidentally, the listing of the immediate predecessors is one of the input requirements when one is using such line-balancing computer programs as CALB (computer-aided line balancing).

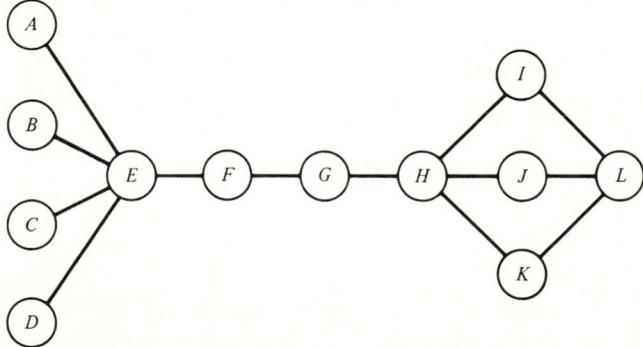

Figure 3-4 Simple precedence diagram.

The precedence chart helps the analyst select a sequence which is one of the most efficient for a product at a given assembly-line cycle time, and where each element has a specific assigned element duration time. It is only after the element and cycle times are known that the line balancing can be done either by hand or by the use of a computer program. The chapter on Line Balancing deals with the selected sequence, considering all possible sequences afforded by the precedence chart, after the element times and cycle time have been added to the problem.

QUESTIONS

3-1 What was Gilbreth's contribution to manufacturing systems analysis?

3-2 What are the five charting techniques used in manufacturing systems analysis?

3-3 How should a person analyze a fabrication chart?

3-4 The fabrication chart is developed directly from what common paperwork items?

3-5 What does the precedence chart illustrate?

3-6 When line balancing with the aid of a precedence chart, is it better to have a series chain of elements or elements in parallel in order to attain efficient line balance?

3-7 Under what general conditions would the area of fabrication be (a) a small area and (b) a larger area?

3-8 What is the difference between a flowchart and a flow-process chart?

PROBLEMS

3-1 From the following list of elements and immediate predecessors, create a precedence chart for mixing the IE Bomb. Some of the restrictions in sequence are for the purpose of enhancing the flavor.

Immediate predecessor	Element
None	Get glasses
Glasses	Add rum A
Glasses	Add rum B
Glasses	Add rum C
Glasses	Add rum D
Glasses	Add rum E
Rum A, B, C, D, E	Lemon juice
Lemon juice, orange	Sugar
Rum A, B, C, D, E	Orange
Sugar	Vermouth
Sugar	Brandy
Hand mix	Olive
Hand mix	Onion
Vermouth, brandy	Hand mix
Olive, onion	Salt edge of glass

3-2 Create a precedence chart without being given the immediate predecessors. The list of elements are for a man getting dressed for work.

1. Remove pajama top
2. Remove pajama bottom
3. Put on undershorts
4. Put on undershirt
5. Put on clean white shirt
6. Put on trousers
7. Fill pockets of trousers
8. Brush teeth
9. Wash hands and face
10. Lather and shave
11. Eat breakfast
12. Put on tie and tie clasp
13. Put on shoes
14. Put on socks
15. Put on topcoat
16. Put on suit coat
17. Put on wristwatch
18. Leave house for work

3-3 Construct a precedence chart for the following elements of work where the elements are identified by numbers.

1. Element 1 must be performed first.
2. Elements 2, 3, 4, 5, or 6 can be done after element 1 is completed.
3. Element 7 can be done after element 2 is done.
4. Element 8 must follow element 3.
5. Element 9 can't be done until elements 3 and 4 have been accomplished.
6. Element 10 must be preceded by elements 5 and 6.
7. Element 6 must also be done before element 11.
8. Elements 7 and 8 must occur before element 12.
9. Elements 9 and 10 must occur before element 13.
10. Element 14 must follow element 12.
11. Element 15 must follow element 13.
12. Element 11 must precede element 16.
13. Element 17 should follow element 14.
14. Element 18 should follow element 16.
15. Elements 15, 17, and 18 must be completed before element 19 can be performed.

3-4 The layout on page 38 is a flowchart of the gear-cover-plate assembly. With the aid of the process chart in Fig. 3-2, convert the flowchart into a flow-process chart.

3-5 With the aid of the process chart in Fig. 3-2 and the flow-process chart created in Prob. 3-4, develop an improved gear-cover-plate process chart and a proposed flow-process chart with the following considerations.

(a) The improvements should not be very expensive, since the gear cover plate is low-volume production.

(b) Anything can be moved in the layout with the exception of the press and spotwelder.

(c) A batch of eight cover plates are presently being assembled per trip around to all the machines. What should be the batch size in the improved method?

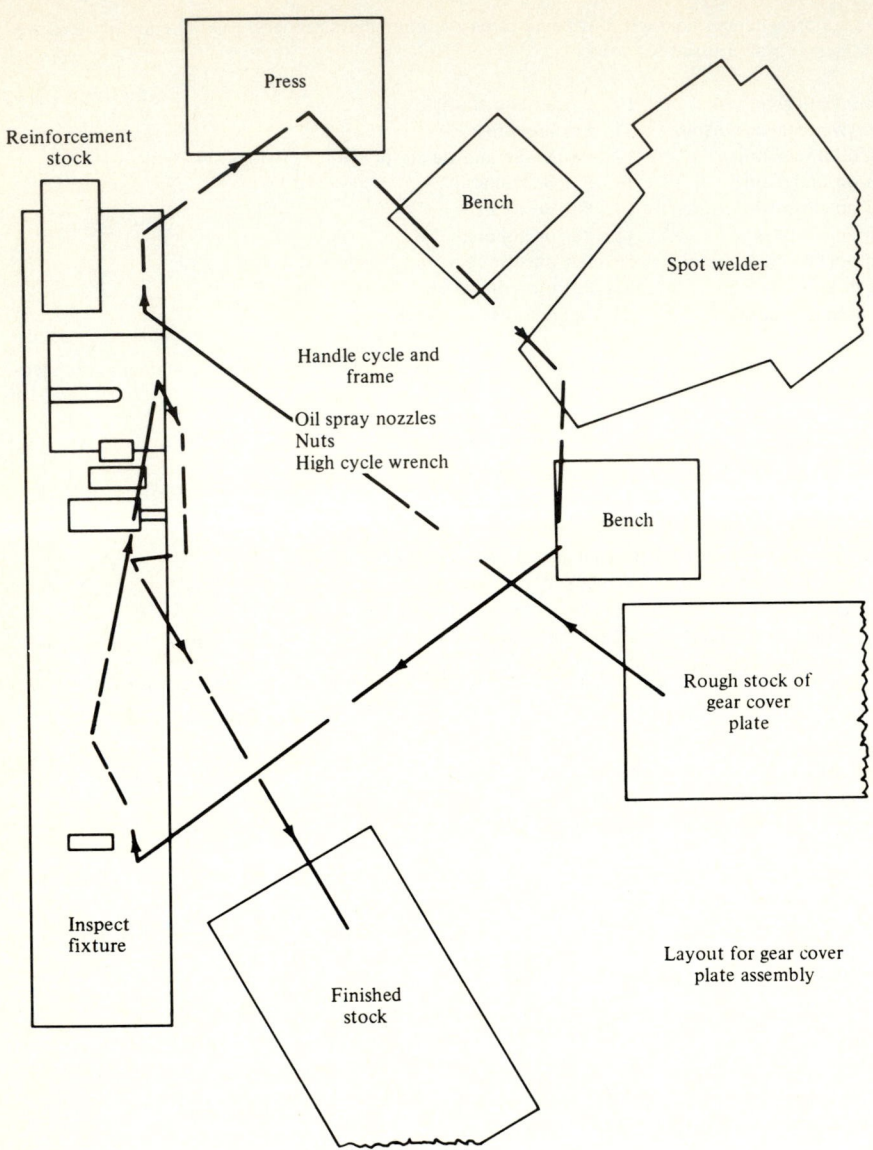

Press

Reinforcement stock

Bench

Spot welder

Handle cycle and frame

Oil spray nozzles
Nuts
High cycle wrench

Bench

Rough stock of gear cover plate

Inspect fixture

Finished stock

Layout for gear cover plate assembly

FOUR

INEFFECTIVE WORKER MOVEMENTS

Analyzing an operation for the presence of ineffective worker movements (IWM) is one of the easiest techniques for improving an operation. It has been said many times that methods is everyone's business, so when productivity improvement is emphasized at all levels of management, this is the technique that can be used by anyone, not just industrial engineers. Whenever a methods-engineering training program is conducted for production supervisors, IWM analysis should always be part of this type of program. The technique is easy to use and the resulting improvements frequently cost nothing; or very little cost is involved in the conversion to the new method.

Effective worker movements are movements that are required to do the operation. In contrast, IWM are movements that should be eliminated or minimized, because they add only expenditure of more time and energy in the performance of work. Therefore, when one is analyzing an operation, concentration is on the detection of IWM in order to find the problems existing in the operation. However, until the analyst is conscious of movements and the significance of movements, he or she is limited in the ability to observe an operation for improvement possibilities. The analyst must first acquire the ability to see the activity of an operator in the form of a series of physical movements. Movement consciousness is an extension of one's ability to observe. When operations are described in terms of movements, both effective and ineffective, they are more easily analyzed and more readily improved upon.

The importance of movement analysis is based upon the fact that the number and extent of movements required to perform a task determines the time, effort, and cost of the operation. It follows then that any reduction in the number or extent of ineffective movements will lower the time and cost of an operation.

When observing an operation, note that some of the things an operator does are effective and therefore contribute to the desired results whereas others are ineffective and add only more time to the accomplishment of the task. For example, the movements required to get over a barrier such as the side of a stock container are ineffective. By tilting the container, such ineffectiveness is reduced.

Some other examples of ineffective movements occur when the operator must get each new part with the left hand and transfer it to the right hand, which immediately indicates that the workplace layout should be changed. An operator performing extensive holds with the left hand during each cycle of work indicates that a holding device or fixture should be provided for the operator. Excessive waits, usually with the left hand, mean that there is an imbalance of work between the hands, in which case, a change in the sequence of doing the work will minimize the waiting time. With the elimination of such IWM, the time, effort, and cost to do the work will be reduced.

CONDITIONS CAUSING INEFFECTIVE WORKER MOVEMENTS

There are several conditions existing in many manufacturing operations which are the most likely causes for IWM. They include such things as the following.

Inadequate Workplace Design

A properly designed workplace must include considerations of most-efficient layout as well as adequate space. The positioning of stock and machine controls should be such that the total distance traveled by the operator's hands in performing the cycle is kept to a minimum. For example, assuming that steps in a cycle are identified with locations of stock or controls, we find that at the completion point of one step in a cycle the operator's hand should be as close as possible to the point in the workplace where the succeeding step is to occur. The size, shape, and location of stock containers should be influenced by the size of the part and its rate of use.

A great deal of investigation has gone into the body dimensions and normal working distances of a typical operator. Many charts are available which recommend practical workplace dimensions. A spread-out workplace can be as ineffective as are cramped quarters at the workplace. Therefore, when an operator is getting and placing parts, the distance moved should be as short as possible without becoming awkward; otherwise, long movements will contribute to a higher cycle time. While the performance demands on the typical industrial operator usually do not justify a physiological investigation, provision of adequate space and reasonable reaching distances are essential to efficient performance.

Lack of Proper Tools and Equipment

An operator must obviously have appropriate tools to do the job. When standard tools are required and the operator is using them properly, the tools are not responsible for ineffectiveness in the operation. However, most manufacturing operations employ nonstandard tools and equipment which are designed for a specific operation. Unfortunately, these designs frequently fall short of meeting the needs of another operation. If a part does not fit easily into a fixture, additional time is required for positioning. If a part must be held by hand while in process, the operator's hands are actually serving as a fixture. Special hand tools can often be provided to simplify an operation. Properly designed guides and locators can also help minimize the positioning movements necessary to locate a part into a jig or fixture.

Condition and Configuration of Materials

The condition of raw materials frequently introduces handling difficulties. Greasy parts may require more time to grasp and position; materials with sharp edges will require extra caution; etc. The shape and dimension of parts also introduce difficulties. Minute parts, common in small assemblies, require a great deal of dexterity and sensitivity in handling. On the other hand, large and cumbersome materials create a variety of handling problems. The characteristics of materials can thus easily complicate the task and, as a result, make it more susceptible to ineffective movements. However, the resulting IWMs can be dealt with by providing such things as counterbalances, automatic feeds, prepositioning devices, etc.

Improper Operator Method

One of the most common causes for IWM can be traced to the operator's method. In a factory employing thousands of operators and undergoing frequent product changes, many operators are put to work with a minimum of job instruction. Thus, an operator will adopt his or her own way of doing things. Even the trained operator will bend to revert to favorite practices. These self-developed methods frequently turn out to be a matter of doing things the hard way. Some examples of this are: frequent passing of parts from one hand to the other; picking up a part and placing it on a bench several times in the process of completing an operation; performing the steps in such a sequence that a machine remains idle waiting for the operator. Each operation should ideally be studied for best method and then each operator should be trained in that method. Most manufacturing operations provide a continuous potential for improvement through application of an IWM analysis. Production supervision trained in IWM analysis can be very helpful in contributing to continuous improvement with proper guidance and incentives by management. This is an untapped resource in too many plants.

TYPICAL INEFFECTIVE WORKER MOVEMENTS

In the foregoing sections, the general causes for ineffectiveness in manufacturing operations have been discussed. While there are many forms of ineffectiveness, there are certain ineffective movements which characterize an operation that can be improved. These movements are defined in the following section. Possible causes are also suggested and are listed somewhat in order of importance; however, the order can vary depending on the types of operations being analyzed. Moreover, the list of IWMs is not necessarily exhaustive, but it should guide an analyst in detecting many problems that will lead to improvements.

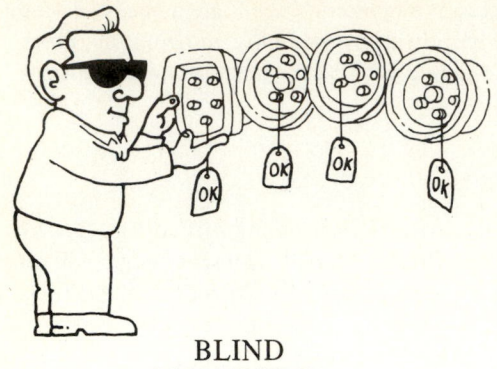

Operator movements made to locations not visible to operator

Possible causes
Poor workplace layout
Inappropriate material containers
Part or equipment inverted
Barrier in workplace area
Characteristic of part

BLIND MOVEMENT

A temporary halt by operator of active muscular movements in order to maintain a definite relation between two or more objects

Possible causes
Holding device absent
Imbalance of hand activity
Poor fixture design
Lack of operator training

HOLD

Operator movements that require unusual body positions and ones which require effort to maintain a position and thereby add to the effort of doing a job

Possible causes
Material outside normal working area
Part or equipment inverted
Inaccessible parts or tools
Barriers in workplace area
Poor placement of handles or controls

AWKWARD MOVEMENT

**CHANGE
OF
CONTROL**

Object transferred by operator from one controlling device to another (left hand to right hand)

Possible causes
Poor workplace layout or improper location of tools
Lack of self-locational aids on part or equipment
Lack of operator training

**COMPLICATED
MOVEMENT**

Operator movements requiring high manual dexterity

Possible causes
Poor design of equipment
Lack of suitable mechanical aids
Physical shape and condition of part or tool
Characteristic of operation

**HIGH
EFFORT**

An operator activity that requires above-average exertion, that is one that requires more effort than would ordinarily be necessary to do the job

Possible causes
Lack of mechanization
Heavy tools or equipment that are not counterbalanced
Barrier that prevents operator from getting close to the job

An operator's waiting with tool, part, piece of equipment, hand, or whole body for following activity

Possible causes
Unbalance of work between hands
Waiting for machine to finish cycle
Waiting for next operator or operation
Lack of standardization or training
Planning further activity

WAIT

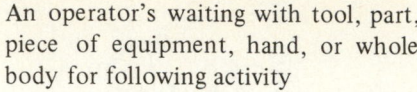

Operator movements which could cause injury to operator or other personnel in the vicinity

Possible causes
Safety guards absent or inadequate
Operator unable to see what he or she is doing
Physical shape or condition of object
Inertia of moving object uncontrolled

HAZARDOUS MOVEMENT

Operator movement guided by the eye, that cannot be completed until the eye has first determined the final position

Possible causes
Poor workplace layout and placement of tools
Lack of self-locational aids on the part or equipment
Lack of standardization or operator training

EYE DIRECTED MOVEMENT

Any operator movement that can be shortened without becoming awkward

Possible causes
Poor workplace layout
Lack of use of vertical space
Operator forced to reach over barrier
Inconvenient material location
Two distant workplaces causing walk

LONG MOVEMENT

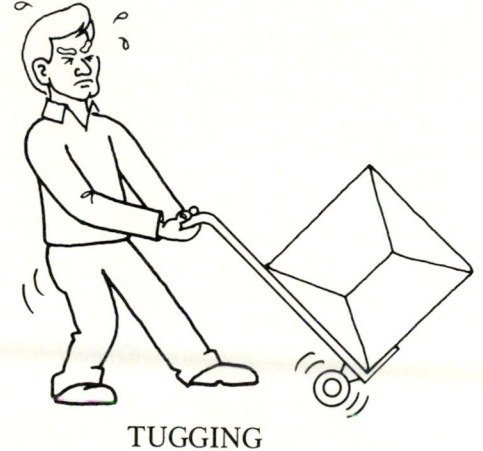

Pulls or strains with difficulty on an object by operator

Possible causes
Lack of separation devices such as suction cups
Lack of adequate counterweights
Inconsistent tolerances or fits
Foreign matter interference (e.g., dirt, oil)
Physical shape or condition of object

TUGGING OR PRYING

A series of repetitive, short-distance operator movements around a proper location before the part is finally located

Possible causes
Lact of self-locational aids on part or equipment
Assembly of two or more parts without guides
Operator unable to see clearly due to obstruction or insufficient light

POSITIONING

FUMBLING

Operator who fails to grasp object securely first time, drops it, and then must regrasp again

Possible causes
Lack of prepositioning device
Dirty or greasy parts
Physical characteristics of part
Improper gloves
Wrong type of container or feed system
Work area too restricted

LOSS OF CONTROL

Object which has to be used again within a few seconds laid aside by operator and then almost immediately picked up again

Possible causes
Wrong sequence of performing work
Lack of use of multiple fixtures
Lack of "palming" a tool or part (retaining control) whenever this is possible; usually done with small tools or parts

OBSTRUCTED MOVEMENT

Operator who must detour from a straight-line movement because of some obstruction in the path of travel

Possible causes
Poor workplace layout
Poor design of safety guards
Fixture design that does not allow sufficient clearance for part placement

Operator who performs additional movements beyond what the operation requires

> *Possible causes*
> Lack of use of power tools
> Poor workplace layout
> Lack of self-locational aids
> Part or equipment inverted

UNNECESSARY
MOVEMENT

INEFFECTIVE WORKER MOVEMENT CONSIDERATIONS

After having become completely familiar with all of the IWM, use Fig. 4-1 as a guide for making an IWM analysis. The following writeup follows the flow of activities in Fig. 4-1.

A Guide for Making an Ineffective Worker Movement Analysis

1. *Observing worker movements.* Both effective and ineffective worker movements are present in an operation when making an IWM analysis. Figure 4-2 is an example of how the analysis should be done. The IWM are listed in the upper-left-hand corner of Fig. 4-2. The analyst should methodically go through the list in sequence looking for only *one IWM at a time;* otherwise, too many IWM will be missed by looking for all of them simultaneously. Only IWMs found in an operation are listed on the form. Incidentally, there can be more than one occurrence of a particular IWM. For example, there may be *one or more* long movements in an operation.
2. *Analyzing for causes.* As each IWM is recorded, the observed or possible causes are listed on the right side of the form. Remember that possible causes were previously listed after the identification of each IWM. This may be helpful in determining possible causes for each IWM during an analysis.

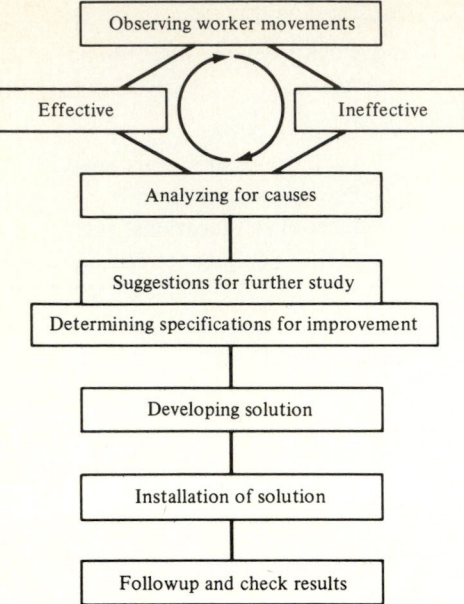

Figure 4-1 Ineffective worker movement analysis procedure.

3. *Suggestions for further study.* When making suggestions for further study, it is common to consult with several individuals, depending on the alternate considerations for improvement. For example, when the need for a fixture is determined, one should consult with a fixture designer to decide whether it should be a single or multiple fixture.

4. *Determining specifications for improvement.* In determining the specifications for improvement, it could be decided that a single fixture would be correct in Fig. 4-2, because two pins are being placed in the fixture simultaneously. Other specifications would be determined accordingly.

5. *Developing solution.* While developing a solution, it is common to make several changes that evolve from several ineffective movements. Note that four improvement possibilities are listed in Fig. 4-2.

6. *Installation of solution.* Note in Fig. 4-2 that "reduce handle travel on press" and "move covers from right to the left of the operator" are improvements that could be made in one day. It would take a while for the fixture to be made, so improvement possibilities 2 and 3 would be implemented when the fixture became available.

7. *Follow up and check results.* The analyst would follow up to make certain that all the improvements were made. After all improvements had been implemented, the analyst could check the results by making a time study to determine the exact amount of time and money saved.

Ineffective worker movement analysis is the most basic of the several forms of operation analysis common to methods work. Accordingly, it is the most easily applied. Substantial savings can result through the use of this technique. In fact, it is

I.E.-71
PRINTED IN U.S.A.

INEFFECTIVE WORKER MOVEMENT ANALYSIS

Date 8/25

Long	Tugging	
Fumbling	Holding	
Waiting	Blind	
Extra Effort	Prying	
Positioning	Eye-directed	
Hazardous	Complicated	
Awkward	Loss of control	
Changes of Control		

Analysis By

Name of Operation Press dowel pins in cover

No.

Department Name

No.

INEFFECTIVE WORKER MOVEMENT	OBSERVED OR POSSIBLE CAUSES
Long--place handle	Handle travel on press too long
Wait--LH while RH gets and places pin	Unbalanced work between hands
Positioning--pins to holes	Holes difficult to see
Awkward--bend over to see hole	Holes in upper ram
Change of control--LH get cover from RH	Cover on wrong side of operator
Holding--LH while RH presses dowels in cover	Lack of a holding device
Blind--placing pins in holes	Holes in upper ram
Eye directed--aligning cover holes with pins	Lack of locational aids
Etc.	

Summary of Ineffective Movements and Causes

1. By providing a fixture, the hold, blind, awkward and positioning motions are eliminated or minimized.
2. Moving the covers to the left eliminates the change of control.
3. Placing the pins simultaneously eliminates the wait.

Suggestions for Further Study or Improvement Possibilities

1. Reduce handle travel on press.
2. Provide a fixture to locate the two pins and the cover.
3. The two pins can be placed into the fixture simultaneously.
4. Move covers from rt. to the left of the operator.

Figure 4-2 Typical ineffective worker movement analysis.

often true that more can be saved per dollar spent on simple changes than the savings gained per dollar spent on some mechanized equipment. Extensive reorganization of an operation may require a more thorough type of analysis, which can be done with the act-breakdown or predetermined method time system analysis. However, much can be done using IWM analysis.

Typical Improvements from IWM Analysis

Some common improvements which are feasible based on IWM analysis are listed below. Potential IWMs eliminated or minimized by the improvements are enclosed in parentheses.

1. Rearrange the workplace layout. (Long, change of control, eye-directed, complicated, blind, awkward.)
2. Change the sequence of the movements to improve the balance of work between the hands. (Wait, hold.)
3. Provide a holding device such as a fixture(s). (Hold.)
4. Have the operator do work during machine process time instead of waiting for the machine to complete the cycle. (Wait for machine.)
5. Use multiple fixtures instead of a single fixture. (Hold, wait, loss of control.)
6. Preposition parts mechanically or manually. (Fumbling, waiting, long, positioning.)
7. Redesign fixture to provide for easy load and unload, and positive location of parts with locators, guide pins, etc. (Positioning, fumbling, blind.)
8. Provide mechanical assists when heavy parts or equipment require a high degree of effort. (Extra effort, hazardous, tugging, prying.)
9. Install guards or devices to improve the safety of an operation. (Hazardous, awkward, tugging, prying.)
10. Simplify an operation by providing special hand tools. (Extra effort, positioning, waiting, holding.)
11. Change part design to simplify assembly or processing. (Fumbling, positioning, complicated.)
12. Train the operator to use the best method with the new facilities. (All the IWMs.)

Proposed Improvement Factors

Before implementing corrective action based on an ineffective worker movement analysis, it is wise to consider the overall effect on the operation. The following factors will help to decide whether a proposed change should be acted upon.

1. Are the potential savings to be realized, in terms of reduced cycle time, sufficient to justify the cost of eliminating ineffective movement in the operation?
2. Will there be a significant reduction in the required operator effort?
3. Will there be a sufficient decrease in hazardous conditions or an improvement in the safety of operating procedures.
4. Will there be a significant improvement in quality or a substantial reduction in scrap?
5. Do the advantages gained outweigh any ineffectiveness introduced by the proposed changes?

These five items are listed only as a caution, so that the analyst will consider as many factors as possible. The analyst must have a positive attitude but be careful of the overall effect on the operation. In most situations, the answer should be yes to the questions that pertain to a particular operation.

QUESTIONS

4-1 If extensive holds (usually by the left hand) are detected when making an IWM analysis, what should be done to improve the operation?

4-2 What change should be made if there is a change of control?

4-3 What potential change should there be if there are extensive left-hand waits in an operation?

4-4 What is a long movement and what frequently causes long movements?

4-5 Give an example of work that an operator could do instead of waiting for a machine to complete its machine cycle.

4-6 What is a common remedy for reducing positioning movements?

4-7 Give two examples of how high-effort movements can be reduced.

4-8 List three possible causes of blind movements.

4-9 What IWM may occur with a new operator who has had no training?

4-10 Give an example of how loss-of-control movements can be minimized with a multiple fixture producing six assemblies per cycle instead of a single fixture producing one assembly per cycle.

4-11 Why should production supervision be trained in IWM analysis?

4-12 List two common causes of eye-directed movements.

4-13 Why is the detection of hazardous movements listed as one of the IWM?

4-14 The IWM prying occurs when getting a part from a stack of sheet-metal parts. What types of devices can be used to eliminate the IWM prying?

4-15 List at least four types of IWMs that may be eliminated by rearranging the workplace layout more effectively.

4-16 A possible cause of a long movement is lack of use of vertical space. Please explain what this means in a workplace layout.

FIVE

THE ACT BREAKDOWN

Manufacturing analysis implies the study of a multitude of factors involving many related activities affecting the productivity of each and every operation. Underlying this study is the basic purpose of effectively utilizing the factors that make up each work space. One area of study in manufacturing analysis is *methods study,* or methods analysis. Methods analysis is not an all-inclusive study of various factors making up the work spaces. It concentrates on effective utilization of necessary manual content and the interaction of this with the work-space components. More simply, it may be defined as follows.

> Methods analysis is the study of the manual content of work as it affects or is affected by work-space conditions.

The work space is defined as everything that makes up the physical arrangement in which the operation takes place and in which the operator must work. This area involves such factors and related activities as

Work-space layout
Material-handling methods
Material
Equipment
Tooling
Environment

Although this book, and specifically this chapter, is devoted primarily to human performance and measurement, the other factors that constitute the workplace can have a decided influence on the performance. If not carefully planned, the interaction of these factors with the manual component can cause a wide variability output. Some variability can be expected in all jobs, but if it is too great, control of the operation or operations in the process system may be lost and a competitive product may become too costly to produce.

Figure 5-1 illustrates the approximate variation in unrestricted output within some defined limits of fixed method. It stresses the necessity for consideration of all factors if the job performance is to be controlled, measured, and predicted within reasonable limits of effectiveness. The tools, materials, equipment, environment, and workplace layout go hand in hand with manual activity in dictating operation performance. It is clear that all factors must be subject to careful study and analysis.

The study may range from a detailed observation to a recording and analysis of the activity. What form or procedure the analyst may use can never be stated specifically. Individual differences, multiple-problem conditions, economics, and urgency of problem solving are but a few of the influences on the approach to be taken. What one analyst may do with a work order may take another analyst through a recording and analysis to reach the same result. First consideration should be given to the recognition of the problem and then the determination of the course of action.

Emphasis on the manual content underscores the importance of human performance as well as the range and scope of human capabilities in the workplace. A general rule to apply in any situation is to start with the question, "What *can* the operator do?" rather than, "What is the operator doing now?" Given this initial consideration, the results are far more likely to prove beneficial and acceptable to everyone concerned.

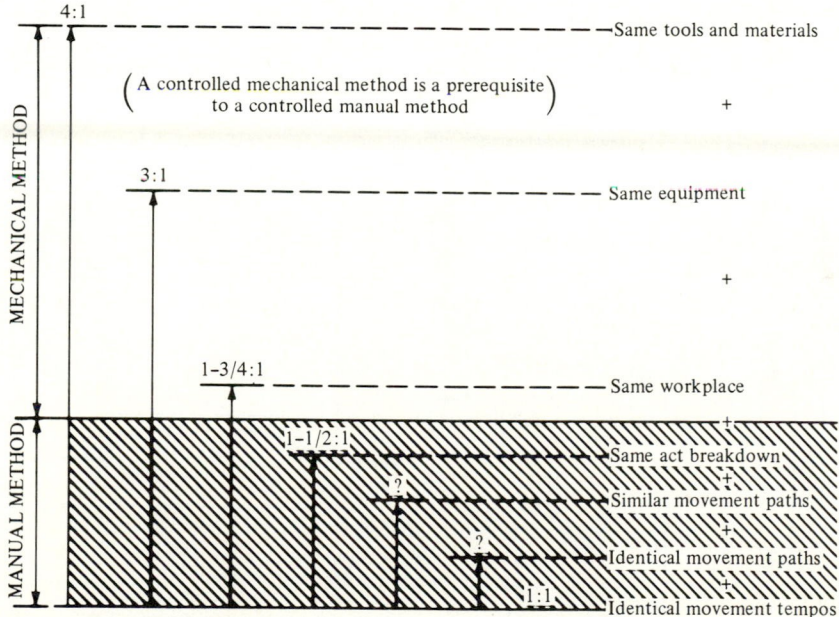

Figure 5-1 Approximate expected variation in unrestricted output within some defined limits of fixed method.

ACT BREAKDOWN

To effectively record, control, and/or predict the manual content, all detail must be recorded. To do this, techniques are needed that are flexible enough to handle any manual activity. In this chapter one such technique called the act breakdown is covered. When systematically applied, it provides an analyst with a detailed description of an operation and perhaps more importantly an insight into improvement possibilities. It breaks a job down into acts and shows the order and correlation of the acts for both hands. To place act-breakdown analysis in its proper perspective with respect to other methods of recording manual and mechanical job content for whatever purpose, reference should be made to Fig. 5-2. Note that the acts fall into an area overlapped by both relatively coarse methods of describing job content (normal stopwatch measurement and analysis by element description) and very detailed and elaborate analysis afforded by motion and movement descriptions associated with the predetermined motion times system. Note also that standard data, which will be covered in a subsequent chapter, evolve from this overlap area in Fig. 5-2.

As a design and analysis tool, act breakdown is sufficient unto itself. However, its unique position midstream in the scale of descriptive detail provides a useful point of departure for establishing a vocabulary base which can be used in describing manual activity. Furthermore, it constitutes a practical and convenient means of developing an awareness of and an ability to describe accurately the manual content of any job. These are essential requirements for anyone concerned with the design of methods,

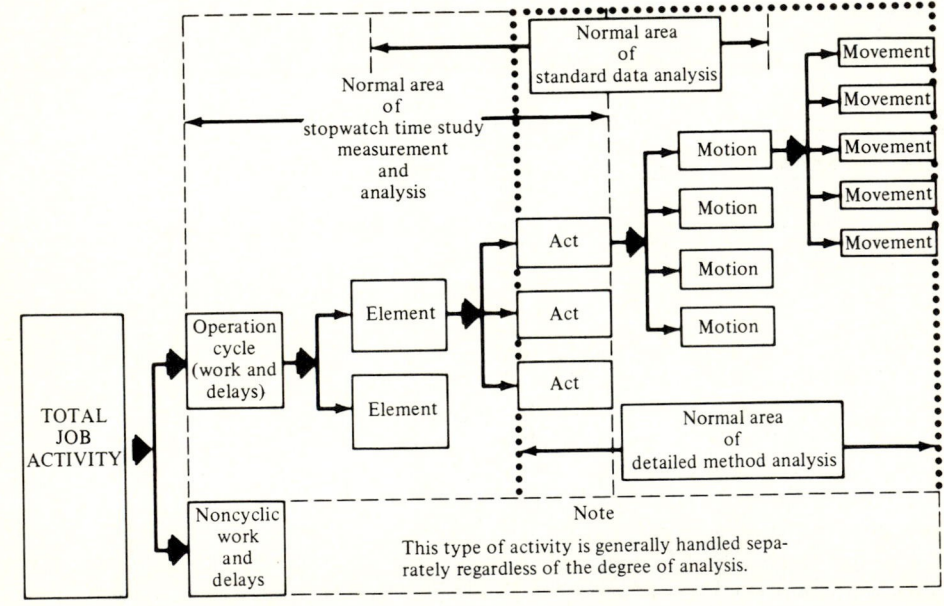

Figure 5-2 Basic components of any type of job study.

tooling and equipment, material-handling facilities, and any factor which impinges upon the worker and his or her job performance.

Act breakdown may be used on all types of operations, but it is most applicable for short-cycle, high-volume, and uniform-method jobs. These conditions should not be considered as precluding its use for long-cycle, low-volume, and inconsistent operator-method types of operations, however. Many other factors may influence the choice of a particular recording technique. Much will depend on the type of problem encountered, the objective of the study, and the skill and experience of the analyst.

ACTS

With the act-breakdown technique, there are terms and a systematic recording procedure to be used. Terms used with the technique are called *acts*. An act is defined as

> A grouping of motions or movements which can be used to describe manual activity for job study.

Excluding body motions for the moment, we find that all manual activity can be described in terms of movements or motions involved with getting things, placing things, and disposing of things. The acts to be used therefore will be get, place, and dispose.

The Get Act

The get act consists of the muscular movements necessary to move to and gain full control (for the purpose intended) of an object. The terminal points of the get act are

Start. When directed muscular action starts to change the position of a body member for the purpose of moving toward (reaching for) an object
Finish. When body member (or transporting device) has secured full control of the object and is in a position to start the next act

The carrier may be the hand or any auxiliary tool or implement controlled by a body member. For example, when the hand moves toward an object in a hopper and the fingers grasp the object so that it is within their control and can be moved as intended, the get act is completed. The definition further implies some subdivisions of activity within the act. These subdivisions are called motions. A motion is a movement grouping smaller than an act, wherein the individual movements have a common objective and have been grouped for convenience in describing method. Motions normally associated with the get act are *move, preposition, gain control, disengage,* and *move clear.* (At this stage of recording, these terms are used only for descriptive purposes and as an aid in analysis for improvement.)

For example, when an operator performs the get act, the following motions may occur:

Get object
Move to (reach for) the object
Preposition carrier during the move in preparation for gaining control of the object
Gain control (for the purpose intended) of the object by closing fingers about the object or closing auxiliary tool such as tongs about the object or executing a contact grasp
Disengage the object from its surroundings (i.e., jumbled parts) or from a fixture recess so that it can be moved as intended
Move clear (withdraw) to start the next motion

It is important to note use of the gain-control motion—as described above. It may not be the endpoint of the get act. Full control as stated in the definition of the get act means when the object can be moved as intended, whereas the gain-control motion ends with the closing of the finger or auxiliary tool about the object. Additional movements may be necessary to separate the object from surrounding objects or to clear the object from a physical barrier before the next act can take place. This is a fine difference which has more than academic interest during motion and movement analysis and application of predetermined method-time systems.

The Place Act

The place act consists of the muscular movements necessary to move an object into a definite position, hold and/or release it there, and possibly move clear.

The terminal points of the place act are as follows:

Start. When directed muscular action starts to change the position of the body member for the purpose of moving an object toward a location
Finish. When body member or transporting device releases or holds the object after being positioned or after moving clear

For example, a place act is performed when the hand (having just gained full control of an object) starts toward a fixture, positions the object in the fixture, and releases or holds the object in positions. As with the get act, there are divisions of activity (motions) within the place act. Motions normally associated with the place act are *move, preposition, position, release control,* and *move clear.* The term "hold" also appears in the definition. This is neither an act nor a motion and lacks movement. It will be discussed later in this chapter.

When an operator performs the place act, it may consist of the following motions or single inactivity (hold):

Place object
Move the object to the fixture
Preposition object in preparation for positioning during move

Position object in fixture
Hold object until holding device is actuated or process starts, or holding interval ends
Release control of object
Move clear to start the next motion

Three possible combinations of activity can occur in the performance of the place act.

1. The operator may move the object into a definite position and release control of the object.
2. The operator may move the object into a definite position, hold the object until a holding device is actuated or process starts, and then release control of object.
3. The operator may move the object into a definite position, hold the object in position for an interval, and then move the object for purposes of placing or disposing, thereby starting another act. In this case, the act would end with a hold.

Of course, the operator can move clear after any one of the three preceding combinations.

Thus, it is clear that several place acts could occur in succession under certain conditions. It is also true that get acts may occur in succession (which implies palming of parts).

The Dispose Act

The dispose act is sometimes referred to as a *simple* place act. In this form of analysis, disposing of an object is treated as a distinct and separate act.

The dispose act consists of the muscular movements necessary to move an object in a given direction and release it *without reference to its final position.*

The difference between the place and dispose acts can be definitely established with respect to whether the operator has put the object into its final position or the object assumes its own final position once it has been released. This is in contrast to normal shop language, wherein dispose is normally used to refer to putting aside the object once the operation is completed. Practice in the use of the terms will eliminate confusion in their application.

The motions associated with the dispose act are *move, release control,* and *move clear.* A typical dispose act may consist of the following:

Dispose object
Move object to pan
Release control of object and object falls into pan
Move clear to start next motion

Additional Terms

In a description of a perfectly balanced manual method, the only terms appearing in the record would be the acts. It is unlikely that this will happen, so it is necessary to designate other terms to be used to complete the recording. Such terms as "wait," "drift," and "hold" will commonly be used for this purpose.

Wait is the interval during which the body member makes no productive muscular movements.
Drift is a slowing down of the performance of a movement.
Hold is the temporary halt of active muscular movement in order to maintain a physical relation between two or more objects or to restrain an object in a physical relation.

A wait will occur when an operator is totally idle, when the operator's hands are idle, or when there are no productive movements on the part of the operator. When the operator, because of some controlling factors on the part of another body member, causes the carrier of an object to slow down its movement, a drift will occur. A drift is defined as the slowing down of productive movement in the performance of that movement. A drift is readily apparent when one observes left- and right-hand activity during an operation. One hand may have more time-consuming activity than does the other hand. The normal tendency is for both hands to complete this work activity at the same time, so that one hand will slow down to absorb the difference in time.

Hold was previously pointed out to be part of a place act, although it can stand alone to indicate a halt in order to maintain a dimensional relation between two objects. It appears by itself in the recording when it is used to highlight ineffectiveness.

One additional term used when recording the method is "process." Since a methods study is concerned with all factors affecting the performance of an operation, process conditions, as related to the manual method, must be indicated.

> *Process* is defined as that part of an operation in which mechanical, chemical, or other means are applied to change the physical conditions of an object.

This term may be further explained as being that part of the total cycle where mechanical, chemical, or other means are used to add something to or subtract something from the object or change its physical condition. It is meant to cover the entire mechanical or chemical process, including travel of the mechanisms involved. Painting, washing, greasing, forming, trimming, turning, shaping, and assembling are examples of process conditions.

MAKING AN ACT BREAKDOWN

In making the act breakdown, certain simple steps have been established so that a uniform procedure can be followed.

Fill Out the Heading

In any recording of data, it is important to relate all pertinent information concerning the particular study to identify the specific activity. Information desired is shown in

Fig. 5-3. The information may be arranged in various ways on any form. It is not the arrangement that is important but rather the fact that all pertinent information is recorded to clearly establish and identify the conditions existing at the time of the study.

Sketch the Work-Space Layout

All the parts, tools, levers, and equipment (see Fig. 5-3) used by the operator must be shown and labeled. Since this may be the only detailed layout of the operation, it is also important that details be drawn to scale or a scale be indicated. A good guide to follow is to ask the question, "Could this operation be reset from the details drawn and be operated as effectively as the day the method was recorded?" In the process of analyzing and improving the operation, the details may of course be rearranged, eliminated, or simplified, which should not detract from the need for recording all the details of the work space at the time of the initial recording.

With the completion of the heading and the sketch, the analyst will have had time to observe the operation at some length and thereby gain some understanding of the method the operator uses, as well as the physical makeup of the work space. Too often an analyst will attempt to record a method without attempting to take time to understand what is taking place. Even though time is spent in sketching the work space, the analyst should spend a short period simply observing the method before attempting any recording.

ACT BREAKDOWN

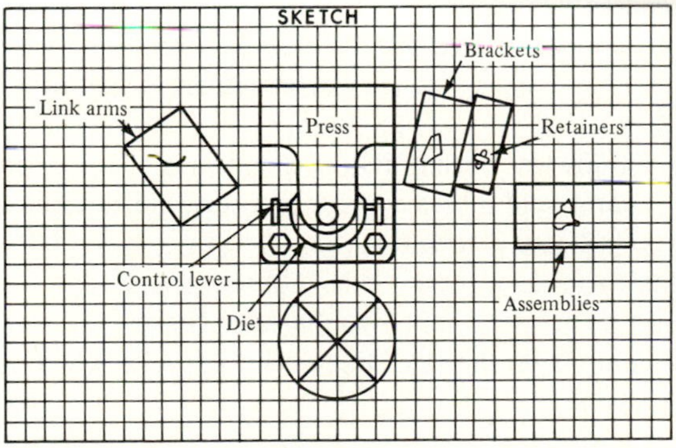

Study File No. AB-902 Date 12-5
Oper. Name-Equip. Description Assemble link arm to bracket and stake Press No. 108S
Tools Used Die D-443A2
Part Description Subassembly
Part No. 850963
Routing Hrly. Cap. 610
Study Hrly. Cap. 732
Analysis By John Doe

LEFT HAND				Process	RIGHT HAND		
Step No.	DESCRIPTION	OBJECT	ACT		ACT	OBJECT	DESCRIPTION
1	Of bench press	Control lever	Get		Get	Control lever	Of bench press
2	For process	Control lever	Place		Place	Control lever	For process
3				V		Control	

Figure 5-3

Select the Starting Point (Balance Point)

The observer should select as a starting point an instant where both hands begin and/or end their acts as nearly as possible at the same time. To find this the analyst should watch the operator for points in the cycle of movements where the operator gets or places a part with both hands, where both hands begin to move at the same time, or where a part is transferred from one hand to the other. Any one of these will provide the observer with a definite point at which to begin. The balance point may not be at the start of the cycle and it may cause some confusion to the new analyst. The finished recording can easily be arranged to have the beginning point of the cycle at the top of the record. This step is mentioned in order to avoid partial-act recording or split-act recording at the beginning of the breakdown.

Record the Method

Identify and record the acts being performed by each hand and fill in the object and explanation column. Do these steps in the following manner:

1. Record the activity or acts selected as the starting point of the analysis, filling in the object and description sections.
2. Identify the next activity performed by each hand and record them according to what each hand does. This may include inactivity such as wait or hold on the part of either hand. The activity of the controlling hand should be recorded first, followed by the hand activity or inactivity related to the other hand. The controlling hand is the hand that is performing constructive movements and governing the action and therefore the time relation between the hands.
3. Continue to record the activity or inactivity of both hands, keeping the recorded information balanced as each step is filled out. Filling out one complete hand description at a time is not considered good practice; it leads only to difficulty in recording, since small waits, drifts, and continued activity may be missed.
    a. If an act, wait, or hold occurs at the same time as similar activity of the other hand, record it as such.
    b. If the hand is continuing an act already begun, denote by placing an x or " in the act column. Repeating the act would indicate a new and separate act. Leaving the act column blank would indicate inactivity.
    c. If the hand or carrier is waiting or holding, leave the act column blank.
4. Identify and record the process in its proper relation to the acts. The process step should be entered in the center column on the same line as the acts with which it is concurrent. Process is indicated by an x.

Figure 5-4 shows an example of how the recorded breakdown would appear.

Once the recording of the method is completed, the objective of the study should be reexamined to determine the next action to be taken. The following may indicate some action steps to be taken for the listed objective:

To complete a recording of method for record purposes the recording can be noted as completed, assigned a study file number, and filed.

To prepare a recording to be used for training operators, proper disposition of the recording should be planned for and instructions prepared to ensure that training can be effectively carried out.

To establish a work standard for the activity, read points should be noted on the recording and the elemental time data recorded and processed.

To determine improvement possibilities, data should be analyzed, alternate proposals developed and evaluated, and recommendations prepared for action.

To plan alternate solutions to a production problem, data should be analyzed for improvement of the operation and necessary mechanical and manual specifications determined to solve the new problem condition.

To plan new methods of operation, several proposals should be developed using manual simulation and mock-up representation of the workplace. For the selected proposals, the necessary mechanical and manual specifications should be determined and a recommendation prepared for action.

ACT BREAKDOWN

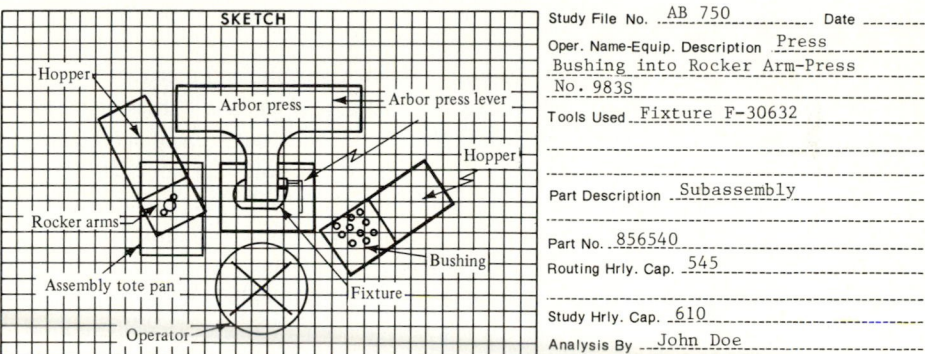

SKETCH		Study File No. AB 750 Date _____
Hopper, Arbor press — Arbor press lever, Hopper, Rocker arms, Bushing, Assembly tote pan, Fixture, Operator		Oper. Name-Equip. Description Press Bushing into Rocker Arm-Press No. 983S
		Tools Used Fixture F-30632
		Part Description Subassembly
		Part No. 856540
		Routing Hrly. Cap. 545
		Study Hrly. Cap. 610
		Analysis By John Doe

Step No.	LEFT HAND DESCRIPTION	OBJECT	ACT	Process	ACT	OBJECT	RIGHT HAND DESCRIPTION
1	In Fixture	Bushing	P		G	Lever	Of Arbor Press
2	Of Arbor Press w/Right Hand	Lever	G		P	Lever	Of Arbor Press
3	Help Right Hand	Lever	P	X	X	Lever	To Press Bushing
4	Wait				P	Lever	To Raise Ram
5	From Fixture	Assy.	G		X	Lever	To Initial Position
6	To Tote Pan	Assy.	D		G	Bushing	From Hopper
7	From Hopper	Rocker Arm	G				Wait
8	In Fixture	Rocker Arm	P				Wait
9	From Right Hand	Bushing	G		P	Bushing	In Left Hand
10							
11	NOTE: $\frac{3}{4}$ turn of Arbor Press Lever is required to lower ram to press bushing into						
12	Rocker Arm						
13							

Figure 5-4 Sample act-breakdown recording.

These are typical examples of problem objectives and the courses of action to be taken. Note that the course of action is determined basically by the objective of the study. Too often the analyst in recording a method attempts to find solutions to the problem in a nonsystematic way, reshuffling the acts into what may be considered a solution to the problem. This may result in a better solution, but a more logical step would be to follow an analytical approach. For the act breakdown, the following approach is used:

Step 1. Question for cause and effect all waits and holds and eliminate all that seem to be questionable.

Step 2. Question for cause and effect all acts and eliminate all unnecessary acts.

Step 3. Question for cause and effect all remaining acts and determine improvement possibilities for each act.

Step 4. Regroup improved acts into a balanced workable method. Add waits where necessary to balance.

Step 5. Determine mechanical and manual specifications necessary to place method into operation.

In applying step 1, the intent is to eliminate all the waits and many of the holds. Wait is always considered to be ineffective, whereas a hold can sometimes be an effective part of the total cycle. The rule would then be to cross out all waits and question whether or not the holds are necessary or unnecessary. If holds are unnecessary, they should be crossed out—which does not mean that holds or waits will not appear in the proposed solution. Removing them from the description is an attempt to eliminate everything considered unnecessary to the completion of the activity. It is better to cross them out of the initial recording than to leave them in, believing they are a necessary part of the activity. They can always be replaced in the proposed method if necessary.

In step 2 the analyst is attempting to determine what acts are necessary to the performance of the activity. The basic principle of methods study to be followed is: The minimum number of acts on any one object are a get and a place. Change of controls, loss of controls, and one hand assisting the other are cases where more than one get and place will occur with any one object. While mechanical methods could be employed to eliminate acts, it should not be considered in developing the initial solution. The analyst should attempt to develop the best improved method by using what is available before considering the partial or complete automation of an activity.

In step 3 consideration is given to minimizing the movements of the operator to accomplish the particular act in the easiest manner and shortest time. The minimum number of movements necessary should be employed for getting and placing objects. Reference again can be made to the motions and the possible conditions that affect the acts. Seeking improvement or elimination of the conditions would be an attempt to minimize the movements involved and thereby improve the act. See Figs. 5-5 to 5-7 for conditions affecting the acts.

For step 4, the analyst should regroup the improved acts into a balanced, workable method. The analyst should first determine if the method is balanced and second if the

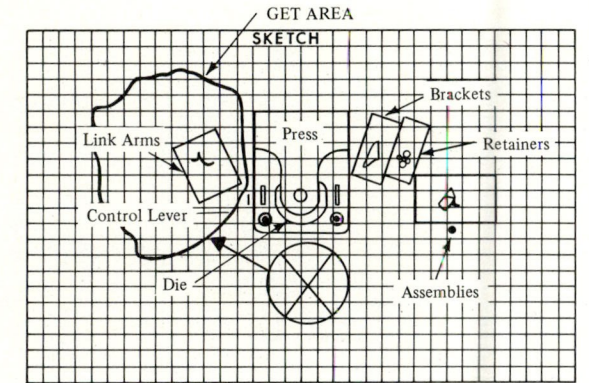

GET AREA

SKETCH

Brackets

Link Arms

Press

Retainers

Control Lever

Die

Assemblies

TERMINAL POINTS

Start:

    Directed muscular action starts to
    change the position of the body member.

Finish:

    When body member or transporting device
    has secured full control of the object
    as intended.

CONDITIONS THAT AFFECT ACT

In addition to *distance* which obviously affects the travel time of body members (recognizing the acceleration, constant speed and deceleration factors involved) the following conditions also affect the method-time relationship of the Motions.

MOTIONS	Characteristics of Object							Characteristics of Transporting Device				Characteristics of Object Travel			Characteristics of Termination Points			Characteristics of Location									Characteristics of Operator	Hazard (Operator)	Senses	Eyes
	Size	Shape	Material	Weight	Resistance	Care	Conditions—Roughness-Color	Size	Shape	Weight	Temperature	Barriers	Direction	Resistance	Tolerance	Target size and Characteristics	Moving or Stationary	Scattered	Stacked	Fixed	Prepositioned	Barriers	Direction	Mixed	Jumbled	Accessibility				
Move	x	x	x	x	x	x		x	x	x	x	x	x	x	x	x	x	x	x	x	x	x	x	x	x	x	x	x	x	x
Preposition	x	x	x	x	x	x		x	x	x	x	x	x	x	x	x	x											x	x	x
Gain Control	x	x	x	x	x		x	x	x	x	x							x	x	x	x	x	x	x	x	x	x	x	x	x
Disengage	x	x	x	x	x	x	x	x	x	x	x	x	x	x	x		x					x	x			x	x	x	x	x
Move Clear	x	x	x	x	x	x	x	x	x	x	x	x	x	x	x	x	x					x	x			x	x	x	x	x

Figure 5-5

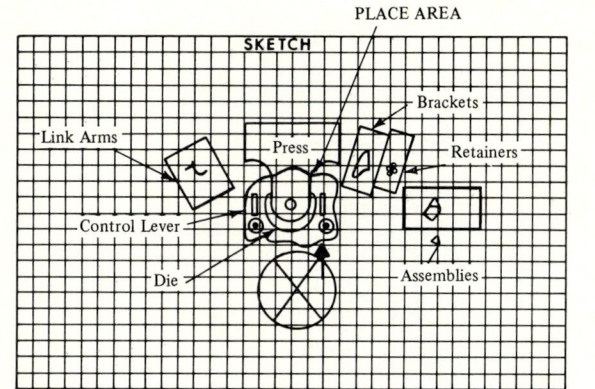

PLACE AREA

SKETCH

- Link Arms
- Press
- Brackets
- Retainers
- Control Lever
- Die
- Assemblies

CONDITIONS THAT AFFECT ACT

In addition to *distance* which obviously affects the travel time of body members (recognizing the acceleration, constant speed and deceleration factors involved) the following conditions also affect the method-time relationship of the Motions.

MOTIONS	Characteristics of Object							Characteristics of Transporting Device				Characteristics of Object Travel			Characteristics of Termination Points			Characteristics of Location										Characteristics of Operator	Hazard (Operator)	Senses	Eyes
	Size	Shape	Material	Weight	Resistance	Care	Conditions—Roughness-Color	Size	Shape	Weight	Temperature	Barriers	Direction	Resistance	Tolerance	Target size and Characteristics	Moving or Stationary	Scattered	Stacked	Fixed	Prepositioned	Barriers	Direction	Mixed	Jumbled	Accessibility				
Move	x	x	x	x	x	x		x	x	x	x	x	x	x	x	x	x	x	x	x	x	x	x	x	x	x	x	x	x	x
Preposition	x	x	x	x	x	x		x	x	x	x	x	x	x	x	x	x										x	x	x	x
Position	x	x	x	x	x			x	x	x	x				x	x	x										x	x	x	x
Apply Pressure	x	x	x	x	x	x	x	x	x	x	x	x	x	x	x		x					x	x			x	x	x	x	x
Release Control	x	x	x	x	x	x		x	x	x	x							x	x	x	x	x	x				x	x	x	x
Move Clear	(x)	(x)	(x)	(x)	(x)	(x)	(x)	(x)	(x)	(x)	(x)	x	x	x	x	x	x					x	x			x	x	x	x	x

Figure 5-6

DISPOSE AREA

SKETCH

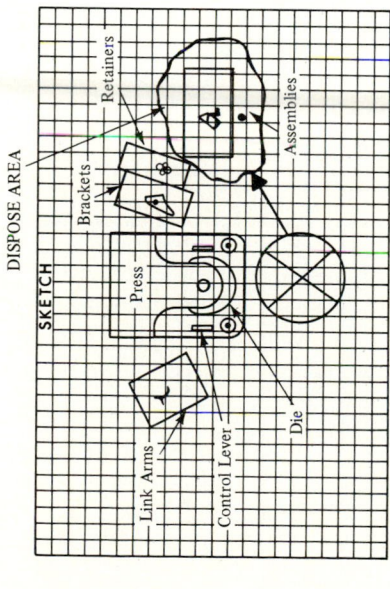

Retainers — Brackets — Assemblies — Press — Link Arms — Control Lever — Die

Start:

    Directed muscular action starts to change the position of the body member.

Finish:

    When body member or transporting device releases object without reference to its final position.

Note: Release and move of object is normally concurrent.

CONDITIONS THAT AFFECT ACT

In addition to *distance* which obviously affects the travel time of body members (recognizing the acceleration, constant speed and deceleration factors involved) the following conditions also affect the method-time relationship of the Motions.

MOTIONS	Size	Shape	Material	Weight	Resistance	Care	Conditions— Roughness- Color	Size	Shape	Weight	Temperature	Barriers	Direction	Resistance	Tolerance	Target size and Characteristics	Moving or Stationary	Scattered	Stacked	Fixed	Prepositioned	Barriers	Direction	Mixed	Jumbled	Accessibility	Characteristics of Operator	Hazard (Operator)	Senses	Eyes
	Characteristics of Object							**Characteristics of Transporting Device**				**Characteristics of Object Travel**			**Characteristics of Termination Points**			**Characteristics of Location**												
Move	×	×	×	×	×	×		×	×	×	×	×	×	×	×	×	×	×	×	×	×	×	×	×	×	×	×	×	×	×
Release Control	×	×	×	×	×	×		×	×	×	×							×	×	×	×	×	×				×	×	×	×
Move Clear								×	×	×	×				×	×	×					×	×			×	×	×	×	×

Figure 5-7

plan is workable. At this stage it may be necessary to place waits and holds back into the plan because of imbalance of acts or activity. Sometimes this cannot be avoided.

In applying step 5, the analyst should carefully analyze each proposal and determine what is necessary to place the method into effect. Mechanical and manual specifications must be noted. Specifications as listed become guides to what has to be done by the analyst, the supervisor, the operator, and related staff functions to ensure the proper installation of the proposal. At this stage an evaluation of the physical specifications will also determine whether or not the method can be done and will also determine the cost of development and installation.

For an example of the results from this five-step procedure, refer to Fig. 5-8 and 5-9. Figure 5-8 shows the act breakdown for the present method of subassembling a bushing and a rocker arm. Figure 5-9 shows the resulting method after an application of the five-step analysis approach.

In this particular analysis, the waits and two acts were eliminated and the remain-

ACT BREAKDOWN

| Study File No. AB 750 | Date |
| Oper. Name-Equip. Description Press Bushing into Rocker Arm-Press No. 983S |
| Tools Used Fixture F-30632 |
| Part Description Subassembly |
| Part No. 856540 |
| Routing Hrly. Cap. 545 |
| Study Hrly. Cap. 610 |
| Analysis By John Doe |

Step No.	LEFT HAND DESCRIPTION	OBJECT	ACT	Process	ACT	OBJECT	RIGHT HAND DESCRIPTION
1	In Fixture	Bushing	P		G	Lever	Of Arbor Press
2	Of Arbor Press w/Right Hand	Lever	G		P	Lever	Of Arbor Press
3	Help Right Hand	Lever	P	X	X	Lever	To Press Bushing
4	Wait				P	Lever	To Raise Ram
5	From Fixture	Assy.	G		X	Lever	To Initial Position
6	To Tote Pan	Assy.	D		G	Bushing	From Hopper
7	From Hopper	Rocker Arm	G				Wait
8	In Fixture	Rocker Arm	P				Wait
9	From Right Hand	Bushing	G		P	Bushing	To Left Hand
10	NOTE: $\frac{3}{4}$ turn of Arbor Press Lever is required to lower ram to press bushing						
11	into Rocker Arm						
12							

Figure 5-8 Present method.

ACT BREAKDOWN

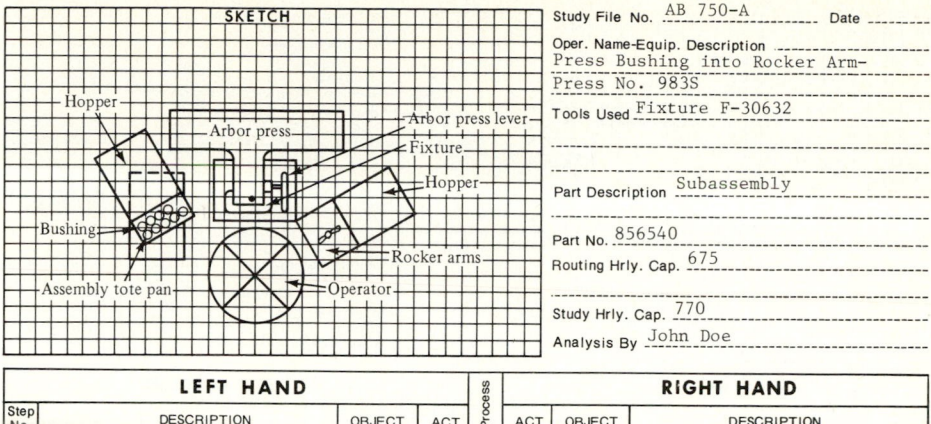

Study File No. AB 750-A ___ Date ___

Oper. Name-Equip. Description ___
Press Bushing into Rocker Arm-
Press No. 983S

Tools Used Fixture F-30632

Part Description Subassembly

Part No. 856540

Routing Hrly. Cap. 675

Study Hrly. Cap. 770

Analysis By John Doe

Step No.	LEFT HAND			Process	RIGHT HAND		
	DESCRIPTION	OBJECT	ACT		ACT	OBJECT	DESCRIPTION
1	In Fixture	Bushing	P		G	Lever	Of Arbor Press
2	Of Arbor Press	Lever	G		P	Lever	Of Arbor Press
3	Help Right Hand	Lever	P	X	X	Lever	To Press Bushing ($\frac{3}{4}$ turn)
4	In Fixture	Assy.	G		P	Lever	To Raise Ram
5	To Tote Pan	Assy.	D		G	Rocker Arm	From Hopper
6	From Hopper	Bushing	G		P	Rocker Arm	In Fixture
7							

Figure 5-9 Proposed method.

ing acts were regrouped into a balanced workable method. Step 3 has not been overlooked, but it was decided that the only changeable condition improving the act performance would be based on reducing the distance of movement with no attempt made to change facilities. In the application of step 5, note that the only possible investigation would deal with whether or not the rocker arm could be placed in the fixture with the right hand. If not, a minor tooling change to make this possible would be investigated or recommended for investigation by the tooling function. The layout sketch on the proposed method would be sufficient for consultation with the layout function or the supervisor of the area. The one remaining specification involves the manual method. Training an operator in the new method would be accomplished by the area supervisor using the recorded method as a guide.

Further development of alternative proposals may involve recommendations for changes in facilities. This may or may not be limited or restricted by job factors mentioned previously. If an air or hydraulic press were recommended, a method as shown in Fig. 5-10 could result. Note that this press is controlled by the activation of palm buttons.

If the analyst were to evaluate whether or not to automatically feed the bushing and also incorporate the use of the air or hydraulic press, the method shown in Fig. 5-11 could be developed.

ACT BREAKDOWN

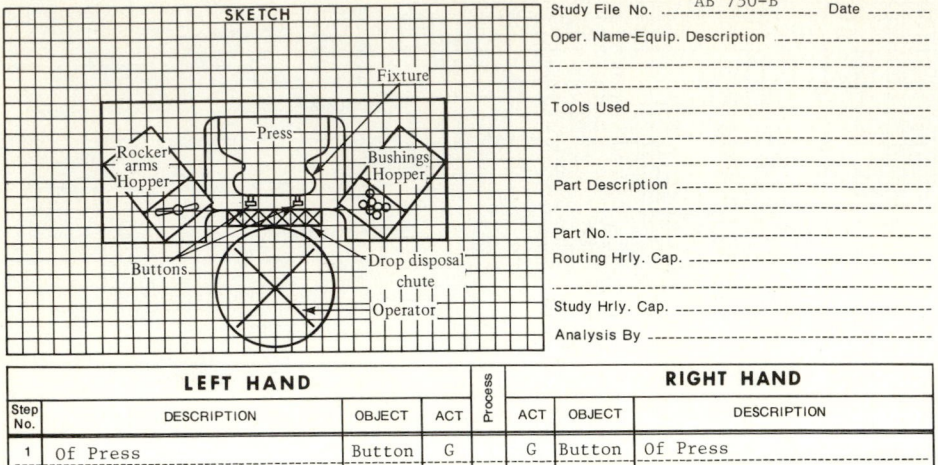

Study File No. ___AB 750-B___ Date _____

Oper. Name-Equip. Description _____

_____

_____

Tools Used _____

_____

Part Description _____

_____

Part No. _____

Routing Hrly. Cap. _____

_____

Study Hrly. Cap. _____

Analysis By _____

Step No.	LEFT HAND DESCRIPTION	OBJECT	ACT	Process	ACT	OBJECT	RIGHT HAND DESCRIPTION
1	Of Press	Button	G		G	Button	Of Press
2	Of Press	Button	P		P	Button	Of Press
3	Hold for Process	Button		X		Button	Hold for Process
4	From Hopper	Rocker Arm	G		G	Assy.	From Fixture
5	In Fixture	Rocker Arm	P		D	Assy.	To Tote Pan
6	In Fixture	Rocker Arm	X		G	Bushing	From Hopper
7	Wait				P	Bushing	In Fixture

Figure 5-10 Second alternative for improvement.

Furthermore, the use of air disposal of the assembly would result in a method shown in Fig. 5-12.

The next proposal might be for a totally mechanical (automated) method. This should be undertaken only if economically feasible or if required because of limiting criteria.

In following the five-step approach, the analyst should be able to develop the best solution within the limitations of improvement possibilities and economics involved. Limitations as stated here mean the degree of improvement that may be accomplished in recognition of economics, life of job, production scheduling, volume, time for improvement to be developed and installed, and production and layout problems surrounding the activity studied. Development of the improvement proposals should be built around first what can be done immediately at minor cost and second what can be planned as a future or long-range type of solution. The normal tendency is to seek the optimum solution without regard for the limitations imposed on the activity. There is likewise a tendency to overlook immediate types of improvements if there is no thought given to the purchase of new physical items. The first question to be asked of any activity is, "What can we do better with what we have?" This approach alone has saved millions of dollars in industry. Many times the solutions developed through minor changes of layout, tooling, and method have resulted in betterment

ACT BREAKDOWN

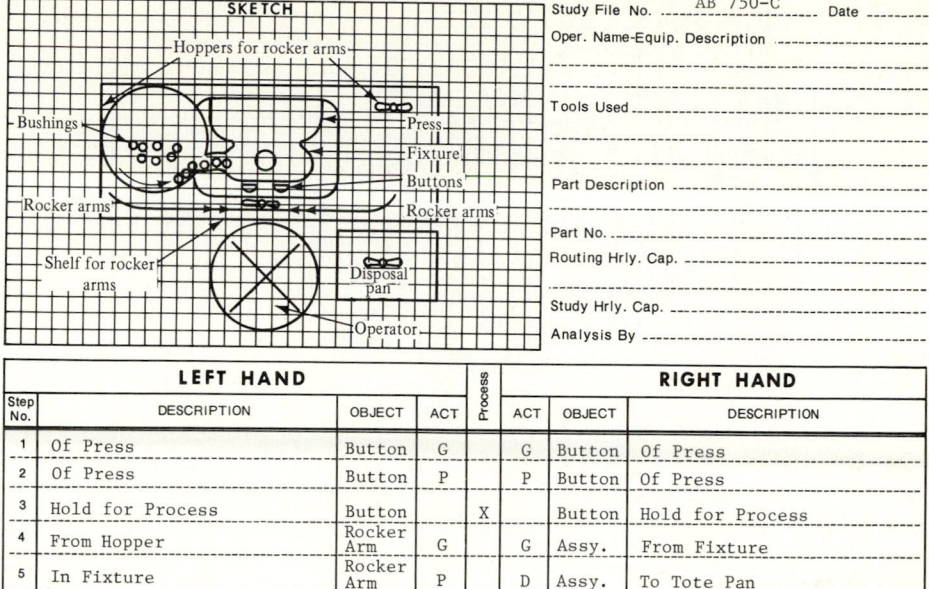

Step No.	LEFT HAND			Process	RIGHT HAND		
	DESCRIPTION	OBJECT	ACT		ACT	OBJECT	DESCRIPTION
1	Of Press	Button	G		G	Button	Of Press
2	Of Press	Button	P		P	Button	Of Press
3	Hold for Process	Button		X		Button	Hold for Process
4	From Hopper	Rocker Arm	G		G	Assy.	From Fixture
5	In Fixture	Rocker Arm	P		D	Assy.	To Tote Pan

Figure 5-11 Third alternative for improvement.

in the activity such as to preclude the need for further expenditures of money for improved facilities.

No attempt is made in the coverage of the act-breakdown technique to bring out evaluation methods. In comparing the present method with proposed methods, the objective of the problem will be the guide. Basically, time and cost would be the factors normally associated with the evaluation and therefore the comparison of one method versus another. Cost of the physical items or changes can be determined in conjunction with other staff functions. Where manual content is concerned, the analyst will have to use known time data (standard data), develop an estimate, and perform a time study of the new method or apply predetermined movement or motion data. The use of the act-breakdown technique without the incorporation of time would result in a calculated guess about savings potential. Analysis of method-time relation is discussed elsewhere in the text.

SUMMARY POINTS OF ACT BREAKDOWN

Definitions

Act. A grouping of motions or movements which can be used to describe manual activity for job study

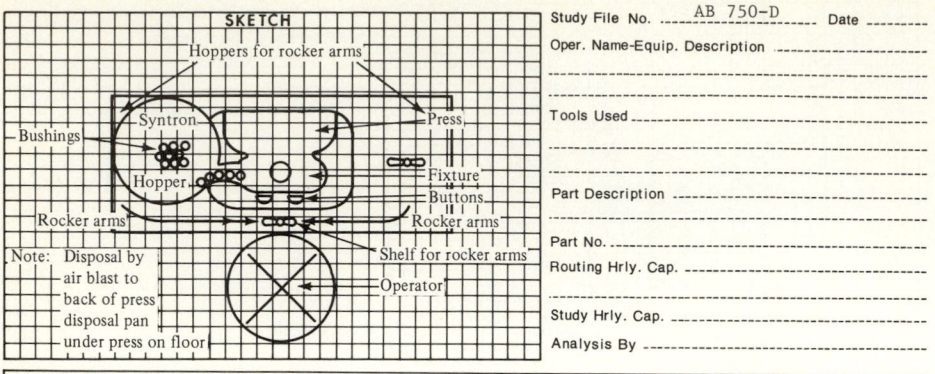

ACT BREAKDOWN

| Study File No. | AB 750-D | Date |

Oper. Name-Equip. Description

Tools Used

Part Description

Part No.

Routing Hrly. Cap.

Study Hrly. Cap.

Analysis By

Step No.	LEFT HAND DESCRIPTION	OBJECT	ACT	Process	ACT	OBJECT	RIGHT HAND DESCRIPTION
1	Of Press	Button	G		G	Button	Of Press
2	Of Press	Button	P		P	Button	Of Press
3	Hold for Process	Button		X		Button	Hold for Process
4	In Fixture	Rocker Arm	P		G	Rocker Arm	From Hopper
5	Of Press	Button	G		G	Button	Of Press
6	Of Press	Button	P		P	Button	Of Press
7	Hold for Process	Button		X		Button	Hold for Process
8	From Hopper	Rocker Arm	G		P	Rocker Arm	In Fixture

Figure 5-12 Fourth proposal for improvement.

Get act. The muscular movements necessary to move to and gain full control of an object (for the purpose intended)

Place act. The muscular movements necessary to move an object into a definite position and hold and/or release it there

Dispose act. The muscular movements necessary to move an object in a given direction and release it without reference to its final position

Rules for Recording

1. Fill out the heading.
2. Sketch the work-space layout.
3. Select the starting point (balance point).
4. Record the method.

Steps in Analysis

1. Question for cause and effect all waits and holds and eliminate all that seem to be questionable.

2. Question for cause and effect all acts and eliminate all unnecessary acts.
3. Question for cause and effect all remaining acts and determine improvement possibilities for each act.
4. Regroup improved acts into a balanced workable method.
5. Determine mechanical and manual specifications necessary to place method into operation.

QUESTIONS

5-1 How is method analysis defined?

5-2 What are the factors or related conditions that make up the physical arrangement in which an operation takes place?

5-3 What is the range of variation to be expected in unrestricted output within some defined limits of fixed method for uncontrolled to controlled method?

5-4 What are some of the influences that may affect the breadth and depth of methods study?

5-5 What is the definition of the get act and what motions are associated with this act?

5-6 What is the definition of the place act and what motions are associated with this act?

5-7 What is the definition of the dispose act and what motions are associated with this act?

5-8 Define the term "wait."

5-9 Define the term "drift."

5-10 Define the term "hold."

5-11 Define the term "process."

5-12 At what point in the cycle should one start recording the acts?

5-13 What is the analytical approach for developing an improved act breakdown?

5-14 Analyze the following method and create an improved act breakdown.

Step No.	LEFT HAND DESCRIPTION	OBJECT	ACT	Process	ACT	OBJECT	RIGHT HAND DESCRIPTION
1	From Hopper	Part	Get				Wait
2	To Right Hand	Part	Place		Get	Part	From Left Hand
3	Drift Toward Button				Place	Part	In Fixture
4	Of Press	Button	Get		Get	Button	Of Press
5	Of Press	Button	Place		Place	Button	Of Press
6	Hold for Process & Release	Button	X	X	X	Button	Hold for Process & Release
7	Wait				Get	Part	In Fixture
8	From Right Hand	Part	Get		Place	Part	To Left Hand
9	To Hopper	Part	Dispose				Wait
10							

5-15 The operator is assembling a cover and two bolts and washers to a body positioned in a fixture on a conveyor. The method being used is as shown. Assume that a suggestion has been turned in to have washers placed on a tray with a sponge bottom allowing the operator to gain control of a washer by placing a bolt through a washer and thereby partially moving the washer on to the bolt. What method would propose incorporating this suggestion?

Step No.	LEFT HAND DESCRIPTION	OBJECT	ACT	Process	ACT	OBJECT	RIGHT HAND DESCRIPTION
1	Wait				G	Cover	From stack
2	In right hand		G		P	Cover	To Body on Conveyor
3	Assist to Align		P		X	Cover	Align to Body
4	From Tray	Washer	G		G	Bolt	From Tray
5	Assemble to Bolt	Washer	P				Hold
6	Wait				P	Subassy	To Cover
7	Wait				X		Start Bolt
8	From Tray	Washer	G		G	Bolt	From Tray
9	Assemble to Bolt	Washer	P				Hold
10	Wait				P	Subassy	To Bolt
11	Wait				X		Start Bolt
12							

5-16 How would you improve the following method?

Step No.	LEFT HAND DESCRIPTION	OBJECT	ACT	Process	ACT	OBJECT	RIGHT HAND DESCRIPTION
1	To Back	Assy	D		G	Shaft	From Hopper
2	Wait (drift)				P	Shaft	In Fixture
3	From Hopper	Spring	G				Wait
4	On Shaft	Spring	P				Wait (drift)
5	Wait				G	Washer	From Hopper
6	Wait (drift)				P	Washer	On Pin
7	From Tray	Key	G		X	"	Hold
8	In Slot Of Shaft	Key	P		X	"	Depress Spring
9	From Fixture	Assy	G				Wait
10							
11							

5-17 How would you improve the following method?

Step No.	LEFT HAND DESCRIPTION	OBJECT	ACT	Process	ACT	OBJECT	RIGHT HAND DESCRIPTION
1	From Pile	Plate	G		D	Assy	To Chute
2	On Fixture	Plate	P		G	tube	From Box
3	Wait				P	Tube	In Left Hand
4	From Right Hand	Tube	G		X	"	" " "
5	Against Ram	Tube	P		G	Handle	Of Arbor Press
6	Hold Tube Against Ram	"	X	X	P	Handle	Down To Engage Tube
7	Of Press	Handle	G	X	X	"	"
8	Assist Right Hand	Handle	P	X	X	"	"
9	From Fixture	Assy	G		P	Handle	Up
10	In Right Hand	Assy	P		G	Assy	From Left Hand
11							
12							

METHODS DESCRIPTIONS FOR WORK MEASUREMENT

Another important segment of a time study is the element description, which is also part of the standardization of the method necessary to establish a work standard.

THE ELEMENT DESCRIPTION

An element can be defined as the subdivision of an operation cycle that can be recognized, described, and timed. Since foreign or irregular elements do not occur every cycle, they are not part of this regular cyclic description. The advantages of a detailed element description are worth the time and effort involved. Some advantages of dividing an operation into elements are that it

1. Makes a better job description
2. Aids in establishing better methods
3. Makes noting small changes in method easier
4. Enables separation of delay times from the body of the study
5. Helps maintain consistency by separating constants from variables
6. Enables comparison of similar elements between jobs
7. Minimizes the number of studies that must be taken to establish standard time data

The element description uses the same terms as does the act breakdown, because these terms are defined and the motions within each act are known. Therefore, *get, place,* and *dispose* will describe the activities and *wait* and *hold* will describe the inactivities of an operation. This standardized language should provide a good word picture of the method used, thereby enabling good communication of the method to other concerned persons. To further ensure a good element description, the following guides should be considered:

1. Stand in a position where all movements of the operator are clearly visible.
2. Observe enough cycles until familiar enough to start the description.

3. Start description at beginning of cycle.
4. Note that each element should have a definite stopping point (read point).
5. Observe that elements should be as short as can be accurately timed.
6. Use only act-breakdown terminology to describe elements.
7. Record distance for each act.
8. Complete the element description before timing the operation, except where the cycle time is too long to be practicable.
9. When possible, record the following activities as separate elements:
   a. Constant time work (element time remains constant)
   b. Variable time work [element time varies with independent variable(s)]
   c. Getting and placing of individual parts
   d. Walking
   e. Waiting for work (human being or machine)
   f. Machine process time
   g. Machine loading
   h. Machine unloading
   i. Machine internal time (work done while machine is producing)
   j. Machine external time (work done while machine is not producing)

When these guides are followed, a good element description is ensured; this will also simplify the development of standard time data. In guide 9, the words "when possible" are used, because there is sometimes a time restriction that does not permit the separation of elements as desired. For example, the machine process time may be too short to time as a separate element for some palm button-operated presses, which is not a problem on most machining-type operations. Getting and placing individual parts may not be a separate element when the operator is handling two different parts simultaneously, which is an example of another type of restriction. The chapter on Standard Time Data explains constant and variable elements, and internal and external time is detailed in the Method Summary Charting chapter.

Types of Element Description

Since there are many diverse operations found in industry, three different types of element description are presented in this chapter. There are many different variables that affect the determination of which description is to be used for a particular operation. These variables will be discussed later in the text after a discussion of the three types of description. Note that all three of the examples describe the same operation, have the same read points, use act-breakdown terminology, have distances for each act, and consist of nine elements in the operation cycle.

Type A description　A description is similar to the act breakdown and should have similar methods-improvement potential. Any waits and holds should be questioned as necessary in the same manner as is the act-breakdown analysis for improvement.

It is evident in Fig. 6-1 that type A is a column-type description, somewhat similar to the act-breakdown format, but has some distinct differences.

Element No.	LEFT SIDE (Hand is understood unless another body member is specified)	Distance nearest to $\frac{1}{2}$ ft.	RIGHT SIDE (Hand is understood unless another body member is specified)	Distance nearest to $\frac{1}{2}$ ft.
1.	Get rod from stock pan	1	Get cap from stock pan	1
	Walk to hand mill			4
	Hold rod		*Place cap on machine bed*	$\frac{1}{2}$
2.			Get cloth from machine bed	$\frac{1}{2}$
			Place cloth to rod joint	
			face and wipe face clean	$\frac{1}{2}$
			Place cloth on machine bed	$\frac{1}{2}$
3.	Place rod to RH	$\frac{1}{2}$	Get rod in LH	$\frac{1}{2}$
	Place rod in fixture			1
	Hold rod in fixture		Get fixture lever	$\frac{1}{2}$
	"		*Place lever to right to close fixture*	$\frac{1}{2}$
4.	Get cap from machine bed	1	Get cloth from machine bed	$\frac{1}{2}$
	Place cap to front of body	$\frac{1}{2}$	Place cloth to cap joint	
	Hold cap		face and wipe face clean	$\frac{1}{2}$
	"		*Place cloth on machine bed*	$\frac{1}{2}$
5.	Place cap in fixture	1	Get fixture lever	$\frac{1}{2}$
	Hold cap in fixture		*Place lever to right to close fixture*	$\frac{1}{2}$
6.	Get feed handle			$1\frac{1}{2}$
	Place (raise) handle to advance work to cutters			1
	Place handle to mill lock slot in rod and cap			
	Place (lower) handle to back work from cutters			1
7.	Wait		Get cap fixture lever	1
	"		Place lever to left to open	
	Get cap from fixture	$\frac{1}{2}$	fixture	$\frac{1}{2}$
	Place cap to front of body	1	Wait	
8.	Hold cap		Get rod fixture lever	$\frac{1}{2}$
			Place lever to left to open	
			fixture	$\frac{1}{2}$
			Get rod from fixture	$\frac{1}{2}$
9.	Walk to roller conveyor			4
	Place cap in stock pan on, conveyor	1	*Place rod in stock pan on conveyor*	1

Figure 6-1 Example of type A element description.

1. Distances are now shown for each act, and the distances can be in inches, feet, centimeters, or meters; use whatever is desired.
2. An element normally consists of several acts, and the last act of the element is underlined, preferably in red, (italicized in Fig. 6-1) to designate the read point where the watch is read.
3. Walking is written across the center as seen in element 1.
4. In element 3, "place rod in fixture" is also written across the center, because both hands are placing the rod in the fixture.

The type A description is the best of the three choices for describing an operation, and it should be used whenever possible. A good description will be ensured if the analyst completes one row of activity and/or inactivity before proceeding to the next activity in sequence. *Never* complete the right-side activity for the entire element or cycle and then return to describe the left-side activity. Some activities and inactivities will be missed if this procedure is followed.

Type B description Type *B* is a narrative form of description (see Fig. 6-2). Since there are no columns for the left hand and right hand, it is convenient to use the abbreviations LH for left hand, RH for right hand, and BH for both hands. There are no columns now to remind the analyst to record the distance; therefore, each time an act is recorded, also *designate* the *body member* performing the work and the *distance* moved. Of course the read points are underlined, preferably in red again, (italicized in Fig. 6-2) and only act-breakdown terminology should be used.

If the method as well as the type *A* description is to be documented, then the type *B* description must make use of the term "while" repeatedly. All simultaneous work activities and inactivities should be indicated by using this expression. In element 2, "LH holds rod *while* RH gets cloth, etc." is a good example of its use. Using the term "while" will enable the analyst to detect waits and holds that otherwise would be missed. This then enhances the analyst's chances of detecting improvement possibilities.

Type C description Figure 6-3 is an example of the type *C* description that is also a narrative form of description. Read points and distances are still shown, and act-

Element No.	
1.	Get rod with LH and cap with RH from stock pan on roller convey-or 1 ft. in front of operator. Walk 4 ft. to Hand Mill and *place cap on machine bed with RH $\frac{1}{2}$ ft. in front of operator.*
2.	LH holds rod, while RH gets cloth from machine bed ($\frac{1}{2}$ ft.) and places cloth to wipe rod joint face clean and *places cloth on machine bed ($\frac{1}{2}$ ft.).*
3.	Get rod in both hands ($\frac{1}{2}$ ft.) and place rod in fixture (1 ft.). Hold in place with LH. *Place lever to right with RH to close fixture ($\frac{1}{2}$ ft.).*
4.	LH gets cap from machine bed (1 ft.) and holds in front of oper-ator while RH gets cloth from machine bed ($\frac{1}{2}$ ft.), places cloth to wipe cap joint face clean and *places cloth on machine bed ($\frac{1}{2}$ ft.).*
5.	Place cap in fixture with LH (1 ft.) *place lever to right* with RH ($\frac{1}{2}$ ft.) *to close fixture.*
6.	Both hands get feed handle ($1\frac{1}{2}$ ft.) place (raise) feed handle (1 ft.) to advance work to cutters, place handle to mill lock slot in rod and cap and place (lower) handle (1 ft.) to *back work from cutters.*
7.	Get lever with RH (1 ft.), place lever ($\frac{1}{2}$ ft.) to left to open cap fixture and *get cap from fixture ($\frac{1}{2}$ ft.) with LH.*
8.	LH holds cap while RH gets lever ($\frac{1}{2}$ ft.), place lever ($\frac{1}{2}$ ft.) to left to open rod fixture and *get rod from fixture ($\frac{1}{2}$ ft.).*
9.	Walk 4 ft. to roller conveyor, place cap in stock pan (1 ft.) with LH and *place rod in stock pan with RH (1 ft.).*

Figure 6-2 Example of type *B* element description.

Element No.	
1.	Get rod and cap from stock pan on roller conveyor (1 ft.), walk 4 ft. to Hand Mill and *place cap on machine bed* ($\frac{1}{2}$ ft.).
2.	Get cloth ($\frac{1}{2}$ ft.), place cloth to wipe rod joint face clean and *dispose of cloth* ($\frac{1}{2}$ ft.).
3.	Place rod into fixture (1 ft.) and *place clamp closed* ($\frac{1}{2}$ ft.).
4.	Get cap and cloth (1 ft.), place cloth to wipe cap joint face clean and *dispose of cloth* ($\frac{1}{2}$ ft.).
5.	Place cap into fixture (1 ft.) and *place clamp closed* ($\frac{1}{2}$ ft.).
6.	Place handle to advance work to cutters (1 ft.), hand mill slots in rod and cap and place handle to *return mill table* (1 ft.).
7.	Get and place lever (unclamp) and *get cap from fixture* ($\frac{1}{2}$ ft.).
8.	Get and place lever (unclamp) other fixture and *get rod* ($\frac{1}{2}$ ft.).
9.	Walk 4 ft. to conveyor and *place both pieces in stock pan* (1 ft.).

Figure 6-3 Example of type *C* element description.

breakdown terminology is still used. However, there is one distinct difference between this description and type *B*: there is no designation of the body members performing the work. Furthermore, the term "while" is not shown and there is an absence of waits and holds. With the conspicuous absence of these items, the method is not as well-documented as are the type *A* and type *B* descriptions.

The type *C* description might be used on an operation with a production run of only one day or several hours per month. A modified type *C* may have to be used on long-cycle operations where the method cannot be recorded before the timing begins. In this case, there will be even less detail and larger elements in respect to time. If more detail is wanted, then midget tape recorders can be used where the element description and time are spoken and thereby recorded on the audio tape; people can speak much faster than they can write. The use of TV equipment to record method and time is another alternative for better documentation; it also offers the much-needed methods-improvement potential for long-cycle operations.

Relative Merits of the Three Types of Element Description

It is apparent that the major differences in the examples lie in the quality and amount of detail recorded. It is also apparent that all indicate what work is performed and how the work is performed but in varying degrees of exactness. For timing purposes, one type seems to be as satisfactory as another, except possibly when irregularities in the observed method are designated.

An approximate evaluation of their relative merits can be determined by considering the degree to which each example fulfills the nine objectives and requirements of the operation description listed in Fig. 6-5. In order to do this, it is necessary to analyze the examples and determine such things as the number of recorded work activities and the number of recorded waits, holds, distances, etc.

The exactness of the recorded worker method must also be appraised at its face value; it has been tabulated as the number of methods possibilities (see Fig. 6-4). For example, the first work activity in the example of type A description shows that the left hand gets a rod from the stock pan at the same time that the right hand gets a cap from the stock pan. Ruling out the absurd possibility of crisscrossing the hands, we find that there is no doubt about the one method employed by the worker in obtaining these two-piece parts. When analyzing the same work activity in the example of the type B description, we find that the worker could follow any one of three methods and still be within the boundaries of the recorded description, viz., he or she (1) could get the piece parts simultaneously; (2) could get the rod with the left hand while the right hand waits and then get the cap with the right hand while the left hand waits; or (3) vice versa (from 2), make three methods possibilities in this very small part of the operation. When determining the methods possibilities of this same work activity permitted by the recorded description in the example of type C, we find that there are at least seven such possibilities; viz., three are the same as those permitted by the example of type B; four others are: (1) get rod with right hand while left hand waits, place in left hand; get cap with right hand while left hand waits, (2) vice versa (from 1), (3) get both rod and cap with right hand while left hand waits, and (4) vice versa (from 3).

Element No.	Step No.	Type A	Type B	Type C
			Methods possibilities	
1	1.	1	3	7
	2.	1	1	1
	3.	1	2	4
2	4.	1	1	8
	5.	1	Indefinite	Indefinite
	6.	1	1	4
	7.	1	1	8
3	8.	1	1	Indefinite
	9.	1	1	5
	10.	1	2	Indefinite
	11.	1	2	5
4	12.	1	2	5
	13.	1	Indefinite	Indefinite
	14.	1	1	5
	15.	1	1	5
5	16.	1	2	5
	17.	1	2	5
6	18.	1	1	Indefinite
	19.	1	1	5
	20.	1	1	5
	21.	1	1	5
7	22.	1	2	Indefinite
	23.	1	2	5
	24.	1	2	5
	25.	1	Indefinite	Indefinite
8	26.	1	1	Indefinite
	27.	1	1	5
	28.	1	1	5
9	29.	1	1	1
	30.	1	3	5

Figure 6-4

Objective or Requirement	Type A	Type B	Type C
1. Accurately and completely describe the method used and the work performed at the time the standard is established so that it can be clearly understood.	100%	75%	45%
2. Facilitate an analysis of the operation in order to establish the best practical method before the recording of times.	100%	70%	20%
3. Facilitate an analysis of the operation which will indicate the possibilities for future job improvement.	100%	70%	20%
4. Facilitate the detection of changes in the worker's method.	100%	70%	20%
5. Contain certain basic standardized terminology (at least within a plant or division).	100%	100%	100%
6. Designate the work performed by left and right hand or other members of the body when the work pattern is such that it can be maintained.	100%	90%	0
7. Designate any one-handed waiting on the part of the worker or automatic or semiautomatic equipment.	100%	0	0
8. Facilitate changes in the work standard when the work content of the job or the method of performing the operation is changed.	100%	75%	45%
9. Show distances in the description and/or a sketch of the workplace layout; show relative locations in either a sketch or photograph of the workplace layout.	100%	100%	100%

Figure 6-5 Percent fulfillment of work measurement objectives by A–, B–, and C–type descriptions.

Figure 6-4 shows the realistic number of methods possibilities in each step or work activity of the operation in the examples. The examples of types B and C are analyzed and compared with the example of type A, which is used as the basis of comparison in all steps. The micromotion analyst might state that the example of type A permits more than one method possibility. From this viewpoint, it is true. There will always be operations where it is desirable to consider the worker's method in the minute detail afforded by micromotion analysis. From a practical viewpoint, however, it is generally unnecessary to describe and analyze operations in such detail for time-study purposes. Therefore, the example of type A is considered to permit only one method possibility in each of the 30 recorded steps of work activities. The data obtained from the foregoing analyses were used to calculate the percentages in Fig. 6-5, which indicate the approximate degree to which nine objectives and requirements of the operation description are fulfilled. The data from the analysis of the example of type A is used for the 100 percent bases.

Guides for Selecting the Type of Description to Be Used

When deciding what type of description to make on a particular operation, one should consider one or more variables that will help one arrive at the correct decision. Often several items will help determine the proper type of description needed for the operation.

1. *Methods-improvement potential.* It would be readily apparent that the type A description should be used after viewing objectives 2 and 3 in Fig. 6-5. Type B

would be somewhat effective in detecting methods-improvement potential, but only if the analyst made liberal use of the term "while" for simultaneous activities and inactivities.

2. *Coordination of body members.* If coordination of body members must be shown, then type *A* is the best. Once again, if the term "while" is used repeatedly, then type *B* would qualify almost as well. Type *C* does not designate body members, so it does not qualify (see Fig. 6-5, objective 6).

3. *Number of units to be run.* Very high production would demand a type *A* or at least a type *B*; whereas, type *C* could be used for very low production.

4. *Number of people performing the same work.* If several people are performing the same work, then type *A* should be used if possible, because methods-improvement potential would be of prime importance too. An improvement of this type of operation would provide more substantial savings with the amount of people involved.

5. *Length of cycle.* When the length of cycle is short enough, type *A* or at least a type *B* should be used, because of greater methods-improvement potential involved. Some cycle times are so long that a type *A* or *B* description becomes impossible, so a type *C* must be used.

6. *Cycle variation.* When there is very little variation in the cycle, type *A* or *B* can be used. Great cycle variations would mean that only a type *C* would be possible. This should not be confused with interruptions of the cycle by foreign or irregular elements which are *not* part of the cyclic description and can be easily handled with code letters and separate descriptions.

7. *Studying delays or indirect labor.* Usually type *C,* or a modified type *C,* are the only ones that can be used, because of variations in the work pattern. If the method cannot be recorded before getting the time values, then underlining read points and recording distances for each act may not be possible; however, walk distances or paces should be recorded in the modified type *C.* However, keep in mind the possible elimination or minimization of questionable work and imposed wait times.

8. *Compiling standard time data.* Type *A* or at least *B* should be used, unless restricted to a type *C* by some of the other variables in this section. Incidentally, compiling standard time data usually uncovers methods improvements as a result of the exposure of many similar operations and operators' patterns of work.

9. *Studying bottleneck or critical operations.* The type *A* description should be used unless restricted by some of the other items discussed here. As an example, if an improvement can be made on a bottleneck operation in an assembly line, then the line flow should be better and more assemblies may be produced.

10. *Grievance studies.* For study of an operation where a grievance has been filed, of course the best possible type of description that would thoroughly document the method would be used. Besides having a good element description, all the job data and the sketch of the workplace should be complete.

Before a time study can be taken, the analyst must obtain a clear understanding of the factors surrounding and affecting the job to be studied. It is important that this be preliminary to the study, since the job conditions must be known in case it becomes necessary to restudy the job later under the same conditions to suggest improvements or changes in method or to make an immediate decision regarding taking or deferring the time study of the operation. The job conditions are the framework of the operation.

There may be minor improvements in the job conditions which can be made immediately before taking a time study. Some of these may be overlooked if the prestudy of the job is not a conscientious effort on the part of the time-study analyst and the production supervisor. The preliminary survey of the job will form the basis for determining the direction of future improvement of the job. Future improvements may be suggested by the study itself or they may result from later study of the job conditions as recorded by the analyst.

Is the Job Ready for Time Study?

The answer to the question, "Is the job ready for time study?" will direct the course of action to be taken by the time-study analyst with respect to the operation to be studied. This answer is determined by the analysis of the job conditions as recorded by the time-study person. The course of action may take two main directions. Either the taking of the time study will be deferred or it will begin immediately.

If the study is deferred, it may be a matter of a few hours or a considerable period of time. The amount of time needed will depend on the corrective action required as indicated by the analysis of the job conditions. If the changes are minor, the supervisor may be requested to make the changes and the operation will then be timed after a brief period of acquainting the operator with the change. A common example of minor change would be moving a stock box closer to the operation.

If the suggested correction is of major character, such as a fixture change or a machine rearrangement, the study will have to be deferred until the corrective action has been taken or a temporary standard set until the change has been made.

If no time study is to be taken, the resulting element description constitutes the major portion of an activity chart and it may be filed as is or used for other methods or work-measurement purposes.

The second course of action may be to take the time study immediately after analyzing the job conditions. This latter decision may be the result of accepting the conditions as standard, in which case the conditions must be such that the job can be performed continually without undue fatigue or effort on the part of the operator. Or it may be that even though the job conditions are not standard, a time study must be taken. This may be because of the limited production involved or a need for a time record of the job as it is being performed. Depending on local plant policy, this may be identified as a "temporary" standard or it may be considered permanent. If it is considered temporary, the conditions should be noted as such, so that there is no question when the job is restudied.

In order to ensure a full development of the picture of the conditions surrounding and affecting the job to be studied, a check sheet covering most common conditions may be used. The items covered in the check sheet are usually presented in the form of questions about the conditions designed to help the time-study analyst determine if the operation is ready for time study. As a result of the analysis, the time-study person can make a more accurate decision about whether or not the job is ready for time study. A representative checklist along with the reasons the items are listed is presented below. Other questions may be required according to the job.

1. *Is the supervisor at the job with you?*
   It is essential that the supervisor be present when the time-study person is analyzing the job, since it is the supervisor whom the analyst should consult when questions on job conditions arise. Since the supervisor must eventually either approve or disapprove the study, he or she should be present when the study is made.

2. *Is the operation being performed safely?*
   This is a primary requisite on the job. If the job is being performed in a way that is hazardous to the operator or to fellow workers, it should not be studied. Rather, corrective action should be initiated and the study deferred until action is taken.

3. *Is the specified material being used?*
   In order to produce a time study reflecting normal conditions, the material should be that which is specified. If the material is not to specifications and the study must be taken because of other reasons, these facts should be noted and the specifications of the actual material recorded.

4. *Are the specified tools and fixtures being used, and are they being used as designed for the job?*
   The tools and fixtures as provided by the various staff departments should be used on the job to ensure normal conditions. Care should be taken to see that they are being used in the manner for which they were designed.

5. *Are speeds and feeds correct?*
   The time-study analyst should check the feeds and speeds of the equipment and determine if they agree with those specified. If they do not and it is necessary to take the study under these conditions, this fact should be noted on the time study.

6. *Is the operator producing parts which meet inspection requirements?*
   This item is closely related to the questions about proper use of tools and fixtures and correctness of feeds and speeds, since these are primary factors which affect the amount of scrap produced. The parts being produced during the study must be good parts, because standards are set on good parts produced.

7. *Is the light, heat, and ventilation on the job that which is normally encountered?*
   Any variation in general conditions as they normally occur on the job must be considered in determining if the job is ready for time study. Abnormal temperatures or burned-out light bulbs should be noted. These conditions must be considered for determining when the operation is to be timed and the type of standard to be set.

8. *Is the operator using the established method of doing the job?*
   This item is extremely important, since variations in method mean variations in time required. The method used on the job should be the method specified.

9. *Is the cutting compound correct for the job?*
   Use of the specified cutting compound on the job ensures machine time that will reflect normal operating conditions and normal tool life.

10. *Is material flowing into and out of the workplace properly?*
    Stock should be provided the operator in a way that shows normal practice on the job. If the operator normally has to get the stock, this condition should exist during the course of the study.

11. *Are the holding devices operating correctly?*
    The mechanism of the holding devices, if any, should be in proper operating condition. Levers and handles should be in the proper position, quick-acting clamps should operate properly, and screw-type clamps should not be too tight or too loose.

12. *Is the machine operating correctly?*
    Parts of the machine that affect the operator's method, such as handle levers, clutches, and quick returns, should all be operating properly to ensure a normal study.

13. *Can the workplace layout be improved by rearranging such equipment as tote pans and chutes?*

14. *Can the operation be eliminated or combined with another operation?*

15. *Can the part be prepositioned before or after the operation?*

16. *Can multiple or combination tools be used?*

17. *Can multiple station fixtures be used?*

Questions 13 through 17 on the checklist are primarily related to methods improvement. They are intended to advise the analyst whether or not he or she can recommend either immediate or long-range job improvement. It should be pointed out that such things as burned-out light bulbs should be immediately replaced and barriers should be removed. Major tool improvements generally require a development time too great to justify a delay in taking the time study. Therefore, a study should be taken on the method as it exists, even though it is not the ideal method.

It is extremely important that the supervisor responsible for this operation be contacted by the time-study person before he or she approaches the job. The supervisor should introduce the operator to the time-study analyst on the initial approach to the job. The supervisor will be interested in the conditions surrounding and affecting the job, since the maintenance of these conditions is his or her responsibility. All the conditions surrounding and affecting the job should be discussed between the analyst and the supervisor. Such discussions will help the time-study analyst determine the course of action as described above. After making a decision, the supervisor must be informed of the action to be taken. He or she should be present during the actual taking of the study, if possible. The human-relations factor involved in a time study of any operation is a vital condition affecting the job.

QUESTIONS

6-1 Define an element of work.

6-2 Can an operation cycle consist of only one element?

6-3 Why is the type *A* the best of the three types of description?

6-4 Why have a type C description, since it is obviously inferior to types A and B?

6-5 Does the read point occur at the beginning or at the end of an element?

6-6 When starting to time an operation, would the analyst start the watch on the first or last read point?

6-7 What term must be used repeatedly, if a very good type B description is desired?

6-8 Why is it important to record all waits and holds in addition to describing the activities?

6-9 Explain the difference between a hold and a wait.

6-10 "Can the workplace layout be improved by rearranging such equipment as tote pans and chutes?" is item 13 of the checklist at the end of the chapter. What ineffective worker movements would indicate that the workplace layout should be changed?

6-11 What activities should be separate elements when not restricted by time or some simultaneous acts?

6-12 Why is it a good idea to have the work supervisor present during a time study?

SEVEN

JOB ALLOWANCES AND THEIR DETERMINATION

An allowance is the time allotted in the work standard to cover any necessary work or delay outside the normal repetitive cycle of an operation. Conversely, the cycle time is the productive interval where one round of elements recur regularly in the same sequence until interrupted periodically by one of the allowances that must be performed.

In the establishment of a work standard, many other things can occur besides the regular cycle of work. In order to set a fair work standard, all necessary work done throughout the entire work shift must be accounted for in the work standard. The time to be allocated for these allowances can be obtained from delay studies, regular time studies, work sampling, memomotion, etc. However, standard time data developed from these studies would be very desirable.

TYPES OF ALLOWANCES

The following seven types of allowances can be considered as a check sheet, so that no legitimate delay is left out of a work standard.

Type 1 Tool Changes and Adjustments

The type I delay covers such items as changing or sharpening worn tools and adjusting tools to maintain the size and/or finish of a product. If the operator must wait while this work is being performed by a maintenance operator, time must still be allowed for this activity. The work includes items such as

1. Cutting tools
2. Grinding and polishing wheels
3. Welding electrodes
4. Electronic and mechanical devices.

Type 2   Stock Handling

Allowance for stock handling will not be repetitive with each piece or cycle, but it will cover intermittent handling of material by the worker within the assigned work area or waiting while this work is done. This allowance includes such items as

1. Coils, bars, and strips
2. Tote pans, skids, and gondolas
3. Component parts
4. Miscellaneous supplies

Type 3   Servicing Equipment

Whenever servicing equipment is a job requirement, the operator will perform work in order to maintain the proper functioning of the equipment or wait while the work is done. Servicing equipment includes items such as

1. Changing or adding coolant
2. Lubricating
3. Making minor adjustments
4. Cleaning chips

Type 4   Job Preparation and Cleanup

Job preparation and cleaning involve work that an employee does as a job requirement in preparation for the day's work at the beginning of the shift, before and after lunch, and before the job can be left at the end of the shift. This pertains to items such as

1. Arranging the workplace
2. Checking operating conditions of tooling and equipment
3. Getting or returning supplies, tools, gages, etc.
4. Putting on and removing protective clothing (health or safety measure)
5. Cleaning up workplace
6. Washing up (health or safety measure)
7. Counting production and other clerical duties

Type 5   Gaging and/or Inspection

Inspection involves the periodic checks an employee is required to make on his or her own work and/or gages or the wait while this is being done in order to maintain a quality part or capable process. Whenever possible, the work should be done internal to the machine cycle, so that the machine time and the inspection time are occurring simultaneously. Examples of this allowance are

1. Visual inspection for flaws
2. Use of a gage for checking dimensions

Type 6   Other Delays

The type 6 classification may be used where plant policy specifies that allowances must be made in the work standard to cover various minor delays that are not covered by the first five types of allowances. The use of this allowance should be limited to

1. When a plant is compelled by company policy to include items of delay which are not specifically covered by the other types of allowances
2. When an allowance is normally made to cover unpredictable and unavoidable minor delays, in which case the allowance should be small owing to the larger coverage by the other five types of allowances

The other-delays allowance might include

1. Infrequent interruptions by supervisors, inspectors, job setters, or other employees
2. Minor interruptions of stock flow

When studies are made to determine the correct time for the preceding six types of allowances, *caution* must be exercised in order to get the proper time values. Consideration should be given to the following questions:

1. Can the delay be *eliminated* or *minimized*?
2. Is the *best method* being used in the performance of the work necessary for the delay item? (This must be done on delays as well as the regular cycle of work.)
3. Is the delay item being performed at the *proper frequency*?

Type 7   Personal

Personal allowance is the time allowed an employee to take care of normal physical necessities. Examples of this allowance are

1. Going to the toilet
2. Getting a drink of water
3. Cleaning safety glasses
4. Wiping perspiration

Other items of a similar nature which deal directly with the employee's personal comfort would be part of this allowance. Some people choose smoking or going to the vending machine as a way of spending part of their personal time.

Either 3 minutes per hour of work or 24 minutes per 8-hour shift is a frequently used value for personal time with no distinction between males and females. This allowance of 24 minutes is normally for nonassembly-line operators who take their own personal relief without having a relief operator to take over their duties. Where a relief operator is employed for assembly-line operators, 46 minutes per 8-hour shift is sometimes used. These values are often negotiated values which are acceptable to management and the union. In order to remain competitive with other companies producing similar products, the personal time allowed should be reasonable.

INCORPORATION OF ALLOWANCES IN THE WORK STANDARD

Allowances must not be included indiscriminately in the work standard. In addition to checking to see if (1) the delay can be eliminated or minimized, (2) the best method is being used in the performance of the work, and (3) the proper frequency is being used, the delay item should meet the following requirements.

Allowance Requirements

The delay item should meet the following requirements before it is included in the work standard.

1. The delay must occur at least once per shift.
2. The delay must be a job requirement.
3. The delay must not be charged to another expense.

When a delay occurs less than once per shift, there should be a separate task standard to cover this work. On a particular day when this work is performed, the task standard would then be used in addition to the regular production standard. A good example of this would be when a worker does his or her own machine setup work several times a month. This at-least-once-on-every-shift limitation makes it possible to establish work standards which can serve as the basis for an accurate measurement of daily efficiencies. With the exception of the personal allowance, the fact that the delay must be a job requirement is self-explanatory.

If a delay is covered by another expense account number, then obviously, the time for this work is already accounted for and does not enter the production work standard. As an example, machine repair is charged to a separate expense.

Allowances for unmeasured delay items under such headings as "miscellaneous delays" and "contingencies" should be avoided. In order to be fair to the worker and management, all delay items should be measured and documented. If a miscellaneous category is used, there should be a list of the individual times for items included in that category. In addition, the types of delays discussed here probably belong in the type 6 other-delays category, which normally should not exceed 10 minutes per shift. Otherwise, it would be apparent that the delay item belongs in one of the first five types of delay allowances. The main point is not to estimate but to measure the time for all delays.

Calculation of Allowances

Calculation of delay times that are allowed in the work standard is a very simple task. Only two units are necessary—minutes per shift and minutes per piece. The delays normally fall into one category or the other. For example, personal time is best understood when quoted as minutes per shift rather than minutes per piece. In contrast, if a part is to be inspected once every 10 pieces, making this calculation in minutes per piece is more convenient.

There are many ways that calculations can be made, but the following example is one of the simplest methods of handling allowances in the calculation of a work standard. This example is abbreviated, so it will not necessarily show all delays needed in a particular operation; the emphasis is on the method of calculation only.

	Minutes per shift		Minutes per piece
Personal	24	Cycle time	0.604
Job preparation and clean up	6	Visual inspection	0.012
Other delays	4	Stock handling	0.024
Tool change and adjustment	6	Remover wrapper	0.010
Total	40	Total	0.650

480 minutes in an 8-hour shift
480 – 40 = 440 minutes per shift
440/8 = 55 average minutes per hour
55/0.650 = 84.6 pieces per hour
1 hour/84.6 = 0.01182 hour per piece

The last two calculated values, 84.6 pieces per hour and 0.01182 hour per piece are the items normally shown on the production, or labor, routing.

The personal allowance of 24 minutes per shift is normally a negotiated allowance, whereas the other minutes-per-shift allowances are usually determined from such studies as work-sampling or delay studies. The cycle time value of 0.604 minute is usually determined from a regular time study. The time for visual inspection, stock handling, and removing of wrappers could have been calculated from a regular time study or delay study. An example of calculating one of the foreign elements would be as follows. If the average time for remove wrapper is 0.10 minute and the number of components within a wrapper is 10 pieces, then 0.10 minute per 10 pieces equals 0.010 minute per piece, as shown in the data.

Fatigue

Much has been done in the past to eliminate or minimize fatigue in industry, so fatigue is much less of a problem today than it used to be. It will be even less of a problem in the future as industry becomes more automated. Fatigue has been and is being minimized by

1. Methods improvements to minimize effort expended
2. Proper selection and placement of employees
3. Job rotation (changing workers periodically from one job to another)
4. Improvement in job conditions
5. Technological improvements in equipment and tools
6. Diversion in activities while performing some of the seven allowances necessary throughout the entire workday, thereby providing a change from the regular repetitive cycle of work

Both the office worker and the production operator will feel the effects of a fair day's work, which is also true for a homemaker. Regardless of the type of job that a person has, each person will become conditioned to the job through days, weeks, months, and years of repetition. Furthermore, in the great majority of operations, the getting and placing of parts and controls is not difficult after skill has been developed through repetition.

One other item must be remembered. During a time study, the analyst is establishing a work standard based on normal performance of the operator over an 8-hour period. The analyst must keep in mind the fact that the operator is to work at that pace for the entire shift, which is why the normal walking rate is approximately 3 miles per hour. A person may be capable of walking much faster but would then become fatigued. All elements of work performed by the operator are considered in the same manner.

There is extensive evidence that many production people can work above the normal rate for long periods of time by getting conditioned to the job over a period of time. In fact, this is what is expected in piece work or incentive-type plans. Most operators will work at an above-normal pace in order to earn more money with an appropriate incentive plan. Since fatigue varies over a wide range between persons doing the same kind of work, the amount of money earned in an incentive system will vary also. Of course other variables, such as the degree of skill in performing the work, will have an effect on output. In addition, what is very fatiguing to one person may not be as fatiguing to another, because fatigue can be mental or physical or a combination of the two.

Many men and women jog a total of a few hours a week to stay in condition. In contrast, many people in industry work 40 hours a week performing repetitive work that automatically conditions them to the job, because of the extensive time devoted to the work performed. There may be an appropriate allowance for the few *consistently* heavy or hot operations commensurate with the conditions of the job. When a fatigue allowance is used, it is frequently an allowance that is negotiated with the union. In order to remain competitive with other companies performing the same type of work, the negotiated allowance must be a reasonable one. However, there should be no additional allowance for fatigue in the work standard for the great majority of jobs.

QUESTIONS

7-1 Why should delays be measured and analyzed?

7-2 Can work sampling be used to measure delays?

7-3 What are the seven standardized delay allowances?

7-4 Give four examples of job preparation and cleanup.

7-5 List four ways of eliminating or minimizing fatigue.

7-6 With respect to delay allowances, how can machine utilization be improved?

7-7 Why is fatigue less of a problem today than it was many years ago?

7-8 How often must a delay item occur before it can be allowed in the work standard?

7-9 If the cycle time and delays in minutes per piece add up to 0.85 minute per piece, what is the work standard in pieces per hour if all the other delays total 48 minutes per shift? Assume an 8-hour shift.

EIGHT

PERFORMANCE EVALUATION

Performance evaluation is a procedure for the establishment of allowed times on the time study which are representative of times that would be required by a worker demonstrating a satisfactory or normal performance level. Some of the other terms used for this particular technique are speed rating, effort rating, pace rating, selecting the allowed time, and leveling. Performance evaluation is done to determine a fair day's work level so that the operator's productivity is fair for management and for the operator. However, there is much that can be done effectively before the time study is taken when the operator's performance is evaluated.

VARIATIONS IN OUTPUT

Much of the variation in output between workers producing the same products can be explained by examining Fig. 8-1.

The Mechanical Method

By merely having the same tools and materials, there can be an expected output variation of approximately 4 to 1. When the same equipment is used by all operators in addition to the same tools and materials, the output variation will drop to approximately 3 to 1. When the same workplace layout is added to the standardization of the jobs, output variation drops to a ratio of $1\frac{3}{4}$ to 1. Remember that eliminating such

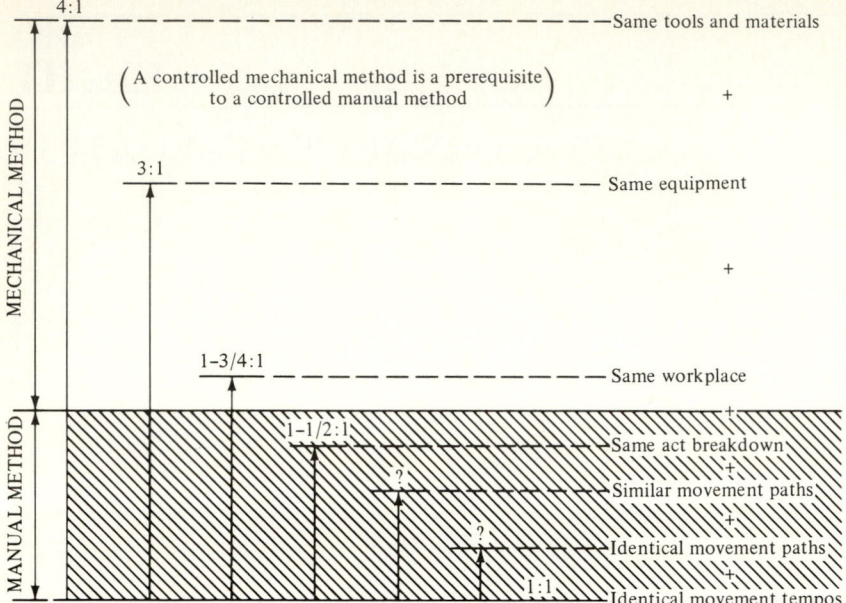

Figure 8-1 Approximate expected variation in unrestricted output within some defined limits of fixed method.

ineffective worker movements as long movements and changes of control can be accomplished by efficiently changing the workplace layout, which helps decrease the output variation.

Please note the important message near the top of Fig. 8-1—a controlled mechanical method is a *prerequisite* to a controlled manual method.

The Manual Method

When operations are standardized further by having the same act-breakdown sequence used by the workers, the output variation ratio drops to $1\frac{1}{2}$ to 1. Waits are minimized by changing the sequence of the acts so that an efficient act breakdown is used.

During the time study, effectively detecting foreign elements that are part of the repetitive cycle will also minimize the problem of rating the performance of the worker. This is an important aspect of timing the operator in addition to rating the operator's performance.

Referring to Fig. 8-1 again, we find that output variation decreases further when similar movement paths and then identical movement paths are added to the standardization. The output variation ceases when identical movement tempos are added as the last item. For all practical purposes, identical movement paths and identical movement tempos are encountered only in mechanical devices. The most important conclusion to be reached from Fig. 8-1 is that when production *output varies, frequently* the mechanical and/or manual *method varies.*

THE MORE-IMPORTANT TECHNIQUES IN GENERAL USAGE[1]

Speed Rating

In the rating technique termed "speed rating," the speed of the movements of the operator is given as the only factor which lends itself to measurement and hence to rating procedure. The extent of method and skill present are revealed in the time study by the actual elements that appear on the study. Differences in the speed of the operators are reflected in the actual time required to perform like elements.

The rating procedure thus consists of judging the pace or speed of the operator's movements in relation to a normal pace and noting the relation as a factor. The rating makes no attempt to correct for deviations from the standard method. This rating is applied to each element and in some cases is applied to each individual reading on the study. The observed time for each element is multiplied by the ratio of observed speed to expected speed to arrive at the expected, or normal, time for the element. Deviations from the standard method must be handled independently of the rating factor. The factor is sometimes expressed on the basis of a standard hour equal to 60 and deviations in speed indicated as a fraction of 60. Therefore, 50/60 would indicate a speed of movements 5/6, or $83\frac{1}{3}$ percent of that expected. A factor of 75/60 would indicate a performance 25 percent above normal. This factor is applied directly to the actual time selected to adjust it to normal. The expression of the factor was derived from the idea that normal is the amount of work that should be done in one unit of time, which is conveniently taken as 1 minute. Thus, a rating of 50/60 indicates that 50 minutes of work is being performed in the hour.

The factor may also be expressed as a percentage, with 100 percent being considered as normal. In this case, a rating of 90 percent indicates a speed equal to 90 percent of that expected. A rating of 125 percent indicates a speed 25 percent above normal. This notation seems to have the advantage of already being in the form in which it will be used when the actual time is extended to normal. It is also the form most often used to make ratio comparisons.

In speed rating, the process of rating is confined to the comparison of speed of movements with a concept of normal speed. On the basis of this assumption, the rating process is made simpler; and with training in developing the concept of normal pace, the observer may become quite proficient in his or her judgment.

Effort Rating

The technique for assessing operator performance, which is termed "effort rating," closely approximates speed rating. Although effort rating may be used by many to name the procedure they employ, this term is associated with Ralph Presgrave, and the following comments are based on his book *The Dynamics of Time Study,* wherein it

---

[1] From *Industrial Engineering Handbook* by H. B. Maynard. Copyright 1971, McGraw-Hill, pages 3-38 through 3-42, by Clifton A. Anderson. Used with permission of McGraw-Hill Book Co.

is discussed.[2] He explains that the term has been selected because of its wide accepta- bility; and when time-study people speak of effort, they have in mind relative produc- tion rates. However, the meaning of effort is confined to the concept of speed of movements.

For an excellent analysis of the problems incident to the evaluation of operator performance, the reader is referred to Presgrave's treatment of the subject. The case for rating speed of movement as the only measurable factor in the process is stated very well. Although skill in the broad sense is recognized as contributing to both method and speed of movement, it is not segregated. Method must be determined and established as a function outside the rating procedure and the rating procedure limited to judgment of the speed of movements.

In this and the speed-rating technique, the concept of a normal speed or effort is built around one speed or tempo. A problem results when one tries to evaluate the per- formance of operators on work which may be differentiated as light or heavy. The tempo of light bench operations is not the same as that evidenced by the operator doing heavy lifting, pushing, or pulling. It is necessary, therefore, to make an additional judgment to distinguish between the two situations if proper time standards are to be derived in all cases.

Pace Rating

The term "pace rating" is employed in some companies, notably the U.S. Steel Cor- poration, to describe the system of performance evaluation in use. Although the tech- nique incorporates most of the ideas of speed rating and effort rating, two other devices are used to assist the person doing the rating and to extend the scope of the applica- tion. Thus it is recognized that all jobs are not performed at the same tempo, so that the pace or speed observed must be related to a concept of normal for the type of work involved. The time-study person uses a number of concepts of normal, depending on the type of work being observed. If the work were limited to one type or a few, the standards, or normals, would be correspondingly limited.

To assist the time-study person in the acquisition of a set of concepts that is uni- form for all time-study people, bench marks have been provided in different types of work. These have been quantified in terms of specific rates of production. Thus, walk- ing on a smooth, level surface, without load, at X miles per hour is one standard. This and other standards can be duplicated or viewed on a motion-picture screen and there- by provide an objective interpretation of the pace described. Rating is expressed as a performance percentage above, below, or at normal, and the ratio or factor is applied to the selected time for the element.

An attempt is made to minimize the effects of other variables by studying opera- tors who are judged to be adequately qualified and trained to do the job in question.

---

[2] *The Dynamics of Time Study* by Ralph Presgrave, 2d ed., McGraw-Hill, New York, 1945.

Objective Rating

A procedure originated by Mundel[3] is perhaps the next logical step following the idea of speed rating. Mundel does rating in two steps, namely, (1) pace rating and (2) a secondary adjustment to compensate for job difficulty.

A normal concept of pace is established against which all jobs are compared. Because no attention is given to job difficulty, a single standard rather than standards for each type of work is given as adequate for this comparison. To assist in judgment of deviations from a normal pace, several step films, each representing some known departure from normal, are recommended for training and practice purposes. After judging pace or speed, the analyst evaluates the job in terms of its difficulty. The factors or categories for which secondary adjustments are added include: (1) amount of body used, (2) foot pedals, (3) bimanualness, (4) eye-hand coordination, (5) handling or sensory requirements, and (6) weight handled or resistance encountered. From experiments and other sources, numerical values were assigned to different degrees of these factors. The summation of the percentage adjustments for each factor constitutes the secondary adjustment.

Leveling

The method of assessing performance, which is referred to as leveling, is described in detail in the Lowry, Maynard, and Stegemerten book on time and motion study.[4] The technique is usually described in any collection of information about performance rating. It is in use in many plants and has gained quite wide acceptance. Close reading of the authors indicates their stress on the need for full understanding and adequate training in the use of the technique in order to get consistent and accurate results.

Four elements are given as constituting the important factors which determine the rate of production that an operator achieves. These four factors are skill, effort, conditions, and consistency. The first two are by far the most important. Each of the four elements carries a somewhat special or limited meaning. It is important that these meanings be understood before application of the technique.

Skill is defined as "proficiency at following a given method." Method is thus excluded from the concept of skill in the definition. The time-study person judges the level of skill by observing such things as hesitations, precision of movements, interruptions to the normal cycle by improper performance, and the general coordination and rhythm of working pace manifested by the operator. Departures from average, or the definition of normal skill, are indicated by grades. Each grade is in turn defined and indicated in chart form as poor, fair, average, good, excellent, or superskill. The skill manifested is thus judged in terms of definitions and compared with a concept of normal or departures therefrom.

[3] M. E., Mundel, *Motion and Time Study,* 2d ed., Prentice-Hall, Englewood Cliffs, N.J., 1955.
[4] S. M. Lowry, H. B. Maynard, and G. J. Stegemerten, *Time and Motion Study and Formulas for Wage Incentives,* 3d ed., McGraw-Hill, New York, 1940.

Effort is defined simply as "the will to work." Effort is considered to be within the control of the operator at all times. It is not measured in terms of foot pounds of work done but rather is judged in terms of the spirit in which the operator attacks the job. It may range all the way from idleness to excess. As will be pointed out later, it is necessary to confine the range of effort observed to narrower limits if the technique is to be entirely successful. Six gradations of effort level are defined, including poor, fair, average, good, excellent, and excessive. Poor effort is thus manifested by a slow-motion style of working, which is very obvious to the observer. Introduction of unnecessary work is also indicative of poor effort, which obviously has an effect on method also. It is generally taken to be a result of poor attitude on the part of the worker. Average effort is defined as that manifested by the operator who works steadily and with a fairly good system. Lost motions are reduced and the operator takes some interest in the work. Excellent effort is exhibited by the operator who plans ahead, reduces lost motions to a minimum, uses the best method available, and takes a keen interest in the work. The operator is anxious to demonstrate his or her superiority.

Conditions are narrowly defined as items which affect the operator rather than the operation. Light, heat, and ventilation, or rather the variation of these conditions from what is normally provided for the given operation, are included in consideration for leveling purposes. Corrections for this factor cover only minor departures from standard. Major items which may affect the method should be corrected before work measurement is begun.

Consistency is established primarily as a factor to call attention to the extent or lack of consistency. The recommendation is made that the cause of inconsistency should be determined and corrected rather than graded. Correction for perfect consistency or poor consistency is a minor factor.

In general, the study is rated as a unit. However, where the operator may be doing familiar work in one part of the cycle and have elements included in another part of the cycle in which he or she is not practiced, the recommended procedure is to grade individually elements which are not performed at the same level as the major part of the study. For long studies, it is recommended that performance evaluations be made periodically to take account of any changes that may develop over the longer period of time.

Numerical equivalents have been provided for each of the grades or levels of the factors. These equivalents are shown in Fig. 8-2. To determine the correction, or leveling, factor, the assigned ratings for each of the four factors are noted and their respective numerical equivalents are added algebraically. The result is added to numeral 1. As an example, a rating of $B2$ skill, $C1$ effort, E conditions, and D consistency would provide correction factors of +0.08, +0.05, –0.03, and 0.00. The algebraic sum is +0.10; added to 1, the resultant leveling factor is 1.10. This factor is applied to the average of the observed time for the element or elements to derive the average (normal) time.

Note that this technique limits the variation that can be compensated for. When an operator slows down to half speed, it is impossible to make adequate adjustment through the leveling factor to correct the actual time to normal time. Within limits of about plus or minus 25 percent of normal, the trained observer can get consistent results utilizing the technique.

Skill			Effort		
+0.15 +0.13	A1 A2	Superskill	+0.13 +0.12	A1 A2	Excessive
+0.11 +0.08	B1 B2	Excellent	+0.10 +0.08	B1 B2	Excellent
+0.06 +0.03	C1 C2	Good	+0.05 +0.02	C1 C2	Good
0.00	D	Average	0.00	D	Average
−0.05 −0.10	E1 E2	Fair	−0.04 −0.08	E1 E2	Fair
−0.16 −0.22	F1 F2	Poor	−0.12 −0.17	F1 F2	Poor

Conditions			Consistency		
+0.06	A	Ideal	+0.04	A	Perfect
+0.04	B	Excellent	+0.03	B	Excellent
+0.02	C	Good	+0.01	C	Good
0.00	D	Average	0.00	D	Average
−0.03	E	Fair	−0.02	E	Fair
−0.07	F	Poor	−0.04	F	Poor

Figure 8-2 Performance rating table for leveling. (*From S. M. Lowry, H. B. Maynard, and G. J. Stegemerten,* Time and Motion Study and Formulas for Wage Incentives, *3d ed., McGraw-Hill, New York, 1940, p. 233.*)

It is helpful to utilize bench-mark performances as a training and checking device, just as is true for the other methods of performance rating. The definitions lack objectivity in themselves, and unless the various levels of performance can be demonstrated, there is a tendency toward inconsistency in interpretation of the various gradations.

The important difference between leveling and speed rating lies in the attempt in leveling to relate the performance displayed by the operator to the causes which result in the various levels of performance. When the operator works in a particular manner, as indicated by the definition which describes his or her performance, the resulting productivity will differ from normal by the amount indicated by the numerical values assigned to each gradation. Somewhat wider scope is thus assigned to the leveling procedure than is the case in speed rating or effort rating, where the judgment is limited to speed of movements only.

Synthetic Leveling

The procedure for determining the performance rate of the operator synthetic leveling, is presented by R. L. Morrow[5] as a means of taking much of the need for judgment out of the rating procedure, thereby attaining more accurate and more consistent time values. The procedure consists of comparing the times for as many of the elements as possible with known standards. There are usually a number of elements in a time study which are common to many time studies, and these at least may be compared. The relation of the elemental standard times to the observed elemental times indicates the level of performance on this study for these elements. The rating is then extended to the entire study. It is important in the interests of accuracy that the elements com-

[5] *Time Study and Motion Economy,* Ronald, New York, 1946.

pared contain the same work requirements. Endpoints, method, and actual work requirements enter into the accuracy of the technique. The assumption that the entire study should be graded alike is necessary also.

Other Techniques

There are variations from system to system as indicated by each of the foregoing techniques. All these systems seem to have one thing in common: the procedure used attempts to establish an arithmetic relation between recorded times on a time study and the allowed time. The purpose behind all these systems is apparently to aid in the establishment of standard time values for elements of work which will then be representative of the time that should be required for a normal worker to perform a specific task. In the foregoing systems, consideration is often given to such factors as skill, effort, conditions, consistency, or speed of movement. One or more of these factors is evaluated by percentages or other numerical expressions in relation to normal. None of these systems seems to completely satisfy the time-study requirements of some companies. Some select the operator closest to or at normal performance; therefore, there is no rating adjustment of the elemental time values obtained in many situations. The cooperation of everyone involved is essential for this system to work.

Normal Operator Selection

It is recognized that time study is a sampling process. Every attempt is made to ensure that the sample is representative of normal or satisfactory conditions, thereby *minimizing the necessity for altering the sample in any way*. Time study is a sample of two major areas—*what* and *how* the work is performed. In order to ensure that the time study is a sample which is representative of normal or satisfactory operating conditions, it is necessary to give careful consideration to these two areas of observation. A sound work standard must be based on standardized operating conditions. Therefore, the first area of observation, *what* work is performed, must be critically reviewed by the engineer and the supervisor to make sure that the work standard includes time for only the work required to be performed. In most cases, determination of what work is required versus what is initially observed is not much of a problem. The second area of observation—*how* the work is performed—calls for a more detailed analysis. That area includes primarily the operator's method of performing the repetitive part of the cycle. Once the method of operation is set, output on a job can still vary owing to the performance of the operator. Performance can therefore be defined as any demonstration, such as output or service of a worker performing a task. It is *primarily affected by the method followed* and may also be affected by the speed of movement.

The objective of performance evaluation is the establishment of allowed times on the time study which are representative of times which would be required of an employee demonstrating a satisfactory or normal performance at a fair day's work level. With this in mind, the engineer and the supervisor should cooperatively evaluate the worker's performance immediately before the actual timing of the operation. This evaluation should be made to determine if the worker is giving a satisfactory or normal performance. In all cases, an attempt should be made to time-study a worker who is demonstrating as nearly as possible a satisfactory performance.

On the other hand, if a worker on a specific operation is below the satisfactory level of performance, the supervisor should get the worker to improve the performance to a satisfactory level. If this fails, the supervisor and the engineer should select another worker who is performing at a satisfactory level. If this fails, then a worker should be selected who is nearest to the normal concept and the times should be normalized (adjusted by rating).

With a better realization in the 1980s that one's company or corporation must compete favorably throughout the United States and the world, there is a growing trend for improved cooperation between union and management in order to survive. This more-positive attitude should help in the time-study procedure, where there is a search for the operator that will demonstrate normal performance, utilizing the best mechanical and manual method.

QUESTIONS

8-1 What is performance evaluation?

8-2 What other terms are used for evaluating the performance of the operator?

8-3 What is the reason for evaluating the performance of the worker?

8-4 How can the mechanical method affect the output of the operator?

8-5 How can the manual method affect the output of the operator?

8-6 Why does Fig. 8-1 appear in this chapter on performance evaluation?

8-7 What is the prerequisite for a controlled manual method?

8-8 In speed rating, a rating of 115 percent would mean what?

8-9 With an observed average element time of 0.100 minute, what would be the allowed time if the speed rating were 110 percent?

8-10 Does effort rating seem to closely approximate speed rating?

8-11 Which large corporation uses pace rating?

8-12 What author originated objective rating?

8-13 In objective rating, when the job is evaluated in terms of difficulty, what six factors are considered?

8-14 What would be the resultant leveling factor with $C2$ skill, $C1$ effort, E conditions, and C consistency?

8-15 What rating procedure consists of comparing the times for as many of the elements as possible to known standards?

8-16 In what way does the normal operator selection procedure differ from all the other rating procedures?

NINE

WORK-STANDARD CALCULATIONS

In the area of work measurement, one of the most common methods of establishing a work standard is the stopwatch time-study technique. Basically, there are only three general steps for using this method.

1. Obtain and record the facts.
2. Investigate and analyze the facts.
3. Standardize the method and time.

The sequence of entries and calculations that are normally encountered in an actual situation will be followed. A sample time study is provided in Fig. 9-1 to illustrate each of the specific steps necessary in order to have a complete time study.

THE MECHANICS OF A TIME STUDY

Job Data

There is great variation in time-study forms throughout the industry. One of the big reasons for this is the variance in the type of job data that is necessary depending on the products that are produced. In the area labeled **A** on the sample time study, the following entries are made:

Part name and number
Operation description and number
Equipment data

Tools
Fixtures
Material
Type of study
Date of study
Effective date
Reason for the study
Observer
Operator name, number, and sex

Recording this information identifies the activity and begins to define the conditions which existed at the time of the study—an essential part of the standardizing process.

Sketching the Workplace Layout

It is not enough to merely specify what machine, tools, and fixtures are necessary to perform the operation. To further standardize the method, a sketch of the workplace layout is necessary. Close observation of part B of Fig. 9-1 makes apparent that all items important to the operation and all objects that the operator handles must be sketched and labeled.

Element Description and Read Points

In addition to standardization of the operation by recording the job data and sketching the workplace layout, the manual acts that the operator does in performing the operation must also be standardized. This is done by making a type A, B, or C element description of the operation. When referring to part C of the sample study, we see that there are three elements and that a type B element description has been made.

When making a type A description, use the centerline to separate the left-hand activity from the right-hand activity. When a type B or C description is used, ignore the centerline, as shown in this example. The analyst uses as many blocks as necessary to describe each element and numbers the elements as shown.

The Recording and Adjustment of Times

In part D of the sample study, the elements are renumbered to show the location of the respective times for each of the three elements. The I shown at this point represents the instantaneous times, or the times that would be recorded directly if the snapback method of timing were used. The C identifies the element time as recorded if the continuous method of watch reading were used. In this example, the continuous method was used and the subtracted times are shown in the I rows. If the snapback method had been used, there would be no numbers in the C rows, because the subtracted times are obtained directly by reading the watch on the read point and then snapping the watch back to zero.

SHEET __1__ OF __1__

TIME STUDY OBSERVATION SHEET
INDUSTRIAL ENGINEERING DEPT.
GENERAL MOTORS INSTITUTE

PART No.	12345
OPER. No.	20
TYPE OF STUDY:	B-Continuous

(A)

PART NAME Crossbar Assembly	MATERIAL 1010 Steel	R.P.M.	SPEED: S.F.P.M.	DATE OF STUDY	10/10
OPERATION DESCRIPTION Spot weld 2 nuts and 2 retainers to crossbar			FEED: IN./MIN.	EFFECTIVE DATE	10/12
EQUIPMENT DATA Federal Spot - welder No. 150	TOOLS 2 welder electrodes No. 258		FIXTURES: Locating fixture No. 5782		

(E)

CYCLE TIME ANALYSIS:

MACHINE TIME	MANUAL		IDLE TIME
	INSIDE	OUTSIDE	

STUDY STARTED   10:10 A.M.   STUDY STOPPED   10:40 A.M.

ELAPSED TIME DURING STUDY 1.74   PRODUCTION/HR. DURING STUDY 345

REASON FOR STUDY   Method change

FINAL STANDARD= 247   PCS./HR. .00405   HOURS/PC.

OBSERVER: E. J. Gordon   (J)

APPROVALS: T. Nelson   H. Roesner

(A) OPERATOR NAME   A. B. Jones

OPERATOR NUMBER 1234   MALE [X]   FEMALE [ ]

REMARKS:

(F)

DELAY CALCULATIONS:

Remove gondola 1.40 min/80 pcs = .0175 min/pc

Get nuts .50 min/100 nuts x 2 nuts/assy. = .0100 min/pc

Get retainers .40 min/100 ret. x 2 ret./assy. = .0080 min/pc

LEVELING FOR METHOD

CALCULATIONS   (.06 + .06 + .06 + .05 = .23)

(.043 x 4 = .172

a = .23 - .172 = .058 ÷ 4 =

.0145 min/pc (avg) ÷ 10 =

.0015 min/pc

TEMPO EVALUATION

NOTES:

Good performance.

SKETCH

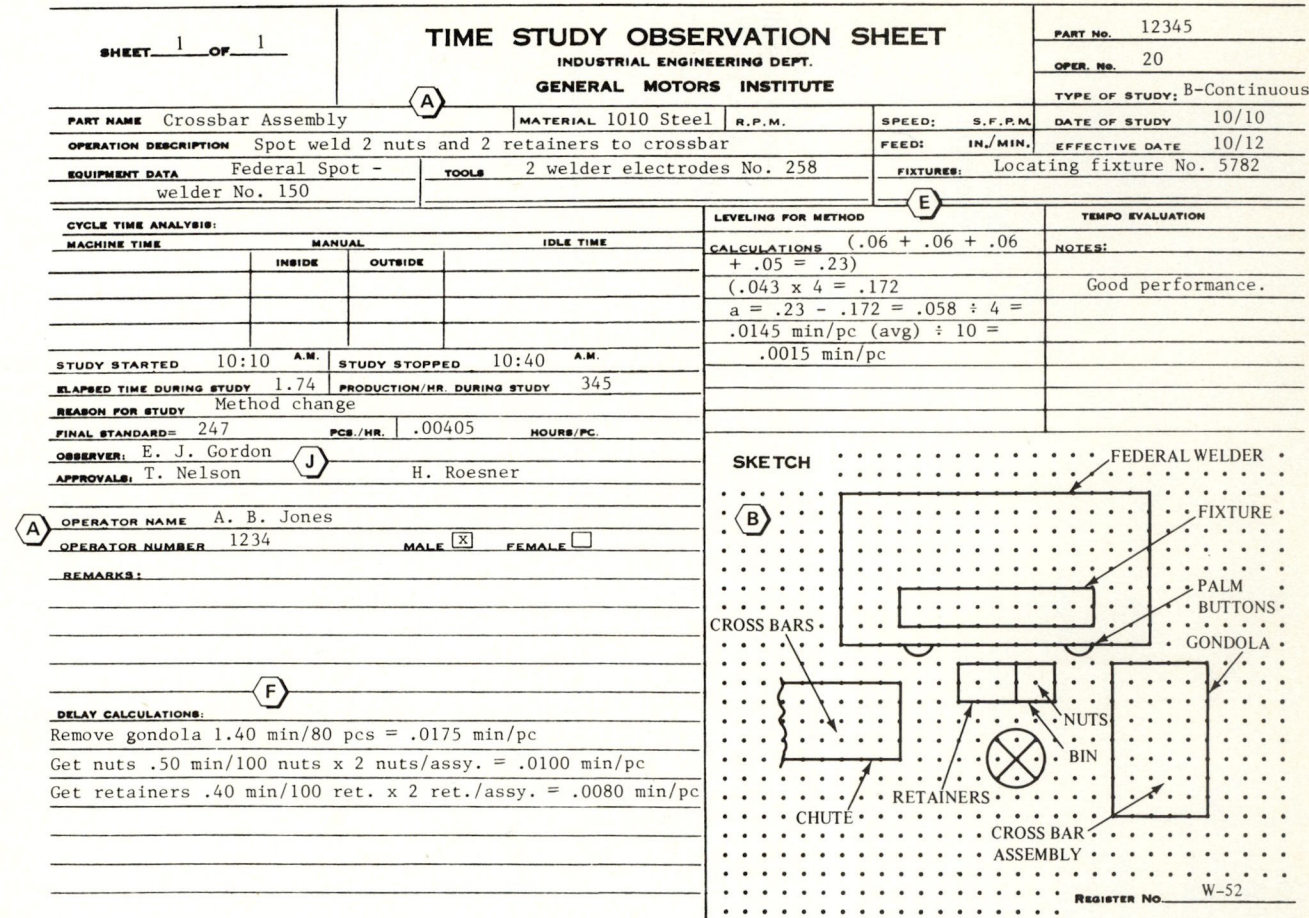

FEDERAL WELDER

FIXTURE

(B)

PALM BUTTONS

CROSS BARS

GONDOLA

NUTS BIN

RETAINERS

CHUTE

CROSS BAR ASSEMBLY

REGISTER No.   W-52

NO.	ELEMENT DESCRIPTION		ELE. NO.	ELEMENT TIME										AVER.	LEVEL-ED AVER.	PER-FORM-ANCE EVAL.	FREQ.	MINS/PC ALLOWED TIME
	LEFT SIDE	RIGHT SIDE		1	2	3	4	5	6	7	8	9	10					
(C) (1)	L.H. finish get 1st. retainer from bin while R.H. get 1st nut from bin 1-1/2, B.H. place (assemble) nut and retainer together 1/2', R.H. place 1st. nut and retainer in fixture 1'; L.H. get 2nd. ret. from bin 1-1/2' while R.H. get 2nd. nut from bin 1-1/2', B.H. place (Assemble) nut and retainer together 1/2'; while L.H. get crossbar 2', R.H. place 2nd. nut and retainer in fixture 1'.		① I	8	7	9	8	8	8	8	7	8	8	.079	.079	110	1/1	.087
			C	8	25	43	62	79	96	13	32	49	66					
			② I	5	6	5	4	4	5	6	3	4	4	.046	.046	110	1/1	.051
			C	13	31	48	66	83	1 01	19	35	53	70					
			③ I	5	3	6a	5a	5	4	6a	6a	5	4	.049	.043	110	1/1	.047
			C	18	34	54	71	88	05	25	41	58	74					
			I															
			C															
(2)	L.H. place crossbar to R.H. 2' and B.H. place crossbar in fixture 1-1/2'		I															
			C															
			I															
			C															
(3)	B.H. get palm buttons 2', B.H. place palm buttons 1" B.H. hold palm buttons during process. B.H., get and place (remove) assembly. from fixture 1/2', and while L.H. starts to get 1st retainer 1-1/2', R.H. dispose of assembly to gondola 3'.		I															
			C															
			I															
			C															
			(G) I															
			C															

CODE	FOREIGN ELEMENTS	DETAIL OF DELAYS:			
			MIN/SHIFT		MIN/PC
(D) a 1/10	Reseat part	PERSONAL	24	gon.	018
—		P & CU	10	nuts	010
—		file		ret.	008
—		elect.	6	a.	002
—					
—					
		TOTAL	40	TOTAL	038

ATTAINABLE HOURLY PRODUCTION = $\frac{60 \text{ MINUTES}}{\text{(ALLOWED CYCLE TIME)}}$ OR ___324___   ALLOWED CYCLE TIME/PC =
                                                .185   .185

FINAL CALCULATION OF STANDARD:

(I) $\begin{pmatrix}\text{ALLOWED/ MIN}\\\text{DELAY / SHIFT}\end{pmatrix}$ $\begin{pmatrix}\text{MIN}\\\text{AVAILABLE}\\\text{FOR WORK}\end{pmatrix}$ $\begin{pmatrix}\text{ALLOWED CYCLE}\\\text{TIME + DELAYS}\\\text{IN MIN/PC}\end{pmatrix}$ $\begin{pmatrix}\text{STD PCS}\\\text{/SHIFT}\end{pmatrix}$ (STD PCS/HR)

480 MIN. - ___40___ = ___440___ ÷ ___.223___ = 1973 ÷ 8 = ___247___

STANDARD HOURS/PIECE ___.00405___

Figure 9-1 Sample time-study and standards calculation.

When there is no deviation from the method specified in the element description, the times are merely recorded as each read point arrives. When something happens that is not in the element description, a code letter is inserted at the point of occurrence and the description is recorded in the "foreign element" section of the time-study form. In this example, the foreign element *a* occurred four times in the third element. In the lower-left-hand corner of the form, the code letter *a* is described as "reseat part." In other words, when the crossbar was placed into the fixture, it did not nest properly and had to be reseated (tapped) in order to be properly seated for welding. All blocks containing a code letter in the body of the study are blocked in, as shown in the example.

The calculations for the columns are done in the following manner:

Average. Straight arithmetical average for *all* entries in the I rows for each element.

Leveled average. Straight arithmetical average for all entries *except* the blocked-in times.

Performance evaluation. Percent rating of the operator's performance if that method of adjusting for normal performance is used.

Frequency. In this example, the frequency is 1/1, because one piece is being worked on during each of the elements. The frequency would be 1/2 if two pieces were being worked on simultaneously, such as milling two pieces at the same time.

Allowed time in minutes per piece. Leveled average $\times$ performance evaluation $\times$ frequency = allowed time in minutes per piece; element 1 = 0.079 $\times$ 1.10 $\times$ 1/1 = 0.087 minute per piece.

Allowed cycle time per piece. Addition of all elements that make up the cycle. *Example:*

$$\text{Element 1 + element 2 + element 3 = cycle time}$$

$$0.087 + \quad 0.051 + \quad 0.047 = 0.185 \text{ minute per piece}$$

Leveling for Method

The calculations for the allowable foreign elements that occur during the recording of times are made in part E of the sample study. The disposition of any other foreign elements which are not to be allowed in the standard is also indicated in this area.

In this example only one foreign element occurred during the study, but it occurred four times. It is possible to have more than one foreign element occurring one or more times during the recording of times. The observed frequency is not necessarily the allowed frequency. In this sample study, reseat part *a* occurred four times, but it is allowed once every 10 pieces (see foreign element section part D). The determination of the proper frequency may be made by observing the operation over a longer time period, or through discussions with persons who know the most about the foreign element. Such a person could be the supervisor, operator, inspector, or maintenance person.

In part E of the sample study, the leveled average is subtracted from each of the four blocked-in times; this equals 0.058 minute total for the four occurrences of reseat part.

$$0.058/4 = 0.0145 \text{ minute per piece} \quad \text{average reseat-part time}$$

$$0.0145/10 \text{ pieces} = 0.0015 \text{ minute per piece} \quad \text{allowed time for reseat part}$$

This last calculation is made to prorate the reseat-part time over the number of pieces as determined by the frequency which is to be allowed. These calculations can be avoided if as part of the investigation of the facts, the cause of the foreign element can be eliminated—something that should be the first consideration.

Delay Calculations

Since the actual timing of the operation may not last for 8 hours, it is logical that other delays will occur during the day when the analyst is not there timing the job. These delays are obtained via delay studies, work-sampling studies, and past-time studies of similar operations. The delays that are calculated in minutes per piece are found in part F of the study. The delays that are allowed in minutes per shift are found in part G of the sample study.

Summary of Delays

The next step is to summarize the delays in minutes per shift and in minutes per piece. This summarization is done in part G also.

	Minutes per shift		Minutes per piece	
Personal	24	Remove gondola	0.018	
Preparation and cleanup	10	Get nuts	0.010	From part F
File electrode	6	Get retainers	0.008	
Total	40	Reseat part	0.002	From part E
		Total	0.038	

Attainable Hourly Production

The attainable hourly production is calculated by dividing the allowed cycle time into 60 minutes, as shown in part H of the study. It is a theoretical figure for an hour's production if no delays or foreign elements occur during the hour. Another method that is popular uses the cycle time plus the delays that occur at least once during each hour for determining the attainable hourly production.

Final Calculation of Standard

The final calculation of the standard is found in part I of the time-study form.

480 minutes per shift − 40 minutes per shift (from part G) = 440 minutes

440 minutes per shift ÷ 0.223 minute per piece (0.185 minute per piece

+ 0.038 minute per piece) = 1973 pieces per shift

1973 pieces per shift ÷ 8 hours per shift = 247 pieces per hour

1 hour ÷ 247 pieces = 0.00405 hour per piece

Completing the Study

The next step is to transpose the final standard in pieces per hour and hours per piece to the front of the time-study form, part J. The time the study was started and stopped and the elapsed time during the study are also recorded in this area. The next step is the calculation of the observed production per hour during the study.

$$\frac{10 \text{ pieces produced during study}}{1.74 \text{ minutes elapsed during study}} \; \frac{60 \text{ minutes}}{1 \text{ hour}} = 345 \text{ pieces per hour}$$

The 345 pieces per hour represents the actual rate of production while the operator was being time-studied. This value can be helpful when getting approval from production supervision on the final work standard, which is only 247 pieces per hour.

In the lower-right-hand corner, the register number is recorded so that the time study can be filed. The tempo evaluation in the upper-right-hand corner is for general information in regard to the operator's performance. The remarks column can be used for supplementary data, such as furnishing ideas for improvement or setting a temporary standard. Last of all, the signatures of approval of the standard are posted by the supervisor, general supervisor, superintendent, or whoever is required to approve the standard in a specific plant.

SUMMARY

The time-study person must employ methods-engineering knowledge to answer the question, "Is the job ready for time study?" When there is sufficient assurance that a good method is being employed, the method and the time are standardized by the time study. Remember, the time-study form is a check sheet. It is a reminder of information that should be posted in order to have a complete study. To understand the mechanics of a time study, the manual method of making a time study has been explained in this chapter. Chapter 11 discusses how many cycles should be timed for a satisfactory degree of accuracy of the work standard.

Today, computer programs are being used to make the time-study calculations, and to provide a suitable printout. Not only is there a reduction of tedious work, but there is more time for the engineer to spend on other projects. Further time savings can be realized with electronic data-collection devices where observed data is timed and automatically recorded in solid-state memory and transmitted directly to the computer.

QUESTIONS

9-1 What are the three basic steps in the stopwatch time-study technique?

9-2 Why is a thorough sketch of the workplace layout important?

9-3 During the actual *timing* of an operator, what does the time-study person do when something happens that is not in the element description?

9-4 Should a time-study person be knowledgeable about methods engineering? Why?

9-5 How can some of the tedious work be eliminated from the calculation of a work standard?

9-6 Give two reasons why a good element description is important.

PROBLEMS

9-1 What was the rate of production in pieces per hour during a time study, if the operator produced 30 pieces during a time period of 21.62 minutes?

9-2 With the following time-study data, calculate the standard in pieces per hour and hours per piece.

Cycle time = 0.54 minute per piece
Foreign element d = 0.035 minute per piece
Foreign element f = 0.018 minute per piece
Stockhandling = 3.85 minutes per 35 pieces
Personal time = 24 minutes per shift
Job preparation and cleanup = 4 minutes per shift

9-3 On the following time study, make all of the necessary calculations in order to get the work standard in pieces per hour and hours per piece.

NO.	ELEMENT DESCRIPTION		ELE. NO.	ELEMENT TIME										AVER.	LEVEL-ED AVER.	PER-FORM-ANCE EVAL.	FREQ.	MINS/PC ALLOWED TIME
	LEFT SIDE	RIGHT SIDE		1	2	3	4	5	6	7	8	9	10					
	Element No. 1		I													100	$\frac{1}{1}$	
			C	6	63	24	93	51	16	77	39	5 01	62					
	Element No. 2		I													100	$\frac{1}{2}$	
			C	18	76	35	2 03	65	29	88	51	15	72					
	Element No. 3		I													100	$\frac{1}{1}$	
			C	34	93	65 A	21	80	48	4 04	69	32	91					
	Element No. 4		I													100	$\frac{1}{1}$	
			C	42	103	74	28	96 B	57	14	80	40	6 00					
	Element No. 5		I													100	$\frac{1}{1}$	
			C	55	17	86	43	3 07	71	34 C	93	55	6 14					
			I															
			C															
			I															
			C															
			I															
			C															
			I															
			C															
			I															
			C															

CODE		FOREIGN ELEMENTS	DETAIL OF DELAYS:			
			MIN/SHIFT		MIN/PC	
A	$\frac{1}{10}$	Rearrange stk.	PERSONAL	24		
B	$\frac{1}{20}$	Tangled parts	P & CU	10		
C	$\frac{1}{10}$	Clip wire	Stock	10		
D	—					
E	—					
			TOTAL		TOTAL	

ATTAINABLE HOURLY PRODUCTION = $\frac{60 \text{ MINUTES}}{(\text{ALLOWED CYCLE TIME})}$ OR ....

ALLOWED CYCLE TIME/PC =

FINAL CALCULATION OF STANDARD:

$$\left(\begin{array}{c}\text{ALLOWED/MIN}\\\text{DELAY / SHIFT}\end{array}\right) \left(\begin{array}{c}\text{MIN}\\\text{AVAILABLE}\\\text{FOR WORK}\end{array}\right) \left(\begin{array}{c}\text{ALLOWED CYCLE}\\\text{TIME + DELAYS}\\\text{IN MIN/PC}\end{array}\right) \left(\begin{array}{c}\text{STD PCS}\\\text{/SHIFT}\end{array}\right) \text{(STD PCS/HR)}$$

480 MIN. - .... = ... ÷ .... = ... ÷ 8 =

STANDARD HOURS/PIECE ....

TEN

ANALYZING THE PROCESS STEPS

The industrial engineer must be able to evaluate the processes used in the plant, which can be accomplished only by gaining as much knowledge as possible about the many basic processes that exist. The part of the operation where work is performed on the product itself is usually called the *process step*. This refers to the particular portion of the operation where physical, chemical, mechanical, or other means are applied to change the condition of the product. Some of the basic processes found in operations are: welding, spraying, machining, casting, forging, pressing metal, soldering, plating, heat-treating, and baking. The rest of the chapter will be devoted to a discussion of the machining processes and the necessary calculations for an efficient operation.

THE MACHINING PROCESSES

In dealing with all processes, the industrial engineer has to determine the essential factors that must be considered in connection with each process. The many factors that affect the feeds and speeds of machining operations must be understood. An ability to calculate these speeds and feeds must then be developed. Whenever the need arises, the technical knowledge of the rest of the organization should be used.

Factors to Be Considered

Some of the essential factors affecting the machining processes are: coolant or lubricant (cutting oil), grade and grain of grinding wheel, type of tool, material in tool, shape of tool, method of machining, manner in which tool is mounted in the machine, design of the machine (rigidity), design and shape of part, method of processing, material to be machined, type of finish, power and speed available, heat treatment of material, size of workpiece, depth of cut, support of work, production requirements, desired life of tool between grinds, cutting speed, feed, approach, overrun, and the geometry of the cutter and part being machined.

Many people have spent years studying all or part of these factors. Their technical information should be used as a guide whenever possible in analyzing a process. Some of the factors may have been arrived at through trial and error (tryout). Often one must accept the results of weeks of tryout and the know-how of others, but in this chapter a few factors that will aid in the necessary calculations for arriving at a fair standard will be discussed.

The mathematics of calculating speeds and feeds can be one of the valuable tools of the analyst. The first concept is that the circumference is the distance around a circular object. The circumference to be calculated might be that of a drill, a milling cutter, or a bar of stock. It can be found by multiplying the diameter of the object by a constant π(pi), which is 22/7, or more exact, 3.1416.

Revolutions per minute is the number of complete turns the part or tool makes in a minute. The equipment may have dials or charts that give us this information, but the only method of knowing for sure is to use a tachometer or a revolution counter and a stopwatch.

Cutting speed, the rate of which the cutting edge of the tool passes through the work, is expressed in surface feet per minute. The main factors affecting cutting speed are: the material being cut, the cutting tool, and the cutting fluid and whether it is a roughing or finishing cut. When turning or boring on a lathe, the cutting tool is held stationary and the work revolves past the tool. Surface feet per minute in this case means the rate at which a point on the circumference of the work passes the cutting tool.

When drilling in a drill press, the work is held stationary and the drill revolves. Surface feet per minute in this case means the rate at which a point on the circumference of the drill is passing a point in the hole being drilled.

When making a cut on a shaper, the work is held stationary and the cutting tool moves. Surface feet per minute in this case means the rate at which the tool is passed along the surface of the work.

On certain automatic or semiautomatic machines, both the work and the tool revolve or move. Surface feet per minute in this case is still the rate at which the cutting edge of the tool passes through the work. If the work and the tool are moving toward each other, the cutting speed is the sum of the two speeds. If the work and the tool are both moving in the same direction, the cutting speed is the difference of the two speeds.

On milling jobs, the work is stationary and the cutter revolves. Surface feet per minute in this case means the rate at which a point on the circumference of the milling cutter is passing the work.

In most cases the cutting speed must be translated into some other term, such as revolutions per minute or strokes per minute, in order to set the machine.

If the allowable surface feet per minute are divided by the circumference in feet, the number of revolutions per minute will be obtained.

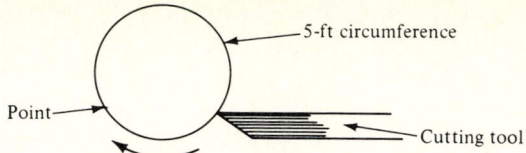

With a 5-foot circumference turning one revolution per minute, it would require one minute for the point to travel 5 feet; or stated another way, the "point" would be traveling 5 feet per minute, which is the definition of cutting speed. Thus,

$$\frac{5 \text{ feet per minute}}{5\text{-foot circumference}} = 1 \text{ revolution per minute}$$

A reverse situation might be to find the cutting speed of a 6-inch-diameter bar turning 90 revolutions per minute.

$$90 \text{ revolutions per minute} \frac{6 \text{ inches} \times \pi}{12 \text{ inches}} = 141 \text{ feet per minute}$$

Another problem might be to determine the revolutions per minute of a drill for a specific job. Drill through at a recommended cutting speed of 60 sfpm.

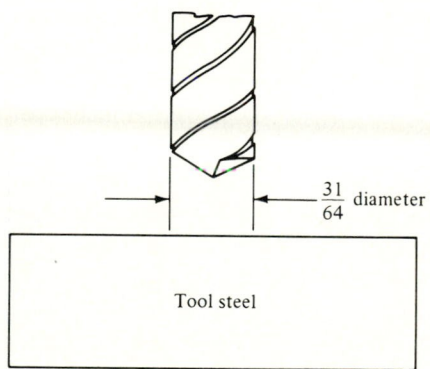

Solution

$$31/64 \text{ inches} \times 22/7 = 1.52\text{-inch circumference}$$

$$1.52 \text{ inches} \div 12 \text{ inches per foot} = 0.127\text{-foot circumference}$$

$$60 \text{ feet per minute} \div 0.127 \text{ foot per revolution} = 472 \text{ revolutions per minute}$$

Still another problem is to determine cutting speed on a milling machine.

Material. SAE 4140 forging, Brinnel 205
Cutter. 12-inch diameter with 14 inserted teeth
Observed rpm of cutter. 200 revolutions per minute

Solution

$$12\text{-inch diameter} \times 22/7 = 37.70\text{-inch circumference}$$

$$37.70 \text{ inches} \div 12 \text{ inches per foot} = 3.142 \text{ feet} = \text{circumference,}$$
$$\text{or feet per revolution}$$

$$3.142 \text{ feet per revolution} \times 200 \text{ revolutions per minute} = 628.4 \text{ feet per minute}$$
$$\text{cutting speed}$$

There are two principal areas of standards work in which cutting speeds are involved:

1. Estimating on new products
2. Time studies on existing operations

Estimating the cutting speed and revolutions per minute in an operation is necessary to find the labor cost. Hence, it is important that estimating calculations be accurate. Time studies involve the determination of cutting speeds having observed revolutions per minute with which to work. The cutting speed actually used on existing operations must be checked for two reasons: first, to check the observed machine time; and second, to determine if the cutting speed is correct for existing conditions.

Feed is the principal factor in the time consumed during the process step and thus directly affects the overall time for the operation. Feed is the rate at which the work, or the tool, or both, advance toward each other. It is usually expressed in inches per minute or thousandths of an inch per revolution.

The feed of a drill, reamer, and lathe is expressed in thousandths of an inch per revolution. The feed on a mill is independent of the spindle speed because chip thickness depends upon the number of teeth in the cutter as well as on the rate of travel of the table. On a shaper or planer, the feed is expressed in thousandths of an inch per stroke. On a grinder, feed is the number of thousandths of an inch which the wheel is fed into the work per pass. It does not refer to the rate of travel of the table.

Calculation Examples

The following examples show the calculation of various factors described previously. The analyst must be thoroughly conversant with these calculations to attain proficiency and effectiveness in setting processing standards. Possibly to better understand and to minimize the chance of error, the following calculations should be done by the method of cancellation of units, with which many people are familiar. This fits in with the units-involved part of Fig. 10-1, whereby the formulas can be derived. Of course, the formulas are also shown in Fig. 10-1.

ITEM	CODE	UNITS	UNITS INVOLVED	FORMULA
Time of cut	T	min	$\dfrac{\text{in}}{\text{in/min}}$	$T = \dfrac{L}{F_m}$
	T	min	$\dfrac{\text{in}}{\text{rev/min} \times \text{in/rev}}$	$T = \dfrac{L}{\text{RPM} \times F_r}$
Feed	F_m	in/min	in/rev $\times$ rev/min	$F_m = F_r \times \text{RPM}$
	F_r	in/rev	$\dfrac{\text{in/min}}{\text{rev/min}}$	$F_r = \dfrac{F_m}{\text{RPM}}$
	F_t	in/tooth	$\dfrac{\text{in/rev}}{\text{teeth/rev}}$	$F_t = \dfrac{F_r}{T_r}$
	F_t	in/tooth	$\dfrac{\text{in/min}}{\text{teeth/rev} \times \text{rev/min}}$	$F_t = \dfrac{F_m}{T_r \times \text{RPM}}$
Revolutions per minute	RPM	rev/min	$\dfrac{\text{ft/min} \times 12 \text{ in/ft}}{(\text{in} \times 3.1416)/\text{rev}}$	$\text{RPM} = \dfrac{\text{SFPM} \times 12}{D \times 3.1416}$
Surface speed or cutting speed	SFPM	ft/min	$\dfrac{(\text{in} \times 3.1416)/\text{rev} \times \text{rev/min}}{12 \text{ in/ft}}$	$\text{SFPM} = \dfrac{D \times 3.1416 \times \text{RPM}}{12}$

L = length of travel of part or tool in inches
T_r = teeth per revolution of tool or teeth per tool
D = diameter of tool or part in inches

Figure 10-1 Basic formulas for machining-time calculations.

Determine cutting time for turning

Length of cut: 6 inches
Revolutions per minute: 570
Feed: 0.007 inch per revolution

Solution

$$\frac{6 \text{ inches}}{570 \text{ revolutions per minute} \times 0.007 \text{ inch per revolution}} = 1.5 \text{ minutes}$$

Determine feed per revolution for turning

Length of cut: $9\frac{1}{2}$ inches
Revolutions per minute: 450
Time: 0.56 minute

Solution

$$\frac{9.5 \text{ inches}}{450 \text{ revolutions per minute} \times 0.56 \text{ minute}} = 0.038 \text{ inch per revolution}$$

Determine cutting time for turning

Length of cut: 11.5 inches
Cutting speed: 60 surface feet per minute
Diameter of work: 3 inches
Feed: 0.050 inch per revolution
Available revolutions per minute: 50, 75, 110, 160

Solution

$$\frac{60 \text{ feet per minute} \times 12 \text{ inches per foot}}{(3 \text{ inches} \times 3.1416)/\text{revolution}} = 76.4 \text{ revolutions per minute}$$

Select 75 revolutions per minute:

$$\frac{11.5 \text{ inches}}{75 \text{ revolutions per minute} \times 0.05 \text{ inch per revolution}} = 3.07 \text{ minutes}$$

The analyst must always recognize that the total length of travel should include the approach and overrun distance whenever one or the other or both are present.

Determine cutting speed and feed for turning

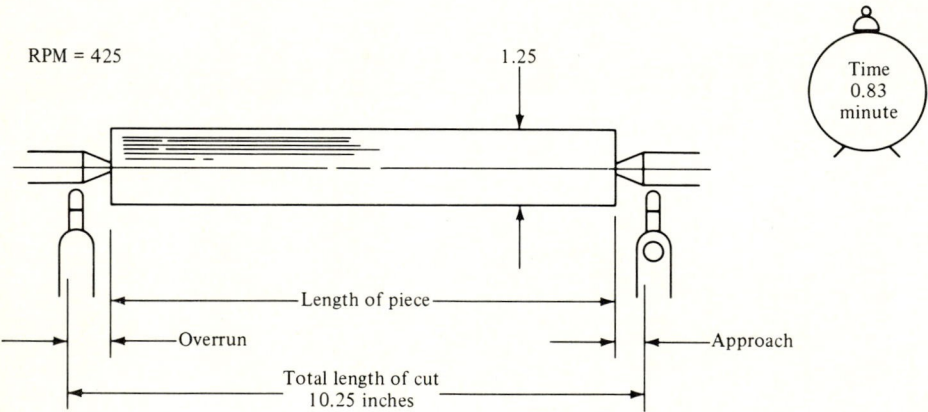

Solution

$$\frac{(1.25 \text{ inches} \times 3.1416)/\text{revolution} \times 425 \text{ revolutions per minute}}{12 \text{ inches per foot}} = 139 \text{ feet per minute}$$

$$\frac{10.25 \text{ inches}}{425 \text{ revolutions per minute} \times 0.83 \text{ minute}} = 0.029 \text{ inch per revolution}$$

Determine cutting speed and feed for drilling

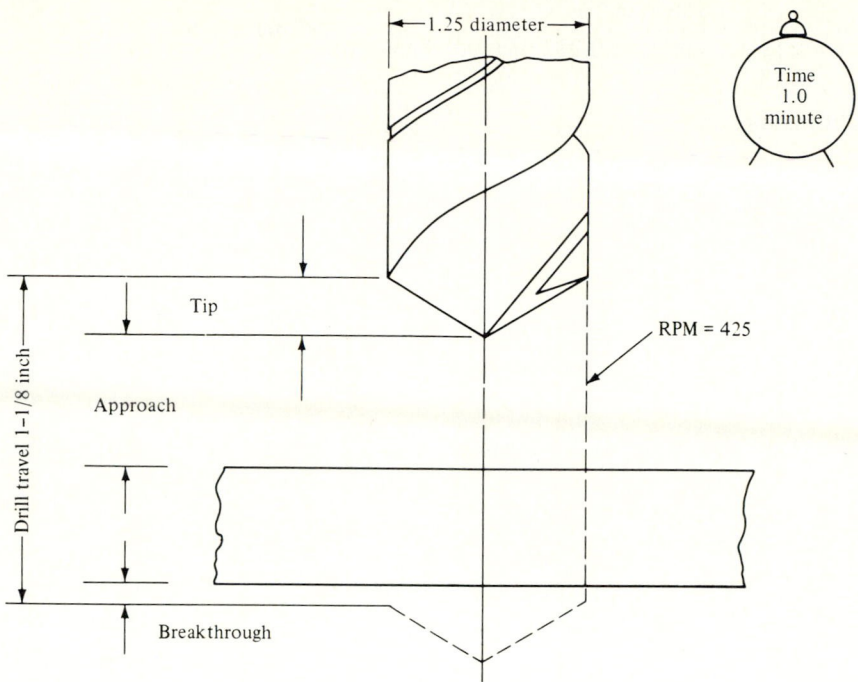

Solution

$$\frac{(1.25 \text{ inches} \times 3.1416)/\text{revolution} \times 425 \text{ revolutions per minute}}{12 \text{ inches per foot}} = 139 \text{ feet per minute cutting speed}$$

$$\frac{1.125 \text{ inches}}{425 \text{ revolutions per minute} \times 1.0 \text{ minute}} = 0.0027 \text{ inch per revolution feed}$$

Determine drilling time

Drill travel: $4\frac{3}{4}$ inches
Cutting speed: 60 surface feet per minute
Diameter of drill: 0.500 inch
Feed: 0.012 inch per revolution
Available revolutions per minute: 180, 230, 290, 370.

Solution

$$\frac{60 \text{ feet per minute} \times 12 \text{ inches per foot}}{(0.50 \text{ inch} \times 3.1416)/\text{revolution}} = 458 \text{ revolutions per minute}$$

Select 370 revolutions per minute:

$$\frac{4.75 \text{ inches}}{370 \text{ revolutions per minute} \times 0.012 \text{ inch per revolution}} = 1.07 \text{ minutes}$$

Determine milling time

Total table travel: 6.4 inches
Table feed: 10 inches per minute

Solution

$$\frac{6.4 \text{ inches}}{10 \text{ inches per minute}} = 0.64 \text{ minute}$$

Determine table feed and chip load per tooth

Mill: 3/16 inch deep
Cutter: 6-inch diameter; 30 teeth
Revolutions per minute: 55
Total table travel: 5.4 inches
Table travel time: 0.25 minute

Solution

$$\frac{5.4 \text{ inches}}{0.25 \text{ minute}} = 21.6 \text{ inches per minute table feed}$$

$$\frac{21.6 \text{ inches per minute}}{30 \text{ teeth per revolution} \times 55 \text{ revolutions per minute}} = 0.0131 \text{ inch per tooth chip load}$$

Up to this point, the total table travel or the total travel of the tool has been given as one value. However, the length of the part being machined is not the total travel. There may be no approach if the operator manually advances the tool or table until contact is made with the part being machined. In contrast, there can be an approach if this is done automatically. Overrun at the end of the cut is common whether it is an automatic or semiautomatic operation. However, there is no overrun when drilling a blind hole.

One other important item is the length of travel (part of the total travel) from the point of contact until the full cut is being made. A sketch is essential for most individuals if the correct total travel is to be determined.

Determine the total table travel

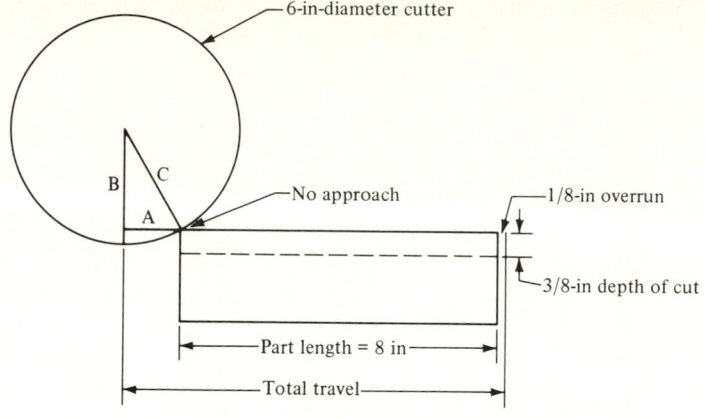

Solution

$$C = \text{radius} = 3 \text{ inches} \qquad B = 3 - 3/8 = 2.625$$

$$C^2 = A^2 + B^2 \quad \text{or} \quad A^2 = C^2 - B^2 = 3^2 - 2.625^2$$

$$= 9 - 6.89 = 2.11$$

$$A = 1.45$$

Total travel = approach + length to full depth of cut + length of part + overrun

$$= 0 + 1.45 + 8 + 0.125$$

$$= 9.575 \text{ inches}$$

The 9.575 inches would then be the total travel distance from lock in to kick out of the automatic feed, which incidentally is *one element* of work. This total length of travel is then used to calculate the cutting time for this one element of work, the machining time. Bringing the part and tool together before cutting and clearing the cutter after the cut is made are usually *separate* elements of work outside the machine-controlled element of work. Of course the mathematics involved in calculating the length from point of contact to the full depth of cut (item A in the problem) will be different, depending on how the cutter is positioned to make the cut. For drilling operations, the distance from the tip of the drill to the full width of the drill must be added in for the full travel of the drill. These situations will be dealt with in some of the problems at the end of the chapter.

Other Considerations

An industrial engineer should also be acquainted with prepared tables found in many handbooks giving approach and overrun distance for given cutters and depths of cut.

It is common to find machines with approach and/or overrun in excess of that necessary to do the job, thereby decreasing the machine utilization. In these cases the settings should be changed to reduce the approach and/or overrun. It may also be necessary to consult table values in order to convert the proper feed in inches per minute into feed per tooth. The limiting factor in this case is the feed each tooth will stand. Prepared tables can also be found for the right cutting speeds depending on the type of tool and the type of material.

In the majority of cases, the observer will be interested in comparing machining time, as recorded by the stopwatch, with the cutting speeds and feeds as calculated on the basis of observation. Once again, a sketch is frequently necessary to get the correct total travel of the part or tool, especially in the planning stages.

When planning machine assignments for an operator, the correct number of machines per operator will affect the layout. It's better to know this before the layout is made than to have to alter the layout later; it can be costly. The chapter on Method Summary Charts will also be helpful in determining the correct number of machines per operator.

Although these calculations are examples of only a few of the many possible influencing factors, they indicate that a working knowledge of the process steps is essential when planning, evaluating, and/or setting standards. Figure 10-1 should be useful in solving the problems that follow. One has a choice of using the method of cancellation of units (units involved section of Fig. 10-1) or simply of using the appropriate formula or formulas.

QUESTIONS

10-1 What are the main factors that affect cutting speed?

10-2 Frequently the cutting speed has to be changed to what term or units in order to set the machine at the proper speed?

10-3 Give an example of a machining operation where there is no overrun.

10-4 Why is approach and overrun used in operations?

10-5 Why should the approach and overrun distances be checked?

10-6 The total travel distance of the part in a milling operation can consist of what four items?

10-7 The total travel distance in a drilling operation can consist of what four items?

10-8 When making a time study of a semiautomatic machining operation, what would be typical read points just preceding the machine-controlled cutting element and at the termination of this element?

PROBLEMS

10-1 At what revolutions per minute should a lathe be set if the length of the part is 12 inches, the dial feed is 0.007 inch per revolution, and the recommended feed for the operation is 4.5 inches per minute?

10-2 If the revolutions per minute dial is set at 1050 and the hole depth is 2 inches, what is the feed in inches per minute if the dial feed is set at 0.004 inch per revolution?

10-3 If the revolutions per minute dial is 100 for a face milling operation and an 8-inch-diameter cutter with 12 teeth is being used, what is the cutting speed?

10-4 With a cutting speed of 350 surface feet per minute and a feed per tooth of 0.0035 inch, what is the table feed when milling a part with an 8-inch cutter containing 10 teeth? There is no approach and there is a 1/4-inch overrun.

10-5 Another milling operation is using a 6-inch cutter with 10 teeth and the feed is 12 inches per minute. If the length of the part is 7.5 inches with 1/8-inch overrun and the cutter speed is 200 revolutions per minute, what is the feed per tooth and what is the cutting speed?

10-6 The cutter used in a face milling operation is 4 inches in diameter and there is no approach; however, there is a 3/16-inch overrun. If the length of workpiece is 6.60 inches and the width of the part being faced is 2 inches, what is the total table travel?

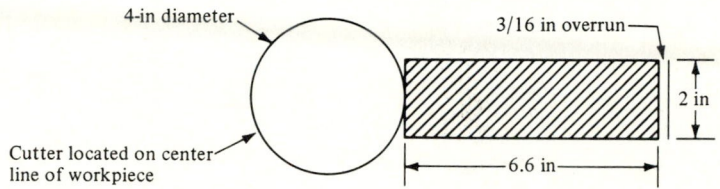

10-7 A 7/8-inch blind hole is to be drilled 2 inches deep with a 1/16-inch approach and of course no overrun. The feed is 0.015 inch per revolution, the cutting speed recommended is 70 surface feet per minute, and available spindle speeds are 200, 300, 400, and 500. The distance from the full diameter to the tip of the drill is one-quarter of the diameter of the drill. What is the drilling time for this element of work? You can make a sketch if needed.

10-8 This is an end milling operation where the recommended feed per tooth is 0.005 inch and the cutting speed is 80 surface feet per minute. The cutter has four teeth and a diameter of 1.5 inches. If the depth of cut is 3/8 inch, the width of cut is 1.5 inches, and the length of the workpiece is 7.7 inches, what is the cutting time? There is a 1/8-inch overrun.

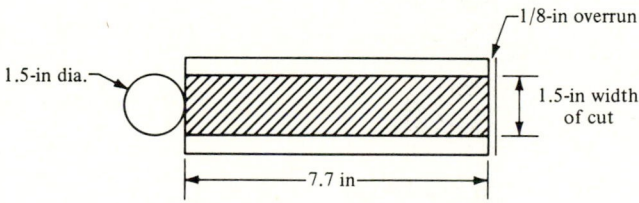

10-9 The workpiece is 11.5 inches, the approach is 1/8 inch, and the overrun is 1/8 inch for this lathe turning operation. If the revolutions per minute speed is 800 and the feed is 0.0055 inch per revolution, what is the cutting time for this element of work? Make a sketch if needed.

10-10 The length of the part is $5\frac{3}{8}$ inches and there is an overrun of 3/32 inch but no approach on this slotting operation. If the milling cutter has a diameter of 5 inches and the depth of cut is 1/2 inch, what is the total table travel?

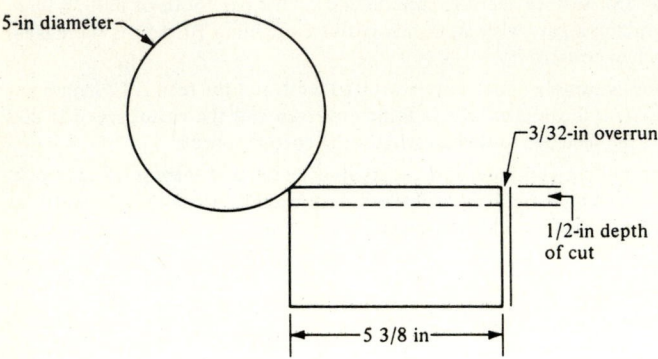

ELEVEN

STATISTICAL TECHNIQUES IN TIME STUDY

Statistics is a science that addresses itself to the collection, analysis, and interpretation of quantitative data. Many of the facets of work measurement are applications of statistical methods, since their results are based on quantitative data. This chapter describes a procedure for evaluating the accuracy of the leveled average times in a time study and/or a determination of the number of observations required to achieve a desired or specified accuracy. The procedure is presented with a minimum of statistical jargon for the reader who is primarily concerned with how to do it. A separate discussion of the underlying statistical concepts follows for those who are interested in the why of the procedure.

GOAL OF A TIME STUDY

The goal of a time study is a number which is representative of the time required to perform some repetitive task in the long run. As pointed out in Chap. 9, this number has two basic components, namely, the allowed cycle time and the delays. The allowed cycle time is determined by analyzing direct measurements of the times required for a series of repetitions of the elements of the work cycle. Despite all the standardizing preparations made before the study (method, workplace, operator, etc.), the observer will encounter variation in the observed times. Some of the causes of this variation are detected by the observer as departures from the prescribed method and the observations are earmarked as foreign elements. The remaining variation is usually due to such things as minute changes in operator movement path and pace, in placement of tools and workpiece within the workplace, or even slight errors on the part of the observer. This unexplained variation is often said to be due to chance and is considered a natural or inherent characteristic of the task under study. The presence of this unexplained variation often causes some concern regarding the "goodness" of the results of the study, particularly the allowed times for specific elements or for the cycle in general.

ACCURACY AND CONFIDENCE

The leveled average computed in a time-study analysis is used to represent the central value of the collection of all the times that have occurred in the past and that will occur in the future relative to the performance of the activity in question. The data of a time study are thus a portion or a sample of a much larger collection or population of time values. The sample average is used as an estimate of the population, or "true," average. The difference between the sample average and the true population average is called the error of the estimate. If a number of studies were to be made on the same task, it is likely that the leveled averages would differ from one another and thus the errors would be different. The term "accuracy" is used to define a maximum error or difference between the study average and the true average. The term "confidence" is used to denote the likelihood or chance that the error of the study is not greater than the accuracy.

It is very important to recognize that the terms accuracy and confidence must not be separated. One should not speak of accuracy without considering the confidence associated with it. A commonly used value for confidence is 95 percent, which is the value embodied in the procedure described in this chapter. When accuracy is mentioned in the following discussion, the confidence should be taken to be 95 percent. After the confidence value has been chosen, the two key factors affecting accuracy are the number of observations (sample size) used to compute the leveled average and the inherent variability of these observations.

ANALYSIS PROCEDURE

As mentioned above, the inherent variability of the observed times is one of the key factors influencing the accuracy of an average. Information regarding this variability is usually obtained through a preliminary sample. The time values from the preliminary sample permit three separate analyses to be performed, namely,

1. Check for the presence of any unusual time values.
2. Determine the accuracy of the average from the preliminary study.
3. Determine the number of observations required to achieve a specified accuracy.

Determine the Average Moving Range

The variability of the times in the preliminary sample is described by a measure called the average moving range $\bar{R}$ of observation pairs. The range R of a pair of observations is simply the difference between their values. The pairing is "moved" across the sample. The first range is the difference between the first and second observation. The second range is the difference between the second and third observation. The third range is the difference between the third and fourth observation, and so on. Only the nonearmarked values are considered in this analysis. The number of moving range values resulting from this procedure will be one less than the number of observations. The average moving range is computed by adding the moving ranges together and dividing by the number of ranges. Consider a preliminary study which resulted in six nonearmarked times for a given element (or cycle):

$$0.13, 0.12, 0.14, 0.19, 0.15, 0.14$$

Five distinct pairs are formed from these six values from which an average moving range can be calculated.

Pair	Observations	Range
1	0.13, 0.12	0.01
2	0.12, 0.14	0.02
3	0.14, 0.19	0.05
4	0.19, 0.15	0.04
5	0.15, 0.14	0.01
Total		0.13

The average moving range $\overline{R}$ is $0.13/5 = 0.026$.

Check for Unusual Values

During the course of a study, the observer should be alert to the occurrence of any events which may influence the time values. As mentioned earlier, such times are earmarked as being unusual. Statistical theory can provide an objective procedure for judging the consistency of the observed times and thus an impartial method of deciding whether a high or low time value will be excluded from the computation of the leveled average even if not earmarked as a foreign element. The presence of such times in a study suggests a possible source of instability in the activity that was not detected by the observer and thus may warrant further investigation.

The check for unusual values is performed on two fronts. One approach is to determine a maximum value or upper limit for the moving ranges. This is accomplished through the use of the graph in Fig. 11-1. Enter the graph at the value of the average moving range $\overline{R}$ on the horizontal scale, then move up to the line and left to the vertical scale to find the upper limit (ULR) for the ranges. Using the example above, note that the $\overline{R}$ scale is entered at 0.026 and the resulting ULR is about 0.084 minute. The largest range in the example is 0.05, which is less than the limit value of 0.084. Thus no problems are indicated relative to internal data consistency.

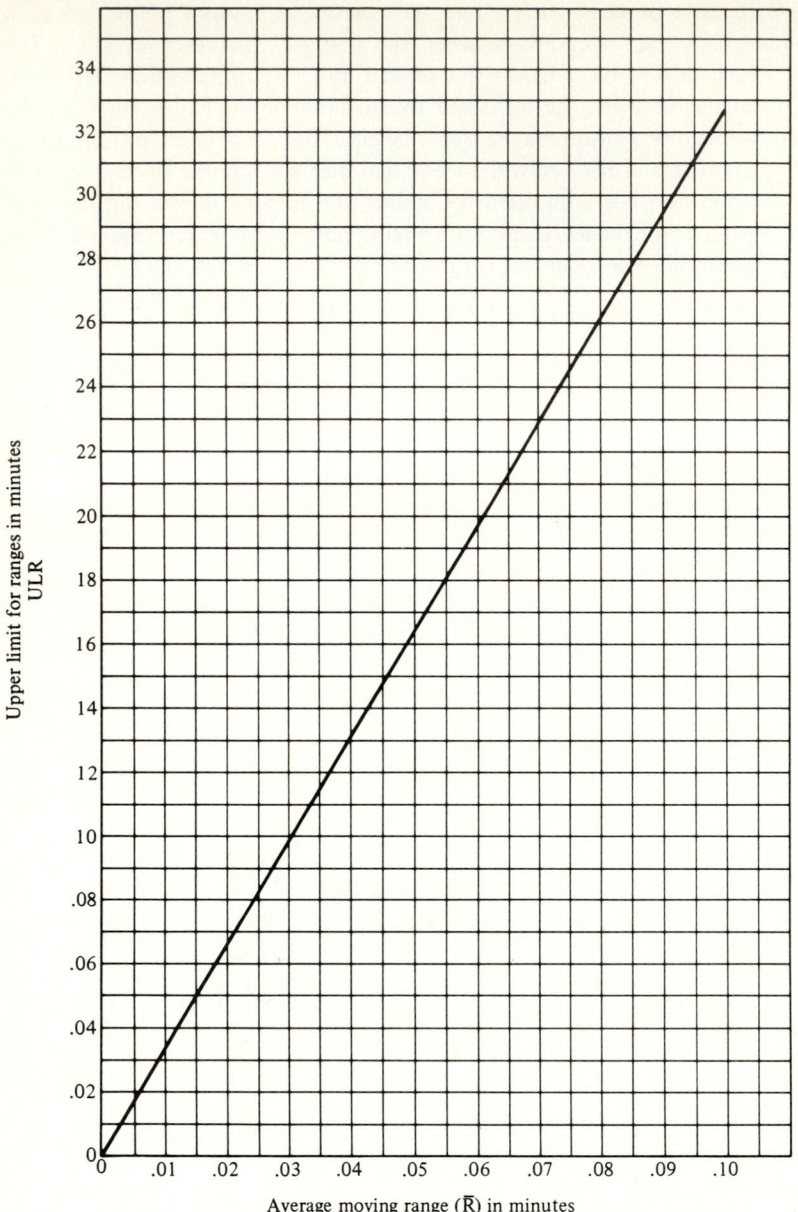

Figure 11-1 Chart for determining ULR.

The second check for unusual readings sets limits for the individual readings. A factor K is obtained from the graph in Fig. 11-2. The upper limit for individual times (ULX) is computed by adding K to the leveled average. The lower limit (LLX) is found by subtracting K from the leveled average. Any times falling outside these limits would be considered "unusual" and thus be suspect as being representative of the process

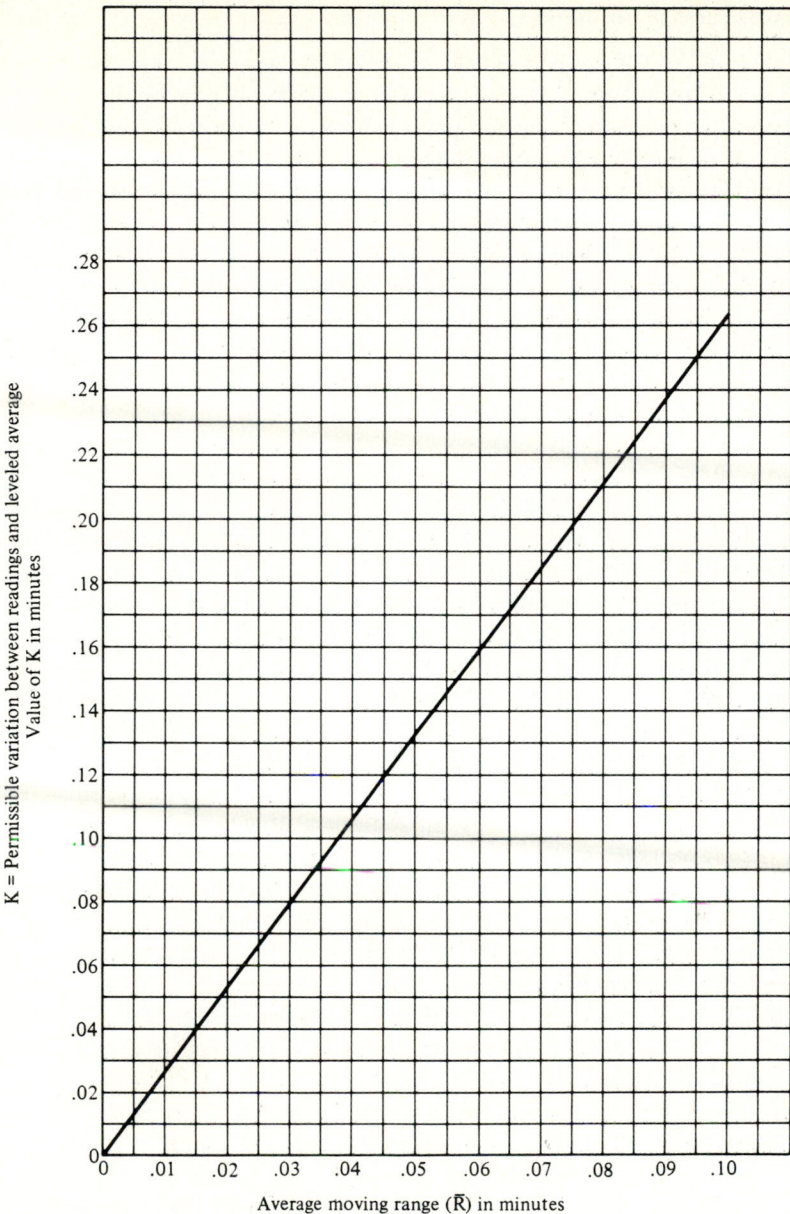

Figure 11-2 Chart for determining value of K.

under study. The value of K is found from Fig. 11-2 in the same fashion as ULR from Fig. 11-1. Using the example value of $\overline{R} = 0.026$ on Fig. 11-2 results in a value for K of about 0.07 minute. The average of the six times in the example is 0.145, so that ULX becomes 0.145 + 0.07, or 0.22, and LLX becomes 0.145 − 0.07, or 0.08. All six time values fall within these limits, so none are judged to be unusual.

Determine Accuracy of Average

The nomograph in Fig. 11-3 can be used to determine the accuracy of an average at the 95 percent confidence level. A point is located on the left-hand scale at the value of the average moving range and a second point is located on the right-hand scale at the number of values used in computing the average under consideration. A straight line connecting these two points will intersect the center scale at the value of the accuracy. Continuing with the example discussed earlier, we see that a point is established on the left at $\bar{R} = 0.026$ and the right-hand point is taken at the sample size of 6. A straight line connecting these points intersects the accuracy scale at about 0.019. Thus based on the sample information, one would conclude with 95 percent confidence that the sample average of 0.145 minute does not differ from the true value by more than 0.019 minute.

Determine Sample Size

The nomograph in Fig. 11-3 is also used to determine the number of observations required to achieve some predetermined accuracy. A point is located on the left-hand scale at the value of the average moving range from the preliminary study. A second point is selected on the center scale at the value of the desired accuracy in minutes. A straight line connecting these two points is extended to intersect the right-hand scale at the required number of observations. Suppose that an accuracy of 0.01 minute were desired in the situation of the example study. Entering the nomograph with $\bar{R} = 0.026$ on the left-hand scale and accuracy equaling 0.01 on the center scale would enable drawing a line that intersects the right-hand scale at approximately 21. Since the preliminary study involved six observations, an additional fifteen observations are required for the desired accuracy.

It is not uncommon to specify the desired accuracy as a percentage of the average. The figures of 5 or 10 percent are often used. Suppose that the 5 percent accuracy specification were applied to the example study situation. The accuracy in minutes would be 5 percent of the sample average of 0.145, or 0.007 minute. Using the nomograph with $\bar{R} = 0.026$ and an accuracy of 0.007 results in a sample size of 45. Thus for 5 percent accuracy, an additional 39 observations would be required to augment the original 6 observations.

These two sample-size determinations demonstrate that at the same confidence level, as the accuracy specification becomes a smaller value, the number of observations required increases. The price of improved accuracy is a larger sample size.

The concerns about process-output behavior in a time study are very similar to those of a quality-control activity. In a time study, attention is focused on process-cycle times (or elements thereof), whereas in quality control the attention is on characteristics of the product or service generated. In both situations interest lies in estimating parameters of the respective output behavior patterns as well as assessing the stability of the patterns. The statistical techniques employed are very much alike.

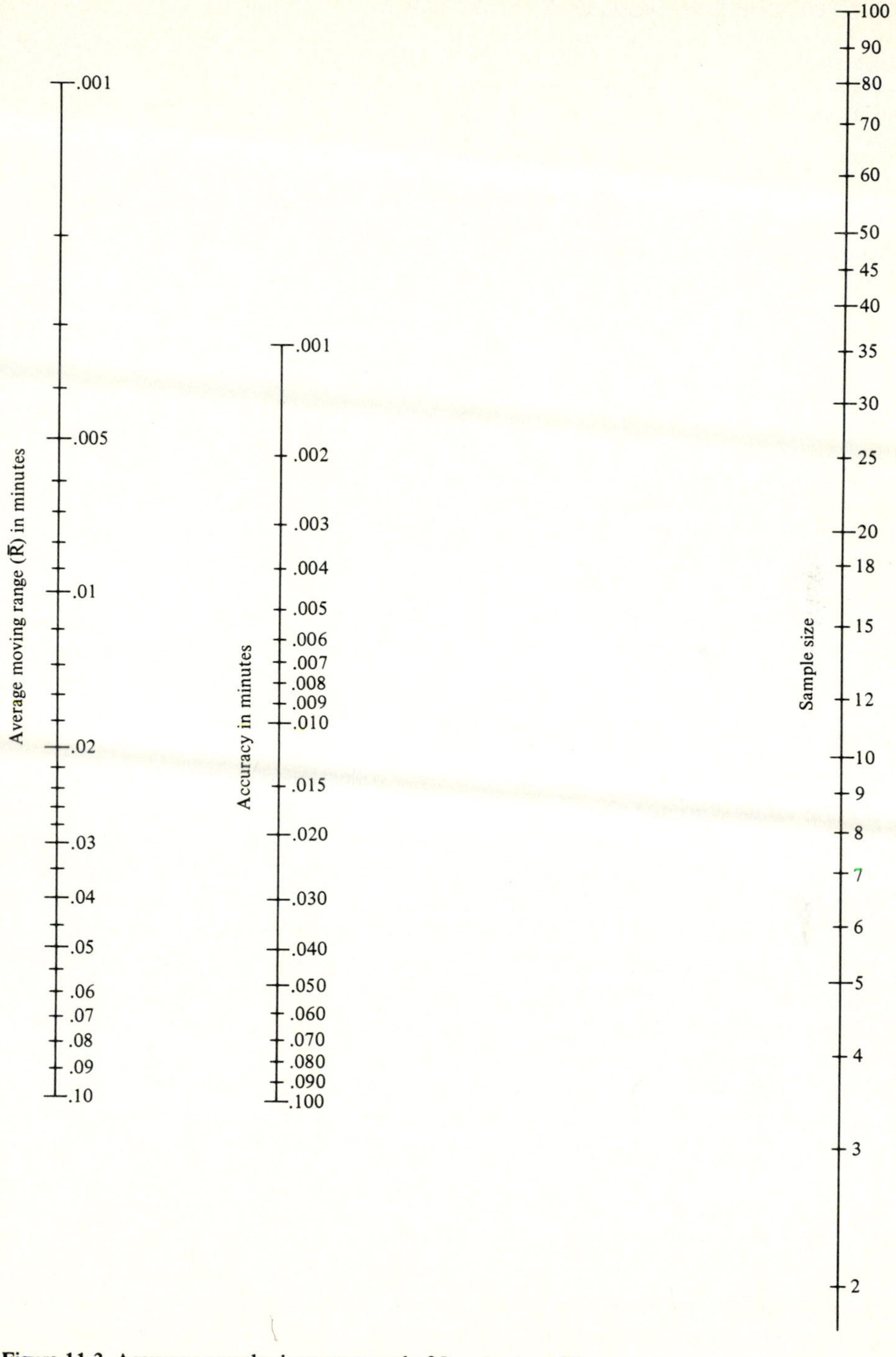

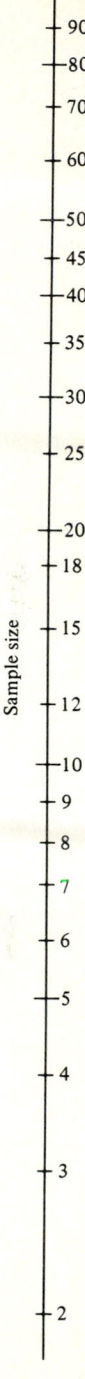

Figure 11-3 Accuracy-sample-size nomograph; 95 percent confidence.

Table 11-1 Descriptive measures of distributions

Characteristic	Symbol	Defining expression
Population mean	μ	$\dfrac{\displaystyle\sum_{i=1}^{N} X_i}{N}$
Population standard deviation	σ	$\sqrt{\dfrac{\displaystyle\sum_{i=1}^{N} (X_i - \mu)^2}{N}}$
Sample mean	$\bar{x}$	$\dfrac{\displaystyle\sum_{i=1}^{n} X_i}{n}$
Sample standard deviation	s	$\sqrt{\dfrac{\displaystyle\sum_{i=1}^{n} (X_i - \bar{X})^2}{n-1}}$

Pattern, or Distribution, Characteristics

The typical pattern of behavior exhibited by a collection of measurements tends to show the values clustered about some central value and appearing with less frequency as they depart in either direction. Such a pattern, constructed from a sample of measurements, is called a frequency distribution, or histogram. It is virtually impossible to capture all the values of a measureable characteristic generated by a process over its life, so the behavior pattern for this totality, or population, is rarely seen in true form. Rather its form is assumed and described by a mathematical model called a probability distribution.

Descriptive measures of these distributions (for both samples and populations) in common use are the mean and standard deviations. The mean is a measure of central tendency of the distribution and the standard deviation is a measure of variability. If the population consists of N values and the sample consists of n values, the symbols and defining expressions for these descriptive measures are as given in Table 11-1.

STATISTICAL CONCEPTS

The output of a repeatable physical process will exhibit variation over time. The output might be a characteristic of the product or service generated by the process or the time required for the process cycle. If the factors influencing the process are stable, the pattern of variability of the output will be stable and thus predictable in the long run.

The following discussion draws together some of the statistical concepts that are applicable to the time-study situation. These concepts form the basis for the charts and nomograph used in dealing with accuracy-sample-size questions.

Normal Distribution

A common probability distribution used to represent populations is the normal, or gaussian, distribution. This behavior pattern is characterized by a bell-shaped curve. Both theory and practice indicate that use of the normal distribution is reasonable until evidence is found in the data to refute the choice. The normal distribution is convenient to work with in terms of determining probabilities if the values of the mean and standard deviation are known. A tabular presentation of normal probabilities is found in most elementary statistical textbooks. For example, an interval of plus and minus one standard deviation from the mean embraces about 68.3 percent of the distribution. An interval of plus and minus two standard deviations from the mean accounts for about 95.4 percent, while plus and minus three standard deviations accounts for 99.7 percent of the distribution. These relations are illustrated in Fig. 11-4.

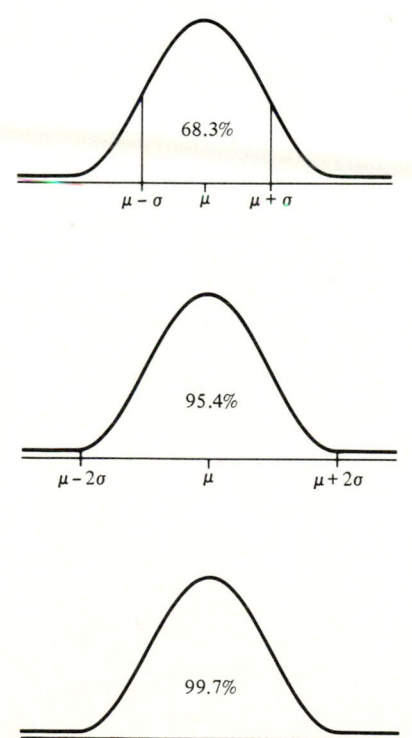

Figure 11-4 Normal probability intervals.

Some Ideas from Quality Control

The application of statistical concepts to industrial situations is well-established in the field of quality control. These concepts give the practitioner insights about what can be expected from a process and also when some type of perturbation seems to be taking place within the process. Two of these well-established concepts are useful in dealing with time-study accuracy. The first is the relation between the range and the standard deviation as measures of variability and the second is an objective means of defining unusual data values.

Range and standard deviation It is often useful to know the value of the standard deviation of a population. The true values of population characteristics are rarely known exactly, so one usually must be satisfied with estimating the values from sample data. The sample standard deviation s is used as an estimate of the population σ. An alternative method of estimating the value of σ is to divide the average range obtained from a number of samples by an appropriate constant. In the case of the preliminary time study, there is only one sample, but it can be viewed as consisting of a series of subgroups of size 2. The average range of these subgroups, as discussed earlier, is divided by a constant, d_2, to yield an estimate of the population standard deviation; thus $\sigma = \overline{R}/d_2$. The value of d_2 for subgroups of size 2 is 1.13. Values for d_2 for other subgroup sizes are shown in Table 11-2.

Defining unusual values In quality control, a control chart is used to identify unusual values of sample characteristics. Values plotted on the chart which fall outside the control limits are considered unusual. The control limits are typically placed at plus and minus three standard deviations (of the characteristic) from the average or mean of the characteristic being plotted. This is the method used to check for unusual ranges as well as unusual individual readings. Figure 11-1 determines the upper control limit for ranges from subgroups of size 2. This upper control limit is defined as $\overline{R} + 3\ \sigma_R$ and is computed by the expression $D_4\overline{R}$. Values of D_4 for various subgroup sizes are shown in Table 11-2. The value of D_4 used in Fig. 11-1 is 3.27, since the subgroup size is 2.

Table 11-2 Constants for determining σ and ULR

Number of observations in subgroup n	d_2	D_4
2	1.13	3.27
3	1.69	2.57
4	2.06	2.28
5	2.33	2.11
6	2.53	2.00
7	2.70	1.92
8	2.85	1.86
9	2.97	1.82
10	3.08	1.78

Individual observations are defined as unusual if they are more than three standard deviations from the leveled average. The three-standard-deviation limit factor is computed as $3\overline{R}/d_2$, or for subgroups of size 2, $3\overline{R}/1.13$. This is the expression graphed in Fig. 11-2.

Behavior of Averages

If one were to draw a large number of samples from a given population and compute sample averages, the averages would exhibit a pattern of behavior. There are three well-established attributes to be expected of this behavior pattern or distribution of averages.

1. The mean of the distribution of averages will be the same as the mean of the population from which the samples were drawn, i.e., the population.
2. The standard deviation of the distribution of averages will be equal to the standard deviation of the population divided by the square root of the sample size

$$\sigma_{\overline{x}} = \frac{\sigma}{\sqrt{n}}$$

3. The distribution of averages is well-represented by the normal distribution. The representation improves as the size of the samples drawn becomes larger. Sample sizes of five or larger are considered adequate.

Confidence Interval Estimates

The previous discussion suggests that when samples are drawn from a population and the sample averages are computed, one would expect about 95 percent of these averages to fall within $2\,\sigma_{\overline{x}}$ of the true mean of the population. Similarly, if only one sample were drawn and the average computed, one would be about 95 percent sure or confident that the value of that average would not be more than $2\,\sigma_{\overline{x}}$ from the true mean of the population. Accuracy A is used to denote this difference between the sample average and true population average which would not be exceeded more than some specified percent of the time (confidence) if the procedure were to be repeated many times. Thus,

For confidence of:

$$A = \begin{cases} \sigma_{\overline{x}} & \text{68.3 percent} \\ 1.96\,\sigma_{\overline{x}} & \text{95 percent} \\ 2\,\sigma_{\overline{x}} & \text{95.4 percent} \\ 3\,\sigma_{\overline{x}} & \text{99.7 percent} \end{cases}$$

The 95 percent confidence is the most commonly used value. The difference between using $2\sigma_{\overline{x}}$ or the more exact $1.96\sigma_{\overline{x}}$ is more of academic than practical concern in defining accuracy at this confidence.

The basic formula for the accuracy of the average of a sample of n observations with an average moving pairwise range of $\overline{R}$ can be developed from the ideas previously discussed.

$$A = 2\sigma_{\overline{x}} = 2\frac{\sigma}{\sqrt{n}} = \frac{2\overline{R}}{d_2\sqrt{n}} = \frac{2\overline{R}}{1.13\sqrt{n}}$$

$$= 1.77\frac{\overline{R}}{\sqrt{n}}$$

This formula can be rearranged to solve for the sample size if A is specified.

$$n = \left(\frac{1.77\,\overline{R}}{A}\right)^2 = \frac{3.13\,\overline{R}^2}{A^2}$$

These formulas are embodied in the nomograph of Fig. 11-3.

CONCLUSION

This chapter has presented one approach to the problem of determining the accuracy and/or required sample size in a time-study situation. There are other approaches to this problem which are based on similar basic statistical principles, even though they use different techniques. One's preference for a particular approach is usually based on a trade-off between simplicity and "statistical elegance." The aim of all the approaches is to bring objectivity into the decision-making process regarding sample-size selection. The results should be viewed as reasonable rather than exact answers to the question.

QUESTIONS

11-1 Define the term "accuracy" as it is applied to a time study.

11-2 What are the two characteristics of a sample that affect the accuracy of its average?

11-3 What characteristic of a sample does the average moving range measure?

11-4 What is the advantage of using calculated limits to define unusual values in a study?

11-5 What are two ways in which the desired accuracy of a study may be expressed?

11-6 What are the three primary characteristics of the behavior pattern (distribution) of sample averages?

11-7 Suppose that preliminary studies were made and the cycle times of operation A exhibited more variation than those of operation B. Which would require the larger time-study sample size if the same accuracy were desired for both operations?

11-8 Suppose that a preliminary analysis resulted in the decision that 20 additional observations were required to obtain an accuracy of 0.01 minute at 95 percent confidence. How would the number of observations be affected (i.e., increase or decrease) if management decided that a confidence of 68 percent would be more appropriate (accuracy still at 0.01 minute)?

PROBLEMS

11-1 A preliminary study of 10 cycles of an operation results in an average moving range of 0.055 minute and an average of 0.92 minute. Determine (*a*) the upper limit for ranges, (*b*) the limits for individual cycles times, (*c*) the accuracy of this study average in minutes, in percent, and (*d*) the number of additional observations required if the desired accuracy is 0.02 minute, 5 percent.

11-2 An operation cycle was broken down into three elements (1, 2, 3) and a preliminary study recorded times for these elements for eight cycles. No unusual times were encountered and the average moving ranges were 0.03, 0.009, and 0.016 minute, respectively.

(*a*) How many additional observations are required for each of the elements to obtain an accuracy of 0.01 minute.

(*b*) Suppose that the final study was made and enough full cycles (all elements) were timed to yield the desired 0.01-minute accuracy on the "worst" element. What accuracy would you expect on the other two elements?

11-3 A preliminary study of 12 observations resulted in an average moving range of 0.16 minute. What is the accuracy of this study? How many additional observations would be required for an accuracy of 0.035 minute? (*Note:* When working values are off the nomograph scale, use formulas.)

11-4 Consider the instantaneous element times (in 0.01 minute) for a preliminary study of 10 cycles.

	Cycle									
Element	1	2	3	4	5	6	7	8	9	10
1	19	24	20	18	22	42^B	21	18	20	23
2	46	52	43	87^A	49	43	45	51	46	96^A

A, part sticks; *B*, fumble part.

(*a*) Determine the leveled average and the average moving range for both elements.

(*b*) Determine the additional observations required for each element to obtain 5 percent accuracy.

(*c*) If full cycles (both elements) are timed to produce the desired accuracy on the worst element as determined in *b*, what final accuracy (in minutes) would you expect for the two elements? Assume that no foreign elements were encountered in the additional readings.

11-5 Rework Prob. 11-3 using (*a*) 68 percent confidence, (*b*) 99.7 percent confidence.

11-6 Consider the continuous watch readings (in 0.01 minute) for a preliminary study on 10 cycles.

	Cycle									
Element	1	2	3	4	5	6	7	8	9	10
1	08	43	73	1.05	60	97	31	63	3.01	37
2	34	66	98	37	89	2.21	53	93	29	61

(a) Determine the leveled average time and the average moving range for each element and the total cycle time.

(b) Check for any "unusual" readings and recompute averages, if necessary.

(c) Determine the number of additional observations required (if any) if the desired accuracy is: (i) 0.005 minute for element 1; (ii) 0.025 minute for element 2.

(d) If only the total cycle time is of interest and is the only figure reviewed, determine: (i) The accuracy of the leveled average from the preliminary study using all of the observations; (ii) The accuracy of the leveled average from the preliminary study if any unusual observations found in b are eliminated.

11-7 Using the observation sheet from a preliminary study as shown below, determine the accuracy of the leveled averages for each of the three elements.

NO.	ELEMENT DESCRIPTION — LEFT SIDE	RIGHT SIDE	ELE. NO.		1	2	3	4	5	6	7	8	9	10
	GET PART FROM CONVEYOR (2') & PLACE TO FIXTURE (2') GET START LEVER (1½) AND PLACE TO ON (½)		1	i	20	23	19	48	23	20	(A)53	22	20	21
				c	20	57	35	(A)96	34	3/14	4/19	52	86	5/19
	WAIT FOR PROCESS, GET FIN. PART FROM FIXTURE (2') & PLACE TO BENCH (2')		2	i	14	16	13	15	(B)60	13	11	14	12	16
				c	34	73	48	3/11	94	27	30	66	98	35
	GET 4 PARTS FROM BENCH (2') AND PLACE TO RACK (4')		3	i	43					39				41
				c	1/16					66				76

CODE	FOREIGN ELEMENTS	DETAIL OF DELAYS MIN/SHIFT	MIN/PC
A	— OPEN CARRIER	PERSONAL	
	— ALLOWED FREQ ~ 1/50		
B	— SPILLED COFFEE CUP		
	— NOT ALLOWED		
	—		
		TOTAL	TOTAL

11-8 Ten cycles were timed in a preliminary check on an operation. The leveled average cycle time for the ten cycles was 4.34 minutes and the average moving range for the nine range values was 0.085 minute.

(a) Determine the largest and smallest values for the observed cycle times if the variation is to be considered "unusual" or "natural."

(b) What is the accuracy of the leveled average cycle time from this study.

(c) If the desired accuracy is 0.025 minute, have enough cycles been observed? If not, how many more observations are required?

TWELVE

WORK SAMPLING

One of the major objectives of work measurement is to establish a specification or standard of time for various work activities. The time-study procedures discussed in earlier chapters are particularly useful in dealing with work activity which follows a well-defined repetitive cycle. The cyclical activity intensively observed forms the core of the time study. The peripheral activity, necessary yet somewhat less disciplined, is incorporated in the overall time specification in the form of delays.

The task of determining how time is utilized in irregular or noncyclical work is not well met with intensive observation techniques. Intensive study is expensive since a considerable length of time, usually a couple of days, is required to yield data on all activities. Secondary problems, such as whether the activity segment observed is truly representative of the long-term activity and whether the continuous presence of the observer influences how the activity was executed, are rarely, if ever, completely resolved in the intensive study. Despite such drawbacks, intensive studies (sometimes called continuous-delay studies) of irregular work are done and yield a chronological record of what transpired during the course of the study. The usual method of processing this information is to set up distinct categories of work and/or nonwork and to assign observed activities to appropriate categories. The end result is an average time per shift or proportion (percent) of shift associated with each category.

Work sampling is a technique which starts with the categories and works backward. Distinct, nonoverlapping categories of activity for the system or facility under study are carefully defined. Observations consist of noting in which category of activity the system is engaged at randomly selected instants in time. The observations are taken over a period of sufficient length to represent the natural influences of the operating environment of the system. This period might range from a day to several months. An estimate of the true proportion of time expended in each activity category is obtained by dividing the number of observations in each of the categories by the total number of observations taken. This process is much like estimating the proportion of times the values 2 through 12 would be expected to appear as the sum on the toss of a pair of dice. One would toss the dice and observe (and record) the results for a number of tosses. In both dice tossing and work sampling, the estimates get better as more observations are made. The "goodness" of the estimates can be addressed in a fashion similar to that employed for time studies in Chap. 11.

SOME USES OF WORK SAMPLING

Work sampling is a technique for getting factual information about a system's operation. It was first employed in the British textile industry by L. H. C. Tippett in 1934 and introduced in this country in 1940 under the name of "ratio delay." Its early application was limited to establishing ratios of delay time to productive time. In reality, it can be applied to virtually any situation where activity can be categorized. The object of the observations may be personnel, equipment, or facilities. Typical categories applied to people are

1. Working
2. Being idle
3. Being out of area
4. Walking
5. Handling material
6. Inspecting
7. Changing tools
8. Cleaning up
9. Handling clerical tasks
10. Talking

Typical categories applied to machines are

1. At work
2. Idle—no operator
3. Idle—no stock
4. Idle—being serviced
5. Idle—interference

The category definitions are prompted by the nature of the activity being studied and the objectives or intent of the investigation.

COMPARISON WITH INTENSIVE OBSERVATION METHODS

There are some advantages and disadvantages of work sampling when compared with intensive observation techniques.

Advantages of Work Sampling

1. The instantaneous method of observation tends to be less fatiguing for the observer and less disruptive for the personnel being studied.
2. The extended time period of the study increases the likelihood of more truly representing natural job conditions. Personnel being studied tend to become accustomed to the presence of observers and thus exhibit more natural work patterns.
3. The study may be interrupted or shelved for a period of time without adverse effects on the results.
4. Several operators or machines may be studied simultaneously by a single observer or several observers.
5. Observers need not be trained time-study personnel. Often people from the area being studied can be utilized as observers after a brief orientation.
6. Total time investment in gathering and processing data is usually less than that of other methods.
7. The accuracy of the study results can be assessed statistically.
8. No timing equipment is required.

Disadvantages of Work Sampling

1. Work sampling is usually not economical for studying a single worker or machine or for studying widely separated workers and machines. Too much of the observer's time is lost in traveling.
2. There is no record of the method employed by the workers. Work sampling merely tells what is being done, not how it is being done.
3. It is difficult to correlate system-output figures and operator-performance levels with study results.
4. Workers may modify their work pattern upon the arrival of the observer in the area.
5. Observers may neglect the importance of randomness and the instantaneous nature of the observations, thus biasing the results of the study.

ACCURACY CONSIDERATIONS

The results of a work-sampling study are percentages, which are estimates of true values that indicate how the total time is allocated to the various activity categories in the long run. The fact that the estimates are percentages often creates confusion when the subject of accuracy is discussed. The term "accuracy" is being used in the same context as it was used in Chap. 11. It designates a maximum difference between the study estimate and the true value of a system characteristic. Confidence is a measure of faith or assurance that this maximum is not exceeded in a particular study. In work sampling, the accuracy is expressed in percent; but the question of percent of what is often not clarified. Two interpretations are possible, giving rise to the expressions "absolute accuracy" and "relative accuracy."

Absolute Accuracy

Absolute accuracy A is the term employed when the accuracy percentage is interpreted as a percent of the total-system activity. Suppose that a study results in an estimate of idle time accounting for 20 percent of the available time. Suppose further that the absolute accuracy at the 95 percent confidence level is 5 percent. It could be said with 95 percent confidence that the study value is within 5 percent of the true value or that the true value for percent idle time is included in the interval from 15 to 25 percent (20 ± 5).

Relative Accuracy

Relative accuracy R is the term used when the accuracy percentage is interpreted as a percent of the category percentage. Reconsider the above example with a study result of 20 percent idle time and a relative accuracy of 5 percent at 95 percent confidence. Now the maximum difference between the estimated and true value (absolute accuracy) for percent idle time is 5 percent of 20 percent, or 1.0 percent. Thus it could be said with 95 percent confidence that the study value is within 1.0 percent of the true value or that the true value for percent idle time is included in the interval from 19.0 to 21.0 percent (20 ± 1.0). Note that this interval is considerably different from the previous one even though the stated accuracy in both cases is 5 percent.

Relation between Absolute and Relative Accuracy

The two types of accuracy are related. This relation is shown in the expressions

$$A = \frac{Rp}{100} \qquad R = \frac{100A}{p}$$

where A = absolute accuracy, percent
p = activity or category percentage
R = relative accuracy, percent

In the example, the idle-time-category estimate was given as 20 percent, so $p = 20$. When the absolute accuracy is given as 5 percent ($A = 5$), the equivalent relative accuracy is found by the expression

$$R = \frac{100A}{p} = \frac{100 \times 5}{20} = 25.0 \text{ percent}$$

When the relative accuracy is given as 5 percent ($R = 5$), the equivalent absolute accuracy is found by the expression

$$A = \frac{Rp}{100} = \frac{5 \times 20}{100} = 1.0 \text{ percent}$$

It is not uncommon to simply use the term accuracy when discussing study results or plans for a study. The example above illustrates why one must be very careful that all parties concerned have a common understanding or interpretation of how the term is used. In any written report, it is wise to include the absolute and relative modifiers when making reference to accuracy.

Sample Size and Accuracy

Chapter 11 discussed the statistical relation between sample size and accuracy for time studies. A parallel relation exists for work-sampling studies. Some mechanics for determining the absolute accuracy of a study and for determining the required sample size to achieve a desired absolute accuracy are given in this section. These procedures are based on 95 percent confidence. A discussion of some of the underlying statistical principles of the procedure is given in the Statistical Concepts section at the end of this chapter.

The charts, tables, and formulas in this chapter are addressed to absolute accuracy. One can easily make the transformation to relative accuracy using the relation of the previous section. The following formulas are useful in determining accuracy or sample size.

$$A = 2\sqrt{\frac{p(100 - p)}{n}}$$

$$n = \frac{4\,p(100 - p)}{A^2}$$

where A = absolute accuracy, percent
n = total number of observations in the study; sample size
p = activity or category percentage

Returning to the earlier example, suppose that the idle-time percentage ($p = 20$) was a preliminary estimate and one wanted to determine the sample size required to yield an absolute accuracy of 5 percent ($A = 5$). The sample size would be computed by

$$n = \frac{(4)\,(20)\,(100 - 20)}{5^2} = 256 \text{ observations}$$

If the desired absolute accuracy were 1.0 percent, the required sample size would be

$$n = \frac{(4)\,(20)\,(100 - 20)}{(1.0)^2} = 6400 \text{ observations}$$

Suppose that the initial figure of 20 percent idle time had resulted from a preliminary study of 100 observations. The machine had been noted as idle on 20 observations ($20/100 = 0.20$, or 20 percent). The absolute accuracy of this preliminary estimate at the 95 percent confidence level would be

$$A = 2 \sqrt{\frac{20\,(100 - 20)}{100}} = 8.0 \text{ percent}$$

An alternative approach to performing the actual computations is provided by the nomograph shown in Fig. 12-1. To determine an absolute accuracy value, the value of p is located on the right-hand scale and the value of n is located on the left-hand scale. The straight line connecting these points intersects the center scale at the value of the absolute accuracy. To determine sample-size requirements, the value of p is located on the right-hand scale and the desired value of A is located on the middle scale. The straight line connecting these points is extended to the left-hand scale and intersects at the value of the required sample size.

Table 12-1 offers still a third approach to the sample-size-accuracy problem. Column headings are selected samples sizes while each row is associated with selected activity percentage, or p, values. The two numbers in each row-column combination represent the limits of the 95 percent confidence interval estimate of the activity percentage, $p \pm A$. Thus the interval or "range of accuracy" has a width of $2A$. For a sample size of 100 and $p = 20$ as in the nomograph example, the interval is found to be 12 to 28 percent. The upper limit, 28, is $p + A$, so that $A = 28 - p = 28 - 20 = 8$ percent, which is the same as the value found from the nomograph.

PLANNING A WORK-SAMPLING STUDY

The value of a work-sampling study will be greatly affected by the care and effectiveness of the planning efforts. One does not just casually collect some data and then try to figure out what the numbers mean. The investment of effort in the planning stage pays off in meaningful and statistically valid results.

Define the Objective of the Study

The first step in planning a work-sampling study is to formulate a concise statement about the purpose or objectives of the study. What type of information is being sought? The objectives will help provide a basis for establishing the activity categories or elements to be investigated. A preliminary survey of the system activity is often made at this time to develop the list of possible activity categories. This survey may be accomplished through direct observation of the system or through conversation with those familiar with the system.

The objectives of the study should give some indication about what accuracy should be sought in the estimates. If the results of the study are to be the basis for decisions regarding the purchase of additional equipment or the addition (or removal) of personnel, one would want more precise estimates than are needed for less costly and/or disruptive decisions such as minor area-layout or duty-assignment modifications. One should be particularly careful at this point that the distinction between absolute and relative accuracy is understood.

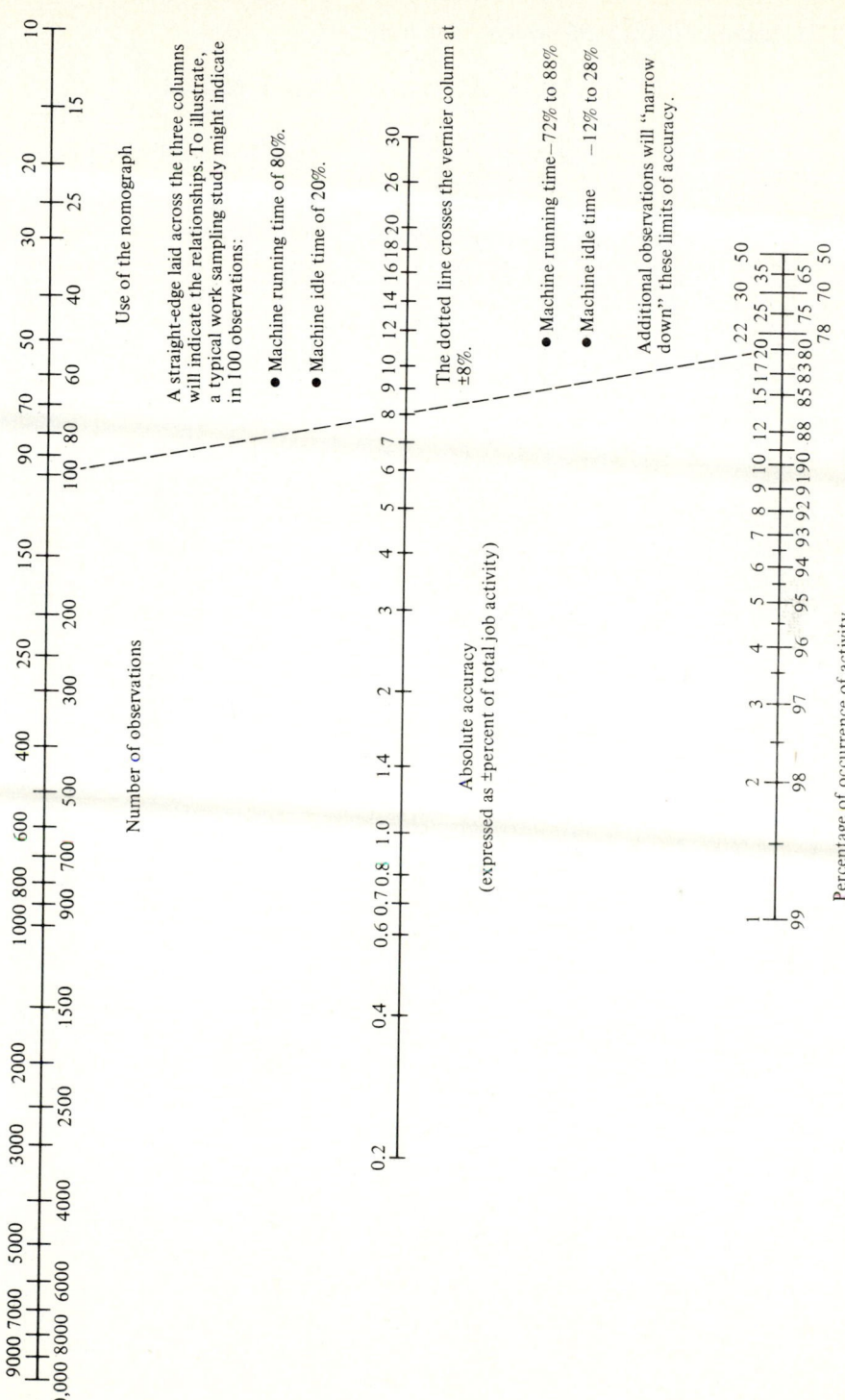

Figure 12-1 Accuracy-sample-size nomograph; 95 percent confidence.

143

Table 12-1 Accuracy limits at 95 percent confidence

> This chart shows the relationship of the number of observations, the size of the activity involved, and the expected range of accuracy.
>
> **Example:** 80% occurrence of "problem item"
> 100 observations
> Range of accuracy 72% to 88%

SIZE OF ACTIVITY INVOLVED (PERCENTAGE OF OCCURRENCE OF "PROBLEM ITEM")

NUMBER OF OBSERVATIONS — RANGE OF ACCURACY IN PERCENT

%	50	60	70	80	90	100	200	300	400	500
1	.00 – 3.81	.00 – 3.56	.00 – 3.38	.00 – 3.12	.00 – 3.12	.00 – 2.99	.00 – 2.41	.00 – 2.15	.01 – 1.99	.11 – 1.89
2	.00 – 5.96	.00 – 5.62	.00 – 5.54	.00 – 5.14	.00 – 4.94	.00 – 4.80	.02 – 3.98	.38 – 3.62	.60 – 3.40	.78 – 3.22
3	.00 – 7.82	.00 – 7.46	.00 – 7.08	.00 – 6.82	.00 – 6.59	.00 – 6.41	.60 – 5.40	1.03 – 4.97	1.30 – 4.70	1.48 – 4.52
4	.00 – 9.54	.00 – 9.06	.00 – 8.68	.00 – 8.38	.00 – 8.14	.08 – 7.92	1.24 – 6.76	1.74 – 6.26	2.04 – 5.96	2.24 – 5.76
5	.00 – 11.17	.00 – 10.62	.00 – 10.22	.12 – 9.88	.40 – 9.60	.64 – 9.36	1.92 – 8.08	2.48 – 7.52	2.82 – 7.18	3.06 – 6.94
6	.00 – 12.72	.00 – 12.12	.34 – 11.66	.70 – 11.30	1.10 – 10.90	1.24 – 10.76	2.64 – 9.36	3.26 – 8.74	3.62 – 8.38	3.88 – 8.12
7	.00 – 14.22	.42 – 13.58	.90 – 13.10	1.30 – 12.70	1.62 – 12.38	1.80 – 12.20	3.40 – 10.60	4.06 – 9.94	4.44 – 9.56	4.72 – 9.28
8	.40 – 15.60	1.02 – 14.98	1.52 – 14.48	1.92 – 14.08	2.28 – 13.72	2.58 – 13.42	4.08 – 11.92	4.88 – 11.12	5.28 – 10.72	5.58 – 10.42
9	.90 – 17.10	1.62 – 16.38	2.16 – 15.84	2.60 – 15.40	2.96 – 15.04	3.28 – 14.72	4.90 – 13.10	5.70 – 12.30	6.14 – 11.86	6.44 – 11.56
10	1.52 – 18.48	2.26 – 17.74	2.84 – 17.16	3.30 – 16.70	3.68 – 16.32	4.00 – 16.00	5.76 – 14.24	6.54 – 13.46	7.00 – 13.00	7.32 – 12.68
11	2.14 – 19.86	2.92 – 19.08	3.54 – 18.46	4.02 – 17.98	4.40 – 17.60	4.74 – 17.26	6.58 – 15.42	7.38 – 14.62	7.88 – 14.12	8.20 – 13.80
12	2.82 – 21.18	3.60 – 20.40	4.24 – 19.76	4.72 – 19.28	5.16 – 18.84	5.50 – 18.50	7.40 – 16.60	8.24 – 15.76	8.74 – 15.26	9.10 – 14.90
13	3.50 – 22.50	4.32 – 21.68	4.98 – 21.02	5.48 – 20.52	5.90 – 20.10	6.29 – 19.71	8.24 – 17.76	9.12 – 16.88	9.64 – 16.36	9.98 – 16.02
14	4.18 – 23.82	5.04 – 22.96	5.70 – 22.30	6.24 – 21.76	6.68 – 21.32	7.06 – 20.94	9.10 – 18.90	10.00 – 18.00	10.54 – 17.46	10.90 – 17.10
15	4.90 – 25.10	5.80 – 24.20	6.46 – 23.54	7.02 – 22.98	7.46 – 22.54	7.86 – 22.14	9.94 – 20.06	10.88 – 19.12	11.42 – 18.58	11.80 – 18.20
16	5.62 – 26.38	6.54 – 25.46	7.24 – 24.76	7.80 – 24.20	8.28 – 23.72	8.66 – 23.34	10.80 – 21.20	11.80 – 20.20	12.34 – 19.66	12.72 – 19.28
17	6.38 – 27.62	7.30 – 26.70	8.02 – 25.98	8.60 – 25.40	9.08 – 24.92	9.48 – 24.52	11.68 – 22.32	12.66 – 21.34	13.24 – 20.76	13.64 – 20.36
18	7.14 – 28.86	8.08 – 27.92	8.82 – 27.18	9.42 – 26.58	9.90 – 26.10	10.32 – 25.68	12.58 – 23.42	13.56 – 22.44	14.16 – 21.84	14.56 – 21.44
19	7.90 – 30.10	8.88 – 29.12	9.64 – 28.36	10.24 – 27.76	10.72 – 27.28	11.16 – 26.84	13.46 – 24.54	14.48 – 23.52	15.08 – 22.92	15.50 – 22.50
20	8.68 – 31.32	9.68 – 30.32	10.44 – 29.56	11.06 – 28.94	11.58 – 28.42	12.00 – 28.00	14.34 – 25.66	15.38 – 24.62	16.00 – 24.00	16.42 – 23.58
21	9.46 – 32.54	10.50 – 31.50	11.26 – 30.74	11.90 – 30.10	12.42 – 29.58	12.85 – 29.15	15.24 – 26.76	16.30 – 25.70	16.92 – 25.08	17.36 – 24.64
22	10.28 – 33.72	11.30 – 32.70	12.10 – 31.90	12.70 – 31.30	13.26 – 30.74	13.72 – 30.28	16.14 – 27.86	17.22 – 26.78	17.86 – 26.14	18.30 – 25.70
23	11.10 – 34.90	12.14 – 33.86	12.94 – 33.06	13.60 – 32.40	14.12 – 31.88	14.58 – 31.42	17.04 – 28.96	18.14 – 27.86	18.80 – 27.20	19.24 – 26.76
24	11.92 – 36.08	12.98 – 35.02	13.80 – 34.20	14.46 – 33.54	15.00 – 33.00	15.46 – 32.54	17.96 – 30.04	19.06 – 28.94	19.72 – 28.28	20.18 – 27.82
25	12.76 – 37.24	13.82 – 36.18	14.64 – 35.36	15.32 – 34.68	15.88 – 34.12	16.34 – 33.66	18.88 – 31.12	20.00 – 30.00	20.66 – 29.34	21.12 – 28.88
26	13.60 – 38.40	14.68 – 37.32	15.52 – 36.48	16.20 – 35.80	16.74 – 35.26	17.24 – 34.76	19.80 – 32.20	20.94 – 31.06	21.62 – 30.38	22.08 – 29.92
27	14.44 – 39.56	15.54 – 38.46	16.42 – 37.58	17.08 – 36.92	17.64 – 36.36	18.12 – 35.88	20.72 – 33.28	21.88 – 32.12	22.56 – 31.44	23.04 – 30.96
28	15.30 – 40.70	16.40 – 39.60	17.26 – 38.74	17.96 – 38.04	18.54 – 37.46	19.02 – 36.98	21.64 – 34.36	22.82 – 33.18	23.51 – 32.49	23.98 – 32.02
29	16.14 – 41.86	17.28 – 40.72	18.16 – 39.84	18.86 – 39.14	19.42 – 38.58	19.92 – 38.08	22.58 – 35.42	23.76 – 34.24	24.46 – 33.54	24.94 – 33.06
30	17.04 – 42.96	18.16 – 41.84	19.04 – 40.96	19.76 – 40.24	20.34 – 39.66	20.84 – 39.16	23.50 – 36.50	24.70 – 35.30	25.42 – 34.58	25.90 – 34.10
35	21.50 – 48.50	22.75 – 47.25	23.60 – 46.40	24.34 – 45.66	24.94 – 45.06	25.46 – 44.54	28.26 – 41.74	29.50 – 40.50	30.22 – 39.78	30.74 – 39.26
40	26.14 – 53.86	27.34 – 52.66	28.30 – 51.70	29.04 – 50.96	29.68 – 50.32	30.20 – 49.80	33.06 – 46.94	34.34 – 45.66	35.10 – 44.90	35.62 – 44.38
45	30.94 – 59.06	32.75 – 57.25	33.12 – 56.88	33.88 – 56.12	34.52 – 55.48	35.04 – 54.96	37.96 – 52.04	39.26 – 50.74	40.02 – 49.98	40.54 – 49.46
50	35.86 – 64.14	37.08 – 62.92	38.04 – 61.96	38.82 – 61.18	39.48 – 60.52	40.00 – 60.00	42.94 – 57.06	44.22 – 55.78	45.00 – 55.00	45.52 – 54.48
55	40.94 – 69.06	42.16 – 67.84	43.12 – 66.88	43.88 – 66.12	44.52 – 65.48	45.04 – 64.96	47.96 – 62.04	49.26 – 60.74	50.02 – 59.98	50.54 – 59.46
60	46.14 – 73.86	47.34 – 72.66	48.30 – 71.70	49.04 – 70.96	49.68 – 70.32	50.20 – 69.80	53.06 – 66.94	54.34 – 65.66	55.10 – 64.90	55.62 – 64.38
65	51.50 – 78.50	52.68 – 77.32	53.60 – 76.40	54.34 – 75.66	54.94 – 75.06	55.46 – 74.54	58.26 – 71.74	59.50 – 70.50	60.22 – 69.78	60.74 – 69.26
70	57.04 – 82.96	58.16 – 81.84	59.04 – 80.96	59.76 – 80.24	60.34 – 79.66	60.84 – 79.16	63.50 – 76.50	64.70 – 75.30	65.42 – 74.58	65.90 – 74.10
75	62.76 – 87.24	63.82 – 86.18	64.64 – 85.36	65.32 – 84.68	65.88 – 84.12	66.34 – 83.66	68.88 – 81.12	70.00 – 80.00	70.66 – 79.34	71.12 – 78.88
80	68.68 – 91.32	69.68 – 90.32	70.54 – 89.46	71.06 – 88.94	71.58 – 88.42	72.00 – 88.00	74.34 – 85.66	75.38 – 84.62	76.00 – 84.00	76.42 – 83.58
85	74.90 – 95.10	75.80 – 94.20	76.46 – 93.54	77.02 – 92.98	77.46 – 92.54	77.86 – 92.14	79.94 – 90.06	80.88 – 89.12	81.42 – 88.58	81.80 – 88.20
90	81.52 – 98.48	82.26 – 97.74	82.84 – 97.16	83.30 – 96.70	83.68 – 96.32	84.00 – 96.00	85.76 – 94.24	86.54 – 93.46	87.00 – 93.00	87.32 – 92.68
95	88.83 – 100.00	89.38 – 100.00	89.78 – 100.00	90.12 – 99.88	90.40 – 99.60	90.64 – 99.36	91.92 – 98.08	92.48 – 97.52	92.82 – 97.18	93.06 – 96.94

NUMBER OF OBSERVATIONS

600	700	800	900	1000	2500	5000	7500	10000 Maximum	%
RANGE OF ACCURACY IN PERCENT									
.20 - 1.80	.26 - 1.74	.30 - 1.70	.34 - 1.66	.37 - 1.63	.60 - 1.40	.72 - 1.28	.77 - 1.23	.80 - 1.20	1
.86 - 3.14	.92 - 3.08	1.00 - 3.00	1.08 - 2.92	1.11 - 2.89	1.44 - 2.56	1.60 - 2.40	1.68 - 2.32	1.72 - 2.28	2
1.60 - 4.40	1.70 - 4.30	1.80 - 4.20	1.86 - 4.14	1.93 - 4.07	2.32 - 3.68	2.52 - 3.48	2.61 - 3.39	2.66 - 3.34	3
2.40 - 5.60	2.52 - 5.48	2.62 - 5.38	2.70 - 5.30	2.82 - 5.18	3.22 - 4.78	3.45 - 4.55	3.55 - 4.45	3.61 - 4.39	4
3.22 - 6.78	3.36 - 6.64	3.46 - 6.54	3.54 - 6.46	3.62 - 6.38	4.13 - 5.87	4.38 - 5.62	4.50 - 5.50	4.56 - 5.44	5
4.06 - 7.94	4.16 - 7.84	4.32 - 7.68	4.42 - 7.58	4.50 - 7.50	5.05 - 6.95	5.33 - 6.67	5.45 - 6.55	5.53 - 6.47	6
4.92 - 9.08	5.08 - 8.92	5.20 - 8.80	5.30 - 8.70	5.39 - 8.61	5.98 - 8.02	6.28 - 7.72	6.41 - 7.59	6.49 - 7.51	7
5.78 - 10.22	5.95 - 10.05	6.08 - 9.92	6.20 - 9.80	6.29 - 9.71	6.92 - 9.08	7.23 - 8.77	7.37 - 8.63	7.46 - 8.54	8
6.66 - 11.34	6.84 - 11.16	6.98 - 11.02	7.08 - 10.92	7.20 - 10.80	7.85 - 10.15	8.19 - 9.81	8.34 - 9.66	8.42 - 9.58	9
7.56 - 12.44	7.74 - 12.26	7.88 - 12.12	8.00 - 12.00	8.10 - 11.90	8.80 - 11.20	9.15 - 10.85	9.3 - 10.69	9.40 - 10.60	10
8.44 - 13.56	8.64 - 13.36	8.80 - 13.20	8.92 - 13.08	9.02 - 12.98	9.75 - 12.25	10.11 - 11.89	10.28 - 11.72	10.37 - 11.63	11
9.34 - 14.66	9.54 - 14.46	9.70 - 14.30	9.84 - 14.16	9.94 - 14.06	10.70 - 13.30	11.08 - 12.92	11.25 - 12.75	11.35 - 12.65	12
10.26 - 15.74	10.46 - 15.54	10.62 - 15.38	10.77 - 15.23	10.87 - 15.13	11.65 - 14.35	12.05 - 13.95	12.22 - 13.78	12.33 - 13.67	13
11.16 - 16.84	11.38 - 16.62	11.54 - 16.46	11.70 - 16.30	11.81 - 16.19	12.61 - 15.39	13.02 - 14.98	13.20 - 14.80	13.31 - 14.69	14
12.10 - 17.90	12.30 - 17.70	12.48 - 17.52	12.62 - 17.38	12.74 - 17.26	13.57 - 16.43	13.99 - 16.01	14.18 - 15.82	14.29 - 15.71	15
13.00 - 19.00	13.24 - 18.76	13.42 - 18.58	13.56 - 18.44	13.68 - 18.32	14.53 - 17.47	14.96 - 17.04	15.15 - 16.85	15.27 - 16.73	16
13.94 - 20.06	14.16 - 19.84	14.34 - 19.66	14.50 - 19.50	14.62 - 19.38	15.50 - 18.50	15.94 - 18.06	16.13 - 17.87	16.25 - 17.75	17
14.86 - 21.14	15.10 - 20.90	15.28 - 20.72	15.44 - 20.56	15.57 - 20.43	16.46 - 19.54	16.91 - 19.09	17.11 - 18.89	17.23 - 18.77	18
15.80 - 22.20	16.04 - 21.96	16.22 - 21.78	16.38 - 21.62	16.52 - 21.48	17.44 - 20.56	17.89 - 20.11	18.09 - 19.91	18.21 - 19.79	19
16.74 - 23.26	16.98 - 23.02	17.18 - 22.82	17.34 - 22.66	17.47 - 22.53	18.40 - 21.60	18.87 - 21.13	19.08 - 20.92	19.20 - 20.80	20
17.68 - 24.32	17.92 - 24.08	18.12 - 23.88	18.28 - 23.72	18.42 - 23.58	19.37 - 22.63	19.85 - 22.15	20.06 - 21.94	20.19 - 21.81	21
18.62 - 25.38	18.86 - 25.14	19.06 - 24.94	19.24 - 24.76	19.38 - 24.62	20.34 - 23.66	20.83 - 23.17	21.05 - 22.95	21.17 - 22.83	22
19.56 - 26.44	19.82 - 26.18	20.02 - 25.98	20.20 - 25.80	20.54 - 25.66	21.32 - 24.68	21.81 - 24.19	22.03 - 23.97	22.16 - 23.84	23
20.52 - 27.48	20.78 - 27.22	20.98 - 27.02	21.16 - 26.84	21.30 - 26.70	22.29 - 25.71	22.79 - 25.21	23.01 - 24.99	23.15 - 24.85	24
21.46 - 28.54	21.72 - 28.28	21.94 - 28.06	22.12 - 27.88	22.26 - 27.74	23.27 - 26.73	23.77 - 26.23	24.00 - 26.00	24.13 - 25.87	25
22.42 - 29.58	22.68 - 29.32	22.90 - 29.10	23.08 - 28.92	23.23 - 28.77	24.24 - 27.76	24.76 - 27.24	24.99 - 27.01	25.12 - 26.88	26
23.38 - 30.62	23.64 - 30.36	23.86 - 30.14	24.04 - 29.96	24.19 - 29.81	25.22 - 28.78	25.74 - 28.26	25.98 - 28.02	26.11 - 27.89	27
24.34 - 31.66	24.60 - 31.40	24.82 - 31.18	25.00 - 31.00	25.16 - 30.84	26.20 - 29.80	26.73 - 29.27	26.96 - 29.04	27.10 - 28.90	28
25.30 - 32.70	25.58 - 32.42	25.78 - 32.22	25.98 - 32.02	26.13 - 31.87	27.19 - 30.81	27.72 - 30.28	27.95 - 30.05	28.09 - 29.91	29
26.26 - 33.74	26.54 - 33.46	26.76 - 33.24	26.94 - 33.06	27.11 - 32.89	28.17 - 31.83	28.70 - 31.30	28.94 - 31.06	29.08 - 30.92	30
31.10 - 38.90	31.40 - 38.60	31.62 - 38.38	31.82 - 38.18	31.99 - 38.01	33.09 - 36.91	33.65 - 36.35	33.90 - 36.10	34.05 - 35.95	35
36.00 - 44.00	36.28 - 43.72	36.54 - 43.46	36.74 - 43.26	36.90 - 43.10	38.04 - 41.96	38.61 - 41.39	38.87 - 41.13	39.02 - 40.98	40
40.94 - 49.06	41.24 - 48.76	41.48 - 48.52	41.68 - 48.32	41.85 - 48.15	43.01 - 46.99	43.59 - 46.41	43.85 - 46.15	44.00 - 46.00	45
45.92 - 54.08	46.22 - 53.78	46.47 - 53.53	46.66 - 53.34	46.84 - 53.16	48.00 - 52.00	48.58 - 51.42	48.85 - 51.15	49.00 - 51.00	50
50.94 - 59.06	51.24 - 58.76	51.48 - 58.52	51.68 - 58.32	51.85 - 58.15	53.01 - 56.99	53.59 - 56.41	53.85 - 56.15	54.00 - 56.00	55
56.00 - 64.00	56.28 - 63.72	56.54 - 63.46	56.74 - 63.26	56.90 - 63.10	58.04 - 61.96	58.61 - 61.39	58.87 - 61.13	59.02 - 60.98	60
61.10 - 68.90	61.40 - 68.60	61.62 - 68.38	61.82 - 68.18	61.99 - 68.01	63.09 - 66.91	63.65 - 66.35	63.90 - 66.10	64.05 - 65.95	65
66.26 - 73.74	66.54 - 73.46	66.76 - 73.24	66.94 - 73.06	67.11 - 72.89	68.17 - 71.83	68.70 - 71.30	68.94 - 71.06	69.08 - 70.92	70
71.46 - 78.54	71.72 - 78.28	71.94 - 78.06	72.12 - 77.88	72.26 - 77.74	73.27 - 76.73	73.77 - 76.23	74.00 - 76.00	74.13 - 75.87	75
76.74 - 83.26	76.98 - 83.02	77.18 - 82.82	77.34 - 82.66	77.47 - 82.53	78.40 - 81.60	78.87 - 81.13	79.08 - 80.92	79.20 - 80.80	80
82.10 - 87.90	82.30 - 87.70	82.48 - 87.52	82.62 - 87.38	82.74 - 87.26	83.57 - 86.43	83.99 - 86.01	84.18 - 85.82	84.29 - 85.71	85
87.56 - 92.44	87.74 - 92.26	87.88 - 92.12	88.00 - 92.00	88.10 - 91.90	88.80 - 91.20	89.15 - 90.85	89.31 - 90.69	89.40 - 90.60	90
93.22 - 96.78	93.36 - 96.64	93.46 - 96.54	93.54 - 96.46	93.62 - 96.38	94.13 - 95.87	94.38 - 95.62	94.50 - 95.50	94.56 - 95.44	95

The definition stage should thus result in a formally stated objective. Second, it should result in a list of distinct, well-described, nonoverlapping activity categories with respective accuracy specifications. Rough estimates of the percentages associated with these categories coupled with the accuracy requirements will permit the computation of sample-size requirements, thereby giving some idea of the magnitude of the study and the time requirements for completion. Such estimates may also result in a reevaluation of the accuracy requirements.

Inform the People Concerned

The supervisor of the area in which the study is to be conducted should be made aware of the basic principles of work sampling as well as the objectives and expected duration of the study. The supervisor's approval and cooperation are assets in the execution of the study plan. The personnel being observed should also be informed of the purpose of the study. In addition to being an exercise in good human relations, informing the subjects of the study in the preliminary stage generally results in minimal disruption of activity in the early stages of observation. Sometimes this initial contact with the people directly involved with the activity brings forth information that yields new insights into the problem area—information from questions which no one had previously bothered to ask.

Formalize the Study Plan

Planning the study to this point should provide a list of distinct categories or elements to be checked along with the number of observations required to achieve the desired accuracy of each. The overall study size should be decided upon by reviewing the individual element sample sizes and making whatever compromises are deemed necessary.

Tour route Once the people or machines that are to be observed have been identified, a route or pattern for the observation process can be developed. The tour may be simply visual, such as that of having an observer in an office area seated at a desk and merely looking up to observe the activity of people at the appointed observation times. A more-complex situation would be that of observing a number of workers or machines scattered about an area through which the observer must travel. A layout of the area can be used to physically show alternative routes and alternative starting points for the routes. The observation points within the routes should be well-defined. Such things as "when one comes abreast with column 10-A" or "when one's foot touches the floor tile with the chipped corner" serve as triggers for the observation.

The alternative tour routes should be assigned a number, as should the alternative entry or starting points. The choice of a tour route and the entry point on that route can then be randomly selected with the use of a random-number table such as Table 12-2. The numbers might also be simply written on slips of paper, placed in a box, and drawn at random from the box to determine the route and entry point, thereby preserving the principles of randomness and instantaneous observation.

Table 12-2 Random numbers

40681	27353	22597	88915	79178	81568	96319	51098	71270	63812	77365
39713	63020	45133	71152	54318	33657	45481	41509	04687	33262	98564
94563	84957	44619	79713	09949	65244	53466	55985	27077	81993	37171
43027	68321	02813	47446	08517	28803	96663	86674	67775	55543	00487
51134	79763	80567	62318	21551	41301	24034	29986	79315	61613	83115
67373	65291	63392	50049	64763	77384	69945	86642	49238	31727	79092
13011	44976	94731	44841	58114	02487	68308	63610	64436	79719	86555
75053	10760	56728	67907	73573	06858	89809	12729	13637	70054	93351
00416	07842	61398	82483	92684	53713	96476	13096	08892	29976	77773
08140	19067	07653	11476	57271	28172	20924	86795	80075	74483	76172
03614	04739	91340	60151	25949	13799	24239	37699	61160	65534	91260
51781	71407	97071	01707	52119	71110	83590	08030	00655	26829	89420
74840	30355	24811	91014	44450	53425	76329	88396	25471	24939	08916
17855	86450	13831	52245	61860	99428	74067	55408	52533	50065	63352
01207	28820	12109	62958	47884	88216	55819	09726	67161	38420	02415
29475	55575	37654	91091	33918	95562	68096	03709	34564	53896	34367
87008	92552	81623	12154	48696	96053	47245	69520	09495	97197	35893
24644	01087	32311	77807	56658	93684	33336	01512	39831	85626	23779
46326	03892	41967	94372	32998	58406	24326	88509	63328	21618	27759
25039	83375	32560	11945	50878	87600	66917	92413	00939	75858	26314
51940	44169	83459	88888	07752	23211	26260	08693	29368	99956	84758
65375	34741	99245	09156	83529	61952	83897	09931	76427	69486	88548
93919	72535	35297	38351	69774	61954	53808	51707	61318	15122	88657
32641	23240	37340	36135	25186	02274	25956	08937	31372	06943	96504
40131	51356	32702	75474	84559	53684	28758	39890	72112	15426	69659
65093	45655	00947	97180	35175	46277	19665	24873	75652	72660	24978
91020	86594	87835	53859	50205	22739	94579	69359	17526	57074	49443
89051	71343	26912	15341	31812	05179	17404	23642	30470	35331	43174
66627	47292	87259	27395	34567	98159	40764	95925	13833	63765	15378
07313	43774	88701	56132	36069	16027	05491	37788	27276	57333	02761
13840	33975	89909	88547	08856	37066	42128	07117	10909	68721	99323
56422	38011	10458	65809	15295	99155	01271	36612	93163	18865	68112
75812	82841	99809	33958	03468	98967	60237	88604	34209	87042	52709
78396	28235	26532	83318	77096	36217	99285	32993	85093	53164	28178
77050	98519	56449	08000	65445	38130	72304	32656	58223	09472	23042
45534	45029	84611	04753	49955	10020	56276	90596	89037	18424	94292
97612	39593	89037	03471	76022	08527	21418	56626	24739	06594	44200
95835	42224	66513	35514	19282	86647	84339	33670	50372	38939	41949
34916	94718	93210	03218	92353	34164	55546	57339	89379	94890	77096
46632	41268	35295	93493	61016	32761	10767	22685	50950	74885	64554
01487	64386	02269	15196	93712	61311	10786	18485	81751	28908	77870
44214	71437	59037	12657	30005	17106	78682	91223	82971	78688	84475
90468	99815	78139	69224	02220	59965	69932	79094	04080	66786	28460
74232	24251	70330	91262	09355	68912	96661	67153	13462	29941	39485
92253	94384	86540	11770	76555	77366	83318	75211	83624	32330	75513
53662	22108	08697	50312	91726	37906	10009	28915	25505	75795	35914
15458	76661	02770	47195	68630	08611	30428	16774	55857	73460	02840
53020	68646	01282	42227	39343	72195	32849	66381	88405	87540	34617
28256	03411	92796	77002	07332	05353	45197	37779	89154	38303	70620
87490	35299	62241	27197	04170	36179	59465	39318	01340	85298	70445
00958	98267	66174	28926	99547	16627	45515	67953	12108	57846	09578
30346	26957	78240	43195	24837	32511	70880	22070	52622	61881	91202
14056	57841	00833	88000	67299	68215	11274	55624	32991	17436	70218
96789	22551	12111	86683	61270	58036	64192	90611	15145	01748	05326
12633	15075	47189	99951	05755	03834	43782	90599	40282	51417	71196
25893	57092	76396	72486	62423	27618	84184	78922	73561	52818	33377
13092	50817	46409	17469	32483	09083	76175	19985	26309	91536	85950
72872	54109	74626	22111	87286	46772	42243	68046	44250	42439	19050
20724	19944	34450	81974	93723	49023	58432	67083	36876	93391	13078
37009	52173	36327	72135	33005	28710	34710	49359	50693	89311	84989
25961	70386	74185	77585	84825	09934	99103	09325	67389	45869	90776
73962	47022	12296	41628	62873	37943	25548	09609	63360	47270	52217
63164	76372	90822	60280	88925	99610	42772	60561	76873	04117	58309
05366	00082	72121	79152	96591	90305	10189	79778	68016	13747	95840
15902	61363	95268	41377	25684	08151	61816	58555	54305	86189	34941
53845	17851	92603	09091	75884	93424	72586	88903	30061	14457	38621
31694	55633	18813	90291	05275	01223	79607	95426	34900	09778	44454
23016	96567	38840	26903	28624	67157	51986	42865	14508	49315	16329
17292	18430	05959	33836	53750	16562	41081	38012	41230	20528	86488
75365	99837	85141	21155	99212	32685	51403	31926	69813	58781	47193
89013	86492	75047	59643	31074	38172	03718	32119	69506	67144	66959
44551	77837	30752	95260	68032	62817	58781	34143	68790	69766	80290
49675	13139	22986	82575	42187	62295	84295	30634	66562	31442	43247
40739	73539	99439	86692	90348	66036	48399	73451	26698	39437	29518
64086	82765	20389	93029	11881	71685	65452	89047	62669	02656	67267
79143	31528	39249	05173	68256	36359	20250	68686	05947	09335	56101
28231	07703	96777	33605	29481	20063	09398	01843	35139	61344	25755
76327	50155	04860	32918	10798	50492	52655	33359	94713	28393	84438
05428	65225	64285	86579	77447	75313	35762	45824	21535	48707	84917
56800	69853	75583	38682	55733	98453	35129	73541	62087	36549	77455

Once the tour is defined, the number of observations from each tour is a fixed number. One should also be able to estimate the time required for the observer to complete a tour.

Tour frequency The number of tours to be made each day usually involves two primary considerations, the first of which is the time period planned for the duration of the study. Is it to be completed in 2 weeks, 1 month, 6 months? The time period should be long enough to reflect the influence of the natural variables affecting the system. The figure of one calendar month (20 working days) is often quoted as a minimum length.

Another consideration is the maximum number of tours that could be made during a day. The maximum number of tours per day is found by dividing the available time per day by the tour length. Taking the maximum tours per day would involve continuous observation, which could introduce a cyclical pattern in the observations and destroy the randomness. A rule of thumb sometimes followed is to divide the above maximum by 4 to achieve a workable maximum.

When the number of tours per day is multiplied by the number of observations per tour, the result is the number of observations per day. The number of days for the study can then be found by dividing the study size by the number of observations per day.

As an example, suppose that a study is to consist of 2400 observations. The tour length is 20 minutes and yields 16 observations. The available time per day is 480 minutes.

$$\frac{480 \text{ minutes}}{\text{day}} \quad \frac{1 \text{ tour}}{20 \text{ minutes}} \quad \frac{1}{4} \quad \frac{16 \text{ observations}}{\text{tour}} = 96 \text{ observations per day}$$

$$\frac{2400 \text{ observations per study}}{96 \text{ observations per day}} = 25 \text{ days per study}$$

If it was decided that the study should be spread over 40 working days for better representation, the following approach could be used:

$$\frac{2400 \text{ observations per study}}{40 \text{ days per study}} \quad \frac{1 \text{ tour}}{16 \text{ observations}} = 3.75, \text{ or 4 tours per day}$$

Random starting times Determination of random starting times for the tours is usually done using a random-number table (Table 12-2), which is a tedious process. Computer programs have been developed for this purpose, or the task can be done on a programmable hand calculator. Regardless of how it is done, some objective means of choosing when and where to start the tours is vital to preserving the randomness of the observations. In an effort to strengthen credibility of a study, the daily sampling will sometimes be stratified. For example, if four tours are to be run per day, rather than selecting starting times from the entire day for each tour, one might stratify or divide the day into morning and afternoon and require that two tours be run in each. One can then randomly select two starting times in the morning and two in the afternoon, thereby "forcing" representativeness on each daily sample. Without stratification, one day might have three tours in the morning and one in the afternoon and another might have all four tours in the afternoon.

Design the observation form Consideration should be given to the convenience of recording the observations. A preplanned data sheet with elements listed and ade-

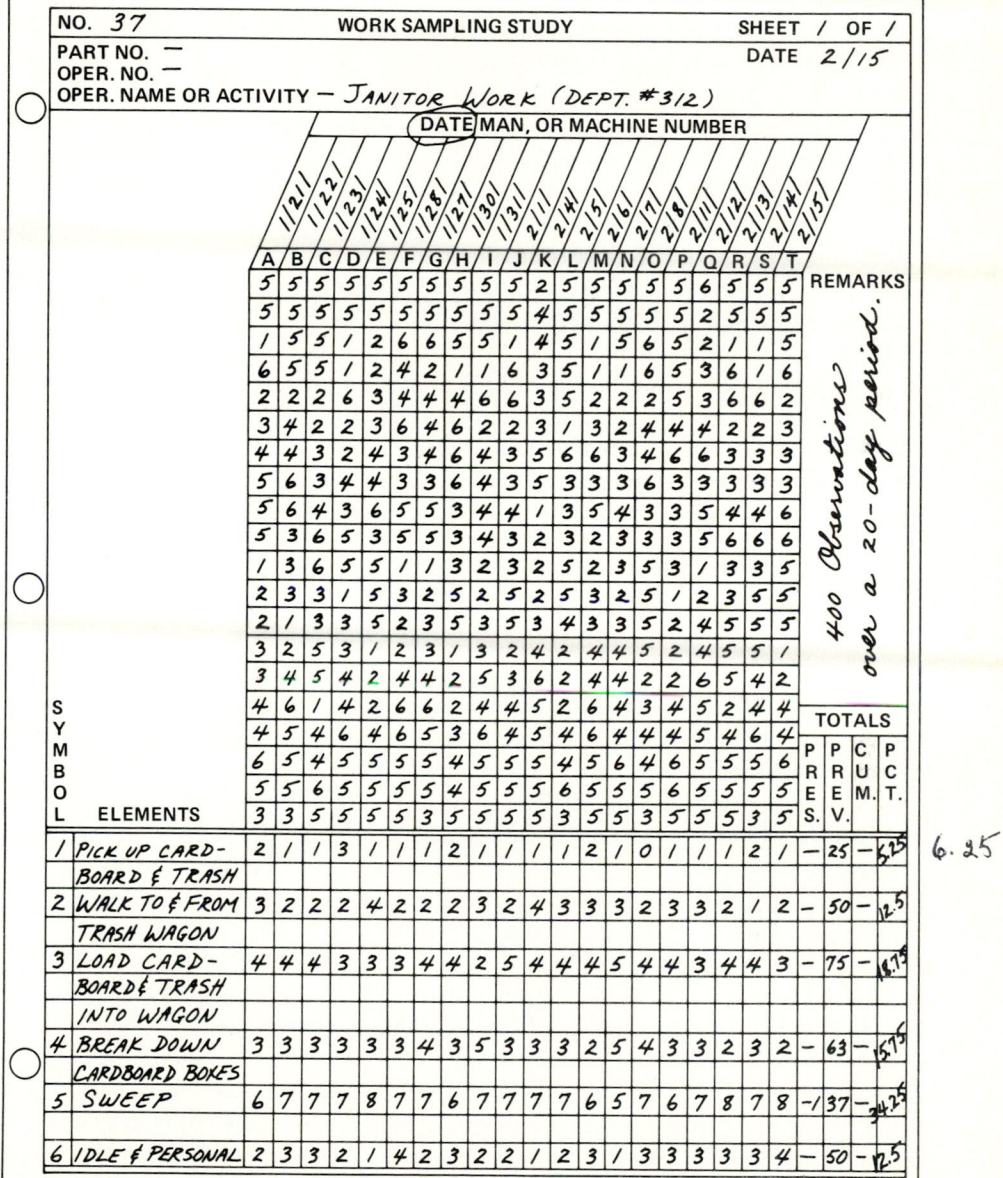

Figure 12-2 Work sampling data sheet.

quate space for recording and making notes is a great asset to the observer. Figure 12-2 is an example of a completed data sheet. The observer records the element code for each observation. A day's observations are in a single column for easy summary.

Conduct the Study

If the planning activity has been effective, conducting the study should be almost mechanical. The key issue is that of the observers' following the plan in terms of random times and instantaneous observations.

In a large study, say 100 or more observations per day, it is good practice to summarize the results daily. One can thereby begin to determine if some of the preliminary estimates are off base and possibly call for a revision in the study size to achieve the desired accuracy.

Charting daily results may serve as a useful tool for detecting any unusual occurrences during the study. A chart is usually set up on one or more key elements rather than on all elements of the study.

Charts may serve a variety of purposes.

Observer bias   If more than one observer is used in a study, a chart of the daily results of each observer may point out a systematic difference between observers. Such a difference may result from different interpretations of the instructions or an inherent bias on the part of the person. Figure 12-3 is an example of such a chart, where observer B tends to give lower values than does observer A.

Control chart   Daily results can be graphically checked for stability by borrowing the concept of a control chart from statistical quality control. The daily result of a key element may be plotted on a chart to which one can add statistical control limits. The control limits give some indication about what the natural variation of the daily results should be. Variation outside the control limits would be a cause of suspicion about an unusual day, or in the early stages of a study, an erroneous initial estimate of the element percentage.

The control limits can be determined by using the formula, nomograph, or table that was used to determine study accuracy. The sample size used in this case would be the number of observations per day and the p value would be the estimated element percentage.

Suppose that the estimated p value is 15 percent and 100 observations were taken per day. From Figure 12-1, one finds $A = 7.1$. The upper control limit would be $p + A$, or $15 + 7.1$, or 22.1 percent. The lower control limit would be $p - A$, or $15 - 7.1$, or 7.9 percent. These values could have been found directly from Table 12-1. One expects about 95 percent of the daily results to fall within these limits if the estimate of p is good and if the system does not experience any unusual disturbances. For example, a batch of bad raw material, which should not have reached the operation, may cause an unusual amount of machine downtime on a given day. Figure 12-4 shows a control chart with the above limits that indicate natural system behavior.

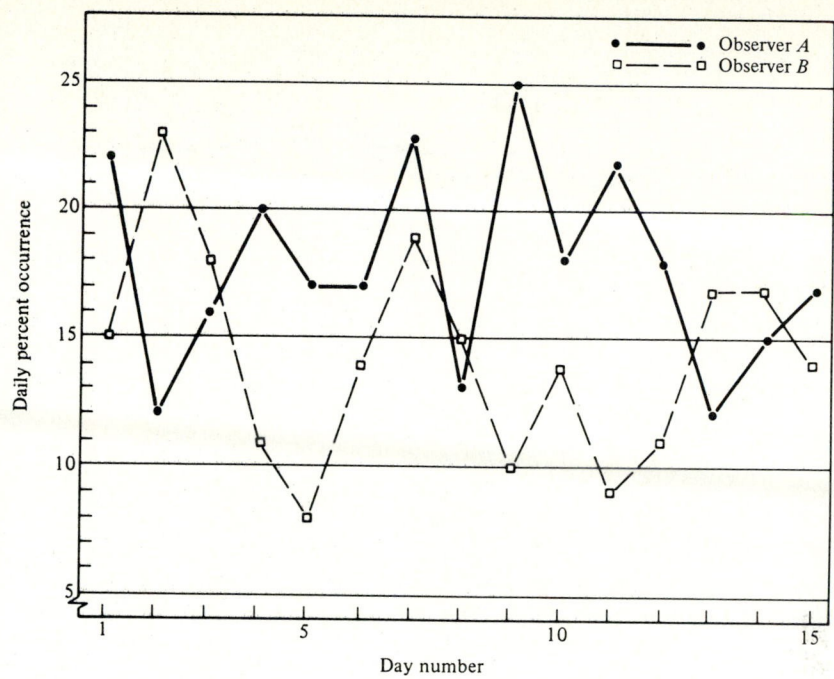

Figure 12-3 Chart of daily results indicating a difference between observers.

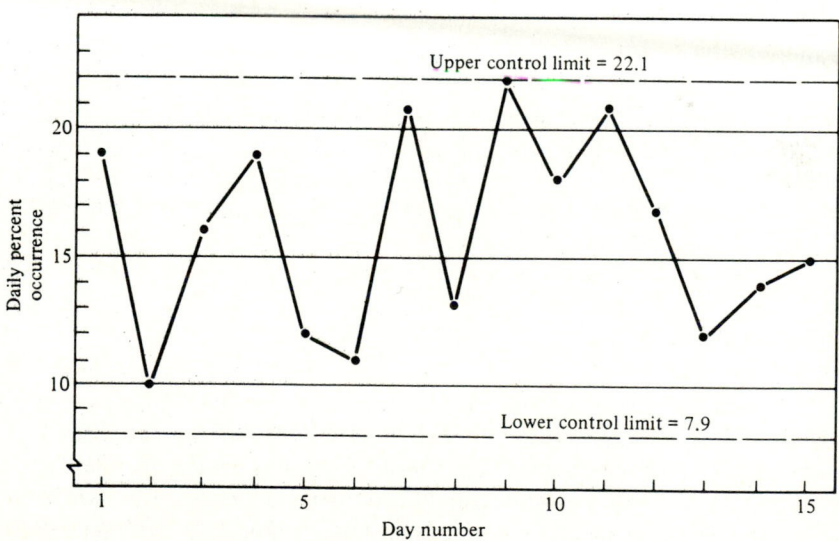

Figure 12-4 Control chart for daily percentages.

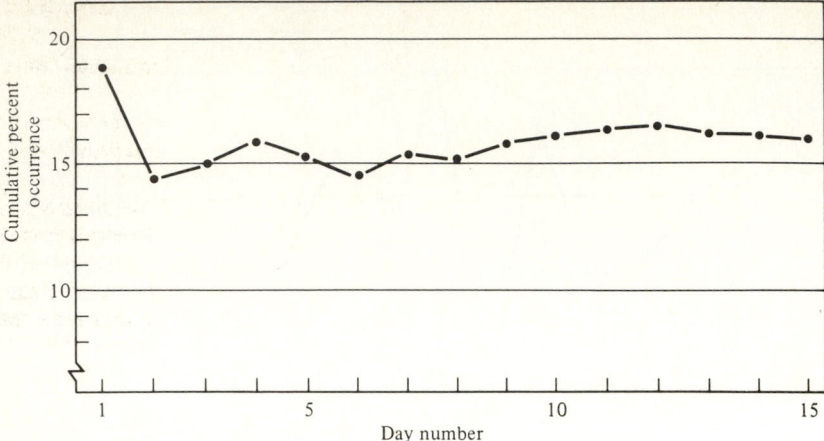

Figure 12-5 Cumulative percent chart.

Cumulative chart The cumulative estimate of p can be plotted on a daily basis and sometimes used to decide when a stabilized value of the percentage has been reached. The daily cumulative value is determined by dividing the cumulative number of observations on the element in question by the total number of observations that have been made. Figure 12-5 shows a cumulative chart for the daily results which are plotted in Fig. 12-4 as individual daily results.

Finalize Results

When the study has been completed, the final report should present the results of the study in a fashion that most effectively addresses the initial objectives. Certainly the report should include the final element percentages and their respective accuracies. The report should specify whether accuracy is relative or absolute. The report should also include any unusual happenings, such as an example of excess downtime due to bad material and an indication of whether those data were included or deleted from the study.

STATISTICAL CONCEPTS

The statistical basis for describing the accuracy of the estimation process in work sampling is basically the same as that discussed in Chap. 11. The primary difference lies in the determination of the standard deviation of the statistic under consideration.

In work sampling, each observation can be considered an experiment, where an activity of interest is occurring or not occurring. After a number n of observations have been made, the statistic x is the number of times the activity of interest was observed to be occurring. If the individual observations were independent of one another and if the system under observation was stable, the behavior of the statistic x is described by the binomial probability distribution. If the statistic x is divided by the sample size n, a new statistic is formed: $p = 100x/n$, which is the percent of occurrences in the sample of the activity of interest. The binomial distribution gives the values for the mean and standard deviation of p values that would be expected if many samples of size n were to be taken. These values are

$$\text{Mean} = \mu_p = p'$$

$$\text{Standard deviation} = \sigma_p = \sqrt{\frac{p'(100 - p')}{n}}$$

where p' is the true population percentage of occurrence of the activity of interest

For large sample sizes, say for $n = 100$ or larger, the binomial distribution can be approximated by the normal distribution, and one would expect about 95 percent of the values of p to fall in the interval $p' \pm 2\,\sigma_p$. Conversely, for a single sample, one can be 95 percent confident that p is within $2\sigma_p$ of p'. Since p' is not known, p is used as an estimate of it, so the definition of absolute accuracy at the 95 percent confidence level is given as

$$A = 2\sigma_p = 2\sqrt{\frac{p(100 - p)}{n}}$$

SUMMARY

Work sampling is one of the most general work-measurement techniques available. It has broad applications in both direct- and indirect-labor areas. It can yield statistically valid results using observers with a minimal amount of training. The validity is dependent on adherence to the principles of randomness and instantaneousness of the observations. The development of the observation schedule to achieve the randomness as well as the processing of interim and final results can be simplified through the use of computer technology.

QUESTIONS

12-1 What is an activity category or element in work sampling?

12-2 What type of information does a work-sampling study provide?

12-3 Describe the two types of accuracy associated with work sampling.

12-4 Why is randomness important in determining observation times?

12-5 For a given confidence level, what two values are required to determine the appropriate number of observations to take?

12-6 What are three methods of determining sample size?

12-7 How does one determine the accuracy to be used in the planning of a study?

12-8 Why would one want alternative tour routes and alternative entry points in the routes?

12-9 How might one investigate differences in observers if more than one observer were used in a study?

12-10 What probability distributions are used in developing the accuracy–sample-size relations?

PROBLEMS

12-1 A study of 425 observations was made of an inspection operation with the results shown below. Determine the percentage and the associated absolute accuracy (95 percent confidence) for each element.

Element	Number of observations
Inspecting	288
Handling paperwork	26
Being idle	51
Going out of area	60

12-2 A study of 250 observations at a fast-food counter resulted in 55 observations of the attendants being idle. Determine the percent idle time along with the absolute and the relative accuracy (95 percent confidence).

12-3 Consider the study in Prob. 12-2. How many additional observations would be required to achieve an absolute accuracy of $2\frac{1}{2}$ percent for the percent idle estimate?

12-4 Determine the absolute accuracy (95 percent confidence) for the six elements shown in Fig. 12-2.

12-5 Construct a plot of A against p for a sample of 400 observations. Let p vary from 0 to 100 percent in 5 percent increments.

12-6 Repeat Prob. 12-5 plotting R against p.

12-7 A tour takes 10 minutes to complete and yields 15 observations. The maximum number of tours per day for an observer has been set at 14. If 3200 observations are required, how many days will be required to complete the data gathering?

12-8 An observer can make 8 tours per day and each tour yields 17 observations. To achieve the desired accuracy, 7200 observations are required. If the study is to be completed within one month (20 days), what is the minimum number of observers required?

12-9 A work-sampling study consisting of 500 observations was made on a fork truck in the shipping area with the following results:

Element	Number of observations
Idle	100
Travel empty	172
Travel loaded	206
Loading or unloading	22
	500

(*a*) Determine the percent of total activity associated with each element.

(*b*) Determine the absolute accuracy associated with each element.

(*c*) Determine the relative accuracy associated with each element.

(*d*) What is the average minutes per shift the truck is expected to be idle in the area?

(*e*) What is the accuracy (in minutes per shift) associated with the estimate in *d*?

(*f*) How many (if any) additional observations would be required if the study of an absolute accuracy were desired on the estimate of percent idle?

12-10 Consider the results of 900 observations on a stamping operation as shown below:

Element	Number of observations
Operating	498
Down—tooling problems	203
Down—no stock	145
Down—operator out of area	54

(*a*) Determine the percent of total activity associated with each element.

(*b*) Determine both absolute and relative accuracy for each of the percentages in *a*.

(*c*) If an absolute accuracy of 1 percent is desired on the last element (down—operator out of area), how many additional observations are required?

(*d*) On the average, how many minutes per shift is the operation expected to be down? With what accuracy (in minutes)?

THIRTEEN

STANDARD TIME DATA

Standard time data (STD) are established normal time values for well-defined elements of work or delay. The values are frequently based on actual time studies established by predetermined methods for gathering, compiling, analyzing, and finalizing the data. Standard-time-data development is one of the most interesting and challenging areas of work measurement because it involves the search for the best correlation between the variables present in an operation and the time that is necessary to do the job.

STANDARD TIME DATA CONSIDERATIONS

The development of standard time data is highly recommended because of the many advantages that are derived during the development of the data and during the use of the finalized data to establish work standards.

Advantages of Standard Time Data

Some of the following advantages will not pertain to all types of industrial work because of the great diversification in the way in which work is performed and rewarded.

1. *STD eliminates some repetitive work for the time-study person.* If no standard time data are developed and used, over a period of years many elements are timed

over and over again. Once standard time data are established, such needless repetition can cease.

2. *STD saves time in establishing work standards.* If the final format of the standard time data is in the form of the calculation sheet, finalized rate table, or multivariable chart, as found in this chapter, then it would be readily apparent that much time can be saved in establishing work standards.

3. *STD allows greater coverage of all work in setting standards.* With the savings of time in setting standards with STD, more time is available for studying other operations or indirect labor areas.

4. *STD leads to greater consistency between similar jobs.* The constant-time elements will always be the same even though they pertain to different part numbers. Actually, the standards will vary based on the size of the variable elements that are in control of the time. In Fig. 13-9, element 5, the time for driving four screws, will always be the same regardless of the operation where the element is performed.

5. *STD helps minimize technical efforts of time-study personnel.* Since the standard can now be easily established with the finalized rate table in Fig. 13-10, only a simple clerical routine rather than a complete time study is involved for time-study people.

6. *STD permits standard to be set before start up.* When a new job is received within the range of the variables of the STD, a work standard can be set before the new job is run, as long as the variables of the new job are known.

7. *STD helps minimize the judgment factor.* Since most STD are based on many time studies, a good *average* normal performance can more readily be expected than can be gotten from one operator's performance during a time study.

8. *Through STD, standards are easily substantiated.* Since STD values are really an average of averages from different time studies, commendable attempts have obviously been made to set accurate work standards. Also, STD furnishes many time studies to defend a disputed standard instead of just one, which is the case when a time study is used to set a standard.

9. *STD reduces grievances that originate in changes from estimated to actual work standards.* Grievances can be reduced when changing from estimated to actual work standards because in many cases an estimated standard is unnecessary when a permanent work standard can be set at the beginning as long as the variables of the new job are within the range of the STD.

10. *STD helps eliminate slowdowns before a standard is set.* Slowdowns are sometimes a problem, primarily in plants where workers are paid so much per piece or per hundred pieces on the incentive system. Workers will do their best after permanent work standards are established; and the incentive system is, in effect, to reward them for the number of pieces produced. With STD the work standard can be set on the very first day of production of the new or revised part.

11. *STD leads to less cost per operation in setting standards.* There is less cost per operation in setting standards because STD saves time in establishing work standards.

12. *STD aids in allocating work for line balancing.* Many assembly plants have the

work elements allocated to each worker for the next model year before the first day's production of the new or revised product; STD makes this possible. In automotive-assembly plants, such preplanning is rather essential.

13. *Persons with less training than qualified time-study persons can be taught to use STD.* As indicated before, with the proper format of some STD, the use of STD can become a clerical-type routine activity whereas the development of the STD requires a well-qualified industrial engineer.

14. *STD promotes standardized processes.* Not only are processes standardized, but processes are corrected when conditions on the job are not normal, such as improper feeds and speeds, as in metal cutting.

15. *STD permits a practical approach for highly repetitive operations.* Highly repetitive operations are natural for STD development whereas infrequent repetitive activities make STD development more difficult. The use of a power tool to drive screws is extensively done in many industrial plants. The hum of power tools can be heard in assembly plants where this type of repetitive operation is performed.

16. *STD aids in methods comparisons.* One of the big advantages of STD development is that of allowing the study of many different operations and the immediate implementation of methods improvements during the initial stages of STD development.

17. *By means of STD, reliable estimates can be made on new jobs.* Estimates derived from STD are more reliable and more quickly determined. In the bottom table of Fig. 13-10, if an estimate were needed on a new job "with sealer," six screws, and a "length plus width" of 10 inches, the extrapolated answer would be 0.0166 hour per job, determined from the horizontal rate of change of 0.0018 added to the adjacent block of 0.0148, which gives 0.0166. This can of course be determined and checked vertically where the rate of change is 0.0001 with a periodic round-off repeat, which is true in this example.

18. *By virtue of STD, standard hour savings can be determined before changes are made.* Standard hour savings can be determined by referring to Fig. 13-10 again. If the present job is assembled with a sealer, four screws, and a length plus width of 10 inches, the standard hours per job is 0.0130 in the bottom table. If a change is requested to assemble this particular assembly without sealer, then the top table value at four screws would be 0.0105 hour per job. The estimated standard hour savings would then be 0.0130 minus 0.0105, or 0.0025 hour per job.

There are other possible advantages that stem from the development and use of STD, but the majority have been listed. Another positive aspect worth mentioning again is that STD development is one of the most interesting and challenging techniques that can be used by an industrial engineer.

When STD Is Especially Needed

If some of the following conditions exist in an industrial company, it should be readily apparent that there is a special need for STD.

1. *Competitor's prices are lower.* If the competitor's prices are significantly lower along with the same degree of quality, STD development, with its price-cutting advantages, would be helpful.
2. *A greater time-study coverage of the plant is wanted.* In the long run, it takes less time to establish work standards with STD, so a greater coverage of all work with permanent work standards is possible with STD.
3. *Consistency between work standards on similar jobs is not satisfactory.* Consistency between work standards on similar operations is assured when standards are set with STD. The constant-time elements have already been averaged, so the element time will be the same for all operations where the element is performed. Similarly, variable-time elements have already-established formulas or tables, so the same answer will be derived with the same value of the independent variable or variables that affect the time.
4. *Permanent work standards or work allocations are needed before start of production.* Many industries have a changeover to a new model each year. Because of modifications in the product, changes are necessary in the work standards and/or assembly lines have to be rebalanced. All this work can be done before next year's production starts if STD is used as soon as the variables of the new products are known.

Generally speaking, if any of the 18 advantages listed for STD are desired, then STD is needed.

Areas Where Standard Time Data Can Be Applied

STD can theoretically be developed on any type of activity, but it should be economically feasible. The less repetition that there is of the elements of work, the more difficult and expensive it becomes to develop STD. STD can be applied for

1. Jobs that are similar in nature
2. Highly repetitive work
3. Jobs that have several standards to be set each day due to numerous combinations of variables
4. Long-cycled jobs that have repetitive elements within the long cycle
5. Delays
6. Indirect labor
   a. Janitorial work
   b. Maintenance
   c. Material handling
   d. Inspection
   e. Etc.

Throughout industry STD has been established in all these areas and in other areas that are not listed here. This list is not all inclusive but merely a representative sample of areas where STD has been successfully developed and applied.

DEVELOPMENT OF STANDARD TIME DATA

To visualize the procedure used in developing STD, refer to Fig. 13-1. This procedure will be covered in detail and demonstrated by means of the problem example.

Gather the Data

Time data can be obtained in either or both of the following ways:

1. From new time studies covering the scope of work under consideration made for the specific purpose of using them on a STD project
2. From time studies made in the regular course of time-study work and filed in such a manner so that they may be analyzed sometime in the future for development of STD

Caution must be exercised in following method 2. Consistent read points must be used on all studies, and all variables that may have an effect on the time must be recorded on each study; this recording is essential.

Other data Included with the time studies made under either method as indicated in the foregoing, other data (in addition to time recordings) should be obtained. It is almost impossible to record too much data along with each time study as it is made. Very often it is found in the analysis stage of development that too little has been recorded on the time studies. Still other data will have to be obtained from any and all sources where the required data are available. Such sources may be the same as those used for purposes of regular time-study work:

1. Supervisors and setup operators connected with the job under study
2. Process or maintenance workers, machine repairers, millwrights
3. Standards department personnel—time-study analysts, supervisors
4. Workers on the job
5. Other standard time data
6. Delay studies
7. Tool records
8. Maintenance records
9. Material records
10. Supply-usage records

Extent of detail of data Time studies should be made covering the range of work to which the standard time data are to be applied. If possible, the extremities of this range should be studied, with the greatest concentration of studies in the area in which the greatest number of jobs occur.

The number of time studies to be taken should be determined in the same way that the number of cycles to be timed were when taking an individual time study. In

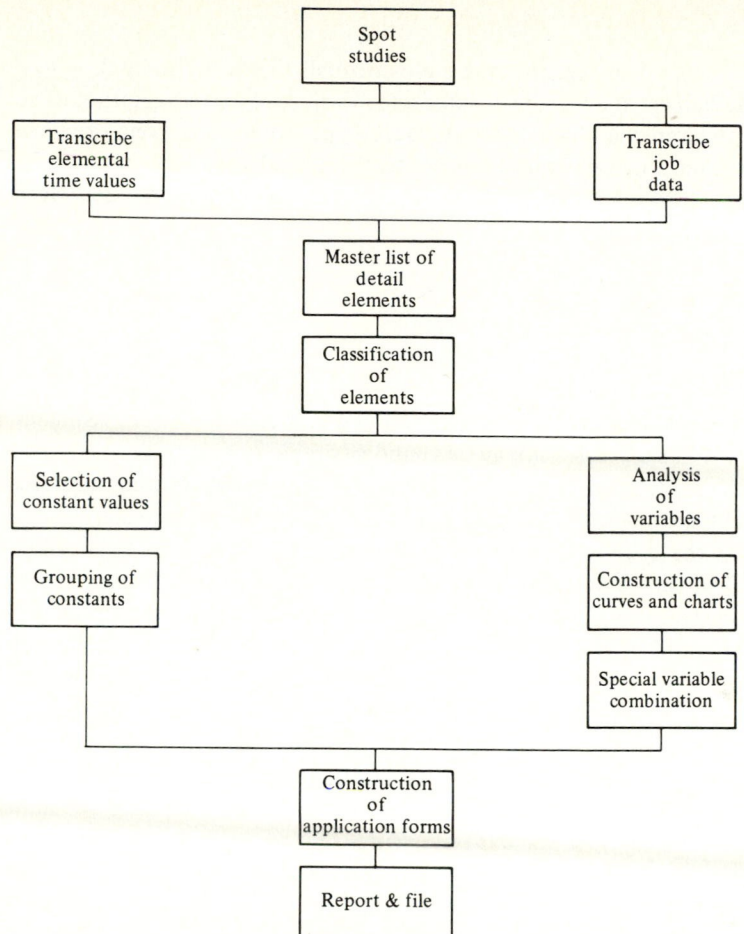

Figure 13-1 Steps in establishing standard-time data.

analyzing the data, it may later be found that more studies are needed, but a good rule of thumb for a starting point has shown that if 10 to 15 percent of the total jobs are covered, sufficient data will have been obtained. Obviously, a larger sample would be better and may be entirely practical in some cases. A larger sample is particularly required where variances in time for a given element may be caused by several different physical characteristics or other factors.

Even though some of the conditions surrounding a job at the time the individual studies are made may appear to have little or no influence on the variances in recorded times, such conditions should be noted on the time study. In analyzing the data later, it may be found that the least likely looking of these, or a combination of these (referred to as "correlation"), may have a direct bearing on the manner in which the actual times vary.

Compile the Data

The purpose of this step is to organize and summarize all the data obtained. If possible, all data should be posted on a spread sheet which will contain a description of all the elements and the variable characteristics, factors, or other conditions obtained when gathering the data. The only times posted on the spread sheet to be used in the actual calculation of the standard time data should be the allowed times from each time study for

1. Regular cyclical elements
2. Regular noncyclical elements (before prorating)
3. Irregular elements (before prorating)

On the latter two types of elements, the data pertaining to the standardized frequency should also be posted. In some cases it may be found advisable to post both the leveled average times and the allowed times to allow comparison or to aid in spotting variances due to minor deviations in method. Often it will be found advantageous to start such a spread sheet early in the stage when the data is being gathered, so that postings can be made as the individual time studies are completed. Actual analysis of the data begins with the posting, inasmuch as out-of-line conditions may be noticed indicating insufficient data were obtained at the time of observation, in some cases. This enables the time-study analyst to be on the lookout for additional data, which may be the cause of such out-of-line conditions, and to record the necessary information on subsequent studies. A sample spread sheet is shown in Fig. 13-2. (*Note*: The operator on this job will run both types of assemblies—with and without sealer—every working day. It is anticipated that work standards will be established for approximately 150 separate assembly part numbers using these standard time data. This assembly has no particular name, since the operation is entirely fictitious; it was developed solely to illustrate the techniques indicated in this procedure.)

Analyze the Data

Constant-time elements   In inspecting the spread sheet, note that the allowed times for some of the elements remain reasonably constant regardless of noted differences in physical characteristics, conditions of the job, or other factors. Such elements may be referred to as constant-time elements. Elements A–1 and B–1 and 3 in Fig. 13-2 are examples. In such cases, the reasons the times to perform such elements of work are constant are usually fairly obvious and may have been known in advance. If the times posted on the spread sheet for a constant-time element are the same, then this figure should be carried forward to the last column on the spread sheet, indicating that this time is normal for this element of work. If the times are not all the same, they should be averaged and carried forward to this final column on the spread sheet. It is assumed that the individual studies were made in accordance with the procedures in this manual for leveling and rating, and therefore, that there should be no manipulation of these figures. The same reasoning must apply as indicated in these basic pro-

Standard Time Data–Reference No. J37-50
Operation–Assemble cover to final assembly
Location–Final Assembly, Dept. A10

No.	Left side	Dist.	Right side	Dist.	Remarks
	Element description				
A-1	Step from roller conveyor to hopper beside prep. bench, get cover and *return to roller conveyor.*			6 '	A-1 element on jobs without sealer.
B-1	Step from roller conveyor to hopper. get cover and *turn to prep. bench.*			3 '	Elements B-1
B-2	Rest end of cover on bench	$\frac{1}{2}$ '	Get brush from holder	1 '	and B-2 on
	Wait		Dip brush in R.S. Sealer	$\frac{1}{2}$ '	jobs with
	Hold cover at 45° angle		Apply sealer to contacting edge of gasket	$\frac{1}{2}$ '	sealer only.
	Wait		Replace brush in holder	1 '	
	Carry cover to roller conveyor			2 '	
3	Assemble cover to frame over shaft extension– *align drilled holes in cover and frame.*	$1\text{-}\frac{1}{2}$ '	Get several $\frac{1}{4}$-20 × $\frac{3}{4}$ machine screws from hopper and palm.	1 '	
4	Hold cover in aligned position.		*Start screws in holes–* 1 to 2 turns, sufficient to hold cover in place.		
5	Wait–hand drifts toward first screw	$\frac{1}{2}$ '	Get Type K Thor electric driver (Spring suspended over top of assembly area)	$1\text{-}\frac{1}{2}$ '	
	Grasp driver bit sleeve on end of driver and help position over first screw.	$\frac{1}{2}$ '	Place driver in driving position	$1\text{-}\frac{1}{2}$ '	
	Drive all screws till torque ratchet slips				
	Release driver				
	Shove completed assembly along conveyor			1 '	
	Additional elements of work and delay				
6	Type 2–Stockhandling –Replenish R.S. sealer in brush can from drum in bay C-17, approximately hopper with screws from keg under prep. bench, twice before lunch and				
7	Type 4–Job preparation –At beginning of shift, get brush from can of solvent, remove excess and cleanup At end of shift wipe out excess sealer on edge of can, get can of night, 2.65 min.				
8	Type 6–Other delays –Receive instructions from supervision concerning schedules, get tack rags				
9	Personal –Operator not relieved by anyone, takes own personal time as required.				

Figure 13-2 Sample spread sheet. (Text for sections 6, 7, 8, and 9 continues on following page.)

cedures themselves. The allowed time on the individual time study reflects the standardized method of performing each particular element of work at normal tempo of movement. Leveling recorded times cannot be done in the office. Neither can rating be done on the spread sheet. Both these things must be done on the job at the time of observation and supported by factual evidence and thus recorded on the study. No times on the spread sheet should be thrown out simply because they are apparently

T.S. No.	37–507	37–511	37–501	37–509	37–510	37–506	37–505	37–516	37–515	37–504
Part No.	531218	530401	530463	529618	531219	530460	529032	532007	530301	530302
No. of Screws →	2	2	2	3	3	4	4	4	4	4
Sealer Used →	No	No	No	No	No	Yes	Yes	Yes	No	Yes
Cover Length →	3.00	3.12	3.14	4.65	4.92	5.14	5.53	5.93	6.32	6.32
Cover Width →	1.50	1.80	1.85	2.00	2.08	2.13	2.64	2.77	2.83	2.83
Element No. ↓					Time in Minutes					
A-1	.0592	.0601	.0583	.0554	.0641				.0620	
B-1						.0430	.0482	.0483		.0501
B-2						.112	.134	.128		.164
3	.0482	.0491	.0523	.0504	.0533	.0477	.0513	.0482	.0513	.0540
4	.103	.0981	.110	.166	.148	.189	.213	.203	.207	.196
5	.147	.167	.175	.202	.223	.220	.232	.242	.255	.267

35 ft. from job, at beginning of shift and after lunch. 3.30 min. each time, 6.60 min. total. Fill twice after lunch, 1.80 min. each time, 7.20 min. total.

solvent and wipe fairly dry on rags, hang on holder above sealer can, open can of sealer, 1.25 min. solvent from under bench, and place brush in solvent; close sealer can, clean up bench for the

from crib, etc. 3.85 min. total.

Standard personal allowance used.

Figure 13-2 (continued)

out-of-line with the others; if any times are thrown out, they should be supported with indisputable facts.

Variable-time elements After isolating the constant-time elements, the remaining elements on the spread sheet can be referred to as variable-time elements. Elements B–2 and 4 and 5 in Fig. 13-2 are examples. The time for such elements is influenced in

T.S. No.	37–514	37–503	37–513	37–508	37–512	37–502	SUMMARY			
Part No.	529035	531220	530304	527623	527625	530305				
No. of Screws →	4	4	6	6	6	8	Total time in minutes	Number of data	Average time in minutes	Allowed time in minutes *
Sealer Used →	Yes	Yes	Yes	Yes	Yes	Yes				
Cover Length →	7.90	8.49	9.48	9.87	9.87	9.10				
Cover Width →	3.51	3.89	3.64	3.26	4.77	8.51				
Element No. ↓	Time in Minutes									
A-1							.3591	6	.0599	.0599
B-1	.0430	.0464	.0472	.0452	.0491	.0460	.4665	10	.0467	.0467
B-2	.175	.164	.152	.176	.174	.210	1.589	10	−	.0579 + .00874 × (Length + width in inches) See Fig. 8
3	.0492	.0531	.0483	.0517	.0470	.0514	.807	16	.0504	.0504
4	.202	.214	.297	.318	.304	.395	3.3631	16	−	.0064 + .0494 × No. Screws (See Fig. 5)
5	.281	.293	.333	.347	.372	.460	4.216	16	−	.0647 + .0482 × No. Screws (See Fig. 4)
6	Note: Covers stocked to hoppers from stock room over assembly floor by stock handler.									13.80 per 8-hour shift
7	Job preparation & cleanup									3.90 per 8-hour shift
8	Other delays									3.85 per 8 hours
9	3.00 min. per hour allowed. Personal									24.00 per 8 hours

*Note: The last summary column is blank until *after* the analysis of variable elements is completed.

Figure 13-2 (continued)

some manner by one or more physical characteristics or conditions of the job. It may or may not be apparent which of these factors affect the time to perform these elements of work.

For the most part, determination of the effect of the various physical characteristics upon the time required to perform an element is a trial-and-error proposition. This process involves graphical analysis of the data and the determination of the relation between the time and each physical characteristic or other condition of the job. To simplify this process, the first step should be that of selecting the most obvious characteristic and then plotting on graph paper the time values for the element from the spread sheet against the various values of this characteristic. Figure 13-3 shows a series of points plotted in this manner for element 5 (Fig. 13-2). This element consists of driving several 3/4-inch machine screws, one at a time, with a type K Thor electric driver.

Since the characteristic of the number of screws has been selected because it obviously has a direct influence on the amount of time necessary to perform this element of work, we can expect that the plotted points will graphically indicate the general trend of the relation. In such a situation, a straight-line curve which does not radically deviate from the plotted points can be drawn by inspection. Figure 13-4 illustrates such a curve. Standard times for values of the characteristic which were not studied can be read directly from this straight-line curve. For example, the time for driving five screws would be 0.31 minute. For some applications, this simplified method of determining time values may be entirely adequate.

For many applications, however, the determination of an equation for a straight-line curve is practical and constitutes a better method of actually using the standard time data. Furthermore, the determination of such an equation is a relatively simple matter, as shown in the following for the straight-line curve in Fig. 13-4.

Extending a line vertically from eight screws until it touches the straight-line curve and then going horizontally until it meets the ordinate yields a value of 0.455 minute. The extension of the straight-line curve crosses the vertical axis for zero screws at 0.065 minute. This figure (0.065 minute) indicates the constant time (intercept) for driving any number of screws and constitutes the normal time required to get the driver, place it into approximate working position, and get rid of the driver after the last screw has been driven.

Subtracting 0.065 from 0.455, we find that the difference of 0.39 includes the normal time required to drive all eight screws and move the driver between screws.

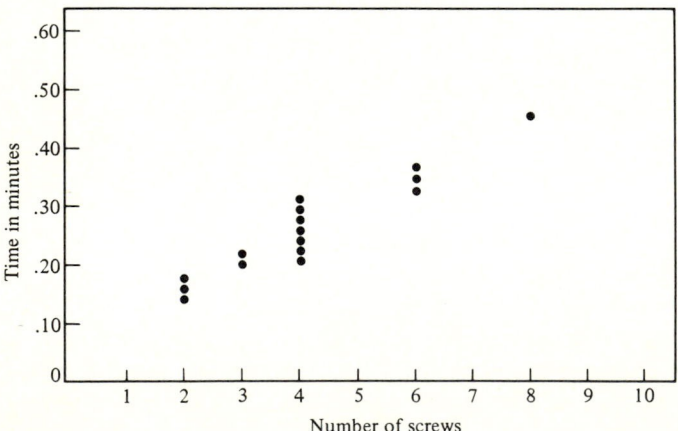

Figure 13-3 Scatter diagram; element 5.

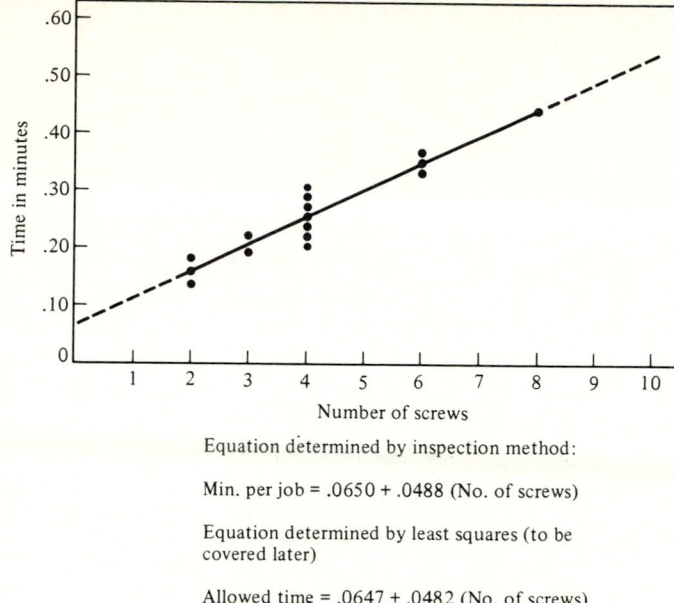

Equation determined by inspection method:

Min. per job = .0650 + .0488 (No. of screws)

Equation determined by least squares (to be
covered later)

Allowed time = .0647 + .0482 (No. of screws)

Figure 13-4 Straight-line curve drawn by inspection; element 5.

Dividing 0.39 by 8 (screws), we get the quotient of 0.0488 minute, which is the normal time required to move the driver to each screw and drive it. This 0.0488
minute is the variable time (slope) per screw.

The time for this element is thus made up of two parts—the intercept, 0.0650 minute,
and the slope, 0.0488 minute.

The time for driving any number of screws (included in the original scope of this
standard-time-data project) can be expressed as

$$\text{Allowed time in minutes} = 0.065 + 0.0488 \text{ (number of screws)}$$

By substituting in this equation, allowed times for driving five or seven screws can
be obtained even though time studies were not made on these numbers. Caution
should always be exercised when obtaining allowed times for values of the variable
characteristics which are outside the scope of the original data. This is called "extrapo-
lation." Referring to the previous example, we find that allowed times for one, nine,
or ten screws might be obtained with reasonable reliability, even though these values
were not originally included in the scope or range of the data gathered. Extrapolating
to obtain allowed times for 15, 20, or 30 screws, however, might produce unreliable
results, since these values are far removed from the known data. In such cases, additional data should be obtained.

Element 4 is the same type of element as 5, as Fig. 13-5 indicates.

Graphical analysis for each of the variable-time elements should be continued
until all have been resolved. For many elements, however, the selection of a charac-
istic for plotting along the horizontal axis (x axis, or abscissa) may not be so easy nor

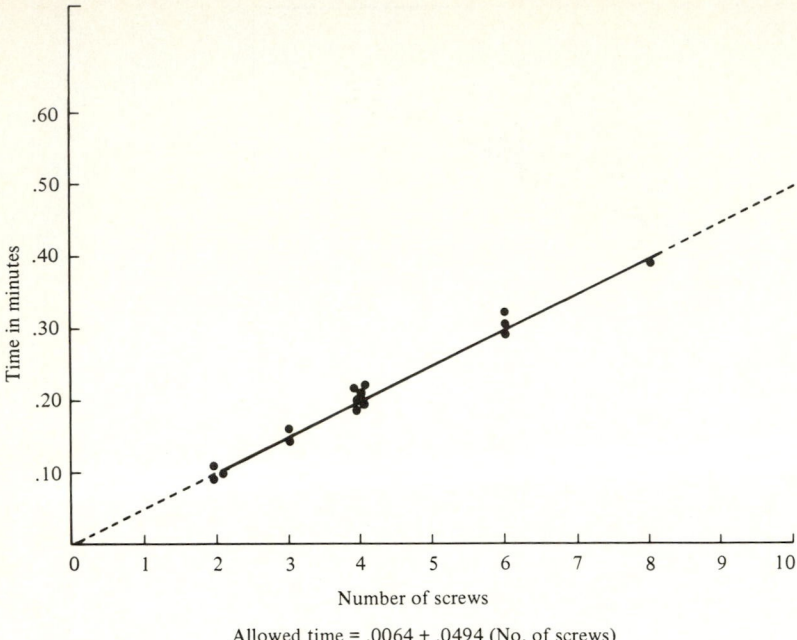

Allowed time = .0064 + .0494 (No. of screws)

Figure 13-5 Scatter diagram and curve for element 4.

may it produce a scatter diagram which indicates a definite trend of the time data in relation to the characteristic. The process of resolving these elements may be more or less tedious, depending on the kinds of elements being analyzed and the experience and ingenuity of the analyst.

When single characteristics fail to produce scatter diagrams which conclusively indicate a good trend for drawing the curves by inspection, combinations of characteristics often aid in or entirely resolve the issue. Examples of such combinations can be found in girth, diagonal, area, length plus width, density, ratios of width to length and diameter to height, squares and cubes of dimensions, and products of two or more characteristics. Element B-2 (Fig. 13-2) is an example of this condition. The time required to apply the sealer to the preassembled gasket seems to vary with the size of the cover. In this case, the summation of the length and width indicates the size and relates directly to the time allowed for applying the sealer on each of the studies. In Figs. 13-6 to 13-8, note that plotting the time data against either the width or the length does not produce a trend as conclusive as that obtained when plotting the time data against the summation of these two characteristics. The curves in Figs. 13-6 and 13-7 were drawn by inspection; the curve in Fig. 13-8 was generated by the method of least squares.

In a similar manner, the search should continue for a scatter diagram which indicates the best trend of the data until all variable-time elements have been resolved. It

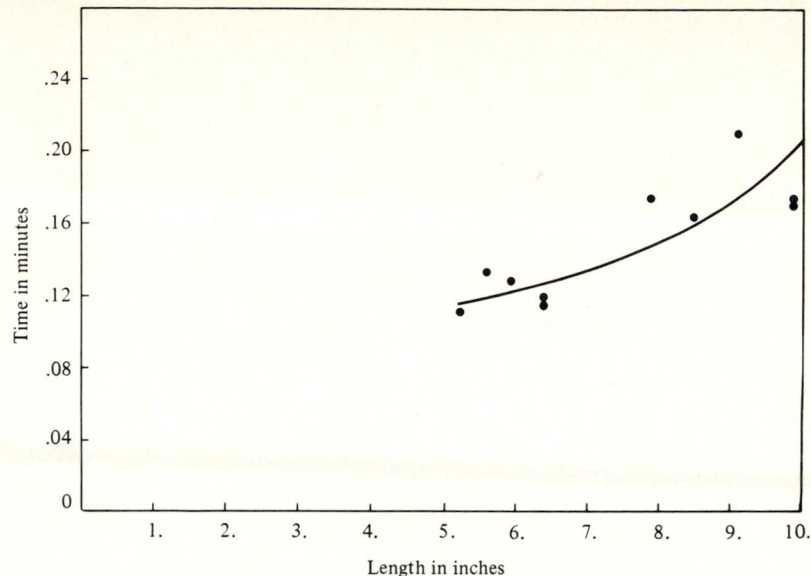

Figure 13-6 Scatter diagram and curve for element B-2.

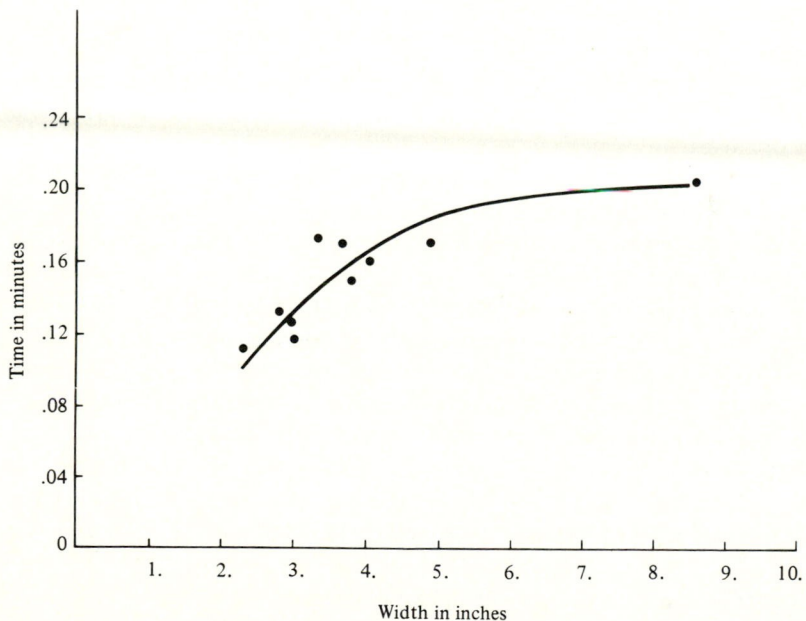

Figure 13-7 Scatter diagram and curve for element B-2.

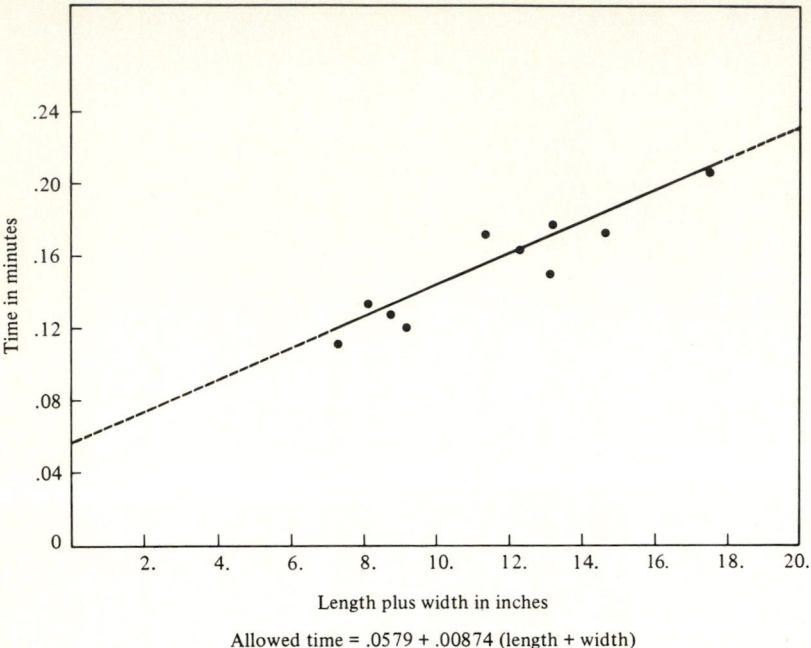

Allowed time = .0579 + .00874 (length + width)

Figure 13-8 Scatter diagram and curve for element B-2.

will be advantageous, usually, to obtain straight lines instead of curves, since the determination of the straight-line equation is much simpler than is that for any of the various types of curves.

Rectilinear graph paper is the simplest type to use, although paper with logarithmic and semilogarithmic rulings may be more appropriate in some situations.

In addition to the inspection method, there are many other ways of determining the curve or line of regression for a scatter diagram. Of these, the least-squares method is one which accurately gives the one curve of best fit. However, the inspection method of curve fitting is by far the simplest and it is fairly accurate when used by a competent analyst. An occasional check with the least-squares method will disclose the relative accuracy of the job being done when using the inspection method. Such checks should be made at the discretion of the individual plant or division.

In the following, the least-squares method of determining the best straight-line curve for the data in Fig. 13-3 (element 5) is exemplified. It also shows the relative accuracy of the curve in Fig. 13-4, which was previously determined by the inspection method.

The general equation for a straight line in two dimensions is

$$Y = A + BX$$

In standard-time-data calculations,

Y = time values (for each particular element)
A = intercept (intersection of the extension of the curve
    and the y axis)
B = slope of curve (amount of change in time for each
    change in numerical value of the characteristic)
X = numerical value of the variable characteristic (for
    example, in Figs. 13-3 and 13-4, the number of screws)

When both the A and B values have been estimated, the straight line of best fit has been determined.

The following normal equations are to be used in solving the equation $Y = a + bX$:

$$\Sigma Y = Na + b\Sigma X \quad \text{and} \quad \Sigma XY = \Sigma Xa + b\Sigma X^2$$

where N = number of data (in Fig. 13-2, 16)

X	X^2	Y	XY
2	4	0.147	0.294
2	4	0.167	0.334
2	4	0.175	0.350
3	9	0.202	0.606
3	9	0.223	0.669
4	16	0.220	0.880
4	16	0.232	0.928
4	16	0.242	0.968
4	16	0.255	1.020
4	16	0.267	1.068
4	16	0.281	1.124
4	16	0.293	1.172
6	36	0.333	1.998
6	36	0.347	2.082
6	36	0.372	2.232
8	64	0.460	3.680
Σ (summation = 66)	314	4.216	19.405

Substituting in the two normal equations, we get

$$4.216 = 16a + 66b \quad \text{and} \quad 19.405 = 66a + 314b$$

Solving these equations simultaneously to obtain the value of b and multiplying the first equation by 66/16, or 4.125, and subtracting from the second equation, we get

$$19.405 = 66a + 314.00b$$
$$17.391 = 66a + 272.25b$$

$$2.014 = \quad 41.75b$$
$$41.75b = \quad 2.014$$
$$b = \quad 0.0482 \quad \text{slope}$$

Substituting in the first normal equation, $\Sigma Y = Na + b\Sigma X$, to obtain the value of a, we get

$$
\begin{aligned}
4.216 &= 16a + (0.0482)(66) \\
4.216 - (0.0482)(66) &= 16a \\
4.216 - 3.182 &= 16a \\
16a &= 1.0348 \\
a &= 0.0647 \quad \text{intercept}
\end{aligned}
$$

The equation for this element, as determined by the least-squares method, is

$$\text{Allowed time} = 0.0647 \text{ minute} + 0.0482 \text{ (number of screws)}$$

An alternate method that may be more desirable would be that of solving for a and b directly using the following equations.

$$
b = \frac{\Sigma XY - \dfrac{(\Sigma X)(\Sigma Y)}{N}}{\Sigma X^2 - \dfrac{(\Sigma X)^2}{N}} = \frac{19.405 - \dfrac{(66)(4.216)}{16}}{314 - \dfrac{(66)^2}{16}} = 0.0482
$$

$$
a = \frac{\Sigma Y}{N} - \frac{b(\Sigma X)}{N} = \frac{4.216}{16} - \frac{0.0482(66)}{16} = 0.0647
$$

Of course, the answers will be the same using either set of equations. A word of *caution*. The equations should be used for linear data only. If the data are nonlinear, then the line of best fit will not be an equation of the first degree. Computer programs are available to satisfy either situation, thereby also minimizing the calculation time necessary and eliminating the error that manual calculations are prone to. If computer programs are used to determine the equation of the line, one should plot the data on graph paper, unless this plotting is also done on the computer. All these applications including nonlinear regression, are commonly used today.

Finalize the Data

The purpose of this step is to arrange the STD to best facilitate its use. The specific arrangement of the data in a particular situation may take any one of several different forms. Such arrangements of data, which should be made at the discretion of the individual plant or division, will depend on

1. The amount of STD
2. The purpose for which the STD will be used
3. The frequency with which the STD will be used

Following are some of the general forms that the arrangement of the STD can take.

1. Preprinted time-study form.

   a. The elements are described and shown in sequence. STD for constant-time elements are preprinted and the formula for the STD for variable-time elements are preprinted with spaces provided for inserting the values of the variables. Arrangement also should include the defined method of handling all allowances which may also be classified as STD. The calculation sheet shown in Fig. 13-9 is an excellent example.

Standard time data–Reference No. J37–50
Assemble cover to final assembly–Dept. A10

Part No. _____ No. of screws ____ Sealer used: Yes / No   Length _____ in.
                                                     Width _____ in.
T.S. File No. _____ Date _____   Total _____ in.

Data applicable for $\frac{1}{4}$ – 20 X $\frac{3}{4}$ mach. screws, type R.S. Sealer, rectangular cover & gasket assemblies (pre-assembled), not over 10 screws nor 20.25" lgth + wdth

El. No.	Abbreviated element description and standard times in minutes for each (details contained in file J37–50)	Allowed minutes per job
A-1	*For jobs without sealer only* Get cover from hopper and return to roller conveyor. .0599 per job	
B-1	*For jobs with sealer only* Get cover from hopper and turn to prep. bench. .0467 per job	
B-2	Brush sealer on contact face of cover and gasket assembly. .0579 + .00874 X _____ (length + width)	
3	*For all jobs* Assemble cover, align holes, get screws from hopper. .0504 per job.	.0504
4	Start screws–1 to 2 turns–in all cover holes .0064 + .0494 X _____ (No. of screws)	
5	Drive all screws. Use type K Thor electric driver. .0647 + .0482 X _____ (No. of screws)	
	Total time for repetitive elements	

	Additional elements of work and delay (details contained in file J37–50)	Allowed min./8 hrs.
6	Type 2–Stockhandling–For sealer 6.60 min. For screws 7.20 min.	13.80
7	Type 4–Job preparation & cleanup–Start of shift 1.25 min. End of shift 2.65 min.	3.90
8	Type 6–Other delays–Schedule instructions, get tack rags, etc.	3.85
9	Personal	24.00
	Total	45.55

Calculation of work standard

Total shift time 480.00 min. less 45.55 min. = 434.45 net working min./shift

434.45 ÷ _____ (total time, el. 1 thru 5) = _____ Jobs per shift

Jobs per shift _____ ÷ 8 = _____ Average hourly production

1. hr. ÷ _____ (average hourly production) = _____ Std. hrs. per job

---

Figure 13-9 Finalized standard-time-data (STD) calculation sheet.

    b. STD and values of the variables are arranged in finalized tables. The finalized rate table shown in Fig. 13-10 on the facing page is an excellent example of this form of STD. When possible, this form should be used, because all necessary calculations have already been made.

2. Tables of STD arranged in loose-leaf binders that may include direct reading graphs, tables, or multivariable charts.
3. An overall formula shown for a complete operation which combines the STD for all constant-time and variable-time elements. When using multiple regression analysis to develop STD, such a formula would be obtained directly from the computer output.

The following points should be considered when finalizing the data in any STD project.

1. If determined, equations should be recorded on each graph.
2. Graphs should be adequately identified for reference purposes.
3. If the element descriptions do not appear in the final form, appropriate reference showing where these details can be found should be included in the final form.
4. The standardized allowances should either appear on the final form or be condensed and summarized if appropriate reference is given.
5. Any limitations on the types of jobs to be covered by the particular STD should be clearly stated.
6. All records of the time studies, spread sheets, graphs, work sheets, computer outputs, and final summary sheets should be dated, initialed by the analyst, given a STD project reference number, and filed.

The finalized STD should be in an easy-to-use form that requires minimum time to determine a work standard. Even needless repetition of calculations can occur in the use of STD if the final format of the STD is not the best. It is not always possible to get the data in the finalized rate-table form shown in Fig. 13-10, but this format should be the goal for the finalized form when circumstances are correct.

MULTIVARIABLE CHARTS

In Fig. 13-10, there are only two independent variables needed to determine the work standard—the number of screws and the total of the length plus the width of the cover. In more-complex problems, there may be three or more independent variables needed to determine the answer. To accommodate more variables for a quick answer, as in Fig. 13-10, construction of a multivariable chart (MVC) is necessary.

    The reader is no doubt already familiar with standard data development—gathering data by making selective time studies, compiling data on spread sheets which contain all possible elements, and controlling variables, analyzing data (determining constants and variables), and finalizing data. In essence, the final form of the STD for use by the time-study person is the selected item for discussion, where more variables are involved in a problem.

Standard time data–Reference No. J37–50
Assemble cover to final assembly–Dept. A10

Part No. _____ No. of screws _____ Sealer used: Yes / No   Length _____ in.
Width _____ in.
T. S. File No. _____ Date _____   Total _____ in.

Data applicable for $\frac{1}{4}$ – 20 × $\frac{3}{4}$ mach. screws, type R. S. Sealer, rectangular cover and gasket assemblies (pre-assembled), not over 10 screws nor 20.25″ lgth + wdth

Assemble without sealer

No. of screws	2	3	4	5	6	7	8	9	10
Std. hrs./job	.00693	.00873	.0105	.0123	.0141	.0159	.0177	.0195	.0213
Avg. hrly prod.	144.	115.	95.0	81.1	70.8	62.8	56.5	51.3	46.9

Assemble with sealer—Standard hours per job

Length + width (in inches)	Number of screws								
	2	3	4	5	6	7	8	9	10
5.26 to 5.75	.00864	.0104	.0122						
5.76 to 6.25	.00872	.0105	.0123		Additional time studies				
6.26 to 6.75	.00880	.0106	.0124						
6.76 to 7.25	.00888	.0107	.0125						
7.26 to 7.75	.00896	.0108	.0126		desirable before extending				
7.76 to 8.25	.00905	.0108	.0126						
8.26 to 8.75	.00913	.0109	.0127						
8.76 to 9.25	.00921	.0110	.0128	.0146	data in this area.				
9.26 to 9.75			.0129	.0147					
9.76 to 10.25			.0130	.0148					
10.26 to 10.75			.0130	.0148	.0166				
10.76 to 11.25			.0131	.0149	.0167				
11.26 to 11.75			.0132	.0150	.0168				
11.76 to 12.25			.0133	.0151	.0169	.0187			
12.26 to 12.75			.0134	.0152	.0170	.0188			
12.76 to 13.25			.0134	.0152	.0170	.0188			
13.26 to 13.75			.0135	.0153	.0171	.0189			
13.76 to 14.25			.0136	.0154	.0172	.0190	.0208		
14.26 to 14.75				.0155	.0173	.0191	.0209		
14.76 to 15.25				.0156	.0174	.0192	.0210	.0228	.0245
15.26 to 15.75				.0156	.0174	.0192	.0210	.0228	.0246
15.76 to 16.25					.0175	.0193	.0211	.0229	.0247
16.26 to 16.75	Additional time studies				.0176	.0194	.0212	.0230	.0248
16.76 to 17.25					.0177	.0195	.0213	.0231	.0249
17.26 to 17.75						.0196	.0214	.0232	.0250
17.76 to 18.25	desirable before extending					.0196	.0214	.0232	.0250
18.26 to 18.75						.0197	.0215	.0233	.0251
18.76 to 19.25							.0216	.0234	.0252
19.26 to 19.75	data in this area.						.0217	.0235	.0253
19.76 to 20.25							.0218	.0236	.0254

Stds. include 45.55 min. delay/8 hrs. Supporting data in File J37–50

Figure 13-10 Finalized STD rate table.

Assume that time studies have been made on selected operations, data were compiled on the spread sheet, data were analyzed in regard to constant and variable elements, and tables were made from the graphs or equations. In making tables from graphs, it is important to draw off even increments of time and let the variable spread be dictated by the time increments. Of course, this is extremely important when there is a nonlinear condition and a slope variation. The size of the increment is also important; it depends on the degree of accuracy desired and the amount of time variation wanted between similar operations. Since a regular time study can take up to several hours to establish a work standard, and since it takes several minutes or more to establish a work standard by the standard data method (excluding development time), by going a few steps more, one can reduce the time per standard (table lookup of calculations) to seconds.

For simplicity, the problem that follows will omit the element description. There has been no attempt to have problems bear any resemblance to any particular type of operation, because the prime concern is to demonstrate the method of consolidation of data. Remember that the time studies were taken and the constant-time elements were determined with the results shown. The variable-element times were plotted and tables were developed from the graphs (see Fig. 13-11).

The nine elements in Fig. 13-11 represent the regular cycle of work. (When a variable is between table values shown, use the larger variable-time value.)

Standard noncyclic times were also tabulated during the time studies with the following results:

Stockhandling	0.02 minute per piece
Personal	24 minutes per shift
Tool change and adjustment	10 minutes per shift
Servicing equipment	4 minutes per shift
Preparation and cleanup	6 minutes per shift

All operators in this area work an 8-hour shift.

Element No.   *Constant time value or variable table*

1 — .05 min.

2

O.D.	1	1.5	2	2.5	3	3.5	4
*Min.	.05	.06	.07	.08	.09	.10	.11

3 — .04 min.

4

Wt. (lbs)	2.5	5	7.5	10	12.5	15	
*Min.	.04	.05	.06	.07	.08	.09	

5

No. of screws	2	3	4	5	6	7	8
Min.	.04	.07	.10	.13	.16	.19	.22

6

No. of screws	2	3	4	5	6	7	8
Min.	.05	.09	.13	.17	.21	.25	.29

7 — .04 min.

8

Length (in.)	6	11	15	18	20
*Min.	.06	.07	.08	.09	.10

9 — .03 min.

Figure 13-11 List of all elements.

Procedure Develop a multivariable chart[1] using *all* the data from the time studies. Show final values in pieces per hour.

Step 1 Combine elements 5 and 6, since these elements depend on the same variable (see Fig. 13-12).

No. of screws	2	3	4	5	6	7	8
Min.	.09	.16	.23	.30	.37	.44	.51

Figure 13-12 Combining elements 5 and 6.

Step 2 Start making the multivariable chart by combining the outside diameter and weight from elements 2 and 4 into one table (see Fig. 13-13).

Step 3 Convert Fig. 13-13 by extracting the time values from the main body and place these time values in sequence along the border (see Fig. 13-14).

Time reference lines to get main body of time values →		1	1.5	2	2.5	3	3.5	4	O.D.
		.05	.06	.07	.08	.09	.10	.11	Min.
2.5	.04	.09	.10	.11	.12	.13	.14	.15	
5	.05	.10	.11	.12	.13	.14	.15	.16	
7.5	.06	.11	.12	.13	.14	.15	.16	.17	← Total time for
10	.07	.12	.13	.14	.15	.16	.17	.18	elem. 2 and 4
12.5	.08	.13	.14	.15	.16	.17	.18	.19	depending on
15	.09	.14	.15	.16	.17	.18	.19	.20	values of O.D.
lbs.									and wt
Wt.	Min.								

Figure 13-13 Combining the outside diameter and weight tables.

Border time (reference line for main body of time values in multi-variable chart)

			O.D.					
1	1.5	2	2.5	3	3.5	4	▼	
2.5							.09	
5	2.5						.10	
7.5	5	2.5					.11	
10	7.5	5	2.5				.12	
12.5	10	7.5	5	2.5			.13	
15	12.5	10	7.5	5	2.5		.14	
	15	12.5	10	7.5	5	2.5	.15	
		15	12.5	10	7.5	5	.16	
			15	12.5	10	7.5	.17	
Wt. (lbs.)			15	12.5	10	.18		
				15	12.5	10	.19	
					15	12.5	.20	
						15		

Example

From previous Fig. 13-13; O.D. of 2.5 and wt. of 10 lbs, the value is .15, so place 10 under 2.5 O.D. and across from .15 min., etc.

Figure 13-14 Creating a vertical time reference line.

[1] Phil Carroll, *How to Chart Data*, McGraw-Hill, New York, 1960, pp. 181–230.

After border times have been listed as shown in Fig. 13-14, place the proper weight in the blank space with the proper (vertical) outside diameter and (horizontal) time to match the previous table. This table now covers all possible combinations of outside diameters and weight in the range of the data.

At this point, the first half of the tables necessary for the multivariable chart is finished. The same combining must now be done with the other two variables, the number of screws (elements 5 and 6) and the length of the part (element 8). Remember that in Fig. 13-12, elements 5 and 6 were already combined.

Step 4 Use the same procedure here as in Fig. 13-13 (see Fig. 13-15).

Step 5 Figure 13-15 is now converted to Fig. 13-16. The procedure is the same as was used in converting Fig. 13-13 to Fig. 13-14.

Step 6 The second half of the MVC is now ready for use. Figures 13-14 and 13-16 are now placed in the exact position as that shown in Fig. 13-17. Figure 13-14 is in position on the left side and Fig. 13-16 is in position at the top. The main body of time values is merely the total of the two intersecting border times or time-reference line values. As can be seen, it is necessary to have a vertical and a horizontal time reference line placed together at 90° to each other without any overlap of values.

For instance, the first border row time value is 0.15 and the first border column time value is 0.09; these two values added together equal 0.24 minute.

		2	3	4	5	6	7	8	No. of screws
		.09	.16	.23	.30	.37	.44	.51	Min.
6	.06	.15	.22	.29	.36	.43	.50	.57	
11	.07	.16	.23	.30	.37	.44	.51	.58	To decrease size of MV Chart, do not use these row values for border times in next table.
15	.08	.17	.24	.31	.38	.45	.52	.59	
18	.09	.18	.25	.32	.39	.46	.53	.60	
20	.10	.19	.26	.33	.40	.47	.54	.61	
(in.) Length	Min.								

Figure 13-15 Combining the screws and length tables.

	No. of screws							In.	
	2	3	4	5	6	7	8	20	L
	2	3	4	5	6	7	8	18	e
2	3	4	5	6	7	8		15	n g
2	3	4	5	6	7	8		11	t
2	3	4	5	6	7	8		6	h

.15|.17|.19|.22|.24|.26|.29|.31|.33|.36|.38|.40|.43|.45|.47|.50|.52|.54|.57|.59|.61 ← border time values

Figure 13-16 Creating a horizontal time reference line.

No. of screws

Length (in.)

			2		3		4		5		6		7		8	20
			2		3		4		5		6		7		8	18
		2		3		4		5		6		7		8		15
		2		3		4		5		6		7		8		11

Reference border times

O.D.

1	1.5	2	2.5	3	3.5	4		2		3		4		5		6		7		8		6
								.15	.17	.19	.22	.24	.26	.29	.31	.33	.36	.38	.40	.43	.45	.47	.50	.52	.54	.57	.59	.61
2.5							.09	.24	.26	.28	.31	.33	.35	.38	.40	.42	.45	.47	.49	.52	.54	.56	.59	.61	.63	.66	.68	.70
5	2.5						.10	.25	.27	.29	.32	.34	.36	.39	.41	.43	.46	.48	.50	.53	.55	.57	.60	.62	.64	.67	.69	.71
7.5	5	2.5					.11	.26	.28	.30	.33	.35	.37	.40	.42	.44	.47	.49	.51	.54	.56	.58	.61	.63	.65	.68	.70	.72
10	7.5	5	2.5				.12	.27	.29	.31	.34	.36	.38	.41	.43	.45	.48	.50	.52	.55	.57	.59	.62	.64.	.66	.69	.71	.73
12.5	10	7.5	5	2.5			.13	.28	.30	.32	.35	.37	.39	.42	.44	.46	.49	.51	.53	.56	.58	.60	.63	.65	.67	.70	.72	.74
15	12.5	10	7.5	5	2.5		.14	.29	.31	.33	.36	.38	.40	.43	.45	.47	.50	.52	.54	.57	.59	.61	.64	.66	.68	.71	.73	.75
	15	12.5	10	7.5	5	2.5	.15	.30	.32	.34	.37	.39	.41	.44	.46	.48	.51	.53	.55	.58	.60	.62	.65	.67	.69	.72	.74	.76
		15	12.5	10	7.5	5	.16	.31	.33	.35	.38	.40	.42	.45	.47	.49	.52	.54	.56	.59	.61	.63	.66	.68	.70	.73	.75	.77
			15	12.5	10	7.5	.17	.32	.34	.36	.39	.41	.43	.46	.48	.50	.53	.55	.57	.60	.62	.64	.67	.69	.71	.74	.76	.78
				15	12.5	10	.18	.33	.35	.37	.40	.42	.44	.47	.49	.51	.54	.56	.58	.61	.63	.65	.68	.70	.72	.75	.77	.79
	Weight (lbs)				15	12.5	.19	.34	.36	.38	.41	.43	.45	.48	.50	.52	.55	.57	.59	.62	.64	.66	.69	.71	.73	.76	.78	.80
						15	.20	.35	.37	.39	.42	.44	.46	.49	.51	.53	.56	.58	.60	.63	.65	.67	.70	.72	.74	.77	.79	.81

Figure 13-17 MVC with variable element times.

Other examples

Horizontal border time	Vertical border time	MV chart time
0.36	0.14	0.50
0.50	0.18	0.68
0.61	0.20	0.81

With all the main body times posted in Fig. 13-17, the total time for elements 2, 4, 5, 6, and 8 can now be read in this manner.

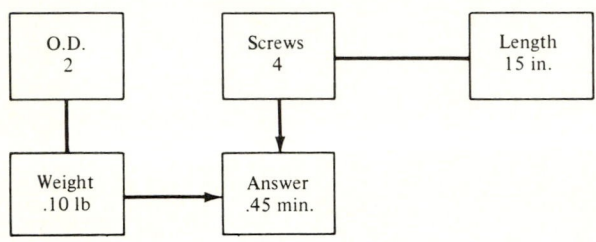

Step 7 Referring to the original data, we find that elements 1, 3, 7, and 9 can now be brought into the MV chart. These are the cyclic constant elements in minutes per piece. The one noncyclic time for stock handling can be brought in at this time because it is also in minutes per piece. The total time is then calculated for elements 1, 3, 7, 9, and stock handling.

	Minute per piece
Element 1	0.05
Element 3	0.04
Element 7	0.04
Element 9	0.03
Stockhandling	0.02
Total constant time	0.18

The total constant time is now added to *each* of the main body of times in the MVC in Fig. 13-17. Now is a good time to remove the time reference lines or border time values. The resulting MVC is shown in Fig. 13-18.

Adding total constant element times to the main body of times in the MV chart was done for simplicity of presentation. To save time, the total constant element time can be added to *either* the reference border time row or column in Fig. 13-17 *before* the main body of times values are added. In this manner, the immediate results will be Fig. 13-18—merely doing two steps in one.

Length (in.)

								2			3			4			5			6			7			8	20
								2			3			4			5			6			7			8	18
							2			3			4			5			6			7			8		15
O.D. in.							2			3			4			5			6			7			8		11
1	1.5	2	2.5	3	3.5	4	2			3			4			5			6			7			8		6
2.5								.42	.44	.46	.49	.51	.53	.56	.58	.60	.63	.65	.67	.70	.72	.74	.77	.79	.81	.84	.86	.88
5	2.5							.43	.45	.47	.50	.52	.54	.57	.59	.61	.64	.66	.68	.71	.73	.75	.78	.80	.82	.85	.87	.89
7.5	5	2.5						.44	.46	.48	.51	.53	.55	.58	.60	.62	.65	.67	.69	.72	.74	.76	.79	.81	.83	.86	.88	.90
10	7.5	5	2.5					.45	.47	.49	.52	.54	.56	.59	.61	.63	.66	.68	.70	.73	.75	.77	.80	.82	.84	.87	.89	.91
12.5	10	7.5	5	2.5				.46	.48	.50	.53	.55	.57	.60	.62	.64	.67	.69	.71	.74	.76	.78	.81	.83	.85	.88	.90	.92
15	12.5	10	7.5	5	2.5			.47	.49	.51	.54	.56	.58	.61	.63	.65	.68	.70	.72	.75	.77	.79	.82	.84	.86	.89	.91	.93
	15	12.5	10	7.5	5	2.5		.48	.50	.52	.55	.57	.59	.62	.64	.66	.69	.71	.73	.76	.78	.80	.83	.85	.87	.90	.92	.94
		15	12.5	10	7.5	5		.49	.51	.53	.56	.58	.60	.63	.65	.67	.70	.72	.74	.77	.79	.81	.84	.86	.88	.90	.93	.95
			15	12.5	10	7.5		.50	.52	.54	.57	.59	.61	.64	.66	.68	.71	.73	.75	.78	.80	.82	.85	.87	.89	.92	.94	.96
				15	12.5	10		.51	.53	.55	.58	.60	.62	.65	.67	.69	.72	.74	.76	.79	.81	.83	.86	.88	.90	.93	.95	.97
	Weight lbs				15	12.5		.52	.54	.56	.59	.61	.63	.66	.68	.70	.73	.75	.77	.80	.82	.84	.87	.89	.91	.94	.96	.98
						15		.53	.55	.57	.60	.62	.64	.67	.69	.71	.74	.76	.78	.81	.83	.85	.88	.90	.92	.95	.97	.99

Cycle time + delays in min/pc.

Figure 13-18 MVC with variable plus constant element times.

Step 8 Last of all, the other noncyclic times must be allowed. Refer once again to the original data. There are four noncyclic items that must now be considered and handled in this manner.

	Minutes per shift
Personal	24
Tool change and adjustment	10
Servicing equipment	4
Preparation and cleanup	6
Total time	44

480 minutes per shift – 44 minutes per shift = 436 minutes per shift

$$\frac{436 \text{ minutes per shift}}{8 \text{ hours per shift}} = 54.5 \text{ minutes per hour available for the other work}$$

All times values in the MV chart in Fig. 13-18 must be divided into the 54.5 minutes per hour.

Example

$$\frac{54.5 \text{ minutes per hour}}{0.42 \text{ minute per piece}} = 130 \text{ pieces per hour}$$

The 130 pieces per hour now replaces the 0.42 minute per piece to form the MV chart in Fig. 13-19. The rest of the calculations are made in the same manner to have the MV chart read in pieces per hour. Possible errors are easily detected while making the final MV chart entries, because of the increasing or decreasing trend of the data.

When changes occur because of product improvement, model change, etc., the production standard will change according to the changes in the controlling variables. The controlling variables can be obtained from

1. Sample parts of the new or changed part
2. Process sheets
3. Operation description sheets
4. Etc.

Periodic studies are necessary, and if there is a change in the work method that affects time, the MV chart and other data must be updated.

In conclusion, a few general points should be made.

1. The MV chart can be used in many other areas of engineering besides time-and-motion study.
2. The MV chart can be used for line-balance-type operations, but should combine only elements of work that must be done by one operator. To aid in attaining an

No. of screws — PCS./HR

O.D. in.							No. of screws (2 → 8) · Length (in.): 20, 18, 15, 11, 6																				
1	1.5	2	2.5	3	3.5	4	2	2	2	3	3	3	4	4	4	5	5	5	6	6	6	7	7	7	8	8	8
2.5							130	124	118	111	107	103	97	94	91	87	84	81	78	76	74	71	69	67	65	63	62
5	2.5						127	121	116	109	105	101	96	92	89	85	83	80	77	75	73	70	68	66	64	63	61
7.5	5	2.5					124	118	114	107	103	99	94	91	88	84	81	79	76	74	72	69	67	66	63	62	61
10	7.5	5	2.5				121	116	111	105	101	97	92	89	87	83	80	78	75	73	71	68	66	65	63	61	60
12.5	10	7.5	5	2.5			118	114	109	103	99	96	91	88	85	81	79	77	74	72	70	67	66	64	62	61	59
15	12.5	10	7.5	5	2.5		116	111	107	101	97	94	89	87	84	80	78	76	73	71	69	66	65	63	61	60	59
	15	12.5	10	7.5	5	2.5	114	109	105	99	96	92	88	85	83	79	77	75	72	70	68	65	64	63	61	59	58
		15	12.5	10	7.5	5	111	107	103	97	94	91	87	84	81	78	76	74	71	69	67	64	63	62	60	59	57
			15	12.5	10	7.5	109	105	101	96	92	89	85	83	80	77	75	73	70	68	66	63	63	61	59	58	47
				15	12.5	10	107	103	99	94	91	88	84	81	79	76	74	72	69	67	65	63	62	61	59	57	56
					15	12.5	105	101	97	92	89	87	83	80	78	75	73	71	68	66	64	62	61	60	58	57	56
						15	103	99	96	91	88	85	81	79	77	74	72	70	67	66	64	61	61	59	57	56	55

Weight lbs

Note: Use larger variables when the variable is between values shown.

Figure 13-19 Finalized MVC in pieces per hour.

efficient line balance, transferable work elements should be kept small when possible.

MVC Considerations

1. When a variable may or may not occur in a particular operation, a zero in the border time and the variable can accommodate this condition.
2. When a constant element may or may not occur in an operation, the element can be treated like a variable with only a yes or no condition.
3. When the time values are in thousandths of a minute for each variable and the MV chart might get too large, the *border time values* can be reduced by:
   a. Selection (see note on Fig. 13-15).
   b. The allowance of a certain percent time increment from one border time value to the next, such as 5 percent. The variable is then put in the proper position in the MV chart across from the border time value that is closest to the real-time value. This all depends on the accuracy wanted in the final table, such as ± 5 percent, ± $2\frac{1}{2}$ percent, ± 1 percent, etc.
4. The MV chart can accommodate many variables (3, 4, 5, 6, etc.) by turning the table inside out and setting up a new time reference line as each additional variable is added.

Using the Finalized Standard Time Data

The format of the finalized STD is very important. The best examples of the most efficient methods of using STD to establish work standards are shown in Figs. 13-10 and 13-19. The primary difference between the two is that the MVC format is necessary when there are three or more independent variables. In both examples all necessary calculations have already been made, so that the work standard in pieces per hour, hours per piece, or both, can be determined directly by tracing through the independent variables pertaining to any particular operation. Incidentally, it would take less time to establish a work standard with this format than it would with many computerized STD programs, because of the extreme amount of organization and consolidation of data. Development of STD for assembly lines is an exception, because the final format cannot read directly in pieces per hour. Instead, elements have to be selected and assigned to individual work stations for one to determine the total work content for an operator at an appropriate cycle time. A computerized line-balancing program utilizing STD would be helpful here, unless the assembly line needed only a few operators.

STD can be used especially for establishing work standards and for determining the work content and time for operators on assembly lines. However, it can also be used for estimating, revising work standards, and checking existing work standards.

When using STD for any of the foregoing purposes, care should be exercised to ensure that the particular job under consideration is within the scope of work covered by the STD and that the elements and time values can be applied to the elements of work and conditions actually in effect on that specific job. Particular attention should be given to the description of each element of work contained in the STD, showing what work is included and how it is performed. If the job under consideration contains the same element of work and is performed in the same manner, the time value for that element, as contained in the STD, can be safely applied. Whenever possible, the actual method and conditions surrounding the job should be checked on the floor prior to using the STD. In addition, each STD project should include at least one sample calculation of a work standard showing direct application of the STD.

Checking and Updating the Standard Time Data

Periodically the STD should be checked to determine its suitability to current conditions on the job; otherwise even minor changes in the job may become cumulative and affect the time required to the extent that the STD are no longer reliable. Such checking can best be done by means of individual stopwatch time studies taken on several representative jobs within the scope of the STD. If the time-study person is thoroughly familiar with the STD, then such time studies need not cover as many cycles as do regular time studies unless out-of-line conditions are observed. All check studies should be filed with the original data.

The STD should be revised if observed changes in working methods or job conditions are concluded to be permanent. Some of the revisions may be relatively minor, but other changes in processes or machines can cause quite extensive revisions, in which case new STD must be developed.

QUESTIONS

13-1 When work standards are set on similar jobs with standard time data, why is the consistency between work standards better than work standards being set by individual time studies?

13-2 How can a work standard be established on a new job by STD before the operation is performed out in the production area?

13-3 Why is it common to expect methods improvements during the development of STD?

13-4 How can standard hour savings be determined using STD before changes are actually made on the part being produced?

13-5 In many cases, why can't past time studies be used in the development of STD?

13-6 What work is involved in gathering data in the development of STD?

13-7 What work is done during the compilation stage of STD development?

13-8 What work is done during the analysis-of-data stage of STD development?

13-9 In the finalization-of-data step of STD development, what types of forms can be prepared for setting work standards?

PROBLEMS

13-1 Using the calculation sheet in Fig. 13-9, calculate the work standard in pieces per hour and hours per piece for a new job with four screws, length of 6 inches, width of 4 inches, and with a sealer used.

13-2 The number of screws driven is obviously the correlating variable. Determine the equation graphically by the inspection method, with the following data for this element of work.

Number of screws	2	2	3	3	4	4	4	5	5	6	6	8
Minutes	0.13	0.15	0.18	0.17	0.22	0.23	0.21	0.26	0.25	0.32	0.29	0.38

13-3 The variable element has graphically been determined to be a straight line, so use the proper mathematical method to determine the equation for the line, as demonstrated in this chapter.

Length of sealer application, inches	5	10	14	18	20	23	26	30
Minutes	0.05	0.07	0.09	0.12	0.13	0.14	0.17	0.19

13-4 Using the method of least squares, determine the equation for this element from the data below. Of course, use the variable that has the best correlation with the times for the element. Do not use multiple regression in this particular problem.

	Time study				
	1	2	3	4	5
Length, centimeters	27	21	18	12	12
Weight, kilograms	1.5	2.0	1.0	1.4	1.3
Diameter, centimeters	2	5	3	1	4
Element, minutes	0.18	0.13	0.11	0.06	0.07

13-5 The time studies have been taken and the following tables have been developed from formulas (or graphs). Combine the following values into a finalized multivariable chart. The time reference lines may be left in the final chart.

Element								
1 Number of clips					2 Length, in			
2	3	4	5	6	5	6	7	8
0.03	0.05	0.07	0.09	0.11	0.05	0.06	0.07	0.08

(Prob. 13-5 continued on next page)

		Element						
3				4				
Number of screws				Number of clamps				
1	2	3	4	1	2	3	4	
0.07	0.10	0.13	0.16	0.02	0.04	0.06	0.08	

13-6 In order to save more time in setting standards, the final multivariable chart developed in Prob. 13-5 should read directly in pieces per hour and/or hours per piece; therefore, incorporate the following delays into the chart.

Stockhandling	0.03 minute per piece
Job preparation and cleanup	10 minutes per shift
Servicing equipment	5 minutes per shift
Tool change and adjustment	6 minutes per shift
Personal	24 minutes per shift

Have the table read directly in pieces per hour.

13-7 Instead of predicting minutes per piece or pieces per hour, have fun predicting the body weight of individuals with the following data.

Weight, kilograms	Chest, centimeters	Waist, centimeters
58.1	88	69
63.5	86	78
74.2	95	88
86.3	108	93
79.2	108	76
65.5	91	73
95.0	108	94
77.7	97	92
72.7	95	84
85.7	108	92

Use a computer multiple regression program to determine the equation for weight prediction with the data above.

FOURTEEN

PREDETERMINED TIME SYSTEMS

In preceding chapters the development of a work standard by several different methods is presented. Several chapters are devoted to the development of work standards through the use of time study. A chapter on work sampling illustrates its use in the development of a work standard. Most of the emphasis is on demonstrating the value of work sampling in getting reliable data on the loss of production due to specific delays, such as machine adjustment, stock handling, and personal, which interfere with the systematic and continuous sequencing of the regular work elements. Work sampling is also used to establish work standards, particularly for support operations, such as those for truck fleets.

The work-sampling chapter was followed by a chapter on the development of standard data, which allows work standards to be set very rapidly by an analyst. Its use is particularly advantageous in the planning and estimating of work standards. To develop a unique set of standard data is very expensive, and rarely can a small company justify the cost. A company's efforts usually result in a set of data which covers a very small percent of its operations.

PREDETERMINED TIME SYSTEMS

In this chapter the use of predetermined time systems (PTS) to establish a work standard will be introduced. A general discussion of the many systems will be followed by a demonstration of the methods-time measurement (MTM-1) system.

All predetermined time systems consist of a set of time data which has been developed from observing many observations of a worker's performance. The observations are usually taken under controlled conditions. Then each system has a unique and systematic procedure which an analyst follows to subdivide a worker's task into elements of work. The elements are then subdivided into motions and body movements, such as those which constitute the act-breakdown technique. While the level of performance was considered to be normal, it is not unusual for a company to make a one-time adjustment of the time values to reflect local performance levels. Proper application of PTS will focus the analyst on the operator's method. If the particular PTS has been followed with precision, the description of the existing method has been done in sufficient detail to allow a rapid application of the time values. A truism such as record the method faithfully and the time will take care of itself applies to the application of PTS.

Advantages of Predetermined Time Systems

Predetermined times can be advantageously used in both direct- and indirect-labor activity for

Developing methods and cycle times in advance of actual production

Improving existing methods

Establishing work standards or portions of work standards

Developing time formulas for standard data

Providing a detailed record for operator training, the shorthand method of which recording of methods and motions results in a highly accurate job description that aids in training and duplicating a method at a later date

Providing a means of obtaining greater consistency in the establishment of work standards and estimating

Eliminating the need for performance rating, since it has been considered in the establishment of the predetermined motion times

Recomputing work standards at a low cost when changes are effected

Analyzing what people can do rather than what they are doing

Planning line or progressive operations and also balancing work and establishing specifications on equipment for such operations

Planning manual requirements and equipment specifications when planning new facilities

Analyzing individual or progressive operations for increased capacity possibilities when faced with expanded schedules

Establishing standardized operation methods in both direct and indirect labor activities since use of the predetermined method time forces the analyst to establish a standard and consistent manual method

In addition to the preceding, understanding and use of predetermined times will contribute to the recognition of the manual factor as being of worthwhile consideration in other phases of the organization's functions. Training engineers, designers, and supervisory employees in predetermined times and their application will tend to make them highly conscious of method and will provide a means whereby they can easily and quickly evaluate all alternate methods in the planning or improvement stages.

This will

Aid product designers to evaluate the method-time factor during the design of products in consideration of assembly, disassembly, processing, and handling problems involved when work is performed by manual labor

Aid in the selection of more effective equipment to maintain the most economic balance between the mechanical and manual components of an individual or progressive line of operations

Develop more effective tool design through the understanding of the necessity for maintaining manual motion balance under minimum motion conditions

Aid in the development of more effective plant layout through the understanding of the necessity for consideration of the planning for minimum manual motions under balanced conditions along with the arrangement of physical factors of the individual- or multiple-work stations

Aid in the settlement of grievances, since greater attention is focused on method and not time

Aid research, such as human engineering and learning time, wherever a time-method relation is a factor

Disadvantages of Predetermined Time Systems

1. Commitment to a system is a long-term one and often requires consultants to be engaged to initially install the system.
2. Training personnel and determining ability of the analysts who are employed by the using company must be considered to ensure that the system is accurately applied.
3. Differences in the time values among the tables advocated by the various systems must be taken into account.
4. So many systems may be available that it can be a difficult task to select the system which best fits the needs of a specific company.

Limitations of Current Predetermined Time Systems

The following limitations should be considered by the user or potential user of predetermined times:

1. There are no known answers to the problems encountered in some manual work, such as buffing, snag grinding, painting, and similar situations where pressure slows down the movements or where the movements are controlled by the time for the process.
2. Predetermined time systems, as a rule, do not make any provision for fatigue. Therefore, caution should be exercised in applying motion times to heavy jobs.

In the area of reduced capacity due to fatigue, human factors data should be applied.

3. Time study is still necessary to verify the results by checking the job on the floor to catch any differences which might exist, so that proper adjustments can be made.

4. A mechanical measuring device, such as a stopwatch or camera, is desirable and should be used as a checking device whenever there are any doubts about cycle times or machine or process times.

5. Most systems are not used to develop times for allowances.

Available Predetermined Times Systems

There are many systems, some of which are available through consulting firms, and the following list is not intended to be exhaustive.

Motion time analysis (MTA)
The work factor system (WOFAC)
Methods-time measurement (MTM)
Basic motion time study (BMT)
Dimensional motion times (DMT)
Maynard operation sequence technique (MOST)
Modular arrangement of predetermined time standards (MODAPTS)
Master standard data (MSD)

These systems are available through consulting firms and associations. An excellent survey and discussion of many of them is given in an article by Brisley.[1] In a subsequent article Brisley discusses the rules and principles for many of the systems.[2] Some on the list, specifically MTM, represent a family of systems.

THE METHODS-TIME MEASUREMENT SYSTEM (MTM)

The MTM family of systems has been arranged in the following classifications by Karl Eady in an article which describes each system with emphasis on accuracy levels, speed of application, and degree of methods description provided.[3]

1. *Generic.* Intended to be used and understood by all; not restricted or particular in application. MTM-1, MTM-2, and MTM-3 are in this category.

[1] Chester L. Brisley, "Work Measurement in the 1980's," *43d Annual IMS Clinic Proceedings,* Industrial Management Society, Des Plaines, IL, 1979.

[2] Chester L. Brisley, "Comparison of Predetermined Time Systems (PTS)," *Proceedings, AIIE Spring Annual Conference,* American Institute of Industrial Engineers, Norcross, GA, 1978.

[3] Karl Eady, "Todays International MTM Systems—Decision Criteria For Their Use," *Proceedings AIIE Spring Annual Conference,* American Institute of Industrial Engineers, Norcross, GA, 1977.

2. *Functional.* Adapted to a particular type of activity such as clerical use, tool use, and microassembly. MTM-C, MTM-V, MTM-M, and MTM-GPD are in this category.
3. *Specific systems.* Developed for a particular industry, such as banking and construction, or developed for a particular company.

While predetermined time data have been in existence since the 1920s, the first to be published was MTM in 1948.[4] It was developed from motion-picture time studies of a large number of operations taken in 1940 at Westinghouse. Since then other data were gathered and the original values were modified and extended. A detailed treatment of motions is given in Karger and Bayha.[5] The original system, called MTM-1, will be described in this chapter.

MTM-1

The time value in the MTM-1 system is referred to as a time-measurement unit (TMU).

$$1 \text{ TMU} = 0.00001 \text{ hour} \qquad 1 \text{ hour } \ = 100,000.0 \text{ TMU}$$
$$= 0.0006 \text{ minute} \qquad 1 \text{ minute} = 1,666.7 \text{ TMU}$$
$$= 0.036 \text{ second} \qquad 1 \text{ second} = 27.8 \text{ TMU}$$

As shown in Figs. 14A and 14B, Tables I through X and the Supplementary Tables 1, 1A, and 2 give the motion-time data for each basic motion.

Anyone using a system such as MTM-1 must consider all the constraints and subtle relations of the individual motions. The definitions of the motions and examples illustrating the use of these would require a much greater treatment than is given here. The tables should not be used without adequate understanding of the proper application of the data.

Table I Reach R Reach is the movement of the hand to a desired destination. There are five classes of reach, referred to as cases. To select the proper category, the nature of the object to be grasped and the environment in which the object is located must be considered, since these affect the amount of time required to perform the reach. Table I includes a description of each case.

Since the distance must be selected, measurement of the movement is based on the actual path of the hand. Except for reaches constrained by physical items in the environment, a curvilinear path is taken by the hand in reaching for an object.

In making normal reaches the hand (or hands) goes through a period of acceleration to a maximum velocity, a period of constant velocity, and finally a period of deceleration to a stop. This is known as a type 1 reach. Type 2 and type 3 reaches are called hand in motion. In a type 2 reach, the hand is moving at either the beginning or

[4] Harold B. Maynard, G. J. Stegemerten, and John L. Schwab, *Methods-Time Measurement*, McGraw-Hill, New York, 1948.
[5] Delmar W. Karger and Franklin H. Bayha, *Engineered Work Measurement*, 3d ed., Industrial Press, New York, 1977.

end of the reach. In a type 3 reach, the hand is moving at both beginning and end of the reach. A hand-in-motion reach never occurs alone; it is always preceded and/or followed by a hand-in-motion move.

Table II   Move M   Move is the movement of the hand when the purpose is to transport an object to a desired destination. There are three cases of move, each of which is described in Table II. To select the proper category, the ease or complexity with which the object enters the environment at the end of the travel must be considered. The actual path of the hand (or hands) during the move is measured.

The three types of moves are the same as those described for reach.

If more than 2.5 pounds is carried, or if a force greater than 2.5 pounds is applied, additional time is allowed, as indicated in Table II. The assumption is that these are one-handed moves; and if the weight or force is applied by two hands, then the weight or force applied is divided by 2 before the weight allowance is calculated. If the object is being pushed or pulled, the weight is multiplied by the coefficient of friction before the weight allowance is calculated.

Table IIIA   Turn T   Turn is the path traced by the hand either empty or loaded with an object by a movement that rotates the hand, wrist, and forearm around the long axis of the forearm. The two variables considered in the table are degrees of turn and amount of force required.

Table IIIB   Apply Pressure AP   Apply pressure is the application of muscular force not greater than the object's resistance to motion. There are two cases, as indicated in Table IIIB, the more complex of which includes a G2 (see Table IV), which allows time for the hand to regrasp the object without losing control of the object.

Table IV   Grasp G   Grasp includes the movements required to sufficiently secure control of an object so that it may be held or moved as intended. Movements associated with grasp, generally shorter than one inch in length, are confined almost exclusively to the fingers and hand. There are five types of grasp, some of which have case variables; the table includes a description of each case from the simplest one of contact to the most complex one of grasping a small part in a jumbled condition. The time to grasp an object varies with the size, shape, condition of part, and environment surrounding the part.

Table V   Position P   Position movements are those required to bring objects into an exact relation with an environment. They include the basic movements of aligning, orienting, and engaging one object with another object, such as a part, fixture, or container. Three cases of shape are treated: symmetrical, semisymmetrical, and nonsymmetrical. In addition, two cases of a handling variable are considered: easy to handle and difficult to handle. Three classes of fit are included: loose, close, and exact.

Table VI   Release RL   Release is the basic movement required to relinquish control of an object by the fingers or hand. There are two cases of release—normal and con-

TABLE I – REACH – R

Distance Moved Inches	Time TMU — A	B	C or D	E	Hand In Motion — A	B	CASE AND DESCRIPTION
3/4 or less	2.0	2.0	2.0	2.0	1.6	1.6	**A** Reach to object in fixed location, or to object in other hand or on which other hand rests.
1	2.5	2.5	3.6	2.4	2.3	2.3	
2	4.0	4.0	5.9	3.8	3.5	2.7	
3	5.3	5.3	7.3	5.3	4.5	3.6	**B** Reach to single object in location which may vary slightly from cycle to cycle.
4	6.1	6.4	8.4	6.8	4.9	4.3	
5	6.5	7.8	9.4	7.4	5.3	5.0	
6	7.0	8.6	10.1	8.0	5.7	5.7	**C** Reach to object jumbled with other objects in a group so that search and select occur.
7	7.4	9.3	10.8	8.7	6.1	6.5	
8	7.9	10.1	11.5	9.3	6.5	7.2	
9	8.3	10.8	12.2	9.9	6.9	7.9	
10	8.7	11.5	12.9	10.5	7.3	8.6	**D** Reach to a very small object or where accurate grasp is required.
12	9.6	12.9	14.2	11.8	8.1	10.1	
14	10.5	14.4	15.6	13.0	8.9	11.5	
16	11.4	15.8	17.0	14.2	9.7	12.9	**E** Reach to indefinite location to get hand in position for body balance or next motion or out of way.
18	12.3	17.2	18.4	15.5	10.5	14.4	
20	13.1	18.6	19.8	16.7	11.3	15.8	
22	14.0	20.1	21.2	18.0	12.1	17.3	
24	14.9	21.5	22.5	19.2	12.9	18.8	
26	15.8	22.9	23.9	20.4	13.7	20.2	
28	16.7	24.4	25.3	21.7	14.5	21.7	
30	17.5	25.8	26.7	22.9	15.3	23.2	
Additional	0.4	0.7	0.7	0.6			TMU per inch over 30 inches

TABLE II – MOVE – M

Distance Moved Inches	Time TMU — A	B	C	Hand In Motion B	Wt. Allowance — Wt. (lb.) Up to	Dynamic Factor	Static Constant TMU	CASE AND DESCRIPTION
3/4 or less	2.0	2.0	2.0	1.7				
1	2.5	2.9	3.4	2.3	2.5	1.00	0	**A** Move object to other hand or against stop.
2	3.6	4.6	5.2	2.9				
3	4.9	5.7	6.7	3.6	7.5	1.06	2.2	
4	6.1	6.9	8.0	4.3				
5	7.3	8.0	9.2	5.0	12.5	1.11	3.9	**B** Move object to approximate or indefinite location.
6	8.1	8.9	10.3	5.7				
7	8.9	9.7	11.1	6.5	17.5	1.17	5.6	
8	9.7	10.6	11.8	7.2				
9	10.5	11.5	12.7	7.9	22.5	1.22	7.4	
10	11.3	12.2	13.5	8.6				
12	12.9	13.4	15.2	10.0	27.5	1.28	9.1	**C** Move object to exact location.
14	14.4	14.6	16.9	11.4				
16	16.0	15.8	18.7	12.8	32.5	1.33	10.8	
18	17.6	17.0	20.4	14.2				
20	19.2	18.2	22.1	15.6	37.5	1.39	12.5	
22	20.8	19.4	23.8	17.0				
24	22.4	20.6	25.5	18.4	42.5	1.44	14.3	
26	24.0	21.8	27.3	19.8				
28	25.5	23.1	29.0	21.2	47.5	1.50	16.0	
30	27.1	24.3	30.7	22.7				
Additional	0.8	0.6	0.85					TMU per inch over 30 inches

TABLE III A – TURN – T

Weight	Time TMU for Degrees Turned — 30°	45°	60°	75°	90°	105°	120°	135°	150°	165°	180°
Small – 0 to 2 Pounds	2.8	3.5	4.1	4.8	5.4	6.1	6.8	7.4	8.1	8.7	9.4
Medium – 2.1 to 10 Pounds	4.4	5.5	6.5	7.5	8.5	9.6	10.6	11.6	12.7	13.7	14.8
Large – 10.1 to 35 Pounds	8.4	10.5	12.3	14.4	16.2	18.3	20.4	22.2	24.3	26.1	28.2

TABLE III B – APPLY PRESSURE – AP

FULL CYCLE			COMPONENTS		
SYMBOL	TMU	DESCRIPTION	SYMBOL	TMU	DESCRIPTION
APA	10.6	AF + DM + RLF	AF	3.4	Apply Force
APB	16.2	APA + G2	DM	4.2	Dwell, Minimum
			RLF	3.0	Release Force

TABLE IV – GRASP – G

TYPE OF GRASP	Case	Time TMU	DESCRIPTION
PICK-UP	1A	2.0	Any size object by itself, easily grasped
	1B	3.5	Object very small or lying close against a flat surface
	1C1	7.3	Interference with Grasp on bottom and one side of nearly cylindrical object. Diameter larger than 1/2"
	1C2	8.7	Diameter 1/4" to 1/2"
	1C3	10.8	Diameter less than 1/4"
REGRASP	2	5.6	Change grasp without relinquishing control
TRANSFER	3	5.6	Control transferred from one hand to the other.
SELECT	4A	7.3	Object jumbled with other objects so that search and select occur. Larger than 1" × 1" × 1"
	4B	9.1	1/4" × 1/4" × 1/8" to 1" × 1" × 1"
	4C	12.9	Smaller than 1/4" × 1/4" × 1/8"
CONTACT	5	0	Contact, Sliding, or Hook Grasp.

TABLE V – POSITION* – P

CLASS OF FIT		Symmetry	Easy To Handle	Difficult To Handle
1–Loose	No pressure required	S	5.6	11.2
		SS	9.1	14.7
		NS	10.4	16.0
2–Close	Light pressure required	S	16.2	21.8
		SS	19.7	25.3
		NS	21.0	26.6
3–Exact	Heavy pressure required.	S	43.0	48.6
		SS	46.5	52.1
		NS	47.8	53.4

SUPPLEMENTARY RULE FOR SURFACE ALIGNMENT

P1SE per alignment: >1/16 ≤1/4"   P2SE per alignment: ≤1/16"

*Distance moved to engage–1" or less.

TABLE VI – RELEASE – RL

Case	Time TMU	DESCRIPTION
1	2.0	Normal release performed by opening fingers as independent motion.
2	0	Contact Release

TABLE VII – DISENGAGE – D

CLASS OF FIT	HEIGHT OF RECOIL	EASY TO HANDLE	DIFFICULT TO HANDLE
1–LOOSE – Very slight effort, blends with subsequent move.	Up to 1"	4.0	5.7
2–CLOSE – Normal effort, slight recoil.	Over 1" to 5"	7.5	11.8
3–TIGHT – Considerable effort, hand recoils markedly.	Over 5" to 12"	22.9	34.7

SUPPLEMENTARY

CLASS OF FIT	CARE IN HANDLING	BINDING
1–LOOSE	Allow Class 2	—
2–CLOSE	Allow Class 3	One G2 per Bind
3–TIGHT	Change Method	One APB per Bind

TABLE VIII – EYE TRAVEL AND EYE FOCUS – ET AND EF

Eye Travel Time = 15.2 × $\frac{T}{D}$ TMU, with a maximum value of 20 TMU.

where T = the distance between points from and to which the eye travels.
D = the perpendicular distance from the eye to the line of travel T.

Eye Focus Time = 7.3 TMU.

SUPPLEMENTARY INFORMATION

— Area of Normal Vision = Circle 4" in Diameter 16" from Eyes

— Reading Formula = 5.05 N Where N = The Number of Words.

EFFECTIVE NET WEIGHT

No. of Hands	Spatial	Sliding
Effective Net Weight (ENW)	1	W	W × F_c
	2	W/2	W/2 × F_c

W = Weight in pounds
F_c = Coefficient of Friction

TABLE IX – BODY, LEG, AND FOOT MOTIONS

	TYPE	SYMBOL	TMU	DISTANCE	DESCRIPTION
HORIZONTAL MOTION	LEG-FOOT MOTION	FM	8.5	To 4"	Hinged at ankle.
		FMP	19.1	To 4"	With heavy pressure.
		LM__	7.1	To 6"	Hinged at knee or hip in any direction.
			1.2	Ea. add'l inch	*
	SIDE STEP	SS_C1	17.0	<12"	Use Reach or Move time when less than 12". Complete when leading leg contacts floor.
			0.6	Ea. add'l inch	
		SS_C2	34.1	12"	Lagging leg must contact floor before next motion can be made.
			1.1	Ea. add'l inch	
	TURN BODY	TBC1	18.6	—	Complete when leading leg contacts floor.
		TBC2	37.2	—	Lagging leg must contact floor before next motion can be made.
	WALK	W_FT	5.3	Per Foot	Unobstructed.
		W_P	15.0	Per Pace	Unobstructed.
		W_PO	17.0	Per Pace	When obstructed or with weight.
VERTICAL MOTION		SIT	34.7	—	From standing position.
		STD	43.4	—	From sitting position.
		B,S,KOK	29.0	—	Bend, Stoop, Kneel on One Knee.
		AB,AS,AKOK	31.9	—	Arise from Bend, Stoop, Kneel on One Knee
		KBK	69.4	—	Kneel on Both Knees.
		AKBK	76.7	—	Arise from Kneel on Both Knees.

SUPPLEMENTARY MTM DATA

1 TMU = .00001 hour	1 hour = 100,000.0 TMU
= .0006 minute	1 minute = 1,666.7 TMU
= .036 seconds	1 second = 27.8 TMU

TABLE 1 – POSITION – P

Class of Fit and Clearance	Case of Symmetry	Align Only	Depth of Insertion (per ¼")			
			>0≤⅛"	>⅛≤¼	>¼≤⅜	>⅜≤½
21 .150"–.350"	S	3.0	3.4	6.6	7.7	8.8
	SS	3.0	10.3	13.5	14.6	15.7
	NS	4.8	15.5	18.7	19.8	20.9
22 .025"–.149"	S	7.2	7.2	11.9	13.0	14.2
	SS	8.0	14.9	19.6	20.7	21.9
	NS	9.5	20.2	24.9	26.0	27.2
23* .005"–.024"	S	9.5	9.5	16.3	18.7	21.0
	SS	10.4	17.3	24.1	26.5	28.8
	NS	12.2	22.9	29.7	32.1	34.4

*BINDING—Add observed number of Apply Pressures.
DIFFICULT HANDLING—Add observed number of G2's.
†Determine symmetry by geometric properties, except use S case when object is oriented prior to preceding Move.

TABLE 1A – SECONDARY ENGAGE – E2

CLASS OF FIT	DEPTH OF INSERTION (PER 1/4")		
	2	4	6
21	3.2	4.3	5.4
22	4.7	5.8	7.0
23	6.8	9.2	11.5

TABLE 2 – CRANK (LIGHT RESISTANCE) – C

DIAMETER OF CRANKING (INCHES)	TMU (T) PER REVOLUTION	DIAMETER OF CRANKING (INCHES)	TMU (T) PER REVOLUTION
1	8.5	9	14.0
2	9.7	10	14.4
3	10.6	11	14.7
4	11.4	12	15.0
5	12.1	14	15.5
6	12.7	16	16.0
7	13.2	18	16.4
8	13.6	20	16.7

FORMULAS:
A. CONTINUOUS CRANKING (Start at beginning and stop at end of cycle only)
$$TMU = [(N \times T) + 5.2] \, F + C$$
B. INTERMITTENT CRANKING (Start at beginning and stop at end of each revolution)
$$TMU = [(T + 5.2) \, F + C] \times N$$

C = Static component TMU weight allowance constant from move table
F = Dynamic component weight allowance factor from move table
N = Number of revolutions
T = TMU per revolution (Type III Motion)
5.2 = TMU for start and stop

TABLE X – SIMULTANEOUS MOTIONS

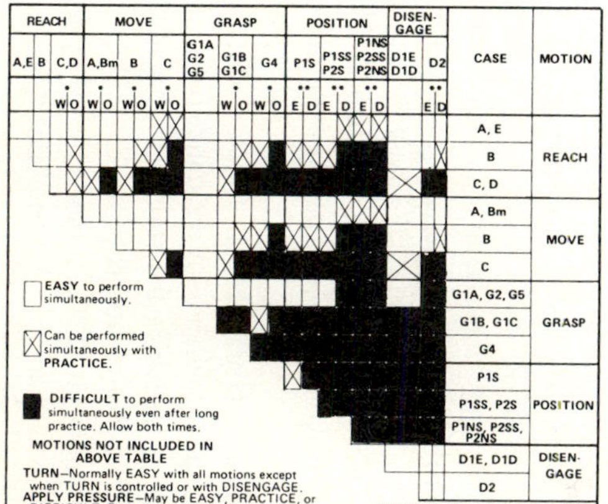

Column groups (left to right): REACH (A,E,B | C,D | A,Bm) · MOVE (B | C) · GRASP (G1A G2 G5 | G1B G1C | G4) · POSITION (P1S | P1SS P2S | P1NS P2SS P2NS) · DISENGAGE (D1E D1D | D2); each with W / O sub-columns.

Row groups (top to bottom): REACH · MOVE · GRASP · POSITION · DISENGAGE.

Right-hand reference columns:

CASE	MOTION
A, E	REACH
B	
C, D	
A, Bm	MOVE
B	
C	
G1A, G2, G5	GRASP
G1B, G1C	
G4	
P1S	
P1SS, P2S	POSITION
P1NS, P2SS, P2NS	
D1E, D1D	DISENGAGE
D2	

Legend:
□ EASY to perform simultaneously.
⊠ Can be performed simultaneously with PRACTICE.
■ DIFFICULT to perform simultaneously even after long practice. Allow both times.

MOTIONS NOT INCLUDED IN ABOVE TABLE
TURN—Normally EASY with all motions except when TURN is controlled or with DISENGAGE.
APPLY PRESSURE—May be EASY, PRACTICE, or DIFFICULT. Each case must be analyzed.
POSITION—Class 3—Always DIFFICULT.
DISENGAGE—Class 3—Normally DIFFICULT.
RELEASE—Always EASY.
DISENGAGE—Any class may be DIFFICULT if care must be exercised to avoid injury or damage to object.

*W = Within the area of normal vision.
O = Outside the area of normal vision.
**E = EASY to perform.
D = DIFFICULT to Handle.

Do not attempt to use this chart or apply Methods-Time Measurement in any way unless you understand the proper application of the data. This statement is included as a word of caution to prevent difficulties resulting from mis-application of the data.

Figure 14-B MTM data tables.

tact. A normal release occurs when the fingers open to move away from the object independently from movements of the arm. A contact release does not involve independent movement of the fingers, so the succeeding reach can be done without waiting for a normal release to occur.

Table VII   Disengage D   Disengage is the basic movement required to break contact between two objects. It includes a recoil, an involuntary movement of the hand, once the objects are separated. There are three cases of recoil. Variables considered are easy and difficult to handle, and care in handling. Another is fit; loose, close, tight, and binding. These are described in the table.

Table VIII   Eye Travel ET and Eye Focus EF   Eye travel is the movement of the eyes between two points of focus. It is a function of the angular degree through which the eyes move, determined by the distance between the two points of focus and the perpendicular distance from the eye to the line of travel. Eye focus involves using the eyes to direct the movement of a body member or to check the characteristics of an object without moving the eyes from the object. Table VIII includes supplementary information. As a rule, the hand, arm, and finger movements are done at the same time as are the eye movements and thus the eye values are required only where all other body movements have ceased and cannot resume until the eye action ends.

Table IX   Body, Leg, and Foot Motions   The leg, foot, side step, and walk motions vary with the distance moved. The turn body, sit, stand, bend, stoop, kneel, and arise are constants.

Table X   Simultaneous Motions   The simultaneous-motion table provides a guide for indicating when both hands can perform motions at the same time. The intersections in the chart are coded to indicate whether or not a motion can be performed simultaneously with each of the motions. For example, it is difficult to perform a P2NS with the left hand while a P2NS or any other position case is being performed by the right hand even after long practice, so both times are allowed.

Supplementary Table 1   Position P   The supplementary position table includes cases for class of fit and clearance. There are three cases of fit and clearance, three cases of symmetry, one case of align, and four cases of depth of insertion. The table includes descriptions and boundaries for the cases.

Supplementary Table 1A   Secondary Engage E2   The engage table includes three cases of fit for each of three cases of depth of insertion.

Supplementary Table 2   Crank C   Supplementary Table 2 has 20 cases for diameter of cranking when light resistance is encountered. The table supplies formulas which include as variables the static and dynamic component weight allowance as well as the number of revolutions turned.

Figure 14-1 illustrates how the symbols are used to represent the motions taken by the left and right hand. Both hands reach together to a container of cylindrical

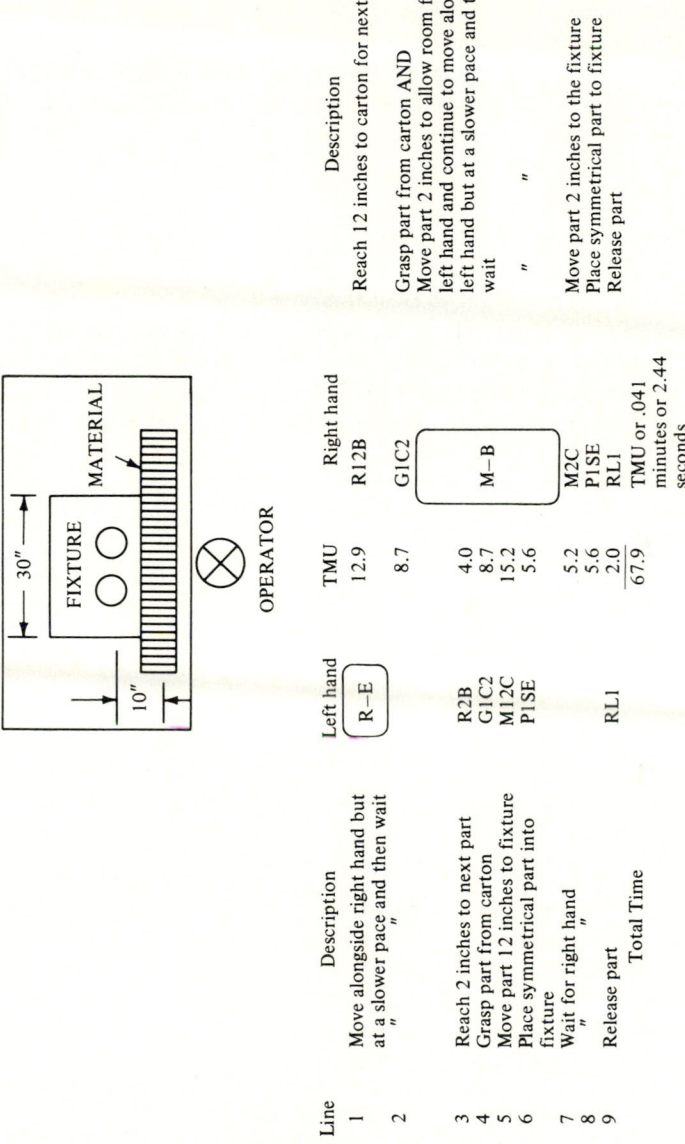

Line	Description	Left hand	TMU	Right hand	Description
1	Move alongside right hand but at a slower pace and then wait	R–E	12.9	R12B	Reach 12 inches to carton for next part
2	" "		8.7	G1C2	Grasp part from carton AND Move part 2 inches to allow room for left hand and continue to move alongside left hand but at a slower pace and then wait
3	Reach 2 inches to next part	R2B	4.0	M–B	" "
4	Grasp part from carton	G1C2	8.7		
5	Move part 12 inches to fixture	M12C	15.2		
6	Place symmetrical part into fixture	P1SE	5.6		
7	Wait for right hand		5.2	M2C	Move part 2 inches to the fixture
8	" "		5.6	P1SE	Place symmetrical part to fixture
9	Release part	RL1	2.0	RL1	Release part
	Total Time		67.9	TMU or .041 minutes or 2.44 seconds	

Figure 14-1 Example of MTM analysis. Each hand gets one part and places it on the fixture. Process time and automatic eject of finished parts are not shown.

parts. The left hand waits near the container while the right hand reaches the first part, grasps it, and moves aside to make room for the left hand. The left hand moves and grasps the second part. Both hands move to the fixture, where the right hand waits while the left hand places the second part in the left side of the fixture. Then the left hand waits while the right hand places the first part in the fixture. Parts are 3/8 inch in diameter and 6 inches long.

During the 1970s some of the systems were placed on computers and some were placed on hand-held calculators. The computer programs[6] are usually interactive, and some have check systems to ensure that the analyst is using the procedure in a proper manner.

QUESTIONS

14-2 What are five advantages of predetermined methods-time systems?

14-2 Can a predetermined methods-time system completely replace a stopwatch system for developing work standards? Explain your answer.

14-3 What are three limitations of most predetermined methods-time systems?

14-4 Why is a predetermined methods-time system superior to a stopwatch system for planning and estimating labor costs for production operations?

14-5 What influences the time for reaching to get an object?

14-6 Can the left hand perform a G4 grasp simultaneously as a G4 grasp is performed by the right hand on a different object?

14-7 In Table III-B why is an APB assigned 16.2 TMUs while an APA is assigned only 10.6 TMUs.

PROBLEMS

14-1 Use Fig. 14-1 and the MTM-1 system to determine the time required to get and place one object using one hand only.

14-2 Use Fig. 14-1 and the MTM-1 system to determine the time required to get and place a cylindrical object in each fixture using both hands as in Fig. 14-1. However, assume that there are two shoulder-high palm buttons which must be operated for each cycle of the process. Assume automatic ejection of the finished parts to a gravity chute leading to a container on the floor. The palm buttons are depressed $\frac{1}{2}$ inch to operate and offer a resistance of $\frac{1}{2}$ ounce. The operator releases the palm buttons immediately after they are depressed.

14-3 Handle the same as Prob. 14-2 except assume that the operator manually removes the parts (one in each hand) from the fixture and places them in the original container.

14-4 In a classroom arrange a workplace and two chairs as indicated in the sketch. Then perform the following task: Start in the seated position at the desk with the eraser in your hand and with the chair far enough from the desk so that you can stand and extend your left leg sideways without pushing the chair away from the desk. Then walk to the first chair and exchange the eraser for the eraser which is already on the chair. Walk to the second chair and again exchange erasers. Then walk to the desk and sit on the chair facing the desk.

---

[6] Delmar W. Karger and Walton Hancock, *Advanced Work Measurement*, Industrial Press, New York, 1982.

Table

Chair

Eraser

4
Paces

App'x
6 paces

Eraser

5 Paces   Chair #2

Eraser

Chair #1

First perform a MTM-1 analysis and then have someone time your performance. Remember to use a normal pace.

14-5 Construct a workplace similar to that in the sketch. The workplace includes two tapered pegs which can be made from wooden dowels. The pegs should be long enough so that a minimum of 15 blanks can be assembled to the peg. A minimum of 20 round blanks approximately the size of poker chips are required. The blanks require a concentric hole the diameter of which should be large enough so that when released over a peg by the operator, they fall to the bottom without resistance.

The pegs should be mounted in a base, which can be constructed from wood or corrugated paper products. The blanks are to be stacked on a surface such as a tray.

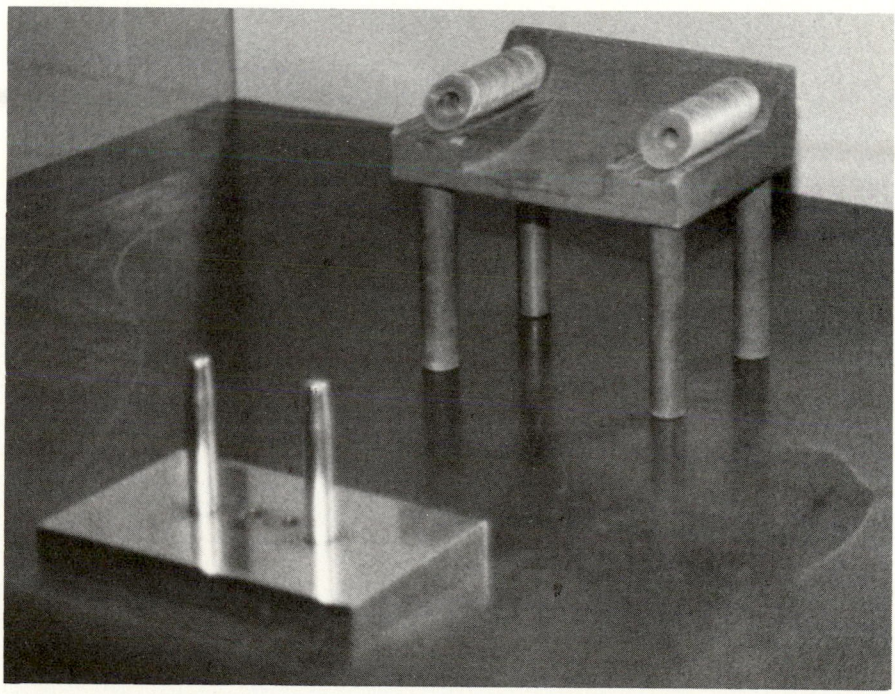

Using one peg, align it in front of the stack consisting of a minimum of 10 blanks such that the curvilinear distance from the top of the peg to the back of the fifth blank is approximately 15 inches. The operator is to use one hand to assemble the blanks to the peg using the following description.

Step	TMUs	Right or left hand
1		Starting at top of peg, reach 15 inches to blank
2		Grasp blank from carton
3		Move blank 15 inches and center blank on peg
4		Release blank over peg

Select the proper values from the tables. How many TMUs are required to assemble one blank? How many minutes?

14-6 Using the same workplace as in Prob. 14-5, assume that the operator must alternate the right and left hand to assemble the blanks. The operator must start with the left hand positioned over the peg and the fingers of the right hand grasping the front blank in the tray.

Step	Left hand	TMUs	Right hand
1	Reach for blank on tray		Move to peg
2	Wait		Place blank to peg
3	Grasp blank		Wait
4	Move blank to peg		Reach for blank on tray
5	Place blank to peg		Wait
6	Wait		Grasp blank

Select the proper values from the tables. How many TMUs are required to assemble one blank? How many minutes?

14-7 Using two pegs and two stacks, the operator must use the left hand to assemble the blanks from the left stack to the left peg. Simultaneously the operator must use the right hand to assemble the blanks from the right stack to the right peg.

First, do an act-breakdown analysis and write a PTS description for the operation following the example in Fig. 14-1. Then select the proper values from the tables. How long does it take to assemble 10 blanks?

FIFTEEN

LINE BALANCING

The manufacture of high-volume products is frequently characterized by the use of fabricating and assembly production lines. Analysis of fabricating lines may include method summary charting and simulation before a suitable economic assignment of operators to machines is achieved. In actual practice, the operator–multiple-machine problem usually occurs during the design of a fabricating line and only occasionally as part of the design of an assembly line. Since the method-summary-chart techniques are covered in great detail in Chap. 17, neither the design of fabricating lines nor the use of method summary charts will be included in this chapter.

INDIVIDUAL BUILD STATIONS

As a rule the design of assembly lines is an iterative process, and practitioners may initially develop an individual build station in which one operator produces a complete assembly. Such a station is also referred to as a one-operator build station which has an inherent advantage of no delay or efficiency loss because of line-balance interference. To produce the required volume, a sufficient number of stations is specified. In Table 15-1 the balance at a cycle time of 46 is an example of an individual build station, that is, one in which one operator produces the complete assembly. If the production requirements were 60 pieces per shift, the number of stations required is calculated as follows:

$$\frac{480 \text{ minutes}}{\text{shift}} \frac{1 \text{ shift}}{46 \text{ minutes}} = 10.43 \text{ assemblies per shift per station}$$

$$\frac{60 \text{ pieces}}{\text{shift}} \frac{1 \text{ shift}}{10.43 \text{ pieces}} = 5.8 \text{ stations required}$$

Six individual build stations would be required to produce the required volume of 60 pieces per shift.

Advantages of Individual Build Stations

Individual build stations allow flexibility for a wide variation of production scheduling up to a limit of $10.43 \times 6 = 62.3$ assemblies per shift in this example. They allow idle stations at the same time that the efficiency of the other stations remains at 100 percent.

If the same production requirement of 60 pieces per shift were to be produced on an assembly line, a cycle time would be calculated as follows:

$$480 \times \frac{1}{60} = \frac{8 \text{ minutes}}{\text{assembly}}$$

From Table 15-1, we find that the percent delay for a cycle time of 8 is either 4.2 or 18 percent, depending on the method by which the operators are assigned. The two assignments which give a 4.2 percent delay require only six operators; and the 18 percent delay occurs because seven operators are assigned to the line. Table 15-1 also indicates that if the line were run with only five operators, the percent delay would be 8, 16, or 23.5, depending on the specific method used to assign elements of work to each operator.

While this example demonstrates the ability of an individual build system to handle a variation in volume without incurring a loss in labor efficiency, it assumes that the actual elemental times for the individual build examples are the same as those for the assembly-line examples. In fact, the description of many of the elements may include enough differences so that the individual elemental times will not be identical for both the individual build and the assembly-line cases; and in most examples, comparable elements would be less for the assembly-line case.

The individual build station would be likely to improve the quality of life of the operators by varying their work pace during the shift and thereby possibly increasing job satisfaction. This may result in higher quality and in greater output per shift.

Many labor contracts include a provision which allows more personal time for operators on paced lines, since such workers must be replaced by relief operators when they require personal time. The increased personal time is a trade-off for the loss of freedom to leave the job at will to attend to personal needs. The contracts usually specify 24-minutes personal time for the individual build case and 46 minutes for the assembly-line case. For large assembly lines the proper utilization of relief operators presents much difficulty, since few operators require relief during the first hour in the shift and the first hour after lunch. One relief operator can therefore relieve a maximum of seven operators. The production supervisor has to assign the relief operators to other jobs during the first hour in the shift and the first hour after lunch.

Individual build stations have the advantage of being able to handle many models. Specific stations can be permanently assigned to a particular model, while others may be changed from model to model on a systematic basis.

A less obvious advantage of individual build stations in most situations has to do with the use of fewer assembly fixtures, which results in less maintenance and fewer

Table 15-1 Comparison of balances obtained at different cycle times

Cycle time	Minimum number of operators Σt_i cycle time	Total number of stations	Number of one-operator stations	Number of multiple stations Two-operator stations	Three-operator stations	Four-operator stations	Total number of operators	Delay in S
3	$15.3 \approx 16$	8	3	3	1	1	16	4.2
4	$11.5 \approx 12$	6	1	4	1	...	12	4.2
5	$9.2 \approx 10$	7	4	3	...	...	10	8.0
6	$7.7 \approx 8$	4	2	1	...	1	8	4.2
7	$6.6 \approx 7$	6	5	1	...	...	7	6.1
7	$6.6 \approx 7$	8	8	...	...	...	8	18.0
8	$5.8 \approx 6$	7	7	...	...	...	7	18.0
8	$5.8 \approx 6$	4	3	...	1	...	6	4.2
8	$5.8 \approx 6$	5	4	2	...	...	6	4.2
9	$5.1 \approx 6$	6	6	...	...	...	6	15.0
9	$5.1 \approx 6$	5	4	1	...	...	6	15.0
10	$4.6 \approx 5$	6	6	...	...	...	6	23.4
10	$4.6 \approx 5$	6	6	...	...	...	6	23.4
10	$4.6 \approx 5$	6	6	...	...	...	6	23.4
10	$4.6 \approx 5$	4	3	1	...	...	5	8.0
11	$4.2 \approx 5$	5	5	...	...	...	5	16.4
12	$4.3 \approx 4$	5	5	...	...	...	5	23.4
12	$3.83 \approx 4$	5	5	...	...	...	5	23.4
12	$3.8 \approx 4$	5	5	...	...	...	5	23.4
12	$3.8 \approx 4$	4	4	...	...	...	4	4.2
13	$3.5 \approx 4$	4	4	...	...	...	4	11.5
14	$3.3 \approx 4$	4	4	...	...	...	4	17.9
15	$3.1 \approx 4$	4	4	...	...	...	4	23.4
16	$2.8 \approx 3$	3	3	...	...	...	3	4.2
17	$2.7 \approx 3$	3	3	...	...	...	3	9.8
18	$2.6 \approx 3$	3	3	...	...	...	3	14.8
19	$2.4 \approx 3$						3	19.3
20	$2.3 \approx 3$						3	23.3
21	$2.2 \approx 3$						3	27.0
22	$2.1 \approx 3$						3	30.3
23	2	2	2	...	...	...	2	0.0
24	$1.9 \approx 2$	2	2	...	...	...	2	4.2
25	$1.8 \approx 2$	2	2	...	...	...	2	8.0
26	$1.77 \approx 2$	2	2	...	...	...	2	11.5
27	$1.7 \approx 2$	2	2	...	...	...	2	14.8
28	$1.6 \approx 2$	2	2	...	...	...	2	17.8
29	$1.6 \approx 2$	2	2	...	...	...	2	20.8
30	$1.5 \approx 2$	2	2	...	...	...	2	23.4
45	$1.02 \approx 2$	2	2	...	...	...	2	48.3
46	1	1	1	...	...	...	1	0.0

rejected parts. In the preceding example, six fixtures would be required in the individual build case; whereas for an assembly line in which the fixtures are attached to an endless conveyor belt, there would be many more fixtures. For a small assembly in which fixtures are at a 2-foot center-to-center distance, an over and under endless belt conveyor might have a belt length of 50 feet. Twenty-five fixtures would be required; and in some installations, at any time, 10 percent of the fixtures are either inoperative or in need of minor adjustment.

Disadvantages of Individual Build Stations

There are many disadvantages associated with individual build stations. Since the same part appears at each of the work stations, more costs are incurred for material handling, in-process inventory, floor space, assembly machines, and the remaining burden costs associated with these.

Since there is a longer operation time (in the preceding example, a 46-minute cycle versus an 8-minute cycle), more time is required to train operators.

Since there are fewer assembly fixtures, the individual build station is usually more complex and more costly. In a pure individual build system, every piece of equipment must be included in each station. The cost of equipment, most of which would have a low level of utilization, frequently is high enough to nullify the advantages of individual build.

JOB ENRICHMENT AND ORGANIZATION DEVELOPMENT

In recent years more attention has been given to the need to increase productivity. As a result more emphasis is being placed on reducing the length of production lines. Shorter assembly lines create a smaller group of people and thus a team approach may be considered. The team may be given decision-making autonomy in many areas previously assigned to supervisors and higher levels of management. In addition the recommendations of the team are sought by management in other areas. This is an outgrowth of the job enrichment and quality-of-work-life philosophy which has a high level of employee involvement in decision making as its cornerstone.

Organization development, an outgrowth of job enrichment and quality-of-work-life philosophies can be an all-encompassing approach, starting with the basic value systems and objectives of the organization. From this the organization structure and the sociotechnical system should jointly evolve. Thus all aspects of the enterprise, including the technical system, are integrated into a coherent design. In these situations assembly lines which allow small teams to vary their work pace are a requirement.

ASSEMBLY TECHNICAL SYSTEMS

Even in this sociotechnical environment the assembly lines must be planned, since whenever two or more people work together in sequence the operators are paced by each other. This is true whether or not the stations are connected by chutes, by belt conveyors with permanently attached fixtures, by synchronous indexing conveyors, or by power and free conveyors in which the operator may temporarily disengage a fixture from the conveyor to create a longer cycle time. In power and free-assembly conveyors, temporary banks of parts may be created between successive operations.

The conveyors may be an over and under type and run in a straight line. They may be elliptical in shape, or through the use of transfer stations they may approach a square shape. The shape of the conveyor may be a circle—for example, a lazy Susan or a powered revolving table occasionally referred to as a dial conveyor.

The operations may consist only of manual elements. These may be interspersed among the manual operations work stations which are semiautomatic or completely automatic. In every case a detail plan must be created which arrives at the least total cost integration of operators, machines, and conveyors.

BALANCING AN ASSEMBLY LINE

Despite the wide array of conveyors available, the first step in designing conveyor systems is to create the elemental descriptions, the time required to perform the elements, and the precedence relation among the elements. Chapter 5 on the Act Breakdown and Chapter 6 that discusses the element description provide a good background for developing elements for precedence charts. Chapter 3 describes how to develop the precedence relations.

Most articles and dissertations on line balancing include the following restrictions:

1. The task or element times are indivisible. They cannot be divided into smaller elements.
2. The cycle time (time in which an operator has to work on a single piece) must be greater than, or equal to, the maximum element time.
3. The work method is fixed.
4. The element times are constant.
5. There is no effect for operator learning or fatigue.
6. The summation of the element times for the jobs to be performed at a single work station must be less than or equal to the cycle time.
7. There is a known precedence relation among the elements.

In this chapter these restrictions will be followed initially and then restrictions 1, 2, 3, and 6 will be relaxed in an effort to find economical assignments.

The following eight-step procedure provides a structure for solving line-balancing problems. The steps will be described first, and then they will be applied to solve a line-balance problem.

Step 1 The following basic information is gathered:

1. The elemental descriptions and times
2. The shipping volume or production requirements (net line speed) in pieces per hour

3. Overall efficiency of the department in which the line operates
4. The space and equipment available and what machines can be grouped
5. A precedence diagram which includes the elemental time values

Step 2 The tooling capacity or line speed is calculated:

$$\text{Line speed} = \frac{\text{production requirement}}{\text{historical or estimated efficiency}} = \frac{\text{pieces}}{\text{hour}}$$

Line speed is the rate per hour at which fixtures, vises, bucks, dollies, or pallets pass a given point while the line is running. If efficiencies are historically below 100 percent, the line speed is adjusted to ensure that the production requirement is met. The adjustment may compensate for missing, malfunctioning, and skipped fixtures and for scrap and parts which have to be rerun. It may compensate for system delays such as conveyor malfunctions, material shortages, and operator shortages. If the adjustment is very large such that most delays are considered, then the system may not have the incentive to correct itself. If the adjustment does not compensate for personal relief time, it is assumed that relief operators are utilized.

Step 3 The cycle time is calculated. This is the elapsed time required for the space between two fixtures to pass a given point.

$$\text{Cycle time} = \frac{60 \text{ minutes}}{1 \text{ hour}} \frac{1 \text{ hour}}{\text{line speed (piece)}} = \frac{\text{minutes}}{\text{piece}}$$

The cycle time is the time available for a worker to perform his or her job on a line. If the cycle time is less than the smallest elemental value, a value equal to or greater than the smallest elemental value is selected for the cycle time.

Step 4 The theoretical minimum number of operators or work stations is found by applying the following three rules and selecting the larger of the resulting two values.

Rule 1

1.
$$N_1 = \frac{\sum\limits_{i=1}^{n} t_i}{\text{cycle time}}$$

where t = element time
$i = 1, 2, 3, \ldots n$
N_1 = minimum number of stations

2. N_1 is rounded up to the next integer value.

Rule 2

1. Divide the cycle time by 2.

2. Count the number of elements which have a time greater than the time computed in 1; call this N_2.

$$N_2 = \text{number of } T_i > \frac{\text{cycle time}}{2}$$

Rule 3 The theoretical minimum number of one-operator stations for the assembly line is the larger of the two values of N_1 and N_2.

Step 5 The theoretical efficiency is calculated for the assembly line:

$$\frac{\text{Theoretical}}{\text{efficiency}} = \frac{\sum\limits_{i=1}^{n} t_i}{(\text{cycle time}) (\text{theoretical minimum number of operators})} \, 100\%$$

This will indicate the best utilization of operators which can be achieved at a given cycle time. Since it does not consider precedence relation, the theoretical efficiency may not be achieved on every line balance.

Step 6 The assembly line is balanced. The tasks (elements) are grouped together to form work assignments at each work station. The assignments must not violate the precedence relations. In addition, the sum of the element times assigned to a work station must not exceed the cycle time.

$$\sum\limits_{i=1}^{n} \text{element time}_i \leqslant \text{cycle time}$$

Step 7 The actual efficiency is calculated.

$$\text{Actual efficiency} = \frac{\sum\limits_{i=1}^{n} t_i}{(\text{cycle time}) (\text{number of work stations})} \, 100\%$$

Since there is one person per work station, the number of stations will equal the number of assigned operators.

Step 8 The results are evaluated. If the actual efficiency equals the theoretical efficiency, the balance derived is the best possible under the given line speed and element breakdown. If the actual efficiency is less, further analysis may be necessary to determine if the tasks or elements can be reassigned. This results in a trial-and-error procedure, which quite often produces a solution with less delay than the first balance.

Example

STEP 1 Given: The Artos Manufacturing Company has a final assembly department that must put together its chief product, a fluid valve, according to the following precedence diagram and times. (*Note:* Letters denote elements. Times are in decimal minutes.) The assembly department historically works at 90 percent efficiency. The Artos Company has a production requirement (shipping commitment) of 480 fluid valves per 8-hour day, or 60 pieces per hour.

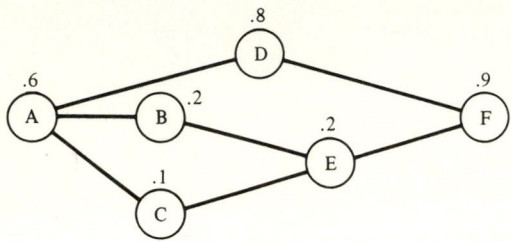

STEP 2 The line speed is

$$\frac{60 \text{ pieces per hour}}{0.90} = 66.7 \text{ pieces per hour}$$

STEP 3 The cycle time is

$$CT = \frac{60 \text{ minutes}}{\text{hour}} \frac{1 \text{ hour}}{66.7} = 0.90 \text{ minute per piece}$$

STEP 4 The theoretical number of operators is selected from the larger of the following two numbers:

Rule 1

$$\frac{\sum_{i=1}^{n} \text{element times}_i}{\text{cycle time}} = \frac{2.8 \text{ minutes}}{0.90 \text{ minute}} = 3.11 = 4 \approx N_1$$

Rule 2

$$\tfrac{1}{2} \text{ cycle time} = \frac{0.90}{2} = 0.450$$

Since three elements, A, D, and F, have times greater than 0.45 the minimum number from rule 2 is three operators (N_2). The larger of the values is given by rule 1; therefore, four operators is the theoretical minimum number required to balance the line.

STEP 5   The theoretical efficiency is calculated as follows:

$$\text{Theoretical efficiency} = \frac{\displaystyle\sum_{i=1}^{n} \text{element times}_i}{(CT)(4)} =$$

$$\frac{0.6 + 0.8 + 0.9 + 0.2 + 0.1 + 0.2}{0.90 \times 4} \, 100\% = 77.8\%$$

STEP 6

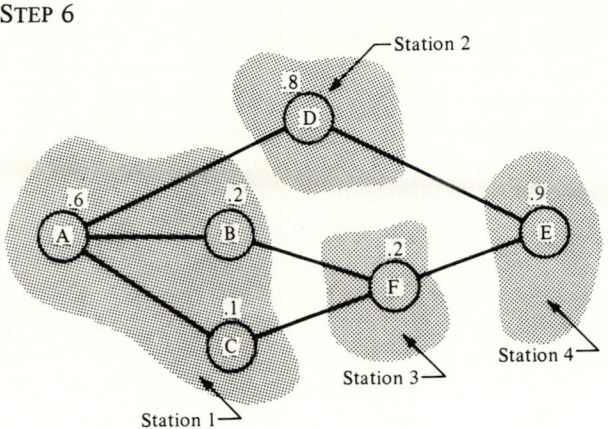

Station	Elements	Time, minutes	Σt_i, minutes
1	A	0.6	
	B	0.2	
	C	0.1	0.9
2	D	0.8	0.8
3	E	0.2	0.2
4	F	0.9	0.9
Cumulative time			2.8

STEP 7   Calculating the actual efficiency,

$$\frac{\displaystyle\sum_{i=1}^{n} \text{element times}_i}{(CT)(\text{number of stations})} = \frac{2.8 \text{ minutes}}{3.6 \text{ minutes}} \, 100\% = 77.8\%$$

STEP 8   Since the actual efficiency equals the potential efficiency, this line balance cannot be improved unless one or more restrictions is relaxed.

The solutions to actual industrial assembly-line-balance problems can usually be improved by relaxing the restrictions listed under Balancing an Assembly Line. The remainder of this chapter will consider many of the general techniques used by practitioners to improve the solutions to assembly-line-balance problems.

Reducing the Total Element Time

In the preceding example the actual efficiency is 77.8 percent, a very poor efficiency. Rule 1 resulted in 3.11 operators, which was rounded up to 4 operators, since a discrete number of operators is necessary to operate the assembly line. If the incremental value beyond 3 operators is multiplied by the cycle time, the result will be the minimum reduction in the total time which would be necessary to change the theoretical number from 4 to 3 operators. In the example, 0.11×0.90 minute = 0.1 minute; an examination of the precedence diagram reveals that deleting 0.1 from element D reduces the time to 0.7 minute. Calculating rule 1, we find that $2.7/0.9$ (new elements total) = 3 operators. The theoretical minimum efficiency becomes 100 percent; therefore elements D and E can be combined into station 2 and element F placed in station 3. This reduces the number of stations to 3 and the actual efficiency is increased to 100 percent. The feasibility and cost of altering D to reduce the time to 0.7 minute must be balanced by the advantage of reducing the cost from 4 to 3 operators.

NONTRADITIONAL TECHNIQUES

Element Sharing[1]

Figure 15-1 shows the precedence diagram for an assembly-line-balancing problem. This problem has a cycle time of 8 and is useful to illustrate the balancing techniques, because it has been used in many articles on line balancing.[2]

The letters in Fig. 15-1 indicate the elements and the numbers represent the time to perform them. The diagram is read left to right and the lines leaving element A indicate that the element must precede elements B, F, G, and H. There is no precedence among elements B, F, G, and H. All elements assigned to a work station are performed by that station on every assembly.

---

[1] John J. Mariotti, "Four Approaches to Manual Line Balancing," *Industrial Engineering*, June, 1970, pp. 35–40, reprinted and abridged by permission of the American Institute of Industrial Engineers.

[2] James R. Jackson, "A Computing Procedure for a Line Balance Program," *Management Science*, vol. 2, no. 3, April 1956.

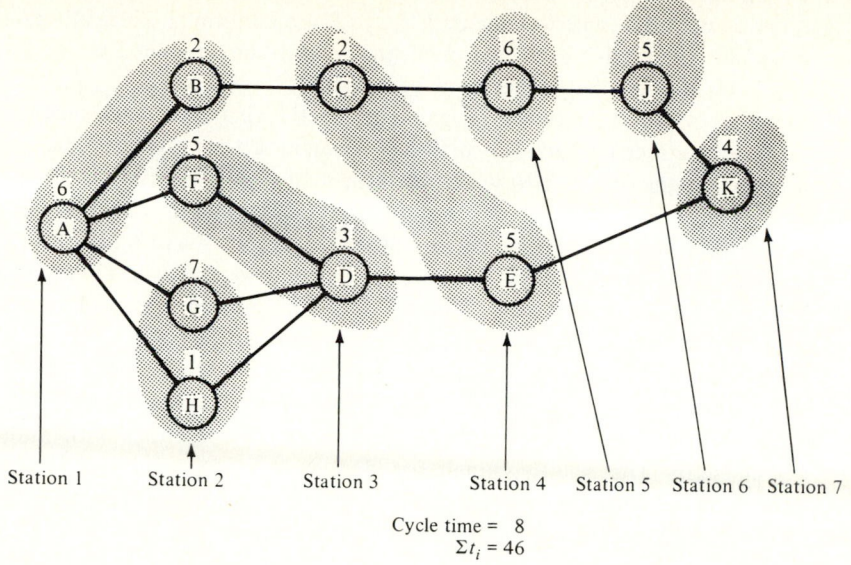

Station 1 Station 2   Station 3   Station 4   Station 5 Station 6 Station 7

Cycle time = 8
$\Sigma t_i = 46$

Figure 15-1 Assembly precedence diagram showing that 90 percent of the delay occurs because of elements I, J, and K. Elements are assigned to stations as shown in the table.

Elements	Time units	Station assignments	Station times	Operators	Delay
A B	6 2 }	1	8	1	0
G H	7 1 }	2	8	1	0
F D	5 3 }	3	8	1	0
C E	2 5 }	4	7	1	1
I	6	5	6	1	2
J	5	6	5	1	3
K	4	7	4	1	4
		$\Sigma t_i \quad =$	46	7	10

$$\text{Delay} = \left(7 \text{ stations } \frac{1 \text{ operator}}{\text{station}} 8 \text{ time units} - 46\right)\frac{1}{56} 100\% = 17.9\%$$

Delay may be calculated in another manner:

Delay = 100% − efficiency   where efficiency is either theoretical or actual

A closer examination of the diagram shows that 90 percent of the delay occurs in work stations 5, 6, and 7, where elements I, J, and K are performed. Since all these elements are greater than half the cycle time c, they cannot be combined with each other and still satisfy the rule that station time be less than or equal to c.

Figure 15-2 shows the same work assignments for the first four work stations, while the last three stations are reduced to two by element sharing. To be a practical solution, the time for the operator to walk upstream to the next assembly must not exceed 0.33 for station 5 and 0.66 for station 6. If the standard station length is based on an 8-time units cycle, the lengths of work stations 5 and 6 might have to be, respectively, 3/8 and 1/8 longer than standard. The work and walk time of the operators as the assemblies pass stations 5 and 6 should be plotted to provide visual reassurance that the station lengths and work assignments are satisfactory.

Some computer algorithms have included the feature of processing a run of assemblies past a station and plotting the path of the operator. This is a very desirable feature, particularly for mixed-model assembly lines and for operations with intermittent work elements. The resulting graph would show how often and how far the operator moves into the adjacent stations. Analysis of the graph can lead the analyst to reassign work elements to prevent interference between operators and to reduce the occurrence of incomplete or faulty assemblies.

Incomplete or faulty assemblies may occur when the operator has traveled down-

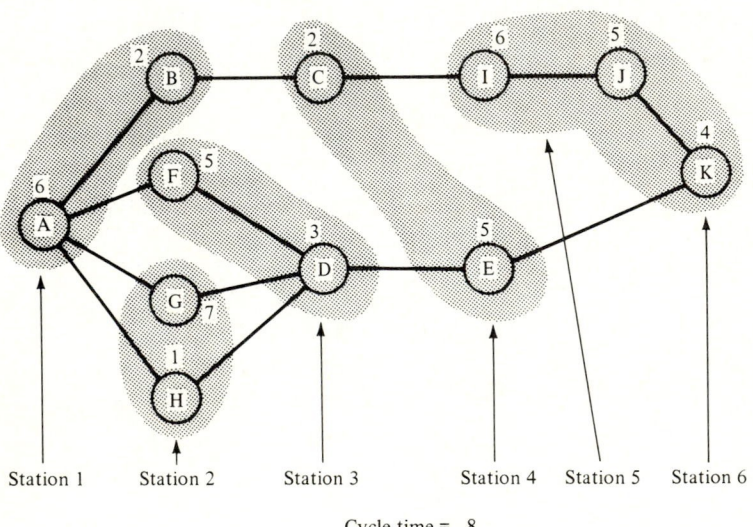

| Station 1 | Station 2 | Station 3 | Station 4 | Station 5 | Station 6 |

Cycle time = 8
$\Sigma t_i = 46$

Figure 15-2 Balance can be improved by sharing elements as follows: station 5 is to perform element J on one-third of the assemblies and element I on 100 percent of the assemblies for a prorated time of $6 + (\frac{1}{3} \times 5) = 7.67$. Station 6 is to perform element J on two-thirds of the assemblies and element K on 100 percent of the assemblies for a total prorated time of $4 + (\frac{2}{3} \times 5) = 7.34$. Delay = (6 stations $\times$ 1 operator per station $\times$ 8 time units – 46) $\frac{1}{48}$ (100 percent). Element sharing by the fifth and sixth station reduces delay from 17.9 to 4.2 percent.

stream a great distance and has difficulty returning to the front of his or her station or is interfering with the downstream operators.

Element sharing may present some personnel problems, particularly in determining the source of rejects. The intermittent nature of sharing creates the same problems for operator 5 as would occur if he or she had to perform an inspection element on every third assembly. The problems caused by being out of the station disappear if an operator-paced free-transfer system can be used. This allows a buffer of assemblies to accumulate between adjacent stations. With this system the assembly is stationary while the operator works and travels to the next station only when released by the operator.

A variation on this, discussed by automotive car assembly engineers, is the variable launch method. Here the spacing between successive models would be proportional to the expected amount of work required on the model.

While an improved balance may be sometimes obtained by element sharing, the practical task of assigning the shared elements among the operators must be mastered. A common solution is that of color-coding the assemblies and assigning each color to a different operator. The operator performs the shared element only upon assemblies marked with his or her color code. Of course, the cost of applying the color code must not exceed the savings expected because of element sharing.

The element to be shared may occasionally be assigned to operators who work in nonadjacent stations. This is advantageous, since it gives more opportunity to make a proper assignment for the shared elements.

There is increased material-handling cost associated with element sharing, since stock has to be delivered to more than one location. More space is needed for the duplicate set of containers and tooling cost is increased for a duplicate set of assembly tooling.

A related approach in automotive assembly is to have an assembly operator ride the conveyor for enough stations to complete his or her assignment. This is occasionally resorted to when a customer's order includes many options which would overload regular operators.

Use of Multiple Work Stations

Figure 15-3 shows another method of balancing the line. If the solution is limited by the restriction which states that only one operator can be assigned to a work station, the minimal number of operators is seven. This gives a delay of 18 percent.

In Figure 15-4, the restriction that only one operator can be assigned to a work station is ignored. The minimal solution now is six operators (four 1-operator stations and one 2-operator station). This gives a delay of 4 percent for a reduction of 14 percent.

The scheduling of the work between operators provides that each operator perform the elements on every other assembly. The forward walk of the operators is proportional to the conveyor speed and to the amount of work assigned to each. The return distance walked by the operator is proportional to the distance between parts, the conveyor speed, and the return-walk rate.

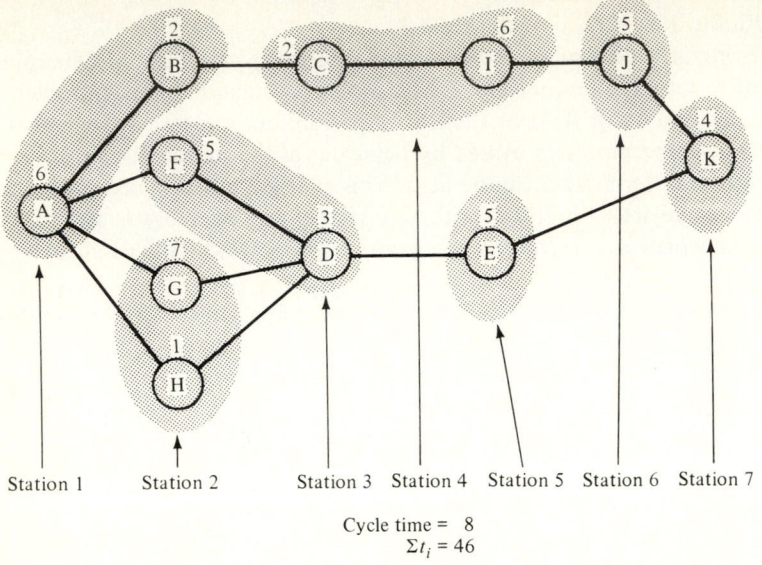

Station 1   Station 2   Station 3   Station 4   Station 5   Station 6   Station 7

Cycle time = 8
$\Sigma t_i = 46$

Figure 15-3 This solution has a minimum number of seven operators. Delay is 18 percent.

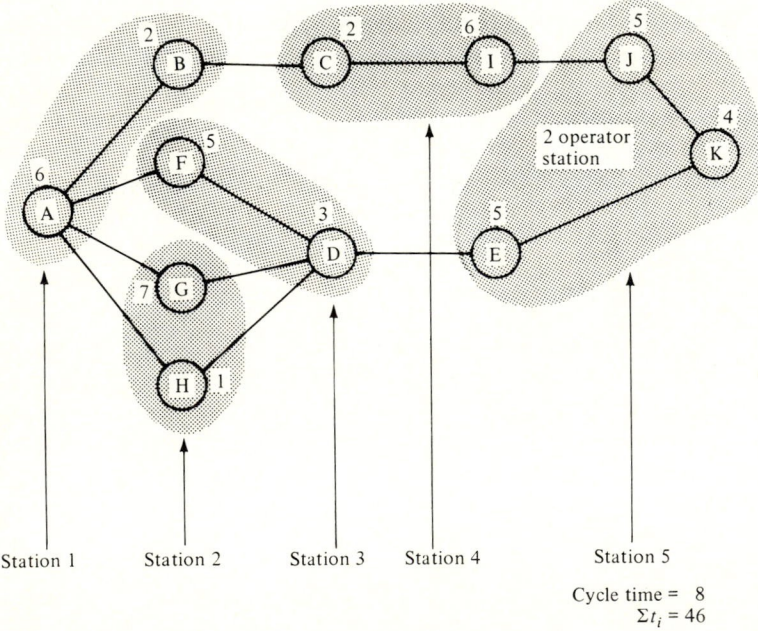

Station 1   Station 2   Station 3   Station 4   Station 5

Cycle time = 8
$\Sigma t_i = 46$

Figure 15-4 If more than one operator can be assigned to a station, this solution can be used giving a delay of only 4 percent.

214

The use of multiple stations enlarges the job assignment of the operator, and should lessen the boredom associated with a small labor-content job assignment, but it does incur cost which must be offset by the decrease in assembly labor cost. These costs are

Increased material-handling cost to deliver goods to more than one point
Increased tooling cost
Increased training time for operators because of the longer work cycle

The learning factor is of particular importance when the daily absence rate of production workers is high.

Cycle Time Less Than Largest Element Time

Figure 15-5 shows the example problem balanced for a cycle time of 5. This is less than the largest element time of 1. To balance the line at a cycle time of 5 requires the creation of one or more multiple stations. The diagram shows seven stations consisting of four 1-operator stations and three 2-operator stations.

A unique advantage of balancing at a lower cycle time than the largest element is that the needs of the customer may be best filled by working at this cycle time. All the advantages and disadvantages of multiple stations apply.

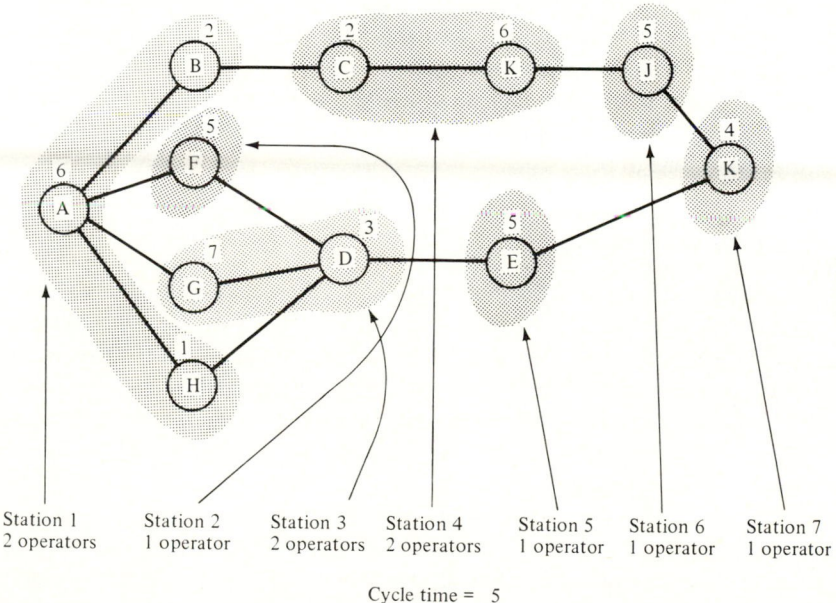

Station 1	Station 2	Station 3	Station 4	Station 5	Station 6	Station 7
2 operators	1 operator	2 operators	2 operators	1 operator	1 operator	1 operator

$$\text{Cycle time} = 5$$
$$\Sigma t_i = 46$$

Figure 15-5 How the assembly line is balanced with a cycle time less than the largest single element.

There is a possibility in some instances of getting better balance by combining element sharing and multiple stations.

Table 15-1 shows various balances obtained for the example problem. The balances were obtained for 32 cycle times ranging from 3 to 46. Since the largest single element is 7, all balances obtained for cycle time less than or equal to 6 violate the restriction that the cycle time is greater than the largest single element. These solutions require one or more multiple stations. To obtain a cycle time of 3, three 1-operator stations, three 2-operator stations, one 3-operator station, and one 4-operator station are required for a total of 16 operators. Multiple stations improve the balance for cycle times 7, 8, and 10.

Examination of the tables shows that the minimum number of operators needed to achieve a cycle time cannot be less than

$$\frac{\sum_{i=1}^{n} \text{element times}_i}{\text{cycle time}}$$

rounded off the next highest integer. (Example: For a balance time of nine, $46/9 = 5.1$ operators.) Therefore, six operators is the minimum possible for the line. Once a balance is achieved with six operators, it cannot be improved; but because of the large balance delay, it would be better to use a cycle time of 8 instead of 9.

If it is essential for a cycle time of 9 to be used, then some methods analysis of the operation should be performed to reduce the large balance delay. Tooling and equipment analysis or a motion analysis to ensure that both hands are gainfully employed should be able to reduce the estimated number of operators required from 5.1 to 5. Once this is done, attempts should be made to balance the line at five operators for the required cycle time of 9.

Dividing the Indivisible Elements

An element is called indivisible if a further subdivision of the element creates a total time greater than the original element time. An example of this is the tightening of five nuts. It is apparent that the least time to tighten the nuts occurs when the tightening tool is picked up once to tighten all five nuts. This would normally be called an indivisible element, because a further subdivision to assign the task to more than one operator would create the need for more gets and disposes of the tightening tool; thus, more effort would be required.

However, there are occasions when a lower balance can be derived by assigning two nuts to one operator, and three nuts to another, even though more work is created. But before this is done, the other alternatives, such as multiple stations and element sharing, should be considered, since there may be less total work effort required with these alternatives. For a situation in which minimum balance may be obtained by any of the three methods, a total analysis should be made, weighing the advantages and disadvantages of each.

The techniques described so far must all satisfy restrictions imposed on the system by fixed facilities or machines in the line and by restrictions of position. Restrictions of position become apparent very quickly in the automobile assembly line. For instance, parts to be assembled on the inside of the automobile may not be assigned to operators who work in the trunk.

Batching

Sometimes when a short-term increase in production is required, another work shift may be established. If the increase in production required is a small fraction of the output from the primary shifts, then batching is sometimes the solution to the added shift. In this arrangement, the number of workers used is a fraction of the normal shift complement. At the start of the shift, the workers operate in the first few stations until they build a suitable bank. Then they walk to the next group of stations to complete the corresponding work elements on the batch. In this way they complete work through all the work stations. When volume is sharply reduced, a solution is to assign each operator to several stations. The operator then performs the work for all the stations upon each of the assemblies.

Banking

For small assemblies, better balance and a higher production rate may be obtained by banking some of the assemblies before the slower operation. The slower operation is then performed on extra time (lunch hours, between shifts, and during off-shift) and the parts produced are banked before the succeeding operation. Repair, relief, setup, or temporary help are often used with this technique.

Proper Allocation of Balance

There are advantages to be gained by controlling the allocation of balance time. Some firms prefer to have balance time spread as evenly as possible throughout the work stations. Worker morale is thus not threatened because of unequal expenditure of effort.

Another point of view is to have as much of the balance as possible concentrated in the lead-off operation. Thus small variations on the lead-off operation do not have an adverse effect on the productivity of the line. In contrast to this, some consider the last operation of a line important enough to warrant allocation of a great amount of balance.

Occasionally, balance time is allocated to specific stations in order to reduce operator effort so that handicapped people may be assigned to these stations. Others assign operators to stations with large amounts of balance as a reward for good service.

Multiple Lines—Multiple Shifts

Frequently, the point of minimum balance is apparently in conflict with the volume requirement. In this case, the following alternatives can be considered:

1. Operate the plant on one shift but create several duplicate assembly lines, each operating at the same cycle time. This cycle time would give minimal balance delay.
2. Operate the plant on multiple shifts, each of which operates at the same delay, but not necessarily the same cycle time.
3. Operate the plant on multiple shifts with the primary assembly line producing at high volume with minimal balance delay. This output would be supplemented by an auxiliary assembly line which operates at a lesser cycle time probably with greater balance delay.

An economic evaluation of alternatives such as those listed should be made before a specific choice is made.

Selection of the Sequence from the Precedence Diagram

The assembly-line problem as presented here is based on the assumption that there is one specified sequence which is essentially unique because of product-design considerations. There are many situations in which the assembly could start with any of several parts designated as the lead-off part to be placed on the line. However, once a specific part is selected as the first part to be placed on the conveyor, many of the assembly sequences are eliminated. As a rule, there are several different sequences, each of which has the same lead-off part, which can be chosen from the precedence diagram that will satisfy the product-design considerations.

One should make a study to determine if the sequence which gives the minimal one-operator assembly time is also the sequence which gives the minimum assembly-line time before one begins to balance. It is apparent that more than one sequence of assembly may have to be developed and evaluated from the precedence diagram during the analysis of assembly-line balancing.

Off-Line Stations and Subassembly Lines

There are occasional situations in which better balance can be achieved by assigning work elements to existing subassembly lines or to off-line stations. If the assembly lines do not exist, an economic analysis might show that one or more could be established profitably. The reverse of this might also be profitable—that is, to remove work from off-line stations or from subassembly lines and to reassign it to the major assembly line.

PROBLEMS

15-1 For this assembly use a cycle time of 0.3, 0.4, and 0.5 minute to balance this line.

(*a*) Calculate rule 1, rule 2, theoretical minimum number of operators, theoretical efficiency.

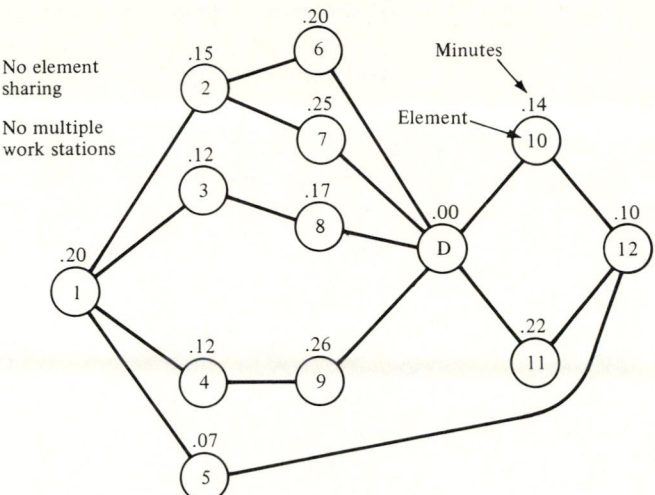

(*b*) Number the stations in their proper sequence and the elements to be performed at them in proper order. These may be placed on the diagram.

(*c*) Calculate the actual efficiency.

(*d*) What is the production in pieces per hour?

(*e*) At $10 per hour (ignore allowances), what is the labor cost per piece?

(*f*) What is the minimum cycle time possible for the line (no element sharing, no multiple work stations)?

15-2 (*a*) For each cycle time calculate the following: rule 1, rule 2, theoretical minimum number of operators, theoretical efficiency.

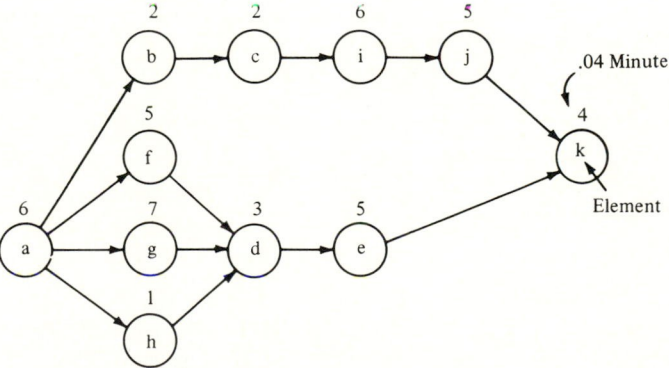

(*b*) Create a line balance for the precedence diagram for each of the following cycle times: 0.07, 0.09 minute.

    (*c*) Number the stations in the proper sequence and elements in each station in the proper order. These may be placed on the diagram.

    (*d*) Calculate the actual efficiency.

    (*e*) Calculate the production output in pieces per hour.

    (*f*) At $10 per hour, what is the labor cost per piece?

15-3 Automotive backup light assembly. Given: The exploded assembly drawing and the list of elements and times.

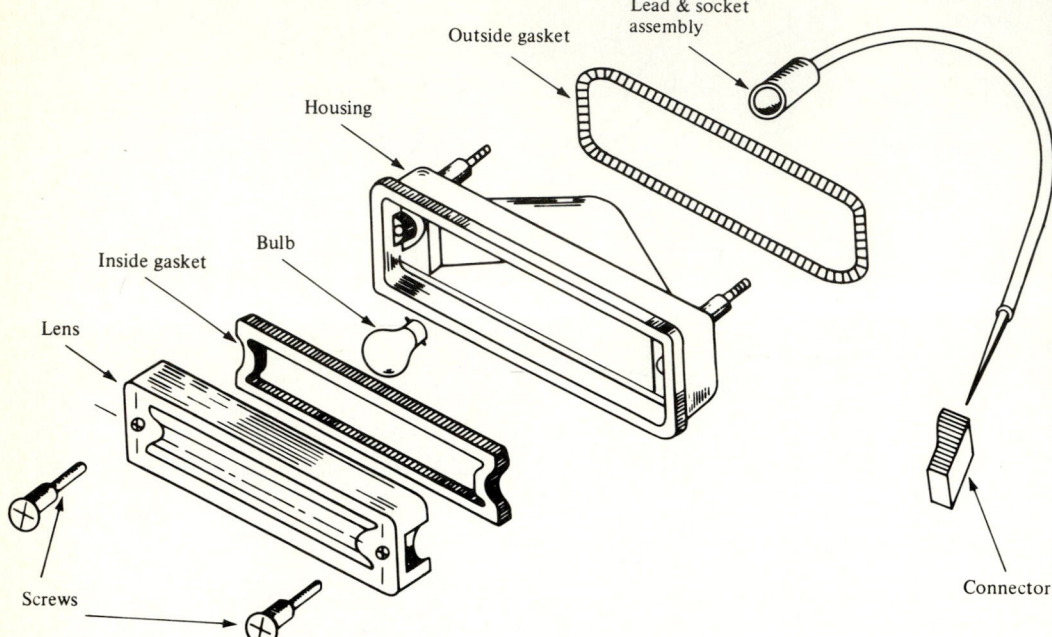

    (*a*) Create a precedence diagram.

    (*b*) Customer demand is 480 pieces per hour.

    (*c*) Balance the line. Assume a 10 percent line loss because of rejects, missing, or inoperative fixtures and line stoppages. Also assume a fixturized belt conveyor.

Element		
Number	Description	Time, minute
1	Assemble outside gasket	0.065
2	Assemble inside gasket	0.053
3	Assemble lead and socket assembly	0.102
4	Assemble bulb to socket	0.073
5	Assemble lens	0.029
6	Assemble two screws and use powered portable screwdriver to tighten	0.112
7	Assemble connector to lead	0.075
8	Inspect and pack	0.097

(*d*) To enrich the problem, search for a cycle time which minimizes the line-balance loss and then determine how the production demand will be met (more hours vs. more than one conveyor).

15-4 What is the significance of rule 1?

15-5 Does rule 2 apply when the proposed cycle time is significantly higher than the largest element time?

15-6 Discuss three ways in which practicing engineers improve line-balance efficiency by violating the traditional constraints.

SIXTEEN

INFORMATION-HANDLING SYSTEMS

A great deal of attention has been directed toward the improvement of products, processes, operations, and movements of the operator. The operator and the physical items used on the job, such as jigs, fixtures, equipment, and parts, have been subjected to such questions as: First, is it necessary? Second, if it is necessary, how can it be improved? There is another field, however, in which little analytical work of this sort has been done. It involves the many operations necessary to carry on the system or network of procedures of the organization. Procedures are necessary in any organization, since there must be a uniform method of doing each job. However, to be effective, the procedure must function properly.

In order to determine if a procedure is functioning properly, one must know several facts about it, such as: (1) What action is taken? (2) Who takes the action? (3) How is the action initiated? (4) When does it take place? (5) Where does it take place? (6) Why is it done? The function of the routine sequence chart is to portray these facts graphically by means of symbols, showing in chronological order what happens, where it happens, how and why it is done, and who does it. The routine sequence chart could be called a routing of a procedure. It follows, then, that the routine sequence chart helps us: (1) understand the procedure(s) surrounding a job and (2) determine the need for, and methods of, improving the job.

THE BASIC ROUTINE SEQUENCE CHART

In order for the routine sequence chart to fulfill the two purposes mentioned, the basic form must contain the following minimum sections. (Refer to Fig. 16-1.)

Sections

1. *Heading.* The heading contains the following items for identifying information:
   a. Name or title of the procedure
   b. Observer's name
   c. Date of recording
2. *Step column.* The step column records the number of steps in the system and the chronological order of these steps.
3. *Places of performance.* The next series of columns tells where the action takes place. Each column represents a department or building or a desk, table, or individual.
4. *Explanation.* The column on the right-hand side is an explanation of what is done and why and how it is done. When time is an appreciable factor, it should also be noted in this column.
5. *Symbols*

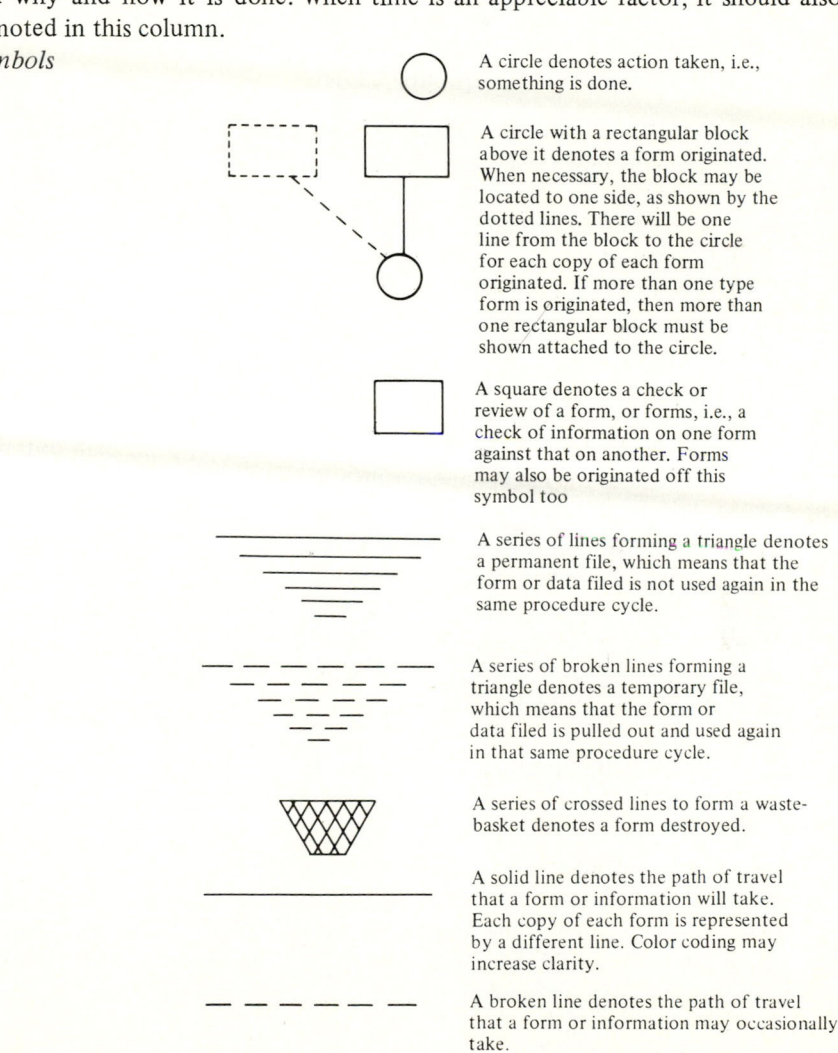

A circle denotes action taken, i.e., something is done.

A circle with a rectangular block above it denotes a form originated. When necessary, the block may be located to one side, as shown by the dotted lines. There will be one line from the block to the circle for each copy of each form originated. If more than one type form is originated, then more than one rectangular block must be shown attached to the circle.

A square denotes a check or review of a form, or forms, i.e., a check of information on one form against that on another. Forms may also be originated off this symbol too

A series of lines forming a triangle denotes a permanent file, which means that the form or data filed is not used again in the same procedure cycle.

A series of broken lines forming a triangle denotes a temporary file, which means that the form or data filed is pulled out and used again in that same procedure cycle.

A series of crossed lines to form a wastebasket denotes a form destroyed.

A solid line denotes the path of travel that a form or information will take. Each copy of each form is represented by a different line. Color coding may increase clarity.

A broken line denotes the path of travel that a form or information may occasionally take.

6. *Legend.* The legend on the chart is made up of abbreviations of the various forms used. Key letters indicate the form and the subnumbers indicate the copy. Some typical examples are as follows:

PR_0 First or original copy of purchase requisition
PR_1 Second or duplicate copy of purchase requisition
Q   Quotation
RB_0 First or original copy of request for bid
M   Material

The preceding symbols are used to identify the paths of travel and to aid in simplifying the writing of the explanation.

Steps in Making a Routine Sequence Chart

To make a routine sequence chart of an existing procedure, there is a certain order of events that should be undertaken, as follows:

1. Select a procedure and record what actually happens not what should happen.
2. Fill in the heading.
3. Determine the party, department, or building where the first action is taken. Put the name of the party or department at the top of the first column under places of performance.
4. Place the proper symbol, usually "form originated," in the top square of this column.
5. Follow the form that initiates "action" with a line indicating path of travel. This line should lead to the next column, which is merely a repetition of steps 3 and 4.
6. Follow the succeeding forms that are originated and send them to a new step if action is taken. If it is filed in the same department, the path of travel may send it to the next step in the same column. One should avoid placing more than one action taken or form-originated symbol in one step, but there may be any number of files or destroys in one step, because inasmuch as it is necessary to explain most actions taken and forms originated, it is inadvisable to place more than one in each step. The files and destroys seldom need explanation, so they can be entered on any step.
7. If a form is held for future reference, whether placed in a file drawer or a basket, a temporary file symbol should be used. When the form is used again, the path of travel should take the form out of temporary file to a point of action under the same heading before advancing to the step where it is used.
8. Place the abbreviation of the form on each path of travel line. At the same time, enter the abbreviation of the form in the legend at the bottom of the page with its identification name. If more than one copy of the form is made, identify each copy by means of a subnumber.

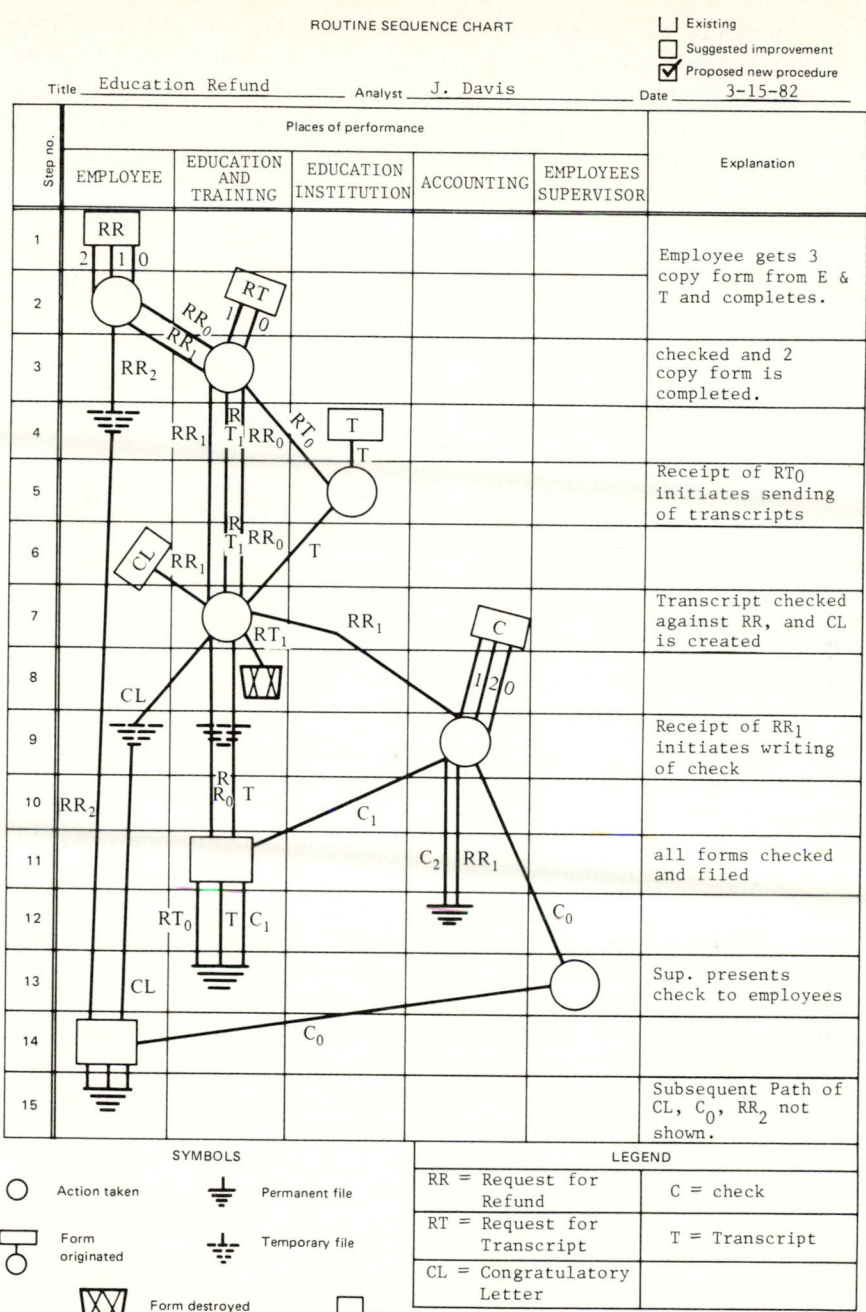

Figure 16-1 Example of a routine sequence chart.

9. In the explanation column to the right, the details of the action taken or form originated may be explained. It is important to avoid repeating what the chart portrays in the explanation column. This column tells how, when, what, and why. When time is an important element, this fact is noted here.
10. The step column merely gives a number to each step for identification.

The Need for Checking the Chart

In any kind of work, accuracy is important. One of the best ways of ensuring this accuracy is to check back on the original job. The reason for such a check is readily appreciated, because even the expert who has been doing the same type of work for an extended period is prone to make occasional mistakes. Even though one person may not be responsible for an inaccuracy of another, he or she may carry the mistake along and thus make all subsequent work inaccurate.

When making a routine sequence chart, note that there is ample opportunity for inaccuracies to creep in. Therefore, if the chart is to be made valid and practical to use, the original work must be checked.

Factors Which May Cause Errors

If the factors which may cause errors are recognized, a more effective job may be done not only in catching the mistakes by means of a check but also in preventing them from entering the job while it is being done. Complete knowledge and understanding of the routine sequence chart will do much to ensure the quality of each chart that an individual may develop.

Gathering detailed information is frequently a difficult job. If nothing concerning the procedure is in writing, information must be gathered by means of contact with other people, which is likely to result in differences in interpretations, dependent upon the respective viewpoints of the individuals contacted. In some cases, standard practice bulletins or written procedures may be used as a source of information. Here again, the ambiguity of words may result in variations between the intent of the author of the bulletin and the interpretation of the observer. Such varying interpretations may cause inaccurate recordings of the procedure.

After all the information and data have been gathered and verified, there remains the problem of accurately recording the facts on the routine sequence chart. Although the procedure is complex, the job of maintaining the proper relation between the form, the sequence of entries, and the flow of the various copies of the forms becomes difficult.

In the process of making the chart, it may be necessary from time to time to make revisions when information is found to have been omitted.

When a complete and recognized method of doing the job is lacking, the resulting nonuniformity of practice may further complicate the observer's task.

The preceding indicates only in a general way the manner in which incorrect recordings may result. Note that there are other causes that will vary widely with the procedures being recorded and the conditions surrounding the job.

Sample Routine Sequence Chart

A sample routine sequence chart is shown in Fig. 16-1. The written procedure follows. It might be worthwhile to check the chart against the written procedure in the following paragraphs as a means of learning how to read a routine sequence chart.

Tuition refund procedure–proposed When a salaried employee has successfully completed an approved course at an educational institution, he or she gets a three-copy request for refund form (RR) from the education and training office (E&T). After completion, the employee keeps copy 2 and sends copy 1 and the original to the E&T office.

At the E&T office the form is checked for legibility and accuracy and if approved, a two-copy request for transcript form (RT) is completed and the original is sent to the educational institution and RT_1, RR_0, and RR_1, are placed in a temporary file. Upon receipt of the transcript (T), E&T checks it against RR and if the transcript is approved, the following items are processed: a congratulatory letter (CL) is sent to the employee, RR_1 is sent to accounting, RT is destroyed, and RR_0 and T are placed in the temporary file.

On receipt of RR_1, accounting prepares the check (C) and two copies. The original is sent to the employee's supervisor, who presents it to the employee while C_1 is sent to E&T and C_2 and RR_1 are permanently filed.

On receipt of C_1 by education and training, C, RT_0, and T are placed in a permanent file.

Checking the Accuracy of the Recording

The check on the original chart must be thorough. It must be from the standpoint of both correctness and completeness. At this point the intent is not to question the purpose of the chart but merely to discover if any part of the actual procedure has been omitted or has been shown incorrectly.

The Check Sheet

To be effective, one's method of checking must be easy to use without requiring an excessive amount of time. A check sheet may well serve this purpose. The questions are so worded as to draw the observer's attention to points where the recording is in error. Also, space is provided on the check sheet to check off the questions and insert comments and remarks, thus making a quick, thorough check possible. (See sample check sheet, Fig. 16-2.)

CHECK EACH POINT CAREFULLY	NO	YES	IF NO	
			STEP NO.	REMARKS
1 Is each copy of each form originated?				
2 Does each place of performance occupy one and only one column?				
3 Does each copy of each form have a definite purpose or use?				
4 Does each copy of each form end in a permanent file or destroy?				
5 Does each copy of each form have a separate line indicating its flow?				
6 Is each flow line identified?				
7 Do the number of lines entering each place of action equal the number of lines leaving each place of action?				
8 Do the number of lines entering each "check" equal the number of lines leaving each "check"?				
9 Do the number of lines entering each temporary file equal the number of lines leaving each temporary file?				
10 Does each step have only one action?				
11 Does the chart read chronologically from top to bottom?				
12 Is the chart properly identified?				
13 Are all explanations complete?				
14 Is each symbol recorded in the legend?				
15 Would color coding aid in classification?				

Figure 16-2 Check sheet for routine sequence charts.

USE OF THE ROUTINE SEQUENCE CHART AS A PLANNING TOOL

The routine sequence chart has two basic uses. It is first an analysis tool and second a planning tool. As an analysis tool, it may be used to review a procedure step by step in order to determine the soundness of the procedure itself. As a planning tool, it can be used to facilitate and expedite formulation of new, previously nonexistent procedures or revision of ones which have been standardized.

Even though the methods of application of the chart as an analysis tool and as a planning tool have many similarities, there exist certain differences. Most of the rules governing the completion of the form are identical in both cases; but because of the differences in the two jobs, there are certain preparatory steps peculiar to the planning of a procedure. On any planning job it is necessary to gather all the relative data and put it into some usable form. This preliminary step of organizing the material will tend to better the quality of the plan, eliminate confusion, and save time.

There are four essential preparatory steps involved in using the routine sequence chart to plan a procedure.

Step 1. Select the end or ultimate objective of the procedure. The procedure to be designed must have an objective or serve some definite purpose if it is to be of value. This end objective may be so defined as to limit the scope of the procedure and thus define the problem.

Step 2. Determine the parties involved in reaching the end objective. Each person or department which is in some way concerned should be noted. In order to obtain an accurate complete list, it may be necessary to determine the nature of the party's concern and the reasons for it.

Step 3. Determine the types of information which must be recorded and/or transferred. The list developed in connection with step 2 may be used here. The function of each party involved in the procedure should then be critically examined and correlated with the items of information which must be recorded or transferred.

Step 4. Determine the means by which the information is to be recorded or transferred. To complete this step form use will have to be investigated. There will probably be some that already exist and others that must be developed. Data will have to be obtained relative to the proposed distribution of copies of these various forms and the methods of distribution.

ADDITIONAL COMMENTS

This chapter has emphasized the design and improvement of a procedure. With the rapid proliferation of computers and word processors, it may be appropriate to analyze all the forms entering and leaving a department. An economic analysis of forms which use a data base common to many departments can be made to determine if they should be placed on a computer system. A study of this nature would uncover other forms which should be placed on a computer system even if they are not based on widely used data-base systems.

A listing of forms entering and leaving a department can be arranged as in Fig. 16-3, which dramatizes the activities performed by the department. Additional information required would include the number of copies per mailing and the frequency of mailings.

A complete analysis of each form, which can be very time-consuming, occurs infrequently, except in companies which establish a forms-control person who approves the release of new forms and studies existing forms. Word processors have stimulated system studies before and after their trial installations. Frequently, the amount of time needed to complete the forms before and after a word processor is installed is required.

A common way to get the time estimates involves each employee's recording the time required for each batch of documents. A work sampling may be done concurrently and the two sets of information can then be integrated to establish the impact of the word processor on the time required to process the information. Since a word

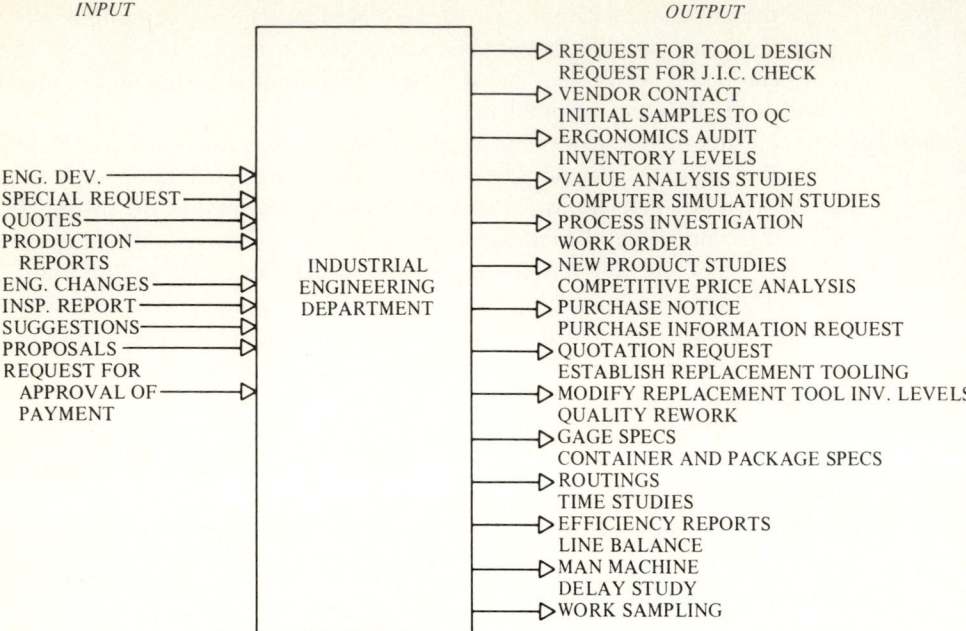

Figure 16-3 Example of an input/output chart.

processor provides other advantages, any final decision may not depend solely on the savings resulting from a reduction in time required to process the information.

The increasing use of computer graphic systems should lead to their use in plotting flowcharts such as the routine sequence charts. Using computer graphics should result in a more systematic charting of procedures. Procedures are currently written, but it is not common practice for flowcharts to be made for each procedure. Computer graphic systems will not only increase the efficiency with which the charts can be drawn but will greatly reduce the time taken to change a chart to reflect a change in procedure.

QUESTIONS

16-1 What five questions are asked when it is necessary to determine if a procedure is functioning properly?

16-2 PR_0 represents which copy of a purchase requisition?

16-3 What represents the third copy of a purchase requisition?

16-4 What is the maximum number of forms-originated or action-taken symbols which should be placed in one step?

16-5 At the end of a routine sequence chart, what should be the final deposition of each copy of a form?

16-6 If it appears that a copy of the form is not used in an action circle or at a check or review step, what action should be taken by an analyst?

16-7 Is there ever a justification for the number of lines entering an action circle not equaling the number of lines leaving?

16-8 What office systems have led to the analysis of procedures and of office work in general?

PROBLEMS

16-1 Analyze the proposed tuition refund procedure and the routine sequence chart, Fig. 16-1.
  (*a*) Does the chart accurately reflect the written procedure?
  (*b*) Apply the checklist, Fig. 16-2, to the chart in Fig. 16-1. Does the chart violate any of the items on the check sheet?
  (*c*) Does each of the copies perform a necessary purpose? If no, why not?

16-2 A production supervisor writes a request for a work order, original and one copy, suggesting some changes in the design of a fixture. The original is sent to the industrial engineer and the copy is temporarily filed. The industrial engineer receives it and after discussions with the supervisor and a study of the workplace, the engineer sketches a proposed revision of the fixture, runs two copies, files the original with the work order request, sends copy 1 to the drafting checker and a copy to the production supervisor, and writes a design revision order. The engineer also sends the original and copy 1 of the design revision order to the checker and copy 2 to the production supervisor; and copy 3 is filed temporarily. The checker adds instructions to the design order request, files the original, and gives copy 1 and the sketch to the detailer.

After the detailer completes the revision, the checker fills out the form, and the drawing, the sketch, and copy 3 are given to the checker after information is recorded on copy 3. After visually inspecting the drawing and comparing it with the sketch and instructions, the checker initials the drawing and runs two copies of the drawing which are sent with the original design request to the engineer. The checker files all paper work in a permanent file.

Upon receipt of the drawings and after comparing them with the sketch and the instructions, the engineer writes a work order. The original and two copies are sent to the tool room, accompanied by copy 1 of the drawings; copy 3 is sent to the production supervisor and copy 4 is filed temporarily. The tool-room supervisor enters an estimate of time, labor, and materials on the work order, files the original and copy 2, and then gives copy 1 to the toolmaker.

When the toolmaker completes the work, the fixture is installed, the production supervisor destroys the forms, and the completed work order is returned to the toolroom supervisor, who files copy 1, makes entries on copy 2 and the original, and sends the original to accounting, where it is permanently filed; copy 2 is sent to the engineer. The engineer files all forms.

Create a routine sequence chart for the preceding procedure. After creating the chart, answer the same questions as in Prob. 16-1. In addition, discuss whether or not the forms which are placed in a permanent file should instead be scrapped.

16-3 The following is a typical procedure used to control the checkout of tools from a tool crib.

When an operator needs a tool from the tool crib, he or she makes out a tool slip in triplicate. The slip is taken to the production supervisor, who checks it for accuracy and completeness and signs the slip.

The operator takes the signed slip to the tool crib, where the attendant checks it for the necessary authorization. If the slip is okay, the order is filled.

The attendant gives the operator copy 3 of the tool slip, with the requested tool, and files the original copy on the checkout board. The second copy is filed in the tool rack. The operator takes the copy of the tool slip and files it in his or her toolbox.

When the operator is finished using the tool, he or she returns it along with the third copy of the tool slip to the tool crib. The tool-crib attendant returns the tool to its rack and picks up the two copies of the tool slip. The first and third copies are returned to the operator, who then destroys them. The second copy is forwarded to the tool record section where the use of the tool is noted on the tool record card. The slip is then filed.

Create a routine sequence chart and answer the same questions as those given in Prob. 16-2.

SEVENTEEN

METHOD SUMMARY CHARTING

A method summary chart provides a graphical representation of manual and process activity on a common time scale. Whether used as a planning device or as a means of studying and analyzing existing operations, there is an advantage in being able to graphically show the time relations among the related activities of a group of people, between an operator and a machine or machines, or the activities of an operator's hands relative to the process equipment. The objective of method summary charting is to efficiently coordinate the operator's activity with the machine(s) or other operator's activity.

That the examples presented illustrate individual machine or crew activities should not be taken as evidence that the concept is not applicable to fabrication and assembly-line situations. The notion of a graphical representation of the time relation of manual activity to machine activity is just as valid in these situations and offers similar potential for use in determining operator loading and relative distribution of work in a group and balancing work assignments to match machine or line times.

One consequence of the trend toward semiautomatic or fully automatic machines is the reduced demand on the operator's time to keep one machine running. The method summary chart is a useful way to depict such relations, offering visible evidence of the feasibility of assigning additional productive work to such operators. It also necessitates a detailed description of the work content, thus ensuring proper planning of manual methods and providing a vehicle for effective operator training on new or revised jobs.

TYPES OF METHOD SUMMARY CHARTS

Method summary charts generally fall into one of the two following categories:

1. Operator-machine charts
   a. Simo chart
   b. Simple-operator–machine chart
   c. Multiple-operator–machine chart
2. Multiple-operator charts (manpower groupings)

Single-Operator–Machine(s) Relations

The most common application of the method summary chart is that for the one-operator–one (or more) machine operation. The need would be apparent in the event that the process time on the machine were greater than the working time of the operator. An example will serve best at this point to illustrate the process of creating an operator-machine chart.

	Work elements	Minutes
1	Unload machine	0.13
2	Load next part	0.12
3	Deburr finished part	0.10
4	Gage finished part	0.10
5	Walk to next machine	0.05
6	Process time on one machine	1.00

In developing the proper assignment of activities to provide effective utilization of the operator's time and the machine cycle, you must categorize the work elements as being either external or internal time relative to the machine process time.

External time is the time required by the operator to perform elements of work which are necessary to cause the machine to go through another automatic cycle. This is work which must be done while the machine is not processing. It is external in relation to the machine.

Internal time is the time required by the operator to perform work which can be done while the machine is processing, but which prevents the operator from working at another station or machine. Walking from one machine to another is treated as internal time on the machine that the operator just left, if the machine the operator has left is still processing.

Process time is the time required for a machine to go through the automatic portion (processing) of its cycle.

Idle time is the time required for the operator or machine to wait for work.

In this example then, elements 1 and 2 must be external and elements 3 and 4 internal elements; and the walk time between machines is internal to the machine that the operator is leaving.

Figures 17-1 and 17-2 show the method summary charts that result from comparing a one-operator–two-machine system to a one-operator–three-machine system for this example. Note that the two-machine system results in a 1.25-minute cycle for two parts (or 0.625 minute per piece) compared with a 1.50-minute cycle for three parts (0.500 minute per piece) for the three-machine system. It can also be observed that the first case results in operator idle time, whereas the second case results in machine idle time.

A useful relation exists which may be used to approximate the number of machines one operator can run efficiently, excluding allowances for downtime for tool changes, stockhandling, or the like, and assuming that the method is identical on machines having the same process time.

$$\frac{\text{Approximate number of}}{\text{machines per operator}} = \frac{\text{operator external time} + \text{machine process time}}{\text{operator external time} + \text{operator internal time}}$$

Using the example data,

$$\text{Number of machines} = \frac{0.25 \text{ minute} + 1.00 \text{ minute}}{0.25 \text{ minute} + 0.25 \text{ minute}} = 2.50$$

Thus, the outcome could be predicted relative to operator-versus-machine idle time before plotting the data on the method summary chart. If the answer is rounded down to two machines, operator idle time results; if rounded up to three machines, the machines will be idle part of the time. This relation is valid only if an operator is running identical machines and handling identical products. There are many other factors

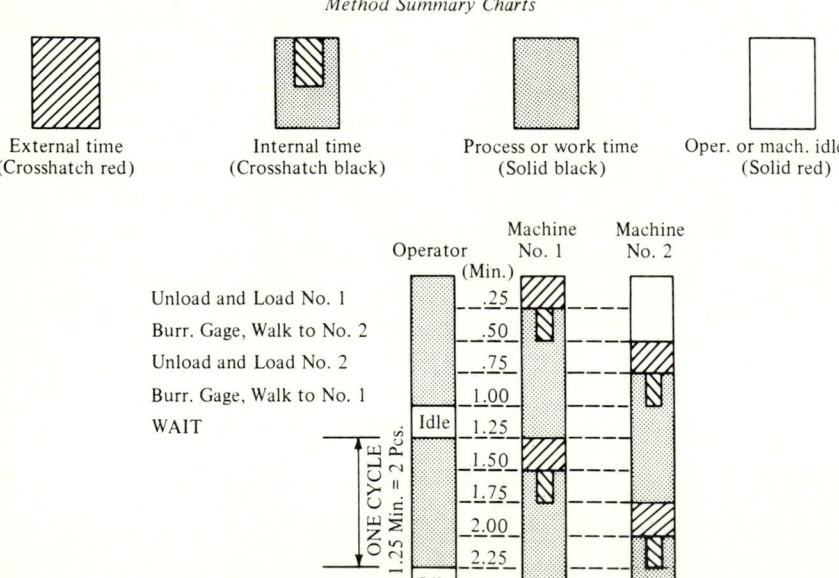

Figure 17-1 One operator–two machines.

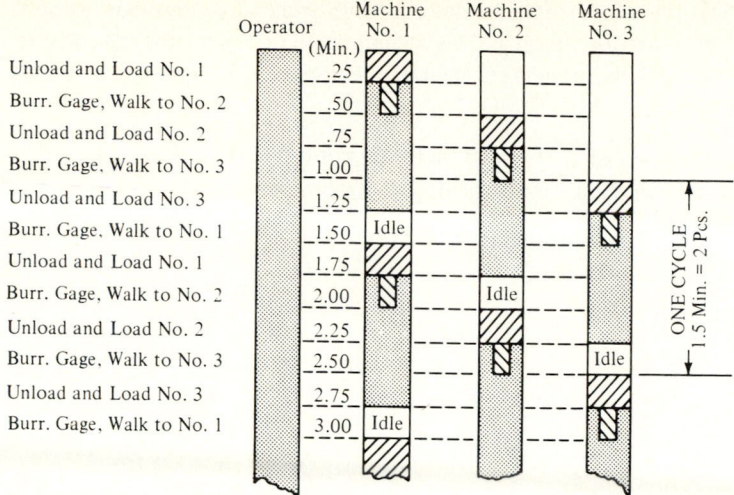

Figure 17-2 One operator – three machines.

which must be considered before reaching a decision about whether the operator should run two or three machines. Some of the decision factors are new equipment cost, equipment availability, schedule requirements, and ultimately the resultant total cost per piece.

A word of caution: the preceding example demonstrates the use of the method summary chart in the one-operator–multiple-machine system only where the work is identical and machine process times are the same. Though this may be the most common situation, there is always the possibility that you may want to consider a system involving one operator running several different types of machines with different work elements for each operation. The following example illustrates the assignment of work for dissimilar machines.

Assume that the following data are obtained for each machine independently:

Machine			
1	2	3	4
External			
1. Unload, 0.25 minute	Unload, 0.25 minute	Unload, 0.20 minute	Unload, 0.15 minute
2. Load, 0.25 minute	Load, 0.70 minute	Load, 0.30 minute	Load, 0.15 minute
Internal			
3. File and walk, 0.50 minute	Walk, 0.05 minute	Gage, dispose, and walk, 0.50 minute	Paint mark on each part and walk 0.20 minute
(Machine cycle, 3.00 minutes)	(Machine cycle, 4.05 minutes)	(Machine cycle, 2.00 minutes)	(Machine cycle, 3.70 minutes)

The following relation can be used to determine the relative amount of operator time used to keep each machine running. This is the inverse of the relation shown previously, where the work and machines were the same. However, this equation is applied to each machine separately.

$$\text{Approximate percent of operator time (utilization)} = \frac{\text{external time} + \text{internal time}}{\text{external time} + \text{machine process time}} \, 100\%$$

For this example, the following is obtained:

Machine			
1	2	3	4
$\dfrac{0.50 + 0.50}{0.50 + 3.00} = 28.6\%$	$\dfrac{0.95 + 0.05}{0.95 + 4.05} = 20.0\%$	$\dfrac{0.50 + 0.50}{0.50 + 2.00} = 40.0\%$	$\dfrac{0.30 + 0.20}{0.30 + 3.70} = 12.5\%$

Summing the results, then,

$$\text{Total approximate operator utilization} = 28.6\% + 20.0\% + 40.0\% + 12.5\% = 101.1\%$$

It can be seen from this result that the operator time has been fully assigned, and it should be anticipated that some machine idle time will result. The method summary chart developed for this system is illustrated in Fig. 17-3. Note that the chart, starting with machine 1 as an arbitrary choice, was developed utilizing the following guidelines:

1. When leaving a machine after completing the work, the operator will proceed to the machine which will next be ready for service.
2. If two or more machines are idle at the time the operator becomes available, the operator will proceed to the machine which has the shortest process time.

The sequence in which the machines should be loaded to obtain minimum idle time for the operator and machines is obtained after charting several cycles as shown. It is apparent that there is some operator, as well as machine idle, time.

The results obtained thus far can be utilized only as approximations of what will occur in practice. The method summary charts in this instance shows the loss in productivity which can be expected to occur in practice. It provides no measure of the machine interference loss resulting from random disturbances, such as breakdowns. This loss is obviously bound to increase as the number of machines per operator increases. Other approaches, such as simulation or various mathematical analyses, have been successfully applied to these situations in order to arrive at a more accurate projection of anticipated results.

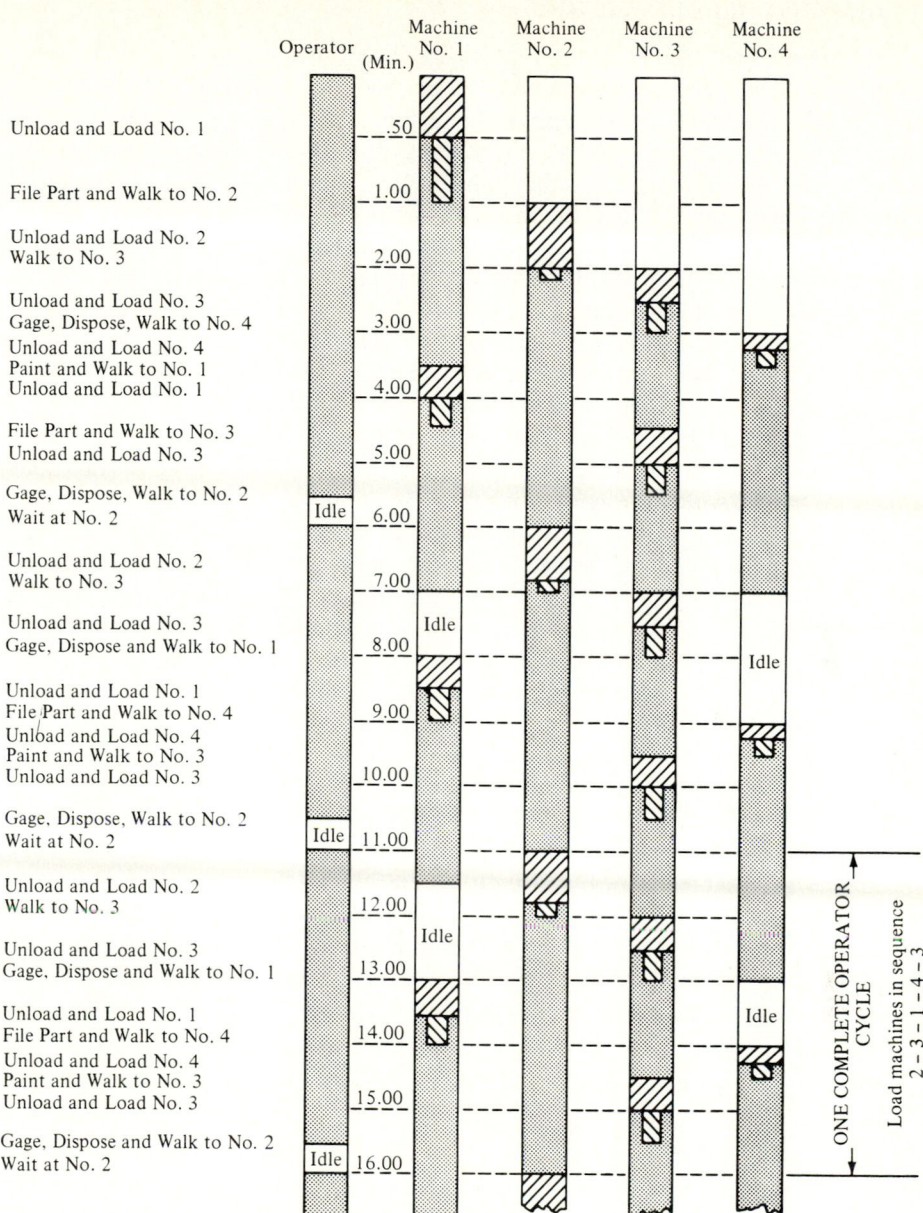

Figure 17-3 One operator–four different machines.

Multiple-Operator–Machine Relation

Several processes and facilities in industry today are of such magnitude that it is not a question of how many machines should a person operate but a problem of how many persons should be used to operate the equipment effectively. Therefore, an engineer might construct a method summary chart of a multiple-operator–machine relation when the investigation reveals that more persons than are necessary are being used to operate equipment. If this is the case, the method summary chart will help determine the correct number of operators needed to service this equipment. Once the chart has been constructed, the idle time and walking time can be analyzed to determine the possibility of performing the necessary elements of work with less operators.

A multiple-operator–machine chart is shown in Fig. 17-4, where there is excessive waiting and walking on the part of all three operators. Remember that wait and walk (long movement) are ineffective worker movements; therefore, they should be eliminated or minimized in this example. The wait and walk time combined adds up to almost a minute for the three operators, which makes it relatively easy for two operators to do the job within the cycle time of 0.525 minute.

In Fig. 17-4, it can be seen that operators 1 and 2 move out of the way and wait 0.11 minute and 0.12 minute, respectively, while operator 3 gets and places the front panel in the fixture. Operator 3 also waits 0.085 minute before placing the panel, because operators 1 and 2 are in the way. Operator interference occurs and causes wait time when too many operators are assigned to a work station, as in this particular example. With only two operators, the containers could also be moved in closer in order to minimize the walking time. Incidentally, the excessive walk and wait times would not be as readily apparent without the construction and analysis of the multiple-operator–machine chart.

The front-end assembly of a car is relatively heavy after being spot-welded, so the operation can be made easier by providing a mechanical unloader, which is not uncommon in sheet-metal operations. Of course, the additional expense should be economically justified with a reasonable payback period, because one operator can now do the operation. After holding the palm buttons for process, the operator will then be free to get the first wheel housing and load it into the fixture for the next cycle, instead of having to wait for the process to end and then unload the assembly manually.

Simo Charts

One of the main reasons for using the method-summary-chart technique is to improve the coordination of the operator with the machine(s). When the simo chart is made, the activity of the left and right hand are shown separately; it is similar to the act breakdown and type A element description (see Fig. 17-5). This separation of the left- and right-hand activity provides the additional advantage of also analyzing the simo chart for improved coordination between the hands in addition to coordinating the operator with the machine.

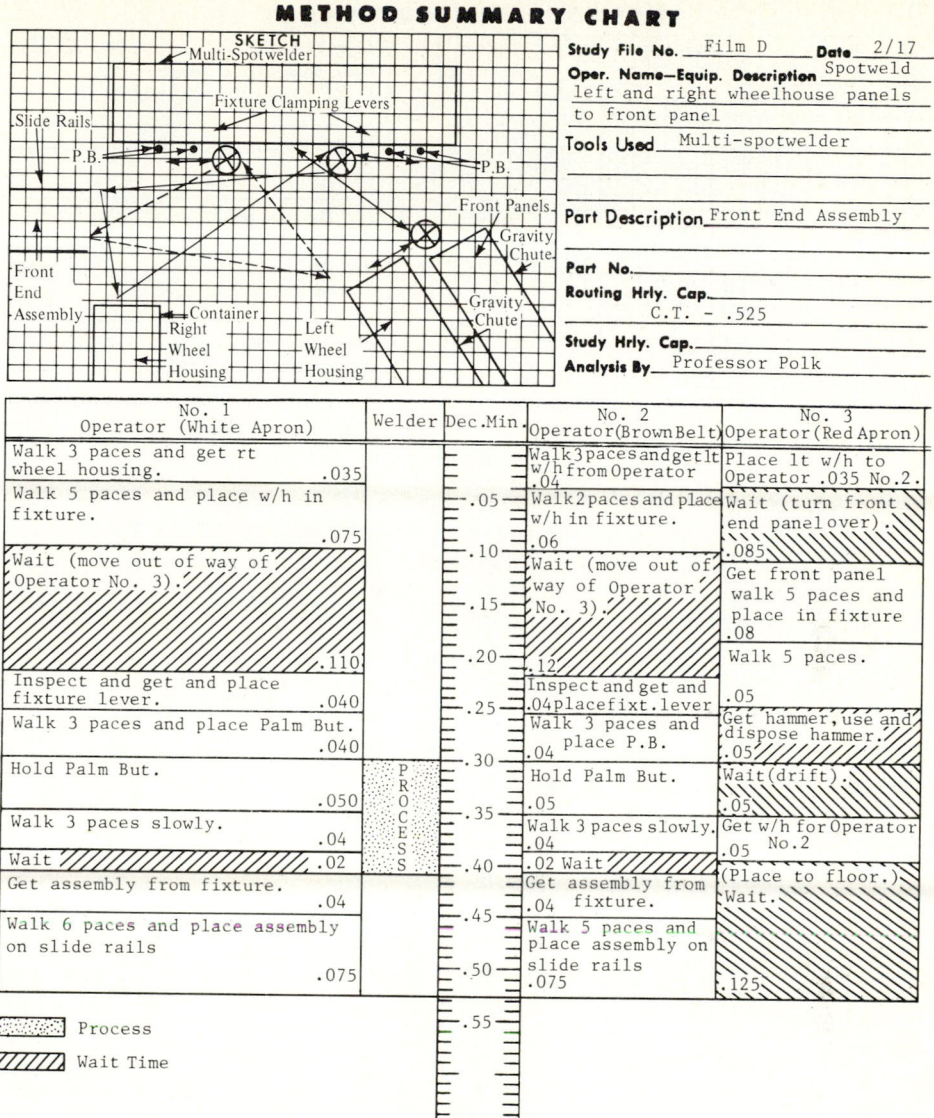

Figure 17-4 Multiple operator–machine chart.

The simo chart is commonly used on fairly short cycle operations when the machine process time is relatively short and the worker is operating only one machine. In Fig. 17-5, a simo chart has been made from the filmed operation "form projection on bridge." The get, place, and wait times have been recorded from a time-and-motion study projector. It is readily apparent that there are extensive waits on the part of the left and right hand caused by compatible acts *not* being performed simultaneously.

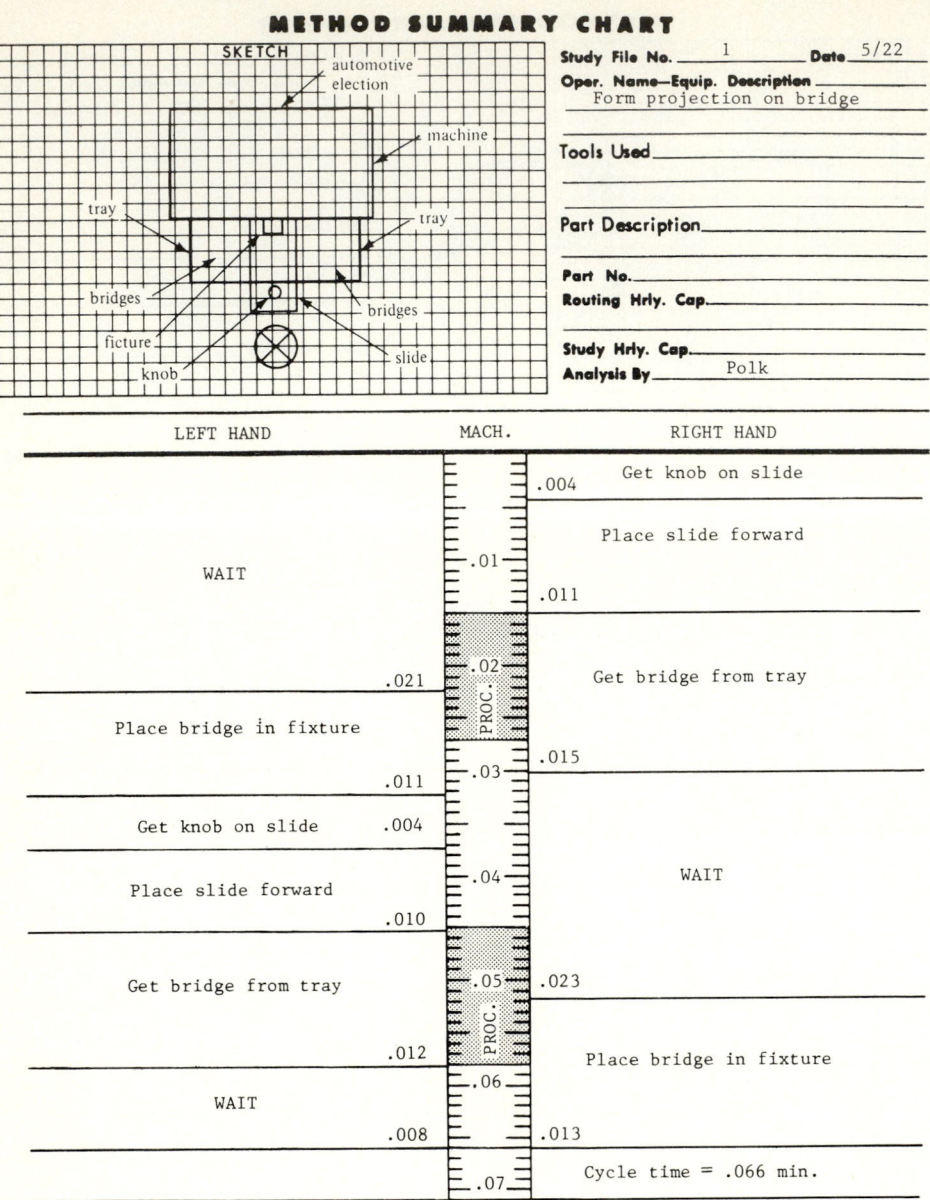

Figure 17-5 Simo chart.

By coordinating the left-hand with the right-hand activity, and coordinating the operator activity with the machine-process time, the resultant improved method is shown in Fig. 17-6; the times shown are actual times from the improved method which will vary somewhat from cycle to cycle. Note that the operator "palms the part" (retains the bridge) while getting the knob on the slide and placing the slide forward.

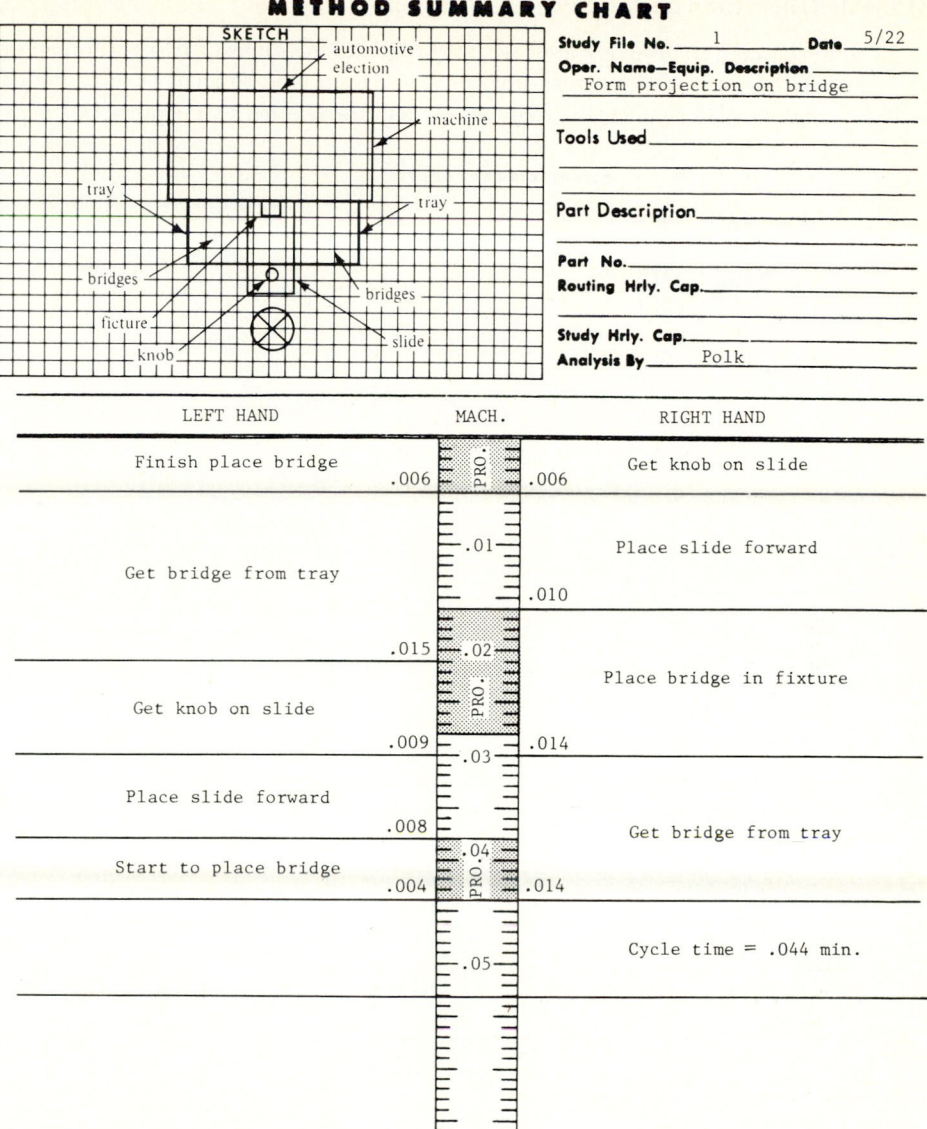

Figure 17-6 Improved simo chart.

Only then does the operator place the bridge in the fixture. Palming the part can easily be done when the parts are not too large. The resultant saving of 33 percent was attained by merely changing the sequence of the acts compatibly with the machine.

No changes were made in the workplace layout or equipment, adjustments which will often improve the method too.

Another advantage of this type of inexpensive improvement is that of increased machine utilization, which in turn means that fewer machines must be purchased to get the required production. This type of savings can oftentimes be substantial.

Multiple-Operator Charts

It is not uncommon to have operators working together in groups of two or more with no machines involved; multiple-operator charts are then used to analyze this type of activity. Either movie cameras or video equipment are also used to capture this type

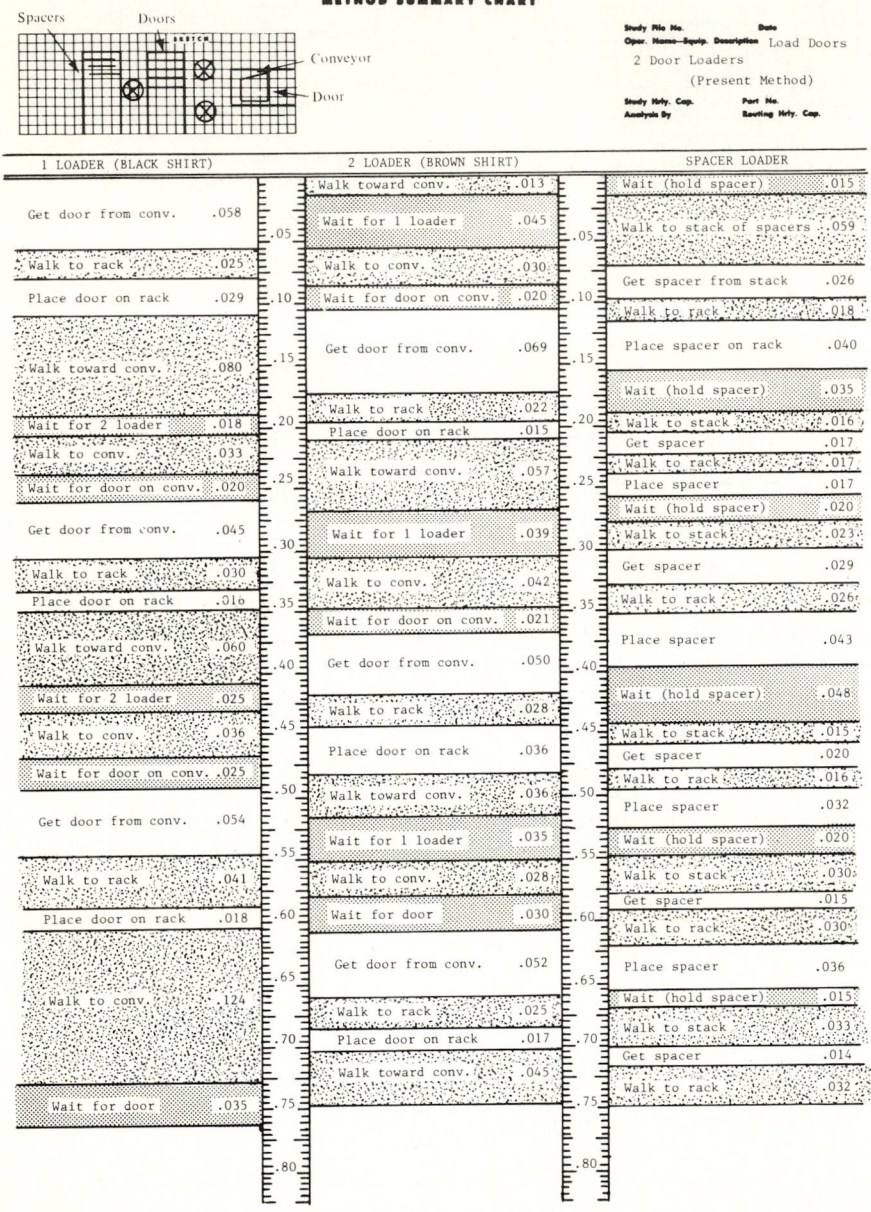

Figure 17-7 Multiple operator chart.

Elements	Number 1 loader	Number 2 loader
Wait		
For conveyor	9%	9%
For other operator	5%	15%
	14%	24%
Walk		
To rack	12%	10%
Toward conveyor	34%	26%
To conveyor	10%	13%
	56%	49%
Get door	22%	22%
Place door	8%	5%

	Space loader
Wait (hold spacer)	25%
Walk to stack of spacers	23%
Walk to rack	17%
Get spacer	14%
Place spacer	21%

Figure 17-8 Summary of door-loading operation.

of activity for analysis. The intent of the analysis is to properly coordinate the activities between the operators and minimize work interference which imposes waits on operators. Work interference can occur especially if there are too many operators assigned to an activity. Of course, improving the workplace layout is considered in the analysis of all method summary charts.

The multiple-operator chart in Fig. 17-7 is for the analysis of a car-door loading operation in which the doors are loaded onto a long rack. In this chart, each door loader is getting and placing three doors each, while the spacer loader is getting and placing six spacers. It should be observed in the sketch that the doors are coming down the conveyor in a horizontal position and are placed in the rack in a vertical position for shipping, which is why the get times of the doors are so large and walk times so extensive.

Figure 17-8 was created to highlight the amount of time spent by each operator on the ineffective worker movements of waiting and walking excessively. This problem will be treated more extensively with the questions at the end of the chapter.

METHOD SUMMARY CHART EVALUATION AND COMPARISON

The method summary chart is a graphical presentation of the method of work performed by an operator when his or her work is coordinated with one or more cycle-time-controlling devices, such as another operator, a machine, or machines. Therefore, it is always to the advantage of the analyst to construct one or more of these charts in analyzing an operation.

Each time an operation or system is improved, the analyst must evaluate the improvement. Therefore, the following example is included as a typical evaluation and comparison of two systems.

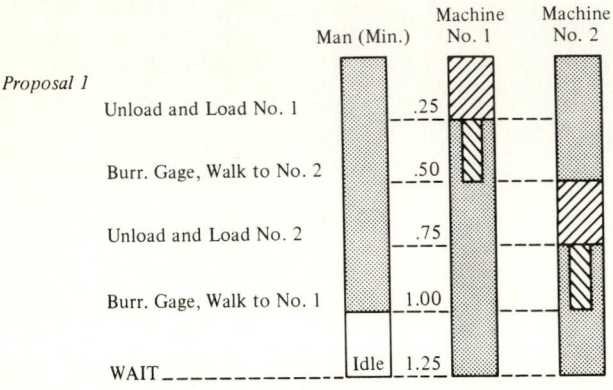

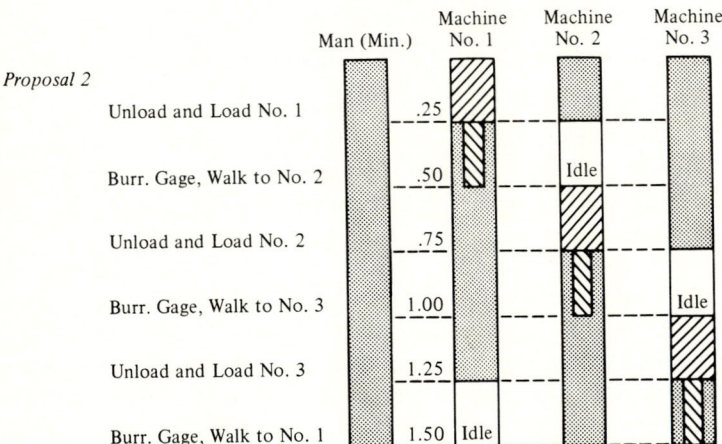

Figure 17-9 Two or three machine proposal.

Sample calculations which can be used as a basis for evaluations and comparing method summary charts are as follows:

1. Basic cycle time.

Proposal 1   1.25 minutes

Proposal 2   1.50 minutes

2. Basic time per piece.

Proposal 1 $\quad \dfrac{1.25}{2} = 0.625$ minute per piece

Proposal 2 $\quad \dfrac{1.50}{3} = 0.50$ minute per piece

3. Allowed cycle time = basic cycle time + (delay allowances) (basic cycle time). (Assume 15 percent allowed for measured delay allowances; use estimates only when direct measurements impossible. Percent varies.)

Proposal 1 $\quad 1.25 + 1.25 \, (0.15) = 1.44$ minutes

Proposal 2 $\quad 1.50 + 1.50 \, (0.15) = 1.725$ minutes

4. Allowed time per piece.

Proposal 1 $\quad \dfrac{1.44}{2} = 0.72$ minute per piece

Proposal 2 $\quad \dfrac{1.725}{3} = 0.575$ minute per piece

5. Production per hour.

$$\dfrac{60 \text{ minutes per hour}}{\text{Allowed time per piece}}$$

Proposal 1 $\quad \dfrac{60}{0.72} = 83$ pieces per hour

Proposal 2 $\quad \dfrac{60}{0.575} = 104$ pieces per hour

6. Daily production.

Pieces per hour $\times$ hours per day

Proposal 1 $\quad$ 83 pieces per hour $\times$ 8 hours per day = 664 pieces per day

Proposal 2 $\quad$ 104 pieces per hour $\times$ 8 hours per day = 832 pieces per day

7. Direct labor cost per piece (assume hourly labor rate of $10 per hour).

Proposal 1 $\quad \dfrac{\$10}{\text{hour}} \dfrac{1 \text{ hour}}{83 \text{ pieces}} = \$0.1205$ per piece

Proposal 2 $\quad \dfrac{\$10}{\text{hour}} \dfrac{1 \text{ hour}}{104 \text{ pieces}} = \$0.0962$ per piece

8. Percent improvement $= \dfrac{\text{cycle time (old)} - \text{cycle time (new)}}{\text{cycle time (old)}}$

or

$$\frac{\text{Time per piece (old)} - \text{time per piece (new)}}{\text{Time per piece (old)}}$$

A comparison of proposal 1 and proposal 2 is presented (1 is considered old or original setup).

$$\frac{0.625 \text{ minute} - 0.5 \text{ minute}}{0.625 \text{ minute}} \; 100\% = 20\%$$

9. Operator effectiveness. This calculation indicates the percent of the cycle time that the operator is working, or

$$\frac{\text{Cycle time} - (\text{waits and holds})}{\text{Cycle time}} \; 100\%$$

Proposal 1 $\quad \dfrac{1.25 \text{ minutes} - 0.25 \text{ minute}}{1.25 \text{ minutes}} \; 100\% = 80\%$

Proposal 2 $\quad \dfrac{1.5 \text{ minutes} - 0}{1.5 \text{ minutes}} \; 100\% = 100\%$

In the case of a simo chart, where the left-hand–right-hand relation is shown, two percentages, one for each hand, are calculated. The resultant percentages are indicative not only of the absolute degree of activity of the operator but also the degree to which the work load is balanced between the two hands.

10. Machine utilization $= \dfrac{\text{process time}}{\text{cycle time}}$ (Process time is read directly from chart)

Proposal 1 $\quad \dfrac{1.00 \text{ minute}}{1.25 \text{ minutes}} \; 100\% = 80\%$

Proposal 2 $\quad \dfrac{1.00 \text{ minute}}{1.50 \text{ minutes}} \; 100\% = 67\%$

This calculation is also made by including the unload and load portion of the cycle in the machine activity time. The disadvantage to this particular method is that inefficient manual activity which reduces the capacity of the machine is not reflected.

11. Amortization of tooling expense. A conversion cost is associated with the installation of many methods-improvement proposals. The savings which are effected by the improvement must pay for the conversion. Only then will a true savings result.

$$\frac{\text{Tooling cost (or conversion cost)}}{\text{Savings per piece}} = \begin{array}{l} \text{the number of pieces that must} \\ \text{be produced to break even} \end{array}$$

$$\frac{(\text{Assume}) \ \$50,000}{\$0.1205 - \$0.0962} = 2,057,613 \text{ pieces to break even}$$

Expressed in another form, when the volume of future production is known:

(Number of pieces × original unit cost) – (number of pieces × proposed unit cost)

must be greater than the proposed tooling or conversion cost before the proposal is economically feasible. This relation might also be shown in the form of a break-even chart (see Fig. 17-10). Distance A on the graph represents the investment required to install the proposed method. The break-even chart depicts graphically the results of the calculations made in the determination of the break-even point. Its primary value exists as a means of showing to management the situation so that the effect of changes can be evaluated. It is possible that management might have additional information, unknown to the analyst, which could alter the course of action taken.

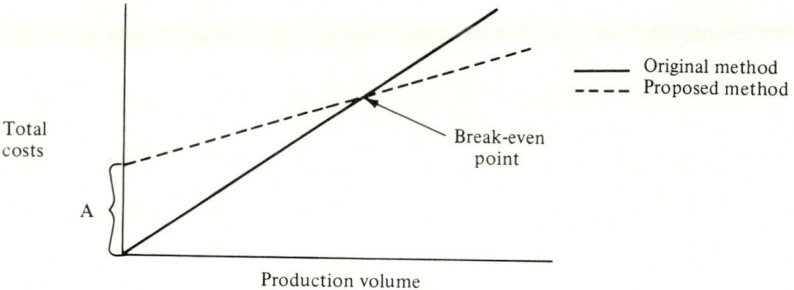

Figure 17-10 Break-even chart.

QUESTIONS

17-1 Which type of method summary chart shows the left- and right-hand activity separately?

17-2 Explain the difference between external and internal time.

17-3 In a multiple-machine assignment, is the walk between machines graphed as internal time to the machine that the operator is leaving or as internal time to the next machine where the operator also does work?

17-4 Can all the different types of method summary charts be used as a planning tool?

17-5 When analyzing an operator-machine chart for improvement, why should the external-time activity be closely scrutinized?

17-6 What is a break-even point?

17-7 How can one determine how many machines an operator should be assigned if the same types of machines will be producing the same products?

17-8 When machine utilization is increased, what inherent savings are there in addition to increased production?

17-9 Should the gauging or inspection of a part be an external or internal element of work?

17-10 In Fig. 17-5, what fairly inexpensive mechanical changes could be made to increase production as an alternative to the improvement shown in Fig. 17-6?

PROBLEMS

17-1 The total cost of converting to the new method is $60,000; in addition, the cost per piece of the present method is $0.85, and $0.58 is the cost per piece of the new method. The payback period is 2 years and the estimated production is 400,000 units during this period of time.

    (*a*) What is the break-even point?

    (*b*) Should the new method be implemented?

    (*c*) How much money would be saved or lost during this period of time if the new method were implemented?

17-2 How much of the operator's time is utilized with the following machine assignments?

	Machine, minutes			
	A	*B*	*C*	*D*
External time	0.12	0.30	0.10	0.12
Internal time	0.20	0.03	0.12	0.18
Machine-process time	1.00	0.80	0.70	1.40

17-3 If the same machines are making the same product, how many machines should the operator be assigned?

	Minutes
Machine-process time	1.46
Walk to next machine	0.03
Inspect and gauge part	0.18
Unload and load machine	0.08
Dispose of part and preposition next part	0.12

17-4 Since there are excessive waits and walks on the part of all three operators in Fig. 17-4, create a new multiple-operator–machine chart with only two operators. Retain the same cycle time of 0.525 minute in order to balance the work with preceding and following operations.

17-5 Create a proposed simo chart with one of the mechanical improvements specified for Question 17-10. Use Fig. 17-5 as a guide for some of the time data.

17-6 What is the cycle time in minutes per door for the door-loading operation in Fig. 17-7.

17-7 Using the cycle time from Prob. 17-6, propose a new multiple-operator chart with two operators and show the new layout also. Use the average get and place times for handling the doors and cardboard spacers. This can be determined from the data shown in Fig. 17-7.

EIGHTEEN

METHODS ANALYSIS AND WORK MEASUREMENT OF INDIRECT ACTIVITIES[1]

Historically, work measurement has been concerned with the measurement of direct labor. One reason is that some direct-labor measurement is required in most cases for product costing and pricing. Another major reason is that direct labor historically accounted for the bulk of the hourly labor in a plant and was the most significant cost to measure and control. From an industrial engineering viewpoint, the measurement of direct-labor operations is a great deal easier and consequently less costly than is indirect labor. For these reasons, the emphasis in the past has been on the measurement of direct-labor operations.

Both evolutionary and revolutionary changes have been taking place in our economy. These changes tend to place much greater emphasis on the measurement of indirect labor. Because of the impact of automation, the traditional relations between direct and indirect labor are often reversed. An example is the automated machining transfer line, where the direct workers are completely replaced by setup and maintenance operators. It is no longer unusual to find a factory where the indirect workers outnumber the direct workers. This condition is further compounded as clerical, technical, and administrative activities become a larger part of the economy. These activities are central to most service industries, which are growing at a rate greater than the economy as a whole. Undoubtedly, the computer and advanced technological improvements such as numerically controlled machine tools are accelerating the growing im-

---

[1] Derived from *Industrial Engineering Handbook* by H. B. Maynard. Copyright 1971, McGraw-Hill, pages 4–31 through 4–35 by William K. Hodson. Used with permission of McGraw-Hill Book Co.

portance of indirect-labor operations. All these developments have created a greater need for the measurement and control of indirect labor.

DISTINCTION BETWEEN DIRECT AND INDIRECT LABOR

The manufacturing cost of a product is usually divided into three major components: labor, materials, and overhead. Labor cost normally is composed of only the direct-labor cost. This is the cost of labor directly involved in the physical manufacturing of the part. Each direct-labor operation has some effect on the part or assembly. The amount of labor required for each part or assembly can be measured directly.

A major part of overhead costs is the cost of indirect labor. A typical indirect-labor cost is janitorial service. Although the cost of janitorial labor can be easily determined, it is difficult to relate the cost of this labor directly to a specific part or product. As a consequence, the cost of indirect labor operations is usually allocated to specific products on a percentage or prorated basis. A typical approach is to allocate indirect-labor costs to products in proportion to their direct-labor hours. This approach assumes that there is a direct relation between the indirect-labor hours and the direct-labor hours. Typical indirect-labor costs include material handling, shipping, receiving, and warehousing; tool cribs; toolmaking; maintenance, janitorial service; inspect and test; factory service and repair, field installation and servicing; clerical workers; chemical and physical laboratory workers; and drafters.

Some of these activities—for example, inspect and test—may sometimes be classified as direct labor if the work content of the operation can be directly related to the job. In industries, such as aerospace, which are oriented to government contracts, a strong attempt is made to classify as many manual operations as possible as direct labor. This classification tends to reduce the indirect labor or overhead costs and to increase the direct-labor hours. Because overhead is frequently expressed as a percentage of direct-labor costs, this greatly reduces the overhead percentage. The magnitude of overhead costs is frequently a factor in the government's evaluation of the efficiency of a contractor. In many cases, however, the apparent efficiency of a contractor is established in the accounting department and not on the shop floor. Low overhead rates may be the result of accounting treatment, and not a true reflection of low costs.

FACTORS INFLUENCING INDIRECT-LABOR MEASUREMENT

Although the basic work-measurement techniques used to measure indirect work are the same as those used to measure direct labor, there is a significant difference in emphasis and method of application. Other more serious differences exist in related areas such as methods, work counts, standard hour calculations, group application of standards, and the like. An analysis of these factors will provide a better understanding of some of the reasons for the differences between direct- and indirect-labor measurement.

Methods

Both direct- and indirect-labor measurement require that the method employed in performing the operation be standardized before the standard time is established. The application of this rule varies substantially between direct and indirect work. On very repetitive direct-labor work, it is not at all unusual to spend from 50 to 100 man-hours on methods work for every one hour spent on work measurement. Furthermore, great emphasis is placed upon training the operator to follow the established method with a high degree of precision. In some cases, each individual motion is analyzed and subjected to the operation-analysis and motion-study approach. The number of motions required to perform the work is reduced to a minimum, and the motions that remain are reduced to the simplest form of motion. Unless an operator is specifically trained to follow the method, motion by motion, it will be difficult for him or her to perform the operation in the standard time allowed.

The other extreme of methods analysis exists in most maintenance activities. Although methods study can contribute substantially to improving maintenance work, the emphasis is different. Instead of concentrating on the methods employed to perform a specific job or operation, attention is focused on the overall methods employed by the crafts person. The overall methods are applicable to all jobs. For example, considerable time should be devoted to studying the various tools used on the job and the methods for transporting and storing these tools. Frequency studies can quickly disclose which tools are most often used. It can then be objectively determined which tools should be attached to a tool belt where they would be quickly available, and which tools should be kept in a toolbox or, in some cases, in a specially designed tool cart.

If the maintenance operators have come up through the shop with little or no formal craft training, the methods work may have to be supplemented by basic training in the proper use of hand tools. The principle to follow is to concentrate on methods studies that will have universal application and to minimize methods studies for specific operations.

Maintenance work represents an extreme example of nonrepetitiveness in indirect-labor work. Other forms of indirect labor, such as janitorial work, tend to be more repetitive, and the study can be directed more toward the methods to be used in performing a specific job. Often, very little thought is given to janitorial work from a methods viewpoint. It seems to be regarded by all concerned as a simple job—one that anyone can do. Consequently, most janitorial people are given very little, if any, instruction on how the job should be done, how frequently it should be performed, and the like. Therefore, methods work in this area can produce substantial returns.

This point illustrates one reason why the application of work measurement to indirect labor produces such worthwhile returns. Practically all direct-labor work is subject to some form of methods study and improvement, particularly in cases where work measurement is applied. As a consequence, the work methods used by direct labor are usually fairly effective. On the other hand, it is unusual to find an application of methods study to indirect-labor operations. In fact, the complexity and variety of work performed by the indirect workers require a much higher order of methods study than do repetitive production operations performed under a standard set of conditions, but the return can be greater than is that on the typical direct-labor job.

Units of Work

Another characteristic of indirect labor that makes it difficult to measure is the lack in it of a single unit of work. The unit of work for most direct-labor operations is the "piece." A time standard can be expressed in terms of minutes or standard hours per piece. The number of pieces produced by the operator can then be counted. The pieces produced multiplied by the standard hours allowed per piece quickly gives the number of standard hours earned for a particular job.

Consider, however, the problems involved in attempting to establish a unit of work for an order picker. An order picker is commonly employed in a finished-goods warehouse. An order for a number of different items in differing quantities is received by the picker. His or her job is to fill the order by walking to the different bins or locations where the items are stored, selecting the correct quantity of each item, assembling the items in a box or truck, and returning the completed order to a packing station.

The unit of work obviously cannot be "an order." The number of different items, usually called "line items," can vary from 1 to 20 or more. The standard time per order will vary accordingly. It is not possible to use the line item as the unit of work, because there are certain elements of work associated with each order that are somewhat fixed regardless of the number of line items. Moreover, the time for a line item will vary substantially depending on the shape and location of the item and whether the item comes in standard package quantities or less-than-package quantities, whether it has to be weighed, and so on. In most indirect-labor applications, one must use a number of units of work and establish a routine for recording the units of work performed. The standard hours earned for each of the units can then be calculated. The problem of establishing work counts is generally a great deal more complicated and expensive than is that for direct labor. In many cases, however, some ingenuity and imagination on the part of the industrial engineer can simplify this problem. In order picking, for example, the job of calculating the hours earned for each order can frequently be combined with the pricing and price extension of the order. If this is computerized, the data base for the time standards can be incorporated in the pricing program. In this way, the standards calculation can be performed as a by-product of the pricing program.

With some ingenuity, the job of collecting work counts and applying time standards can be greatly simplified despite the fact that many more variables are involved than is the case in most direct-labor operations. This does, however, tend to increase the administrative costs of indirect-labor programs.

Measurement of the Work

The standard techniques for measuring direct labor are time study, predetermined motion times, standard data, and work sampling. All these are also used for measuring indirect labor, although their application is quite different.

One of the most common studies on direct labor is an individual time study of a single operation. The operation is normally divided into a number of elements, each of which is repeated in a standard sequence. A time study is then made of the operation, usually covering 10 or 20 pieces. The same sequence of elements is followed for each piece.

This type of study rarely occurs on indirect work—which may be frustrating to the industrial engineer whose previous work-measurement experience has been limited to direct labor. A main characteristic of indirect labor is that it is nonrepetitive by nature. If a series of time studies is made of the order-picking operation, one study for each order picked, it is likely that there will be 20 different studies for 20 different orders. The number of line items, the location of the items, and the quantity of the items picked will vary considerably from one study to the next.

Because of the nonrepetitive nature of indirect-labor operations, the work must be carefully analyzed and planned before any attempt is made to measure it. One of the primary purposes of this preplanning is to develop methods improvements and to standardize the methods used for performing the work. Standardization of the work is important because it enables predetermination and synthesis of what the operator should do to perform a given job. A secondary benefit of this analysis is that it furnishes a great insight into the nature of the work and its characteristics, the major elements of the work, the variable factors that exist in these elements, the sequence of the elements, and the like. All this information is essential to the design of the work-measurement system.

Because of the variable sequence of the work elements and the variables that may exist within a given work element, it is essential to rely heavily on the standard data and the building-block concept of work measurement. Either time study or predetermined motion times can be used to develop the detailed elements needed to construct the standard data.

Multiple regression analysis The procedures discussed in this chapter for measuring indirect labor emphasize for the most part the traditional approach to this problem. This approach involves studying each activity of the indirect-labor operation and establishing time standards for them by the use of time study, predetermined motion times, standard data, or work-sampling techniques. Although the returns from most indirect-labor measurement programs are well worthwhile, the measurement procedure is often tedious, time-consuming, and relatively expensive. A number of attempts have been made to simplify the work-measurement aspect of the problem by the use of mathematical techniques, the most promising of which is multiple-regression analysis combined with work sampling.

Two or more units of measure must usually be used to calculate the output of indirect-labor operations accurately. The multiple-regression-analysis technique provides a means of correlating several units of measures, called "predictors" in multiple-regression terminology, with the time required to perform the job.

The multiple-regression model is an equation that relates the predictors (units of measure or variables) to the response (standard time to perform the work). The standard format is

$$Y = b_0 + b_1 X_1 + b_2 X_2 + b_3 X_3 + b_4 X_4 + \cdots + b_i X_i$$

Assume that a shipping operation consists of filling orders by the use of a fork truck. The truck operator picks up an empty pallet and proceeds to the various stock locations where he or she loads the necessary cases for the orders on the pallet until the orders are filled or the pallet is loaded. He or she then transports the pallet to an order-assembly area. The objective is to determine a method for measuring the time required per pallet load. A preliminary analysis of the operation indicates that the predictors, in this case, may be any of the following:

$$X_1 = \text{number of cases packed per pallet load}$$
$$X_2 = \text{number of orders per pallet load}$$
$$X_3 = \text{weight of packed material per pallet load}$$
$$X_4 = \text{volume of cases per pallet load}$$

A work-sampling study is then made of the operation. During the course of the study, observations are made of the work and nonwork elements for each of the operators. The data are adjusted by performance rating factors to provide a leveled observation percentage of the working time. Records are also maintained of the actual hours worked, the number of cases packed, the number of orders, the weight of the packed material, and the volume of the cases for each pallet loaded. All the data for each pallet load are then placed in a computer program for multiple-regression analysis. Because of the complexity of the calculations, a computer is the only economical way of using multiple regression for problems of this magnitude.

The computer solution provides values for the coefficients b_0, b_1, b_2, b_3, and b_4. The program also provides correlation coefficients for each of the predictors.

By examining the various correlation coefficients and the correlation between the predictors, an individual firmly grounded in the mathematics of regression analysis can determine which of the predictors are significant and which are not. After such an analysis, it may be decided that the predictors of weight and space provide very little additional predictive capability to the predictors of the number of cases and number of orders, and the final formula might look like this:

$$Y = 5.02 + 3.37X_1 + 0.45X_2$$

where Y = standard minutes per pallet loaded
     X_1 = number of cases packed per pallet
     X_2 = number of orders per pallet load

The values for the coefficients b_0, b_1, and b_2 are, respectively, in minutes, 5.02, 3.37, and 0.45. The standard time for a pallet made up of six cases and two orders can be calculated by inserting the predictor quantities into the formula and solving for the standard time:

$$Y = 5.02 + 3.37 \, (6) + 0.45 \, (2)$$
$$= 26.14 \text{ minutes}$$

Although regression analysis is a powerful tool and shows great promise in the field of indirect-labor measurement, it has the potential of being grossly misapplied by industrial engineers who use the programs on a "cookbook" basis. It should not be used without the counsel of an individual who is completely familiar with the mathematics of regression analysis.

GETTING A PROGRAM STARTED

Experience has shown that a program of methods engineering on indirect operations requires careful planning to gain the full support of management and the cooperation of the supervisors and employees involved—especially in cases where no previous analyses have been made in the indirect areas.

Obtain Management Support

Active management support is essential in starting and in maintaining a successful program. Generally, top management need only be informed of an undesirable situation and approval will be readily obtained to make the necessary studies and analyses. In other cases, top management itself may provide the impetus needed for getting a program underway by requesting that an analysis be made in a particular area on a certain type of indirect work.

In developing a program for management, you should consider the following steps:

1. Determine the indirect area with promising potential that appears the most desirable and the most practical to approach.
   a. Observation of inadequate equipment or tools or improper use of equipment
   b. Observation of idle or balance time or poor work patterns
   c. Examination of plant reports, labor reports, budget performance, etc.
   d. Development of the relation of indirect to direct labor
   e. Recognition of direct-labor delays caused by indirect labor
   f. Receipt of comments and suggestions from visitors or vendors
   g. Determination of where chronic or excessive overtime exists
   h. Comparison with performance of other departments or plants
   i. Suggestions received under a formalized program directed at a given area, which may serve as an indicator that a study is needed
2. Inform management of apparent losses as determined or indicated by one or more of the things spotted under point 1. In giving this information to management, you should bring out the apparent causes of these losses. An indirect area with promising potential, one that appears the most desirable and most practical to approach, could be used as a case example.
3. Cite the advantages of a methods engineering program for indirect-labor operations.
   a. Maximum use of manpower
   b. Improved competitive position
   c. Better service to production
   d. Better control of overtime

    e. Improved psychological effect on direct labor, because direct-labor employees sometimes see situations where indirect employees do not have full jobs or do not produce at the same level of effectiveness as they do

    f. Equalization of work assignments

    g. Better means of judging supervisor's effectiveness

    h. Improved budget forecasts

    i. An aid for focusing attention of management on the specific area with the greatest potential

4. Obtain approval on starting a program in a specific area or areas of the plant. If enough attention is paid in making the preliminary survey, the indicated results will, in most cases, convince management that time should be spent in analyzing indirect operations.

Select the First Area to Be Studied

It is very important that the first area studied be carefully selected. In making this selection, consideration of the following pertinent factors will be found helpful. Their relative importance is not indicated, inasmuch as any one factor could be the controlling one in a particular situation.

1. *Potential savings.* The first area selected probably should be one where the greatest amount can be saved with the least amount of expenditure, resulting in a large percentage savings which is readily apparent for all to see.
2. *Anticipated degree of cooperation of supervision.* Successful completion of analyses will be more likely in an area where the supervision is known to be cooperative. Because of the lack of standardization of operations in many indirect areas, supervision's willingness to clarify instructions and work assignments is extremely important.
3. *Anticipated degree of cooperation of the employees.* It is desirable to select an area in which employees are cooperative.
4. *Number and experience of methods engineers available for work of this kind.* In many cases there may be only one person available for this kind of work to begin with—and possibly only on a part-time basis. The past experience of individual methods engineers and actual familiarity with the work done in an indirect area may be an important consideration.
5. *The time and difficulty involved completing analyses in a specific area.* It is desirable to select an area in which the analyses can be completed in a relatively short time so that the results of such a program can be clearly demonstrated. An initial analysis which drags out for several months is not desirable. The first area selected may logically be one where the jobs are the easiest to standardize. Progressive moves can be made from repetitive work into areas where the type of work is less repetitive.
6. *Amount of clerical work required to maintain eventual records and controls.* Since time data may be established on some of the jobs studied and manpower

controls of some kind will be instituted, the first area analyzed might be one in which a minimum amount of clerical work will eventually be required to maintain the records and controls.

7. *Availability and utilization of floor space and equipment.* Floor space and equipment can be important factors to consider when space is at a premium or equipment is difficult to obtain.
8. *New department or process.* A new department or process might furnish a good opportunity to move into a particular indirect area for the first time, especially when new employees are involved.

Obtain Area-Supervision's Support

It is extremely important to have genuine support and cooperation of supervision (supervisor, general supervisor, and superintendent). The following detailed outline is recommended as a sound basis for obtaining such understanding and support.

1. The plant manager, works manager, or factory manager announces the program to top supervision and explains why the program is necessary.
2. The head of methods or industrial engineering then explains, in detail, to the superintendent, general supervisor, and supervisor how the program will operate. In this explanation the following points can be covered.
   a. Benefits to supervision
      (1) Equalization of work assignments
      (2) Elimination or minimization of delays and other losses
      (3) Aid in substantiating or forecasting necessary manpower
      (4) Aid in making improvements in methods, working conditions, equipment, etc.
      (5) Aid in specifying (designing and recording) operator method
      (6) Assistance in elimination of delays and unnecessary work caused by other departments
      (7) Better opportunity for personal recognition
      (8) Improvement in budget performance
      (9) Assistance in training employee
      (10) Means of providing followup to ensure that the method is maintained
   b. Methods engineering's responsibilities
      (1) The way analyses are made, i.e., the means of getting information and data. (Since many indirect supervisors are not familiar with methods engineering techniques, it is recommended that they be given special attention at this time.)
      (2) Analysis of data
      (3) Improvement and standardization of work assignments
   c. Responsibility for determination of performance of indirect manpower compared with the time data or other measures (efficiencies, budgets, etc.), a responsibility that will vary from plant to plant, depending on the type of control used

    d. Supervision's responsibility

        (1) Must provide methods engineering with current manpower assignments, work content, frequency of occurrence of work and tools, and equipment used

        (2) Must examine results of analysis with the methods engineer for the purpose of making improvements in the job

        (3) Must initiate and follow up on acceptable improvements in the job

        (4) Must approve the specified method.

        (5) Must follow up to see that assignments are made in conformance with the established and specified method

        (6) Must confer with the methods engineer so that the specified method can be kept up to date

    e. How employees are to be informed.

        (1) Given reasons why methods studies are to be made.

            Improve the overall job characteristics wherever possible.

        (2) Told how the results of the studies will benefit the worker.

            Equalization of work assignments

            Improvement in safety

            Improvement in methods and working conditions

            Better measure of performance for individual recognition

3. This action can best be accomplished by means of training programs.

Select Methods or Industrial Engineering Personnel To Do the Job

It is important to select a methods engineer who has the following qualifications:

1. Analytical ability and good judgment because of unusual situations often encountered
2. Initiative
3. Ability to *get along with people*
4. Wide range of skills and knowledge of techniques
5. Selling ability

Obtain Cooperation of Employees to be Studied

The initial notification of the workers is an important step in gaining their eventual cooperation. It is suggested that the supervisor tell the workers that they are to be studied, covering the points listed below. The methods engineer will be able to assist the supervisor at this time.

1. Reasons why the analysis is to be made
    To improve the overall job characteristics wherever possible
2. Itemization of how the results of the analyses will benefit the worker
    a. Equalization of work assignments

b. Improvement in safety

c. Improvement in working conditions

d. Reduction in effort needed to do the job

GENERAL PROCEDURE IN ANALYZING INDIRECT OPERATIONS

The action of analyzing indirect operations for improvement possibilities should follow the steps outlined in the methods engineering approach, as shown in Fig. 18-1.

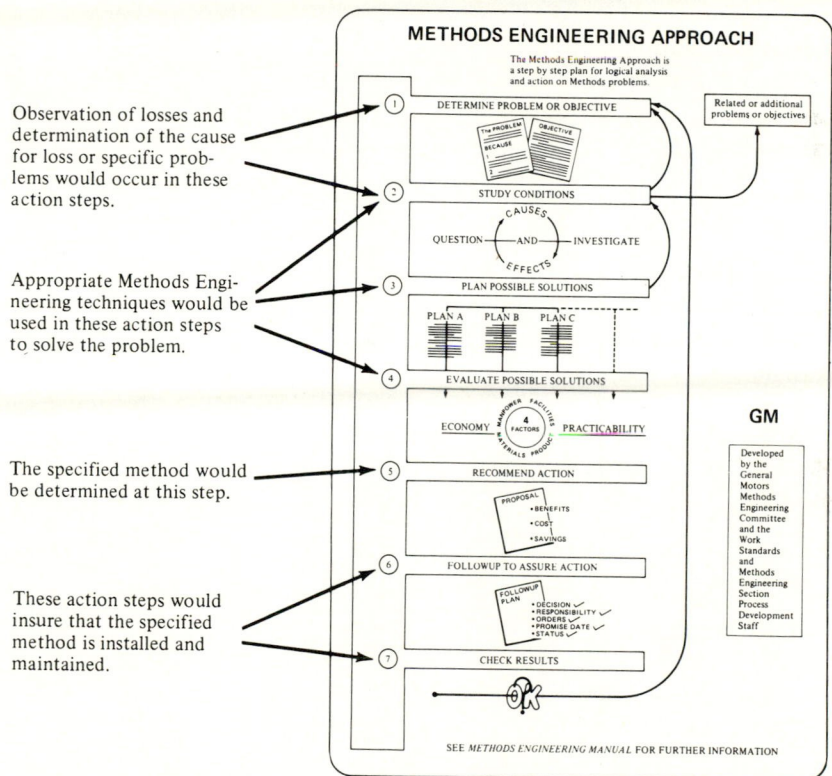

Figure **18-1** Methods-engineering approach applied to indirect labor. *(Developed by the General Motors Methods Engineering Committee and the Work Standards and Methods Engineering Section Manufacturing staff. © Copyright 1953, General Motors Corporation.)*

Determine How Losses Can Be Observed

Losses can be observed and recorded by the following means:

1. Work sampling
2. On-the-floor observations (checks and surveys)
3. Results of time checks (time study)
4. Delay studies or full-shift observations
5. Improvement proposals
6. Analysis of special reports
   a. Efficiency reports
   b. Manpower reports
   c. Comparison of standard to actual performance
7. Budget analyses
8. Scheduling analyses
9. Customer complaints and warranty charges
10. Competitive bids
11. Cost comparisons (actual versus estimates)
12. Team-planning approach
13. Idea exchange between plants

Techniques to Be Used

The techniques that may be used for *observing* losses *or* for *planning* and *evaluating* possible solutions include the following:

1. Methods-engineering approach
2. Possibility analysis on the floor (check sheets, activity check studies)
3. Flow and process analysis
4. Act breakdown
5. Activity charts
6. Method summary charts
7. Memomotion studies, TV taping, etc.
8. Routine sequence charts
9. Predetermined method time systems
10. Workplace layout
11. Human factors data
12. Work-sampling studies
13. 3-D layouts
14. Multiple regression or stepwise regression
15. Standard time data

STATUS REPORTS AND CONTROL PROCEDURES

The measurement of accomplishment in the indirect-labor areas is essential. Such measures point out the effectiveness of the improvement effort as well as the continued need for such effort. They also provide recognition for groups or individuals.

Status Reports

Measurement of accomplishment may be done in one or more of the following ways:

1. Cost comparisons (actual versus estimates; old versus new)
2. Reduction in standard time
3. Budget reduction in dollars and rate
4. Work-sampling comparisons (before and after)
5. Reductions in amount of equipment used or requested
6. Reductions in maintenance of equipment
7. Reductions in floor space
8. Better working conditions and/or reduced work effort
9. Reduction in work force or record of manpower (before and after)

Control Procedures

Determination of the controls is essential and should be considered before the study in order to maintain the results of the effort that will have been expended. These may or may not be based on work standards. Controls may take many forms, some of which are:

1. Budget controls
2. Improvement progress reports (related to budgets)
3. Efficiency reports
4. Performance reports (weekly)
5. Ratio of direct labor to indirect labor
6. Periodic work sampling

QUESTIONS

18-1 Is it usually easier to make work-measurement studies on direct than on indirect labor?

18-2 Why is the measurement of indirect labor becoming more important?

18-3 The manufacturing cost of a product is usually divided into what three major components?

18-4 Overhead cost is frequently expressed as a percentage of what other cost item?

18-5 Does maintenance work or janitorial work tend to be more repetitive or less repetitive with respect to the overall job activity?

18-6 Is work sampling ever used to study indirect labor?

18-7 Is top-management support desirable when studying indirect-labor operations?

18-8 Why should the first indirect-labor area to be studied be selected and not merely picked at random?

18-9 How may the worker benefit from the results of indirect-labor studies?

18-10 Appropriate methods-engineering techniques, such as work-sampling studies, would be used in which three steps of the methods-engineering approach?

18-11 If a work-sampling study is to be used to study an indirect-labor area, what are some of the categories (nonwork items) that would be used in addition to the work categories of a particular area?

18-12 Why is janitorial work more suitable for standard time data development and use than are some other areas of indirect labor?

18-13 How can indirect-labor studies ultimately provide more recognition for indirect-labor workers?

18-14 Is the ratio of direct labor to indirect labor on an increasing or decreasing trend?

NINETEEN

METHODS PLANNING

Many facets of methods analysis and work measurement have been covered in the preceding chapters; some in more detail than others. Emphasis, for the most part, has been placed on the understanding of the methods-analysis and work-measurement philosophies, the problem-solving approach and its application, and the various techniques of analysis. The contents have been presented in this manner so as to develop the individual's awareness of the scope of these two functions and the methods and techniques of solving problems. In some instances, application of the concepts and techniques to actual operations for study and/or improvement will bring out poor workplace design characteristics that would indicate the need for more effective planning during the initial design stages. This is in contrast to the insufficient initial design stage followed by continuous improvement analysis. By no means should it be considered that effective initial design will solve all problems. Since people are involved and conditions change, it is to be expected that there will be a continuous need for reexamining the operating systems and their components. Thus, the point of interest has to do with how this knowledge and awareness of methods analysis and work measurement can be directed in the planning stages.

PLANNING IN GENERAL

First, it must be pointed out that the application of methods-analysis and work-measurement principles and techniques to system design is merely one phase of the entire planning spectrum. Total planning is an involved process of people, systems, organization, and decisions. It is not a new responsibility but one that has become more important as changes have occurred in our economic conditions and as competition continues to force a greater emphasis on planning and the economic considerations of alternatives of system design.

Each individual function of an organization has some means whereby a phase of the planning for the production of products is accomplished. Fresh viewpoints are continually being presented. These new ideas must be blended with the experiences and knowledge of past and present procedures so that understanding and use is achieved. For example, in recent years, the designers have been exposed to more scientific processes of "operations research," "mathematical models," and "systems engineering." These newer concepts have, to some degree, added more quantitative means to the total structure of planning or decision making.

The system design is initially involved in the broad phases of product-need analysis: design intent and evaluation; design concept; physical model and prototype test; and then design for mass production (see Fig. 19-1).

There must be a need for a product either fostered by an enterprising individual or group or generated by an expressed need of the consumers. Once the need is clearly defined in such terms as function, design limitations, and real value, that is, use, desire, or economic feasibility, initial design characteristics must be investigated and evaluated. In other words, some justification must be given to proceed into the actual designing, building, and testing of a prototype. The analysis of the prototype in view of original objectives is a further check on whether or not it is feasible to proceed and consider the mass production and sales of the product. Since the initial design and prototype are not necessarily designed for mass-production techniques, it follows that analysis and design for mass production are most often necessary. It is at this stage that the system design can be undertaken. The question is, "Where do the designers start?"

Logically, it would be difficult for each function to undertake a phase of the design process without there first being a general agreement with all functions involved concerning the product design and specifications. The manufacture of the product is the cause of system design, so the product design must be carefully analyzed from all viewpoints before each function proceeds to detail a phase of the design. The analysis will be successful only if functions affected by the product-design specifications are

Product need and function	What is it supposed to do?
Design intent and evaluation	Size, weight, shape, environment, reliability, financial considerations
Design concept Physical model Prototype test	Identify critical characteristics Form and dimensional geometry Manufacturing problems
Design for mass production	Design versus manufacturing Economics of manufacturing

Figure 19-1 Initial phases of product design and analysis.

a part of the examining body. This is the beginning of the formation of the team concept.

Individuals representing the examining body should have the opportunity to question the design specification as it relates to the economics of

Product design
Material specifications
Processing sequence and selection
Equipment and facilities
Tooling and devices
Plant design and layout
Manpower utilization
Quantity and quality requirements

As shown in Fig. 19-2, attention of each function involved is initially focused on the product for a critical analysis of its specifications. Each product-design specification must have purpose, function, and value. To complicate the design with details is to invite waste of the physical and human resources.

The opportunity to discuss all aspects of the product need, design, and specifications in order to arrive at the best-known design according to the factors mentioned previously sets the stage for subsequent action.

Functions having direct responsibility for a phase of the system design and development should, at the conclusion of this examination, be in accord with respect to specific assignments to be accomplished by each. The many decisions and design details involved in the system development must be continually coordinated, because each will affect other development plans and decisions. Each factor of design will in turn become the focal point for the attention of the team until all factors fit together, much like a jigsaw puzzle, to complete the system design. The integration of all factors is certainly not a one-way flow but is rather a continuous coordinated process as the design progresses toward completion. Shown in Fig. 19-3 is an example of a basic plan-

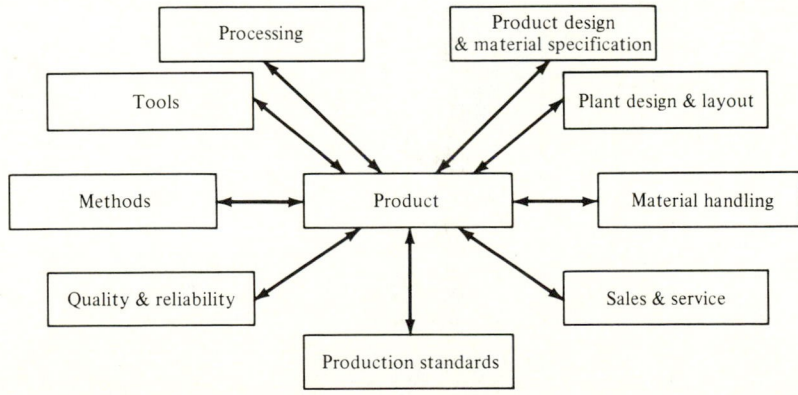

Figure 19-2 Typical examples of functions involved in design process.

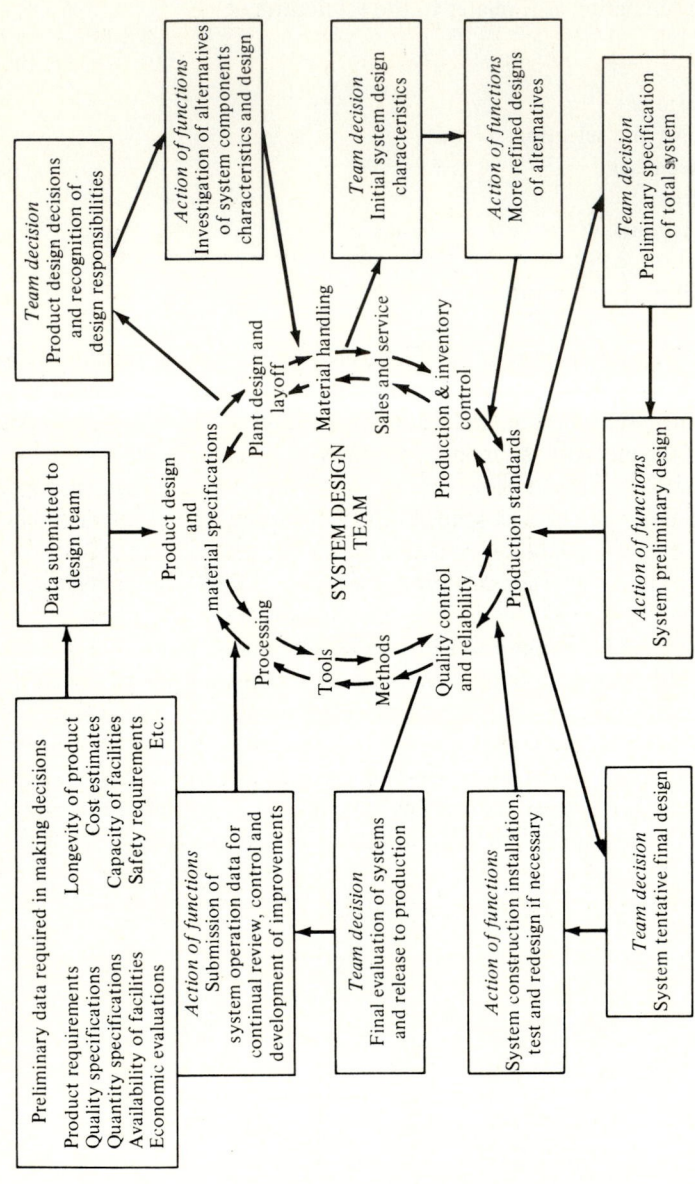

Figure 19-3 Basic design process.

ning process that includes additional preliminary information needed beyond that of product specifications.

Further examples of the detail involved in each design of components of the system are shown in Fig. 19-4. Besides the detailing of the specifications of the systems design and the coordination needed for the design process, another influencing factor to be recognized is that of human nature. Human nature normally seeks the easiest

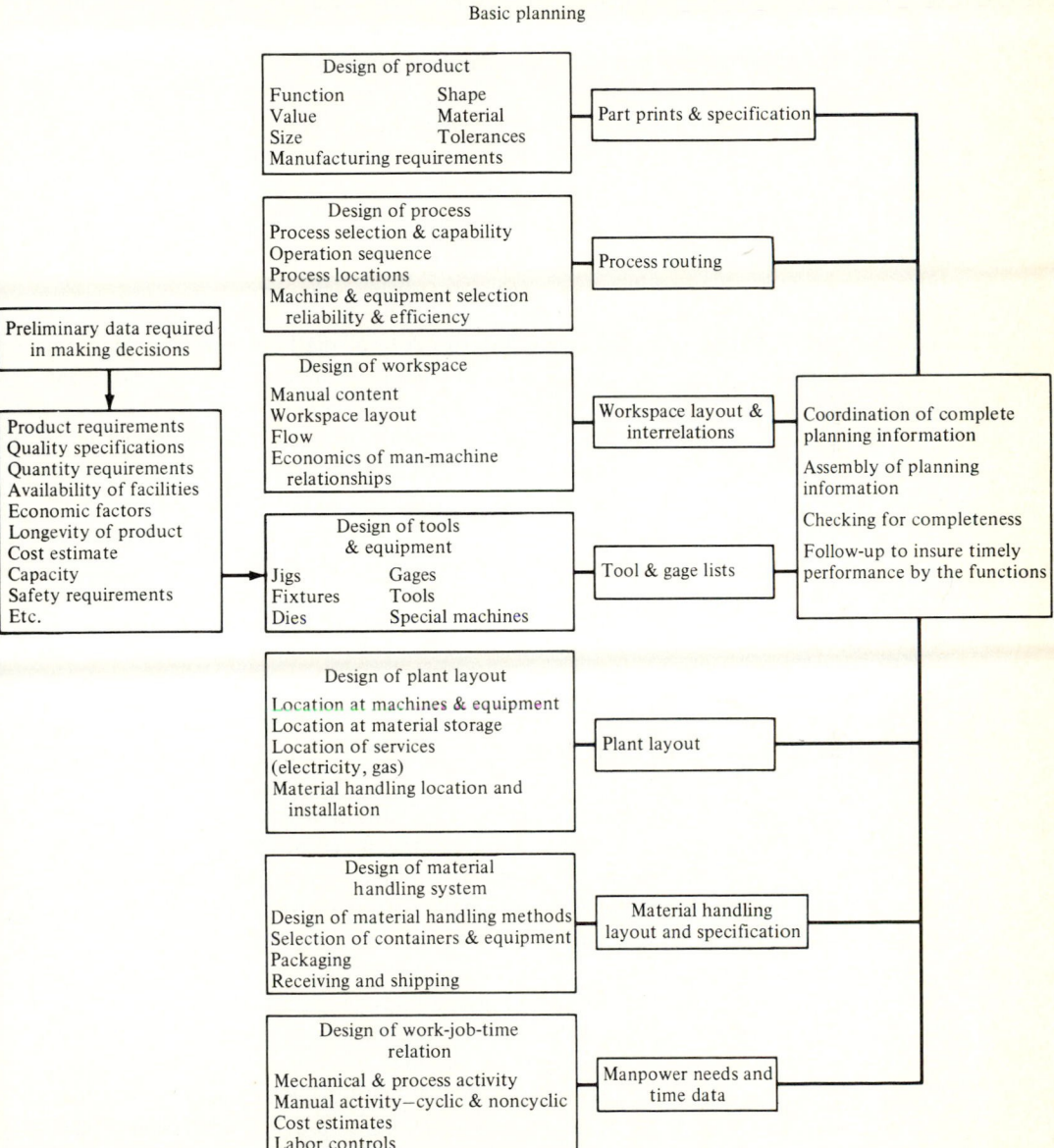

Figure **19-4** Details involved in planning process.

way to a decision. Accordingly, plans for design are frequently built upon experiences, proven examples, and knowledge. Participation in planning over a period of time by an individual or group sometimes develops a pattern or an approach that becomes stereotyped. Decisions and design development are repetition of past designs, even though the problem is different or conditions have changed. The challenge of the assignment is forgotten because of the pressure to get the assignment completed, which is a danger signal—a signal indicating that the production planning structure, although formalized, is not operating effectively. There are individuals who constantly say that there is not enough time. Such a position becomes an easy way out. It has been recognized that planning takes time, and reasons for inadequate planning are easier to find than is a concerted effort to accomplish assignments. Careful structuring of the development stages with factual data rather than opinions is one assurance that the best design, within the limitations of the problem situation, will be developed.

METHODS PLANNING

Although the planning activities of every function are worthy of discussion, the remainder of this chapter will emphasize the procedure of methods planning. Methods planning covers two fundamental categories of planning, improvement of the existing system or a plan for design of a new system.

When planning for improvement, one's first step is to make the present system as effective as possible with minimum expense. This in turn provides the base for economic comparison with other alternatives. It is generally found in improvement planning that more restrictions are placed on designs inasmuch as previous investments have been made and cannot always be scrapped in favor of a totally new design. Regardless of the category of planning, the design process is the same, beginning with product analysis and eventually ending with installation, operation, and control of the system.

THE TRADITIONAL APPROACH

If the opportunity arises to design a new system, the methods function can follow one of two procedures in contributing to the design, classified as the traditional approach and the creative approach. In the traditional approach the methods function, as a member of the planning team, would take the agreed-upon specifications established by other functions and coordinate the design of the components into individual- or multiple-work stations and then assist in the evaluation of the design. In this approach severe limitations are placed on methods design, since each specification established by other functions builds one more section of fence around the possible expansions of alternatives. For example, a machine capable of accomplishing the process may have a length of process cycle which would cause either a poor utilization of manpower or an excessive number of machines to provide the desired production. Or a material-handling device may lead to a need for excessive time for the operator to obtain parts.

The traditional approach has been so-named because it seems to be the one most followed. The limitations of this approach may cause the specification of physical components to govern the design, which is not to imply that the designs of the physical components are wrong, since they may enable achievement of the specifications. They may influence other components to the extent of reducing the total effectiveness of the system. Without close control and coordination, the total process may become indifferent and thus follow rather than lead.

Lead time is determined and production planning is scheduled in view of each function's responsibilities and the extent of time needed to accomplish its specific assignments. Invariably, each function except the last in sequence assumes that because of the great length of lead time that ample time is available, resulting in frequent adjustments of deadlines at the expense of functions which follow. The plan for testing and tryout frequently ends up to be the actual production run, with debugging and rebuilding of details of the plan being done during the production period. The end result is overtime, poor-quality products, and dissatisfied customers. Everybody is mad at everyone else—a poor environment for constructive concentration of time and effort for accomplishing the goals set forth. In this situation, a picture is formed in the minds of the people involved that is something like the following.

The product engineer conceives a complicated gadget or device without regard to manufacturing problems and passes it to the next function involved in the planning process with this challenge, "I conceived this beautiful design and now you try to build it—don't bother me with your questions, just build it."

The process engineer, with this charge, proceeds to set up a process sequence including process selection and equipment specifications without regard to process capability, equipment reliability, or economic considerations. To be sure, the product can be fabricated and assembled, but not without additional or further complications. The process engineer, in turn, passes this plan to the next function, seeking not only revenge upon the product engineer but also passing the previous challenge on to the tool and die engineer.

The tool and die engineer takes the plans for processing and designs the necessary tools, fixtures, jigs, and gadgets to fit the equipment specified and the process selected and tries to locate, hold, and process parts according to product specifications. It may be somewhat of a Rube Goldberg contraption, but it will work— but woe be the person that has to use, maintain, or repair it.

The methods engineer gathers the mass of data and attempts to design the work space, incorporating the previous plans with those of manpower, flow of material, and other production requirements. Hampered by previous decisions and limited in vision and creativeness, he frequently ends up with a design that serves as an excellent study during an improvement program. Exhausted in efforts to finish one design without time to consider further alternatives, the engineer informs plant engineering that the design is completed.

Plant engineering goes to great lengths to arrange the equipment and provide the necessary facilities for the system layout and operation. Of course, the equipment may not be serviced—material is not directly at hand for use, environmental conditions are not satisfactory, efficiency of operation will be impaired; but the plans look very impressive, with multiple-colored tapes, wide aisles, and row upon row of machines and equipment carefully placed to create the illusion of efficiency. Through blind adherence to procedure the plan is then installed, only to find that a 1-inch dimension should have been 1 foot. This is naturally to be expected, since it has happened many times and a period of adjustment and realignment has always been necessary.

Further in the process, a frustrated individual called the production supervisor enters the sequence of activities. Upon the supervisor's shoulders is placed the responsibility for operating the system efficiently, which means producing a quality product per the production requirements with minimum labor difficulties and by use of all the mass of gadgetry and plans previously designed, developed, and installed. Frustrated by the physical and human details and condemned by efficiency, scrap, cost, and quality paper work, the supervisor is a sight to behold.

This story could go on and on if one wished to bring in all the functions of personnel affecting the manufacturing system. The story is only meant to satirize certain aspects of the planning process. It is hoped that all organizations have more intelligent and effective processes than the one described, since all organizations have people with abilities and skills necessary for good production planning.

THE CREATIVE APPROACH

In contrast to the traditional approach is the creative approach to planning—an approach that is meant to create ideas without the limitations imposed on the design because of existence of facilities or systems or a loosely coordinated traditional approach. To begin with, some basic fundamentals should be understood.

It must be recognized that the survival of the organization is dependent on the production of quality goods produced by the most economical means and sold at a price acceptable to the consumer. Planning will be effective only when it is realized that coordination of all functions of the organization with each function is necessary and that production is of most importance. The production force is oftentimes looked down upon, being regarded as a secondary consideration and a responsibility of the production management group. But it is a source of valuable information developed through experiences of operating and utilizing the designs and plans of the staff groups. Without the production of products, there would be no need for functions in indirect or staff areas. Without the total coordination of individuals involved in the manufacturing system, including the production supervisor, the concept of planning becomes that of individualistic effort on the part of each responsible function, with resulting frustration and development of a poor plan for the manufacturing system design. As represented in Fig. 19-5, total design is a responsibility of the team involved.

Since the methods function is a logical member of the team, it must contribute to its fullest extent. Likewise, with the applications of methods principles and fundamentals being a part of all people's responsibility, the methods function itself cannot do the whole design. In the application of the creative approach, all functions are

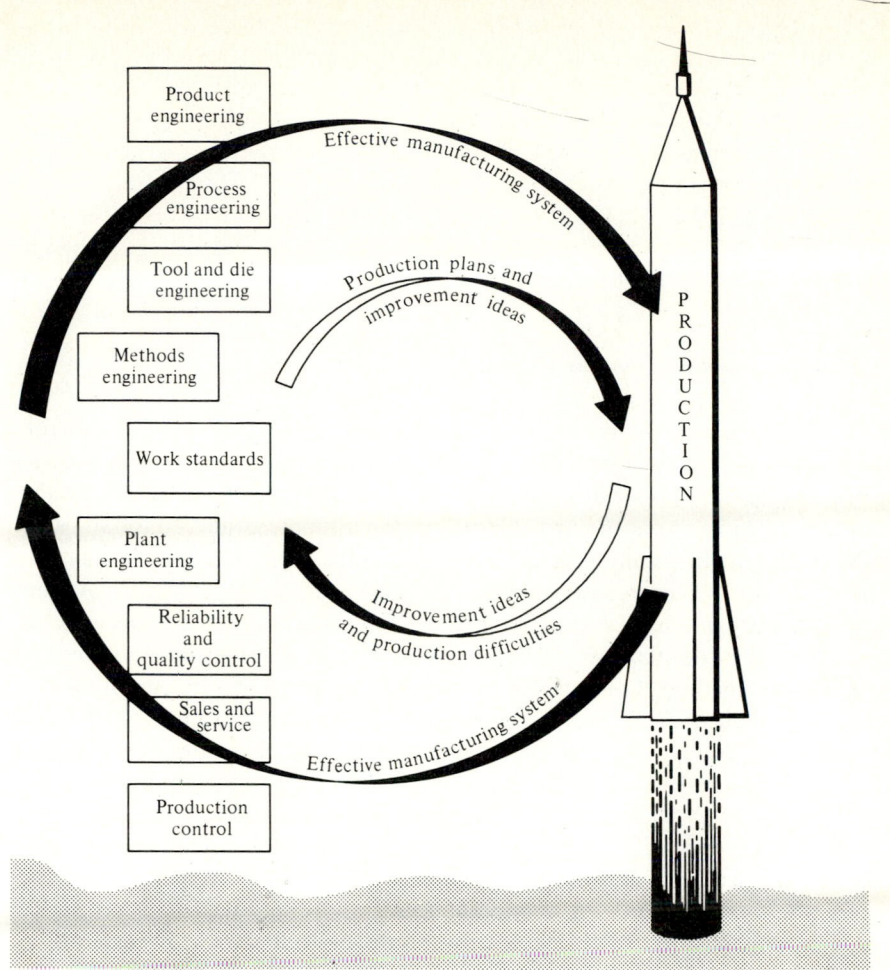

Figure 19-5 Design for production.

therefore called upon to contribute ideas for development of the system design. The specifications are developed first for the ideal manual method, which is zero manual method. Thus, the creative approach appears to be a complete reversal from that of the traditional approach—so different that some critics would call it a radical approach. Regardless of the criticisms, it does offer many challenges to the thought processes of individuals involved in the manufacturing system design. The creative approach tends to direct a person to plan activity around the most economical number of manual acts and movements of the operator. Therefore, this approach presents a conflict with the previous approach of determining mechanical requirements first and then allowing the requirements to influence the manual needs of the activity. It nonetheless tends to direct people's thinking toward the best plan for an activity instead of encouraging them to continue to follow old and timeworn procedures and customs.

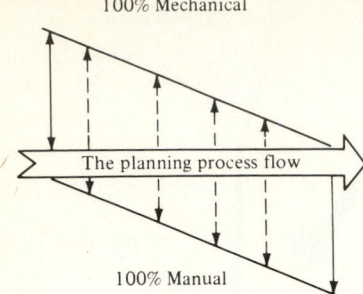

Figure 19-6 The alternatives of workspace design.

Sound reasoning tells us that the best plan for any activity has been that of following the one developed with the ultimate or ideal situation in mind and then loosening up the mechanical or manual specifications until the economical level for the condition presented has been reached. Therefore, the ultimate condition for any situation, if it can be economically justified, is to have a fully mechanized set of plans for the activity. This has been recently labeled "the automation of processes." At this stage in the planning, mechanical specifications or features may be too complicated for development and/or too expensive. The next best plan is one that incorporates the minimum manual method. Continued loosening up on the mechanical specifications and expanding of the manual specifications eventually develop into a plan that can be economically justified. An example of the preceding is best illustrated in Figs. 19-6 through 19-11. Figure 19-6 brings out the investigation of the ideal process or complete automation of processes as the first stage, followed by the reduction of the mechanical specification and expansion of the manual specifications. Note that reference to mechanical and manual specifications pertains to all components of the work-space or system design and the means specified to accomplish each stage of the integrated activities and thereby achieve the purpose or objective of the system.

MOTION ECONOMY

The planning process is guided by two basic principles of motion economy:

Principle 1. The minimum number of acts to be used on any one object should be a get and place. (Remember. An act is a grouping of motions or movements for purposes of job study. A get act is the muscular movement required to move to and gain full control of an object. A place act is the muscular movements required to move an object into a definite position and hold and/or release it.)

Principle 2. The minimum number of movements to be used in getting or placing any one object should be a simple full-arm (FA) and one-finger (F) movement.

In other words, the principles say to use the minimum of manual movement which necessarily direct our use of the fingers or arms, since they are the lowest classification of muscular movements and take the minimum time for movements. As noted in the examples diagrammed, the manual descriptions appear to be very brief, but careful analysis will show that all specifications can be listed for the design of the station. Our attempt is not to become specific in design detail but rather to list specifications for the designer.

Movement time data shown in Fig. 19-7 are the basis for analysis of the examples shown in Figs. 19-8 through 19-13. Data are for unrestricted movements and used for comparison purposes only.

Figure 19-8 shows an application to a simple work-space design. The product has been questioned and design specifications have been approved. In addition, the need for the specific operation has been agreed upon as being necessary, but no decision has been reached about how the operation should be done. Furthermore, the complete mechanization process has been analyzed and evaluated. The next stage is thus to loosen up the mechanical requirements and add the minimum manual specifications to do that part of the operating cycle which has been removed.

Figures 19-9 and 19-10 show a slight reduction in the mechanical or process-development specifications with the additional manual content specified.

Table A – Constants

Symbol	Movement	Time
F	Finger	12
HD	Head	30
E	Eye focus Eye reaction Eye interpretation	20 30 30
ET	Eye travel	50

Table B – Variable with travel distance

Symbol	Movement	Time for straight line travel inches							
		1	4	6	12	18	24	30	36
H	Hand	12	21						
LA	Lower arm	12	21	25	32	37	41	45	
FA	Full arm	12	25	30	41	50	56	62	67
BB	Body bend	62	68	73	85	98	110	123	
FT	Foot	22	28	32					
LL	Lower leg	31	33	34	38	43	47		
FL	Full leg	36	43	47	60	74	87	100	

Figure 19-7 Movement time data (ten-thousandths of a minute).

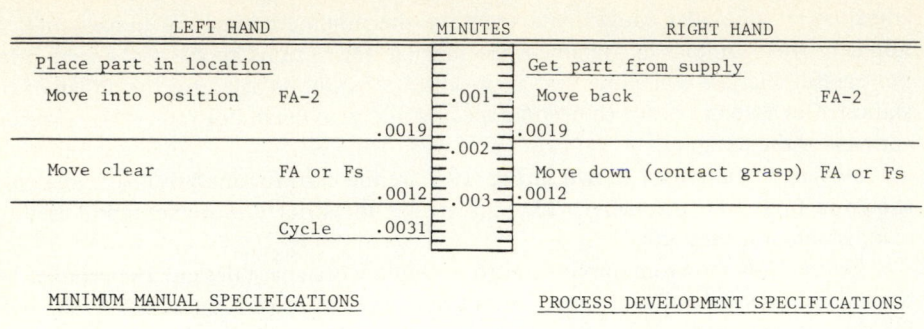

MINIMUM MANUAL SPECIFICATIONS

Get Act

1. Part must be in fixed location.

2. Gain control must require
   contact grasp only.

3. No separation or selection
   allowed.

4. Distance of part from place point
   must not exceed 2".

Place Act

1. Must be able to place during
   process.

2. Part must slide into position.

3. Part must position or preposition
   with approach (move in) movement.

PROCESS DEVELOPMENT SPECIFICATIONS

1. Automatic ejection of part.

2. Automatic process.

3. Maximum process time - .0031 min.

Figure 19-8 Example cycle; minimum manual method.

In Figs. 19-11 to 19-13, analysis shows that the process-development specifications are further decreased and the manual specifications are increased.

Within the range of work-space design there are many possibilities. Some individuals may say that time does not allow the consideration of all alternatives. Experience, knowledge, and careful analysis will quickly reduce the possibilities to a practical number for detailed analysis. The point to be kept in mind is that one should not automatically create barriers to the possibilities and continue to follow past practices of design. Creative planning forces the analyst to solve the problems and not let past practices and experiences be the guidelines for work-space design.

Complete analysis of each component of the system by the creative planning process gives us the many building blocks and their combinations for the eventual design of the total system. In this manner, the following will have been determined:

1. Capacity of alternatives
2. Combinations of processes

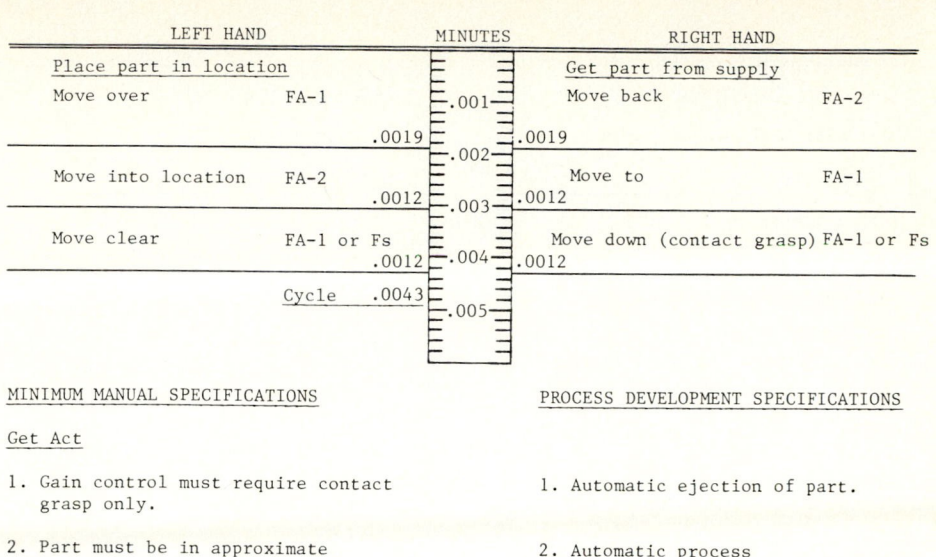

LEFT HAND		MINUTES	RIGHT HAND	
Place part in location			Get part from supply	
Move over	FA-1	.001	Move back	FA-2
	.0019	.0019		
Move into location	FA-2	.002	Move to	FA-1
	.0012	.003 / .0012		
Move clear	FA-1 or Fs		Move down (contact grasp) FA-1 or Fs	
	.0012	.004 / .0012		
Cycle	.0043	.005		

MINIMUM MANUAL SPECIFICATIONS

Get Act

1. Gain control must require contact grasp only.

2. Part must be in approximate location.

3. Distance of part from place point must not exceed 2".

Place Act

1. Must be able to place during process.

2. Part must slide into position.

3. Part must position or preposition with approach (move in) movement.

PROCESS DEVELOPMENT SPECIFICATIONS

1. Automatic ejection of part.

2. Automatic process

3. Maximum process time - .005 minute.

Figure 19-9 Second-best method.

3. Mechanical specifications of each work-space alternative
4. Minimum manual specifications
5. Process times for efficient operations

The development of each alternative presents many challenges to each of the functions involved in the detailing of the design. What must be done is established in the analysis of the manual description. How to do it is left to those functions contributing to the total design. Alternatives are, therefore, designed on the basis of an objective set of specifications rather than totally on experience or past practice.

Further application of the creative approach to each part of the system design, the determination of the interactions between each design component and work-space design and the balancing of the utilization of components, provides the design of system alternatives. Coordination should again be emphasized along with the development of

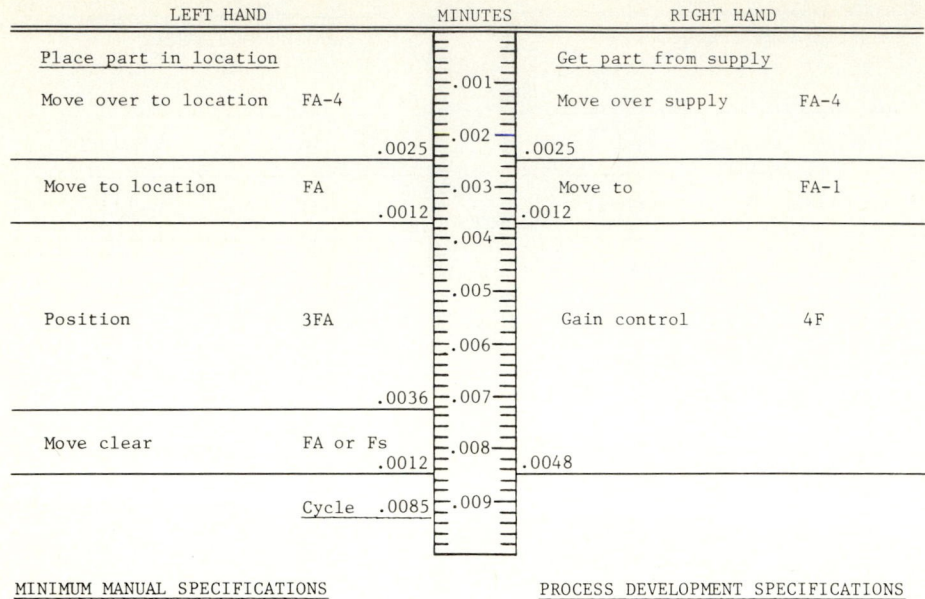

MINIMUM MANUAL SPECIFICATIONS

Get Act

1. Part must be in approximate location.

2. Distance of part from place point must
   not exceed 4".

3. Must be able to grasp 4F.

Place Act

1. Must be able to place during process.

2. Part must position simple position
   movements 3FA.

PROCESS DEVELOPMENT SPECIFICATIONS

1. Automatic ejection.

2. Automatic process.

Figure 19-10 Third-best method.

the team concept so necessary for effective planning. Two approaches to planning have thus been presented:

1. The traditional approach of determining the mechanical or physical specification and, finally, the manual needs for each alternative of the work-space design
2. The creative approach of determining the manual specifications and through analysis establishing the physical or process-development specification

Critics can be found for each approach.

The challenges of the system design involve more than that of attempting to meet specifications established during the planning processes, because planning is done by people. Acceptance of these following challenges should tend to create the proper en-

LEFT HAND		Minutes	RIGHT HAND		Minutes
Place part in location			Get part from supply		
Move up	FA-3	.0022	Move over supply	FA-8	.0034
Move over	FA-8	.0034	Move down	FA-3	.0022
Move down	FA-1	.0012	Move to	FA-1	.0012
Position	3FA	.0036	Wait		.0036
Release control	F	.0012	Gain control	4F	.0048
Balance delay		.0036			
Cycle .0152					

Figure 19-11

LEFT HAND		Minutes	RIGHT HAND		Minutes
Get button			Get button		
Drift			Move out	FA-6	
Move up	FA-15		Move up	FA-15	
Move to	FA-1	.0088	Move to	FA-1	.0088
Place button			Place button		
Move in	FA-1		Move in	FA-1	
Hold for process			Hold for process		
Move clear	FA-1	.0074	Move clear	FA-1	.0074
Drift to supply		.0112	Place part		
Get part			Move down	FA-15	
Move to			Move to	FA-6	
Gain control		.0060	Position	3FA	
			Release control	F	
			Balance delay		.0172
Cycle		.0334			

Figure 19-12

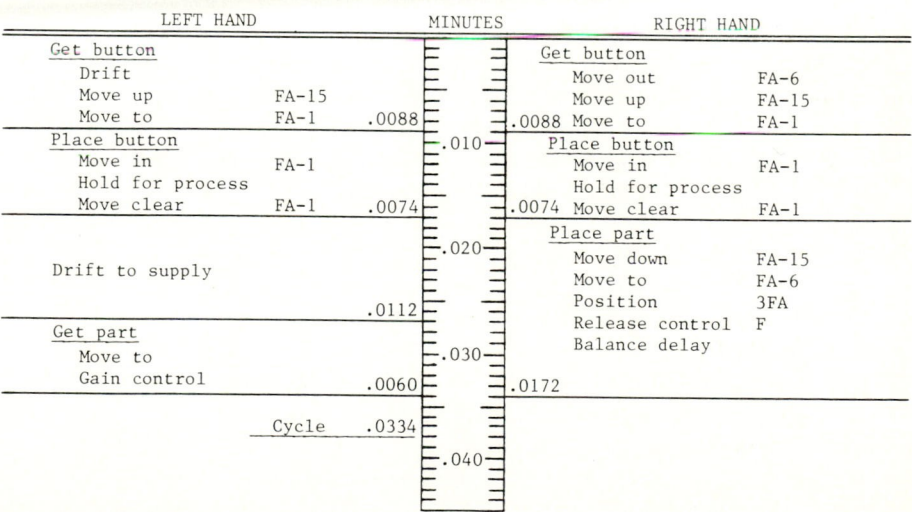

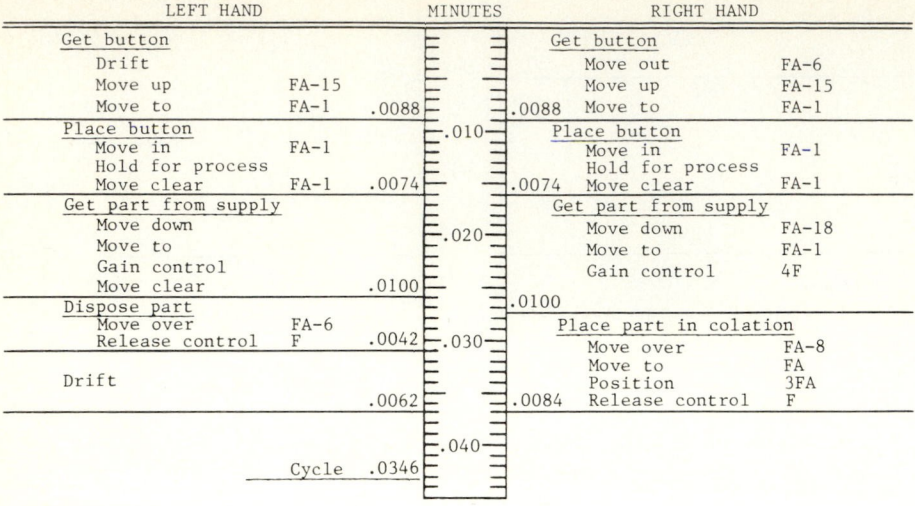

Figure 19-13

vironment for planning and forming a team approach to planning and the creative philosophy of planning.

1. Organization goals and objectives rather than individualistic goals should be foremost in the minds of the team member.
2. The maturity of people is shown through their constant research for new and better ways of doing useful work.
3. System design and analysis involve the many functions of an organization and the strength of the organization is measured by the cooperative and coordinated efforts shown toward effective system design.
4. A progressive group of people continues to build upon its skills and knowledge rather than attempting to live and feel secure on the basis of its experiences.
5. Depth in specialization is important, but breadth in understanding of the workings of the organization, the interplay of functions, and the contributions of the members of the organization are necessary to make for the coordinated team.

QUESTIONS

19-1 What are the broad phases of system design that precede the design for mass production?
19-2 What is the initial step in systems design?
19-3 What are the two fundamental categories of methods planning?
19-4 What are the two general approaches to planning?
19-5 What are the alternatives of work-space design?
19-6 What is the methods principle relating to acts that is followed in creative planning?
19-7 What is the methods principle relating to movements that is followed in creative planning?

BIBLIOGRAPHY

Advanced Methods and Work Measurement, General Motors Institute, Flint, Mich., 1973.

Advanced Work Standards, General Motors Institute, Flint, Mich., 1963.

Alford, L. P., and J. R. Bangs (eds.): *Production Handbook*, Ronald, New York, 1944.

Barnes, Ralph M.: *Motion and Time Study Design and Measurement of Work*, 7th ed., Wiley, New York, 1980.

Better Methods in Work Standards, General Motors Institute, Flint, Mich., 1945.

Brisley, Chester L.: "Comparison of Predetermined Time Systems (PTS)," *Proceedings, AIIE Spring Annual Conference*, American Institute of Industrial Engineers, Norcross, Ga., 1978.

——: "Work Measurement in the 1980's," *43rd Annual IMS Clinic Proceedings*, Industrial Management Society, Des Plaines, Ill., 1979.

Carroll, Phil: *How to Chart Data*, McGraw-Hill, New York, 1960.

Eady, Karl: "Todays International MTM Systems—Decision Criteria for Their Use," *Proceedings AIIE Spring Annual Conference*, American Institute of Industrial Engineers, Norcross, Ga., 1977.

Filipetti, George: *Industrial Management in Transition*, Irwin, Homewood, Ill., 1953.

Gilbreth, F. B.: *Bricklaying System*, Myron C. Clark, Chicago, 1909.

——, and L. M. Gilbreth: *Applied Motion Study*, Sturgis and Walton, New York, 1917.

Jackson, James R.: "A Computing Procedure for a Line Balance Program," *Management Science*, vol. 2, no. 3, April, 1956.

Karger, Delmar W., and Franklin H. Bayha: *Engineered Work Measurement*, 3d ed., Industrial Press, New York, 1977.

——, and Walton Hancock: *Advanced Work Measurement*, Industrial Press, New York, 1982.

Konz, Stephan: *Work Design*, Grid Publishing, Columbus, Ohio, 1979.

Lowry, S. M., H. B. Maynard, and G. J. Stegmerten: *Time and Motion Study and Formulas for Wage Incentives*, 3d ed., McGraw-Hill, New York, 1940.

Mariotti, John J.: "Four Approaches to Manual Line Balancing," *Industrial Engineering*, June, 1970, pp. 35–40.

Maynard, H. B. (ed.): *Industrial Engineering Handbook*, 3d ed., McGraw-Hill, New York, 1971.

——, G. J. Stegmerten, and John L. Schwab: *Methods-Time Measurement*, McGraw-Hill, New York, 1948.

Methods Analysis and Planning, General Motors Institute, Flint, Mich., 1955.

Methods Analysis and Work Measurement, General Motors Institute, Flint, Mich., 1963.

Moodie, C.: "Customized Assembly Line Balancing," *Industrial Engineering*, April. 1969.

Morrow, Robert Lee: *Time Study and Motion Economy*, Ronald, New York, 1946.

Mundel, M. E.: *Motion and Time Study*, 5th ed., Prentice-Hall, Englewood Cliffs, N.J., 1978.

Nadler, Gerald: *Work Design,* Irwin, Homewood, Ill., 1963.

Niebel, Benjamin W.: *Motion and Time Study*, Irwin, Homewood, Ill., 1955.

Polk, Edward J.: "Converting Multiple Regression Output to Multivariable Charts, Work Study," Sawell, London, Eng., October 1971, pp. 13–17.

——: "G M Trains Its Engineers in Methods, Work Standards," *Industrial Management*, October 1970, pp. 12–14.

Prenting, Theodore O., and Nicholas T. Thomopoulos: *Humanism and Technology in Assembly Line Systems*, Hayden, Rochelle Park, N.J., 1974.

Presgrave, Ralph: *The Dynamics of Time Study*, 2d ed., McGraw-Hill, New York, 1945.

Salvendy, Gavriel (ed.): *Handbook of Industrial Engineering*, Wiley, New York, 1982.

Starr, Martin K.: *Operations Management*, Prentice-Hall, Englewood Cliffs, N.J., 1978.

Sutermeister, Robert A.: *People and Productivity*, McGraw-Hill, New York, 1969.

Taylor, F. W.: *The Principles of Scientific Management*, Harper & Brothers, New York, 1911.

Taylor Society, *Scientific Management in American Industry*, Harper & Brothers, New York, 1929.

Thompson, Clarence B.: *Scientific Management*, Harvard University Press, Cambridge, Mass., 1922.

Time Study in Work Standards, General Motors Institute, Flint, Mich., 1945.

INDEX